Urban Legends

Carrie E. Beneš

Urban Legends

Civic Identity and the Classical Past
in Northern Italy, 1250–1350

The Pennsylvania State University Press
University Park, Pennsylvania

Unless otherwise noted, all photographs and maps have
been taken or prepared by the author.

Library of Congress Cataloging-in-Publication Data

Beneš, Carrie E., 1974–
Urban legends : civic identity and the classical past in
northern Italy, 1250–1350 / Carrie E. Benes.
p.   cm.
Includes bibliographical references and index.
Summary: "Explores the role of the classical past in the
construction of urban identity in late medieval Italy.
Focuses on the appropriation of classical symbols, ancient
materials, and Roman myths to legitimate the regimes of
various Italian city-states"—Provided by publisher.
ISBN 978-0-271-03765-3 (cloth : alk. paper)
1. Italy, Northern—Civilization—Roman influences.
2. Italy, Northern—History—To 1500.
3. City-states—Italy, Northern—History—To 1500.
4. Cities and towns, Medieval—Italy, Northern—Hstory.
5. Group identity—Italy, Northern—History—To 1500.
6. Padua (Italy)—History—To 1500.
7. Genoa (Italy)—History—To 1500.
8. Siena (Italy)—History—To 1500.
9. Perugia (Italy)—History—To 1500.
I. Title.

DG607.B46 2011
945´.104—dc22
2010036079

FOR MY FATHER,
Beacus vir qui invenit sapientiam

Contents

Illustrations

Maps

Figures

Acknowledgments

In a study of intellectual networks and influence, it seems particularly apt and necessary to emphasize that this book is not the work of a single scholar working in isolation. The study began in the Department of History at UCLA, and I have benefited from the aid of many people over the years. Richard and Mary Rouse, in particular, offered mentorship, assistance, and constant encouragement; they are an inspiration. At UCLA, Patrick Geary, Ronald Mellor, Carole Newlands, Geoffrey Symcox, Simon Teuscher, and Brent Vine all provided support; in Florida, David Harvey, Anne Latowsky, Nova Myhill, and David Rohrbacher assisted beyond the call of duty. The project also owes much to the collegial advice and comments provided at various stages by Christopher Baswell, Consuelo Dutschke, Edward English, Carmela Franklin, George Gorse, Anthony Grafton, Samantha Kelly, Carol Lansing, Lester Little, Thomas McCarthy, Edward Muir, Barbara Rosenwein, Gervase Rosser, Ingrid Rowland, Magnus Ryan, Father Michael Sheehan, Quentin Skinner, Randolph Starn, Benjamin Victor, and Lila Yawn. Special thanks go to my parents, and to Thomas.

Individual sections of the study were presented to the UCLA European History Colloquium, the California Medieval History Seminar at the Huntington Library, the University of Bristol conference "Urban Witness: Multilingualism in the Medieval Italian Commune," and the Medieval Academy of America. The UCLA Department of History, the Andrew W. Mellon Foundation, the Beverly Walsh Scholarship Fund, the National Endowment for the Humanities, and the New College of Florida Provost's Office all provided assistance with research and travel.

I am also grateful to the staffs of Cambridge University Library; the Biblioteca Medicea-Laurenziana and the Biblioteca Nazionale Centrale, Florence; the Biblioteca Civica Berio, the Archivio di Stato, and the Biblioteca Universitaria, Genoa; the British Library, London; the Getty Research Institute, Los Angeles; the Archivio di Stato, Lucca; the Biblioteca Ambrosiana, Milan; the

Biblioteca Universitaria, Padua; the Bibliothèque Nationale, Paris; the Istituto di Filologia Romanza of the Università degli Studi and the Biblioteca Augusta Comunale, Perugia; the American Academy in Rome; the École Française de Rome; the Biblioteca Comunale Intronati, Siena; the Biblioteca Apostolica Vaticana; the Biblioteca Nazionale Marciana, Venice; and the Biblioteca Comunale, Verona.

Note on the Text

Except where counter to established usage (e.g., in the case of Petrarch), the names of people who lived before 1500 appear cited and alphabetized in full; for example, Dino Compagni appears in the appendix, the bibliography, and the index as "Dino Compagni," and not as "Compagni, Dino." With the same proviso, medieval names are generally cited in Italian: Jacobus de Voragine, for example, appears as Jacopo da Varagine, but Marsiglio de' Mainardini as Marsilius of Padua. For consistency and ease of reference, Greek and Latin authors are cited by conventional appellations rather than by their full names: Sallust rather than Gaius Sallustius Crispus. Citations to classical and medieval works are by conventional book and chapter or line number, supplemented by page numbers in a modern edition. All translations are my own except where noted; references to published English translations are given where available.

A final note: Medieval Latin and Italian orthography is notoriously idiosyncratic and inconsistent. All spellings appear here as written or published.

Map 1   Northern Italy around 1300. Map after Larner, *Italy in the Age of Dante and Petrarch*. Names of cities featured in this study appear in capital letters.

Introduction

What is history but the praise of Rome?

—Petrarch, *Invectiva contra eum qui maledixit Italie*

In 1422, the city council of Montelupo, a small town in southern Tuscany, sent a diplomatic mission to the nearby city of Siena. Its ambassador was charged with the delivery of a gift from the government of Montelupo to that of Siena, and he carried an official letter that read as follows:

> Magnificent and powerful honorable lords:
>
> With our citizen Nanni Matteo Lapetti we are sending to Your Magnificences, whom we have always loved, this wolf. And although this animal is naturally fierce and ravenous, nonetheless this particular wolf is even tamer and gentler than a puppy, for our sons have nourished it since it was taken from its mother's womb. Prepared for your honors and good wishes and given at Montelupo the seventh day of May, fifteenth indiction, 1422.
>
> Your servants, the Council and Commune of the region of Montelupo, in the contado of Florence.[1]

Considered broadly, Montelupo's wolf-gift reflects medieval Europe's fascination with unusual and symbolic animals. The kings of England began keeping animals in the Tower of London in the thirteenth century, and Emperor Frederick II's contemporary menagerie was famous across Europe; Matthew Paris's English chronicle both describes and illustrates the elephant that Frederick sent to the city of Cremona in 1241 to impress visiting English crusaders, as well as the one presented in 1255 to Henry III of England by Louis IX of France.[2]

But the wolf-gift is still more significant if considered in local context. First, and most obviously, Montelupo is Italian for "Wolf Mountain," so the wolf was an obvious reference to the city's own name. Second, as the ferocity of wolves was legendary, a domesticated wolf might have suggested the diplomatic value of friendship over conflict, peace over war, and civilization over brutality.[3] Third, and most important, the wolf had been Siena's symbol since at least the middle of the thirteenth century, so the Montelupesi were presenting the Sienese with nothing less than a live civic mascot. Evidence suggests that the Sienese had begun keeping live wolves in the Palazzo Pubblico (their seat of government) almost a century before Lapetti's mission.[4] It probably was not a continuous practice, as captive wolves were relatively rare—but that very fact would have made the wolf from Montelupo a valuable gift indeed.

Hence, the Montelupesi were offering the Sienese an animal that appealed to and embodied the Sienese sense of identity. According to local legend, Siena had been founded by the twin sons of Remus (the brother of Romulus, who founded Rome); the boys, Aschius and Senius, had been banished from Rome as infants by their jealous uncle and suckled by a she-wolf in the wilderness. Upon growing to manhood, they founded Siena and made the wolf that had nourished them the symbol of their new city. Leaving aside the highly suspicious parallels between this foundation legend and that of Rome,[5] it is evident that the Montelupese wolf would have appealed to the Sienese not only because it was a live version of the town's civic symbol but also because that symbol was rooted in Siena's venerable past, underscoring its republican roots and association with ancient Rome. The republican regime that ruled Siena between 1278 and 1355 had emphasized this connection strongly, and it was once again a major focus in the years after 1400. Thus, by drawing attention to the features of the city that its citizens thought valuable—its republicanism, political autonomy, ancient foundation, and relation to classical Rome—the wolf both represented Siena and defined its past and present. The Montelupesi would have known this perfectly well. Their choice of offering demonstrated their desire to maintain good relations with Siena despite their official alliance with Florence, Siena's main rival.

In fact, anyone who heard about the Montelupese gift would have understood its broader implications. Roman foundation legends like that of the Sienese twins and their wolf-nurse were widespread throughout late medieval Italy. The foundation legend was a common and potent source of medieval identity and propaganda; institutions as diverse as monasteries, kingdoms, family dynasties, and universities created origins for themselves that served contemporary moral and political goals. Chronicles recounted how Romulus's brother, Remus, founded Reims and how Theodosius II chartered the University of Bologna, while Wace's *Brut* (c. 1155) recounted the Trojan origins of the Britons on behalf of the Anglo-Norman king Henry II.[6] Such legends bestowed specific historical connections to their subjects—connections to King Arthur, Charlemagne, ancient Rome, or a Christian saint—and these in turn increased the subjects' pride, legitimacy, and prestige. Constructions of collective identity could celebrate a saint's foundation of a monastery as well as a hero's foundation of a kingdom or a dynasty; the phenomenon took many shapes.

Many European cities had foundation legends—London, Paris, and Cologne are three well-known examples—but the popularity of the civic origin legend in Italy far exceeded that north of the Alps.[7] Virtually every city in medieval Italy had one, and scholars compiled multi-page lists matching each city with its founder.[8] Nowhere else did myths of civic foundation become so broadly known that their content could be alluded to at will in public art and literature—or with the bestowal of diplomatic gifts.

This focus on the mythic past largely resulted from the Italian peninsula's unique sociopolitical situation at the end of the Middle Ages (map 1). Italy had been the most urbanized area of Europe since antiquity, and during the eleventh and twelfth centuries it became increasingly wealthy due to the growth of urban activity and commerce. Politically, however, the Italian peninsula grew more and more chaotic.[9] Its traditional overlords were the pope and the Holy Roman Emperor, but their authority, as well as that of the landed nobility, was gradually eroded by distance and inattention. Economics also had a share in this evaporation of power: starting in the eleventh century, commercially successful townsmen and local nobles formed groups called communes in towns throughout central and northern Italy, whose members swore to protect urban political rights and economic privileges.[10] In this they were little different from many other towns in medieval Europe that received charters from a reigning monarch.[11]

However, the situation in Italy was unique because this trend toward political decentralization went much further than it did elsewhere in Europe, so that by the end of the thirteenth century the pope and the emperor had lost all significant influence over political affairs.[12] Effective imperial power in Italy collapsed along with the Hohenstaufen line after the deaths of Frederick II and his three heirs—Conrad, Manfred, and Conradin—between 1250 and 1268. By 1310, the papacy had moved to Avignon, leaving Rome and central Italy at the mercy of local aristocratic vendettas.[13] The Italian towns had essentially become self-governing city-states; the relatively simple communes of the twelfth century gradually developed into complex municipal bureaucracies—republics, as they styled themselves.[14] Nevertheless, the political situation remained volatile because the removal of external pressures led to greater competition within the Italian peninsula. Newly independent city-states began to maneuver among themselves for territorial domination and political influence, each commune seeking any opportunity to improve its position, either real or perceived, at the expense of its neighbors. Needing to define, legitimate, and ennoble their newly gained autonomy, these cities turned to the Roman past for both concrete and symbolic sources of identity.

This book argues that appropriations of the classical past in the Italian city-states attest to a broader interest in classical antiquity than has traditionally been credited to late medieval Italy. Rather than seeing interest in ancient Rome as limited to a small circle of intellectuals, I contend that the use of Roman myths and physical remains in communal ideology indicates a diverse and widespread engagement with the classical past, one fostered by the relatively sophisticated lay urban culture of the late medieval Italian cities. Italy was the only place in Europe where the public notarial system had survived continuously from the time of the Roman empire, enough that lay notaries retained the professional writing function that the church had assumed in northern Europe.[15] The writing required in the complex world of late medieval commerce, however, was increasingly done by members of the middle class, and recent studies have highlighted "pragmatic literacy," the wide spectrum of possibilities between literacy and illiteracy in the modern sense, depending on one's knowledge of Latin or bookkeeping, one's ability to read and write multiple kinds of script, and other considerations.[16] The university-trained lawyers and notaries who maintained communal records were only the most official writers in a society in which some forms of literacy regularly extended into the lower classes.[17] Inhabitants of the Italian cities therefore had a complex understanding of the role played by writing in the preservation of the past.[18] Contemporary education provided the raw material in the form of Roman authors and texts, and city-state government demanded competent diplomats, politicians, and ideologues. As the usefulness of feudal allegiance to the pope or emperor faded, governments were forced to invent their own ideals and ideologies. Hence, each city's ruling body adapted symbols of classical Rome, used ancient materials, and incorporated Roman myths to create an urban identity both in relation to its own past and in relation to the social and political networks in which it functioned.

Communes used various media to assert and advertise their civic identities—not only texts but also statues, coins, inscriptions, and frescoes. Communal governments propagated such materials widely and deliberately. They commissioned histories, officially approved them, and had them read publicly. They organized events to honor mythical founders, and they incorporated Roman themes into public art and architecture. If the impetus for this trend came from a Latin-literate ruling class, it was nonetheless concerned with spreading the message through as much of the urban population as possible and far beyond the city walls. In an unstable political climate, image was everything. So the Sienese wolf guarded the gates of the city; the Trojan founder of Perugia appeared on the city's main public fountain; Hercules was stamped onto the Florentine currency; and the arch of Augustus in Fano dominated that city's municipal seal. These examples suggest that it was just as important to ensure the wide promulgation of one's civic connection with Rome as it was to establish it in the first place.

Historians have traditionally studied these uses of the Roman past in terms of the reappearance of classical scholarship prior to the Renaissance of the fifteenth century.[19] To chart the revival of interest in classical remains as part of the history of epigraphy or numismatics, scholars like Roberto Weiss and Remigio Sabbadini recorded instances of early fourteenth-century Italian intellectuals attempting to read and reproduce classical inscriptions or copying classical coins into their manuscripts.[20] Others have followed the history of particular cultural artifacts, tracing the fortunes of the Regisol, a famous classical statue in Pavia, or noting mentions of the Veronese amphitheatre in medieval chronicles.[21] Until recently these classical or antiquarian studies stood in isolation from the larger historiography of late medieval Italy; the resurgence of interest in the classical past was assumed to have been the work of individual scholars exploring subjects out of purely academic curiosity. Petrarch's interests in the classical past, for example, are presented as having been shared by few of his contemporaries.[22] Similarly, studies of the "prehumanist" schools of Padua and Verona have tended to document a growing interest in classical Roman subjects without taking into account the source or broader context of that interest.[23]

Rather than considering these manifestations of classical interest in and of themselves, or as precursors of a movement yet to come, I propose a broader scope, examining how classically inspired objects and texts functioned in a late medieval context. I shall address questions such as, what role did they play in the construction and use of communal identity? How was the classical tradition appropriated, manipulated, and reapplied? Who decided that it was necessary, and whose knowledge of the ancient past provided the material for these ideological trends? I incorporate approaches from semiotics and cultural anthropology insofar as they address how particular objects, legends, and symbols acquire cultural significance, and how that significance is used in the articulation of collective identity.[24] Since, for example, the Perugian commune's use of the Roman SPQR symbol can be understood as a statement of either republican independence or allegiance to the papacy, close attention to social norms, authorial intent, and audience expectations is essential for a proper understanding of late medieval classicism.

In particular, much of my methodology derives from the growing volume of work on historical memory and its relation to the construction of personal and collective identity.[25] In *The Past Is a Foreign Country*, David Lowenthal stresses the communal nature of remembering: "Historical knowledge is by its very nature collectively produced and shared; historical awareness implies group activity."[26] Within the field of medieval history, numerous recent studies have analyzed the methods by which medieval people produced and shared their sense of the past. Susan Boynton and Samantha Herrick, for example, are only two of the most recent scholars to explore the social purpose and construction of religious foundation legends—on behalf of the monastery of Farfa in Boynton's case and the duchy of Normandy in Herrick's.[27] Gabrielle Spiegel helped to initiate a similar analysis of the rhetorical strategies and goals of secular historiography, such as that provided by Felice Lifshitz and Leah Shopkow for Norman historians. From a more contemporary perspective, Patrick Geary has revealed the similar motivations of modern-day European nationalists who use stories of medieval origins to advance their cause.[28] These studies have emphasized the defining moment of the origin in medieval (and modern) historiography, both how it constitutes a group as a group—whether monastery, diocese, duchy, or nation—and how it frames ideals and aspirations for members of that group.

Taking this approach with the medieval Italian republics will require the consideration of political, economic, and social issues, as well as art and literature. The historiography of late medieval and Renaissance Italy has traditionally fragmented along disciplinary lines, but historians and art historians of the past thirty years have done much to integrate previously separate historical disciplines.[29] Randolph Starn and Loren Partridge, for example, have clearly connected the commissioning and production of art with contemporary political ideology in their study of Italian halls of state between 1300 and 1600, while Quentin Skinner, Diana Norman, and others have analyzed the classicizing political theories underlying communal art.[30] A growing body of work by Italian scholars like Anna Imelde Galletti and Paolo Brezzi has focused on the *coscienza cittadina*, or civic consciousness, of medieval Italian cities, integrating religious and intellectual changes with political and economic ones.[31] The work of these scholars has produced a better historical understanding of late medieval and early modern Italy on a broad scale, connecting more dynamically the economic and sociopolitical aspects of the culture with intellectual and artistic change. It is within this interdisciplinary paradigm that I wish to locate my study of urban identity formation and communal self-promotion.[32]

In particular, I hope to transcend geographic as well as disciplinary boundaries, avoiding the concentrated approach common in Italian medieval history, where entire books often focus on a single town or province. While such studies are important for understanding particular areas in depth, they can obscure the fact that trade and communication were extensive up and down the Italian peninsula, as well as into the rest of Europe. The cultural history of Italy in the late Middle Ages should not be too stringently compartmentalized.

Some clarifications of scope will be necessary. Despite my emphasis on community, city, and society, I think it important to note that the choice and propagation of civic foundation myths were not democratic or grassroots events. In most cases, a city's image, both to its own citizens and to external observers, was the conscious result of actions taken by the group in power in that city, and the image projected was intended, consciously or unconsciously, to bolster that group's claim to legitimate authority. In the republican city-states, the groups in power were usually oligarchies made up of the wealthy and educated members of society, consisting of the local nobility and successful commercial classes in varying proportions.[33] My point is not that these groups were merciless manipulators of public opinion but that the parameters of any collective identity are to a large extent set by those in charge of the collective.[34] The people, events, and stated ideals of Roman history served as material by which ruling groups could define collective identity and foster unity among their citizens, as well as express their cities' power, legitimacy, and ancient right to self-government in the political chaos that was late medieval Italy. Roman history was an ideological tool.

I do not mean to suggest, however, that it was an exclusive tool. Much has been made of the imperial and monarchic ideologies surrounding imperial rulers or claimants like Frederick II, Henry VII of Luxembourg, and Ludwig of Bavaria—all rulers whose reigns fall within the scope of this study.[35] Likewise, Hans Baron advanced the idea that republicanism was essentially unknown in

Italy before its revival by Florentine intellectuals on the eve of the fifteenth century.[36] The basic difficulty with both of these theses is their assumption that there was only one understanding of the Roman past at any given point in late medieval Italian history. I argue the contrary: the details of Roman history were flexible enough, and its perceived utility great enough, that it was used by proponents of every type of political system. Brendan Cassidy's recent book on civic ideals in medieval Italian sculpture addresses republics, *signorie* (petty lordships), the kingdom of Naples, the papacy, and the Holy Roman Empire alike.[37] For republican Florence and Siena, ruled by citizen oligarchies, to glorify their city's real or manufactured Roman roots was to support the existence, goals, and ideals of the present republican regime, as well as to argue on historical grounds for the city's right to self-government. In exactly the same way, however, to emphasize the ruling family's noble and illustrious Roman roots was to support hereditary authority in cities that were ruled by local lords, like Verona under the della Scala (especially Cangrande) and Ferrara under the Este.[38] Finally, emperors and imperial claimants could cite the precedent of five hundred years, if not fifteen hundred years, of Roman emperors before them. Frederick II's legal, artistic, and political claims to the role of a second Augustus are only the most dramatic example of this trend.[39] All of these examples were essentially contemporary; Roman roots were clearly considered an asset regardless of political allegiance.

Likewise, this was not an intellectual trend pursued only in the biggest, most influential, and most "culturally developed" cities in Italy. Florence and Venice have received much attention from historians for their cultural achievements, but this greater attention has tended to give the impression that they were unique in adopting classicizing self-images by which they represented their republicanism.[40] This is misleading; the promulgation of origin myths lauding a city's supposed Roman or classical roots was a general trend visible on every level, from Venice and Genoa (populations circa one hundred thousand in 1300) to comparatively small cities like San Gimignano and Asti (circa eight to fifteen thousand in the same period).[41] A broad cultural interest in city foundations is evident in the lists of civic origins that frequently appeared in both Latin and vernacular historiography; these lists only became more popular as the fourteenth century progressed. They tend to be organized alphabetically or chronologically for ease of reference, and they frequently include origin information for forty or fifty different Italian cities.[42]

Thus, my focus on the use of Roman history in the republican cities of northern and central Italy is not intended to identify a unique historical episode.

Rather, my study examines a significant part of a larger cultural phenomenon—namely, the adoption, appropriation, and reuse of Roman history by virtually every political entity in medieval Italy over the course of five or six hundred years—ending, in the fifteenth century, in the concentrated revival of Roman literature, art, and culture generally called the Italian Renaissance.[43] Here, I limit myself to a range of autonomous city-states throughout northern and central Italy, excluding the cities of southern Italy and Sicily, which remained under reasonably effective feudal control (e.g., that of Frederick II or Charles of Anjou) and do not show these trends to the same degree.[44] Furthermore, my chosen time span of 1250 to 1350 reveals the republican cities of northern and central Italy at a crucial moment with especially strong ideological incentives: during those hundred years, the absence of strong imperial and papal figures on the Italian peninsula encouraged self-government, but at the same time the instability of the political situation saw the rise everywhere of local lordships, or *signorie*—and not all experiments in republican government proved internally successful. City-states that wished to retain their autonomy had to defend it, which meant providing good ideological and historical reasons for independence, to both the involved citizenry and potential aggressors. Sometimes this "armoury of ideological weapons" was insufficient, but it was inevitably considered a crucial part of any city's arsenal.[45]

This study frames four case studies with two more thematic chapters. Chapter 1 introduces the classicizing foundation legend as forged in the urban culture of late medieval Italy. I attempt to give a sense of the phenomenon's breadth in the century between 1250 and 1350, not only citing evidence from a wide variety of cities but also elaborating on the many ways in which a commune could characterize its relationship to its classical past, real or invented. It might argue that the city was founded before Rome or by the Romans, or it might identify with specific Roman virtues or heroes. It could advertise its chosen myth through physical monuments, works of historiography, or public art. Chapter 1 demonstrates generally why foundation legends were considered important and why Roman foundation legends were considered better than other kinds.

Building on that, each of the next four chapters examines in depth a city with a well-defined classical foundation myth from the turn of the fourteenth century: Padua, Genoa, Siena, and Perugia. These four cities vary in size and are geographically distant from one another. Further, reflecting the cities' particular circumstances, each chapter focuses on a slightly different span of years between 1250 and 1350. I have chosen these four cities, first, to show that they represent a general phenomenon rather than exceptional occurrences; second, because they demonstrate effectively the wide range of the phenomenon in subject, method, and purpose; and third, because they have not received extensive historiographical attention, particularly in English-language scholarship—as compared, for instance, with Florence and Venice.

Padua (chapter 2) claimed to have been founded by Antenor, the only Trojan besides Aeneas to have escaped the burning of Troy; in the late thirteenth century, locals claimed to have dug up Antenor's bones, which were then treated with all the reverence due a holy relic. Genoa's long tradition of municipal historiography resulted, also late in the thirteenth century, in the production of two long and popular histories of the city (chapter 3), both of which attest to its foundation by a third escaped Trojan named Janus, who gave his name to the new town—hence Janua, the medieval Latin spelling of Genoa. In contrast to Genoa, Siena's foundation myth (chapter 4) did not appear in written form until the fifteenth century, but a number of visual sources attest to its importance from the late thirteenth century onward: the twins Aschius and Senius and their nurturing wolf appear not only on the wall of the Sienese communal council chamber, at the feet of the personified commune, but also on the town seal and in civic sculpture. Finally, in 1293, Perugia's ruling council commissioned a long epic poem on the deeds of its founder, Eulistes (chapter 5), who also appears on the monumental public fountain that was built at the same time in Perugia's main piazza.

Each of the four central chapters traces the origin of a given story or myth, as well as its adoption and reappropriation for use in the late medieval period. At the same time, each chapter correlates the development of its city's classicizing myth with its particular sociopolitical and economic circumstances. The evidence available for each city varies, and each city's purpose in propounding its myth was different; hence, these studies demonstrate the wide variation within the larger phenomenon. Although each of the myths analyzed in these chapters emphasizes a different aspect of the Roman past, they all served a similar contemporary function: to articulate each city's sense of historical identity and legitimate its current regime as a logical successor to, or even the continuation of, Roman rule.

Returning to a broader perspective, the final chapter investigates the human side of the phenomenon—specifically, how classical foundation legends were invented, delineated, and propagated, and, as far as possible, who was responsible. It explores the connections among authors, scholars, lawyers, notaries, merchants, and politicians as part of an educated elite that shared classicizing ideas and priorities across the Italian peninsula and beyond. It then focuses on the urban community, investigating how local elites influenced and were influenced by the rest of the city's population—how their knowledge of Roman history was transmitted to the less educated through political processes, public events, and popular literature, but at the same time how the existing oral culture could affect the ways in which the elite shaped their vision of their city's origin myth. Finally, the chapter considers the competitive implications of audience: if each city had its own foundation myth and such myths were widely known, to attack a city's founding hero was to attack its civic honor on a regional or peninsular scale.

Like better-known polities of the fifteenth and sixteenth centuries, therefore, the late medieval city-republics of northern and central Italy attributed their foundations to legendary classical heroes and historical figures; they uncovered and remounted Roman inscriptions; and they displayed ancient images on their coins. This study situates those efforts as part of the conscious identity-formation of the Italian city-states. At the same time, it contextualizes the wider relevance of the classical tradition in the society that brought forth early humanism, and it characterizes the Italian cities' use and knowledge of ancient Rome as a dynamic engagement with the classical past that was more wide-ranging than historians have traditionally recognized.

APPROPRIATING A ROMAN PAST

Drawing the threads from her distaff,
she would regale her family with stories
of the Trojans, and Fiesole, and Rome.

—Dante's description of a traditional Florentine matron

Civic honor was a serious business in the communes of late medieval Italy. The peninsula's network of independent city-states was notoriously unstable: alliances were rapidly formed and broken as each commune attempted to increase its own influence and reputation at its neighbors' expense. As a crucial part of a city's self-image, a foundation legend established and promoted a civic sense of honor, detailing a past that exalted the city's own illustrious origins while at the same time denigrating any such pretensions by its neighbors. The pasts outlined in such legends varied wildly and frequently contradicted one another. Medieval Florentine historians, for example, derived their city's name from words like force, flower, and sword (*forza*, *fiore*, and *fiorenza*). At the same time, they claimed that nearby Pistoia was so named because a terrible plague (*pistolenzia*) had occurred there in the first century B.C.[1] The past was hotly contested and constantly rewritten.

For reasons ranging from the symbolic to the practical, the northern Italian republics relied heavily on the events of Roman history when constructing their historical narratives. The city of Rome had retained much of its ancient aura as the center of Christian Europe, the *caput mundi* (head of the world) and the *urbs aurea* (golden city). Seeking to build on that glory, medieval cities from London to Constantinople claimed the title of *Roma secunda* (second Rome); the same was true of many Italian cities, such as Milan and Pisa.[2] On the other hand, the northern Italian communes' connection with their Roman past went beyond the merely theoretical. Roman historical and literary works spoke to their needs as republics and city-states, and the widespread presence of Roman remains across the Italian peninsula inspired a sense of cultural continuity despite the passage of more than a millennium. Classical sources such as Virgil, Sallust, Livy, and Lucan were both authoritative and useful for medieval Italian scholars and public officials attempting to demonstrate publicly the benefits of a civic system of ethics. Classicizing projects unified a city's population by providing it with a glorious past, one that pointed the way to an equally glorious future while simultaneously illustrating how that future could be achieved.

In creating their various versions of history and spreading their message, civic mythmakers embraced a broad range of media. Between A.D. 1250 and 1350, classicizing intent appears in forms as diverse as public frescoes and sculpture, legal decrees, architecture, civic ritual, coins, seals, and historical literature. Predictably, the choice of medium varied with the objective. In a manuscript culture, voluminous civic chronicles are more useful for enshrining a certain version of past events as canonical than for sharing that version with large numbers of people; public sculpture, on the other hand, has a limited narrative scope but is likely to reach a broader audience.[3] These are extreme examples. Most manifestations of the civic past served both of these functions to some degree, and they reinforced one another when used in tandem. Most cities articulated their chosen past in several different media at once, thus encouraging widespread public familiarity with the legend and its implications.

This chapter explores how the magistrates and scholars of the thirteenth- and fourteenth-century Italian republics articulated their sense of their Roman past. While the general trend was to promote a classical past as a means to civic glorification, a number of different approaches could achieve this goal. The medium was only one consideration. Perhaps more fundamental was the nature of a city's relationship with classical Rome: Did the city predate Rome, or was it founded by the Romans? Were the city's magistrates more interested in familiarizing their citizens with Roman civic virtues or classical political structures? Depending on their interests, communes generally incorporated Roman history into civic history in one or more of three ways: by championing a civic foundation related to or modeled on that of Rome; by integrating the early history of their city with the better-known history of Rome; and by appropriating celebrated features of Roman culture as their own. This chapter will address each of these themes in turn.

Adopting a Romanizing Civic Origin

The preternatural achievements that medieval literature attributed to the ancient Romans provided a sturdy set of coattails for any medieval city that desired to call attention to its ancient lineage, illustrious history, and political influence. For example, the passage most often cited by modern historians to demonstrate the civic self-confidence of the late medieval city-states comes from Giovanni Villani's chronicle of Florence, written in the late 1330s. Villani (c. 1276–1348) declares that he was inspired to write his history after returning from a visit to Rome during the first Jubilee in 1300: "Considering that our city of Florence, the daughter and creature of Rome, was rising and had great things before her, whilst Rome was declining, it seemed to me fitting to collect in this volume and new chronicle all the deeds and beginnings of the city of Florence."[4]

Villani's characterization of Florence as a "daughter and creature of Rome" is only the most famous in a long line of similar descriptions by late medieval Florentine historians and civil servants.[5] Fifty years earlier, an inscription (figure 1) placed on the wall of the Florentine palace of the *podestà*[6] (now known as the Bargello) enumerated in cramped Lombard capitals Florence's similarity to ancient Rome due to her "good health," good fortune, and expanding political influence.[7] With very little variation, local accounts of the early history of Florence attribute the city's origin both to Rome and to nearby Fiesole, a small town in the hills above Florence. Hence, as cited in the epigraph to this chapter, Dante refers to the tales of Rome, Troy, and Fiesole that constitute the history of Florence. These tales epitomize three ways in which a city's origin might engage with ancient Rome: a city could be founded directly from Rome; it could be founded (for example, from Troy) in a process paralleling the history of Rome; or it could be shown (as was claimed of Fiesole) to predate Rome altogether. As Villani's statement implies, the desire to equal or better the history of Rome drove each of these claims.

Since the Romans were well known to have founded many cities in and beyond Italy, the most obvious of these possible connections was foundation by the Romans. Medieval tradition related the founding of Florence as follows: Fiesole, in some accounts founded by the mythical hero Atlas as the first city in Europe, rebelled against domination by the Roman republic. A Roman army under Julius Caesar accordingly destroyed it and established a new town populated by both displaced Fiesolans and conquering Romans on the plain of the river Arno below the old site of Fiesole. A dispute erupted because Julius Caesar,

Fig. 1 Inscription on the Bargello (Palazzo del Podestà), Florence, c. 1255.

against the wishes of the Roman senate, wanted to name the new city Caesarea after himself. Hence, until the city was built and the name Florentia adopted, it was known simply as "little Rome" or "daughter of Rome" (*piccola Roma* or *filia Romae*). Further, the senate decreed that each Roman noble who wanted to name the new city should be given a part of it to build in imitation of Rome. The chronicle attributed to Ricordano Malispini stresses repeatedly how "everything [was] made and built in the style of Rome," "like that of Rome," and "in the same fashion as those in Rome."[8] The idea was that whichever Roman finished his section first should have the privilege of naming the city, but the senators were so eager that all of them finished in a single day.[9] Eventually they agreed to name the city after Fiorinus, a Roman senator who had died in battle with the Fiesolans, because he had been the first to build on the site. Etymological puns characterizing Fiorinus as the flower of the Romans (*fiore de' romani*) and a flower of chivalry (*fiore de' cavalieri*) generally attend this part of the story.[10]

The "little Rome" analogy connecting Florence with Rome functions on a number of levels. According to the medieval legend, not only the city's physical structures but also its name and people derived from ancient Rome. Villani emphasizes that the original population of Florence was a microcosm of its Roman parent body: "It was peopled by the best of Rome and the most capable, sent by the senate in due proportion from each division of Rome, chosen by lot from the inhabitants."[11] The original population of Florence was thus a balanced reflection of the Roman population and also an improved one, since only the "best" Romans were sent to Florence as colonists.

There are at least five full accounts of the origins of Florence from the century around 1300, beginning with Sanzanome's *Gesta Florentinorum* and ending with the Malispini chronicle.[12] Although each contains unique details and explanations of events, their many common elements demonstrate the interrelated nature of their various narratives. In fact, the basics of the legend were well enough known that even authors whose focus was not Florence's early history repeated the phrases ascribing the city's origin to the Romans, elevating the idea to the status of an epithet. The chronicle of Dino Compagni (1246/47–1324), a detailed analysis of Florentine politics between the years of 1280 and 1312, ignores the city's history before 1280 but nonetheless refers to Florence in the introduction as "this noble city, daughter of Rome."[13] Similarly, the 1339 *Florentie urbis et reipublice descriptio* characterizes the people of Florence as "begotten from the stock of the Romans."[14] Roman descent was clearly a major part of medieval Florentines' collective identity.

Although Florence is the best-known example, numerous other Italian cities advertised their foundation from Rome with similar details and rhetorical techniques. The Romanizing claims of Florence's chief rival, Siena, are considered at length in chapter 4 of this book. Roman foundations also figure into the mid-thirteenth-century *De laude civitatis Laude,* a poem on the rebuilding of the city of Lodi after its destruction by the Milanese in the twelfth century. The poem's anonymous author puns repeatedly on the Latin form of Lodi (Lauda, meaning "praise") to exalt his city and its historic independence:

> This was a flourishing race, from the earliest citizens of Rome,
> For the ancient city had been rebuilt twice out of ruins,
> Which Pompey's sword taught to praise [as] trophies.[15]

The author emphasizes his city's antiquity, connection to Rome, perseverance, and military prowess. His diction is notable chiefly for its extreme conventionality, featuring words that will recur repeatedly in this study—race, citizens, flourishing, ancient, and trophies. These words describe a present intimately connected with its past in a way that the inhabitants of a newly rebuilt city may have felt necessary. Since Lodi was rebuilt at a slight distance from the destroyed city, for example, there would have been no visible ruins. Works like the *De laude* would therefore have reminded the Lodesi of their city's antiquity despite a civic appearance of extreme modernity.

In the same way, a short courtly poem on the origins of San Gimignano attributes the city's foundation to "two noble shield-bearers, Silvius and Mutius, of the Roman people, descended and born of the best knights."[16] Descent from the ancient Romans imbued their heirs with a noble heritage—noble in the sense of imparting lofty ethical and political principles, but also in the literal sense of being aristocratic. It is always the Roman nobility, most frequently senators, who are cited in such legends. Like Villani's colonists, Silvius and Mutius are not only Roman but "born of the best knights."[17] These tropes of Roman descent and its various benefits appeared and reappeared in remarkably similar form across late medieval Italy, from Milan and Florence to smaller cities like Todi, Viterbo, and Pistoia.

If a Roman foundation increased a city's prestige, one could argue that a history paralleling or predating that of Rome would be still more effective. In fact, many Italian cities promulgated mythical origins during this period that were not specifically Roman; ancient Rome was the frame of reference, if not the direct subject, for most of these. It was the standard to surpass, and as a result, many non-Roman legends display Romanizing traits. The possession of a history paralleling that of Rome argued for historical parity. Equal antiquity, it was thought, should result in equal prestige, especially if the contemporary fortunes of the city in question surpassed those of Rome. On this basis, a number of medieval cities in northern Italy's Po Valley claimed Gallic foundations. Specifically, they attributed their origins to invading Gauls under Brennus, since the Gauls were the only early tribe known to have sacked Rome, as Livy narrates in book five of the *Ab urbe condita*.[18] Milanese historians took up this trope in the early fourteenth century, as did many smaller cities in Milan's orbit, such as Bergamo, Brescia, and Asti.[19]

In the same way, stories of little-known Trojans permeate the historical literature. Classical Rome's claims to a unique ancestry had always supposed that Aeneas and his immediate family had been the only Trojan survivors of the war, although Virgil and Livy both mention in passing the exploits of Antenor, the legendary founder of Padua (Roman Patavium).[20] In the Middle Ages, however, the list of Trojans who survived the war and went on to found other cities grew dramatically. Kingdoms and cities across Europe acquired Trojan founders, each more improbable than the last. Colette Beaune has explored the Trojan origins claimed for the Capetian kings of France, and Sylvia Federico those for the Anglo-Norman kings of England. Based on these claims, the encyclopedic *Livres dou Trésor* by the Florentine Brunetto Latini (c. 1220–1293/94) even includes a legend explaining King Arthur's Trojan ancestry.[21] Trojan descent was as popular in Italian cities as it was elsewhere in Europe; for example, the cities explored in chapters 2, 3, and 5 of this book all claim Trojan descent in some way. Padua was allegedly founded by Antenor, Genoa by a "Trojan prince" named Janus, and Perugia by a Trojan (or possibly a Greek) veteran named Eulistes.

The uncertainty of Eulistes' affiliation in the Trojan War introduces a contrasting example: cities that claimed parity with Rome not through Trojan ancestry but through the Greeks, who had actually won the war. The overwhelming influence of Roman historiography and the myth of Rome on medieval Europe probably limited the popularity of claims to Greek ancestry. Roman sources naturally display a strong bias toward the Trojan side. Nevertheless, some cities elaborated their descent from or affiliation with the Greeks, probably to challenge Rome's traditional authority on the Italian peninsula. Most such cities were located in southern Italy—unsurprisingly, given the area's ancient affiliation with Greek politics and culture (and its classical appellation of Magna Graecia). Following Solinus and Servius, for example, medieval historians such as Riccobaldo da Ferrara (c. 1245–1318) and Guglielmo da Pastrengo (c. 1290–1362) attribute the founding of Benevento and Arpi to the Greek hero Diomedes in the years after the Trojan War.[22]

The best-documented city affirming Greek affiliation is Pisa, a maritime power in southern Tuscany. Medieval chronicles assert that it was built by the mythical Greek figure of Pelops, son of Tantalus and grandfather of the Atreides, whose familial woes caused the Trojan War. The chronicle attributed to the Pisan Dominican Bartolomeo da San Concordio (c. 1262–1347) claims further that, before he came to Italy, Pelops founded a city in Greece after which the entire Peloponnesian Peninsula was named.[23] Yet Pisan accounts of the past do not stop at linking the city's foundation with Greek mythology. Ranieri Sardo's fourteenth-century chronicle presents a traditional Pisan view of the Trojan War: "And we find how the Pisans gave aid to the Greeks when they were on the battlefield at Troy, and destroyed [the city]."[24] Pisan historians made much of their city's historical connections with Rome, but its purported Greek origin and affiliation during the Trojan War apparently provided a kind of independent historical prestige that direct dependence on Rome did not.[25]

Claiming pre-Roman origins could also be a way of outshining the prestige of Rome's own history. Pisa's participation in the Trojan War meant that the city necessarily predated the war. In fact, Pisan chronicles repeat many times and in great detail how much older their city was than Rome. The chronicle attributed to Bartolomeo da San Concordio contains numerous statements on Pisa's significantly greater antiquity. After a description of the foundation of Pisa by Pelops, for instance, the chronicle adds, "And it is certain that this time, in which [Pisa] was built, was a long time before the city of Rome was founded."[26]

Such statements appear regularly in contemporary histories and chronicles. Ranieri Sardo emphasizes that Pisa was founded in the third age of the world, thirty years before the sack of Troy, whereas "Rome was built in the fourth age, or the fifth, in the 4056th year from the beginning of the world. . . . Therefore, Pisa existed 268 years before Rome."[27] Claims by Dominican historian Galvano Fiamma (1283–after 1344) on behalf of Milan strike a similar chord. Having informed his reader that Milan, originally called Subria, was a great city that controlled all of Lombardy long before Rome grew into its power, he reminds the reader redundantly that "it was built in a most ancient time, before Rome."[28] The superlative *antiquissimo* (most ancient) and the number of times Galvano reiterates the point reveal his view of the significance of the Roman comparison.

Extending the emphasis on extreme antiquity, many legends locate their city origins in primeval times, long before the foundation of Rome or any other Italian city. Numerous cities claim to have been the first city in Italy, founded by the first rulers of Italy at the dawn of the world. We have already seen one version of this claim in Florence's binary origin myth, as it argues that the city originated not only with the Romans but also with the ancient Fiesolans, and that Fiesole was the first city in Europe. As Villani puts it, expanding on a description in the earlier *Chronica de origine civitatis,* "it was the first city built in . . . Europe, and therefore it was named *Fia Sola* [it shall be alone], to wit, *first,* with no other inhabited city in that said area."[29] To explain, the *Chronica* and Villani relate how Fiesole was founded by the classical grab bag of Atlas, Jove, Electra, and Apollo as, respectively, the first postdiluvian city in the world and the first city in Europe. (The Malispini chronicle justifies the former claim by explaining that Atlas was closely descended from Noah.)[30] According to all of these sources, Atlas and Electra, the rulers of Fiesole, had three sons named Italus, Sicanus, and Dardanus, who divided the world among themselves. Italus ruled Italy from Fiesole, while Sicanus claimed Sicily. Dardanus, to whom the rest of the world was assigned, traveled to the eastern Mediterranean to found Troy (thus making the medieval Florentines the ancestors of the Romans). Returning to Italus in Fiesole, Villani recounts how "he [Italus] begat great rulers which after him governed not only the city of Fiesole and the country round about, but well-nigh all Italy, and they built many cities there. And the said city of Fiesole rose into great power and lordship, until the great city of Rome reached her state and lordship."[31] If Fiesole was the first and most important city in primeval pre-Roman Italy, then medieval Florentines (so the argument ran) were merely reclaiming their ancestors' former glory.

The idea of descent from Noah, as was claimed for Atlas, was widespread in this context, since it was the best way to guarantee the unsurpassable antiquity of one's city and people in a Christian world. Galvano Fiamma's story of Milan's foundation as Subria in the "most ancient time" rests on the idea that Subres, the founder of Subria, was the great-grandson of Noah through Tubal, son of Japheth (as enumerated in Isidore's *Etymologiae*).[32] In the Middle Ages, Tubal was generally recognized as the founder of Ravenna, but Ravennese chronicles usually connect him to Noah through Ham rather than Japheth.[33] On Ravenna's fortunes after its foundation, however, Ravennese chronicles emphasize the same points as Fiamma and the Florentine chronicles: "And the city of Ravenna flourished for a long time. . . . And Ravenna was the seat of the kingdom, [a city] in which barons and soldiers and nobles all gathered, and all of Italy was subject to it, up to the time of the Romans."[34] The legend claims that Ravenna was the most important city in Italy from the peninsula's earliest human inhabitation after the flood up to Roman domination, leaving little glory for any other city.

Beyond using classical mythology and biblical stories, primeval accounts of pre-Roman civic glory relied on one other major source, namely, the world chronicle of Eusebius of Caesarea (c. 325), as it had been updated and translated into Latin by Saint Jerome (c. 380). In the Middle Ages, Paul the Deacon (Paulus Diaconus, c. 720–799) and others expanded Eusebius-Jerome into an ongoing tradition of universal histories.[35] Eusebian accounts attest to five rulers of Italy before Aeneas—Janus, Saturnus, Picus, Faunus, and Latinus—and medieval Italian historians often cite them as pre-Roman founders of cities or in broader Trojan or Noetic accounts. Janus was supposedly the first king of Italy and the founder of medieval Genoa, but he also appears in Brunetto Latini's *Trésor* as a descendant of Noah in the sixth degree.[36] In the same vein, the chronicle of Ricordano Malispini relates that Capys, the legendary founder of Capua, was the grandson of King Latinus.[37]

Cities that wished to improve their historical prestige in relation to Rome and their neighbors, therefore, took several different approaches to their civic foundation, though all used the classical history of Rome as a historical benchmark. Three paradigmatic ways of accomplishing this were, first, to claim foundation from Rome itself; second, to vaunt an early history mirroring that of Rome (such as foundation by the Trojans, Gauls, or Greeks); and third, to assert a primeval foundation entirely predating that of Rome. Individual legends often incorporate more than one of these characteristics; with the help of elastic logic, one Genoese account embraces all of them at once.[38]

The details vary considerably from city to city, and even from chronicle to chronicle. Nonetheless, these three types of mythical foundations share a common preoccupation with the legendary history of Rome. Those that do not confront the history of Rome directly are always in some way competing with it as well as with one another. In most cases, the competitive spirit is explicit: chroniclers attempt to extinguish every possible doubt as to their city's primacy and antiquity, on whatever grounds they base their claims. All of these legends may thus be described as Romanizing, since all engage directly with, and imagine themselves within, the canonical Roman past. Using this framework of three basic models for a Romanizing engagement with the past, the rest of this chapter examines the ways in which medieval Italian scholars and public servants tried to support their claims.

Retroactive Networking

Along with claiming the direct foundation of one's city by classical literary and mythological figures, the most common means of "improving" a civic past was by merging local history with the better-known exploits of the Romans, Trojans, or others. The implication was that the Romans were biased and had thus told the story to their own advantage. A city gained prestige if, like Pisa, it had taken part in well-known historical events such as the Trojan War. Thus, cities sought to increase their glory in the medieval present through a practice I shall call retroactive networking—by incorporating historical figures and events into the local history of the city, or, inversely, by arguing for the city's hitherto unrecognized contribution to famous historical events. Many cities, for example, attributed their foundation or other local events, like the building of a monument, to Julius Caesar; the prestige derived from the value attached to Caesar's name. In the same way, Milan and Pavia attached much importance to their association with the later Roman emperors and Lombard kings of Italy. Civic glory was gained retroactively by association with events and people already recognized as glorious by the history, literature, and art of medieval Italy.

Caesar's fame also drives the myth of Rimini (Roman Ariminum), a city south of Ravenna on the Adriatic coast where an arch of Augustus (figure 2) and a bridge built by Tiberius still stand. Taking advantage of these classical remains from at least the turn of the fourteenth century, Rimini advertised itself as the place where Julius Caesar crossed the Rubicon.[39] The commune erected a commemorative stone much like a modern historic site marker (figure 3). It became the focus of local pride; the account of Caesar's exploits by Petrarch (Francesco Petrarca, 1304–1374) in his *De viris illustribus*, written in the 1330s, explains, "When I was a boy, I was shown the stone in the middle of the piazza where it is said that Caesar spoke."[40] Caesar's famous crossing of the Rubicon was especially momentous since the medieval world thought of him (rather than his great-nephew Octavian, later Augustus) as the first Roman emperor. The crossing of the Rubicon thus symbolically divided republic from empire. Having been the site of this famous event increased Rimini's consequence.

In the same way, Florentine sources associate the rebellion of Fiesole against Rome with the Catilinarian conspiracy of 63–62 B.C. They explain that when Catiline fled north from Rome, he went to Fiesole. The Romans had to destroy the city in order to crush the rebellion; the story thus attributes the rebellion and destruction of Fiesole to a more historically significant force than Fiesolan

Fig. 2 Arch of Augustus with medieval crenellations, Rimini, first century A.D.

Fig. 3 Marker where Julius Caesar allegedly made his speech after crossing the Rubicon, Rimini. This fifteenth-century stone replaced an earlier monument.

ill temper or Roman imperialism. The anonymous *Libro fiesolano* takes the story one step further, finishing with:

> And this Catiline, noblest king [*sic*] of Rome, had a son called Hubert Caesar [Uberto Cesare], who was a wise man of the greatest valor. . . . And when this Hubert was fifteen years old, he returned to Rome and was confirmed [in his rights], and pardoned by the senate and the consuls. And all the Romans gave him much honor, and his inheritance was restored to him . . . and he went to rule over Florence with seven companions, among them both Romans and Fiesolans. And he was lord over all of them and held the city for the government in Rome. And so it happened that this Hubert Caesar took a Fiesolan wife and had sixteen children, who multiplied greatly in their realm, as it pleased God.[41]

This version of the story resolves Catiline's involvement with the rebellion of Fiesole and the associated founding of Florence by reconciling Catiline's family with the Roman community through his son. It also specifically attributes the initial merging of the Fiesolan and Roman peoples to the boy, who is given the magical name of Caesar in an effort to increase the legend's symbolic value.[42] One chronicle of Todi, a small city in Umbria, creates a similar genealogical link by claiming that the early Roman hero Coriolanus descended from the early rulers of Todi rather than from local Roman stock.[43]

The practice of incorporating famous figures from Roman history into local history was widespread, involving not only historical celebrities like Julius Caesar and Catiline but also literary and mythological figures. Mantua based a good part of its fame on having been Virgil's birthplace; the city erected at least two statues of the poet in the thirteenth century (see figure 4).[44] Sulmona did the same with the poet Ovid, who was depicted in public statuary and on the Sulmonese civic seal and coinage.[45] The later Roman author Macrobius was celebrated by the inhabitants of Parma, who placed his statue on the façade of their cathedral, and the Paduan veneration of the great Augustan historian Livy will be discussed in chapter 2.[46]

Medieval scholars may have particularly valued Roman authors as ancestors for the immediacy of their works; they could only read about Catiline, but they could experience the words of Livy, Ovid, or Virgil personally. Moreover, medieval pedagogy fostered an acute familiarity with classical works. Notarial education required the close study of ancient letters as models for medieval legal and contractual practice.[47] Virgil in particular—the most respected of all classical

Fig. 4 Statue of Virgil on the Palazzo Broletto, Mantua, c. 1227.

writers—had a medieval reputation that verged on the divine. He was considered not only a poet but also a magician, and accounts of his feats permeated the Italian peninsula throughout the Middle Ages.[48]

Mythological figures such as Hercules also appear frequently in early civic history. Since most such stories were taken from Livy or from Ovid's *Metamorphoses*, they represented a link to the classical Roman past while at the same time providing a pre-Roman milieu. Citizens of Todi, for example, divided their origin in half, producing a legend much like that of the Florentines. The first half attributes the events surrounding the city's foundation to a son of Remus named Senna.[49] The other half of the legend traces the city's origin to a pre-Roman city called Eclis, renamed Todi centuries later by the city's patron saint, Fortunatus. According to the legend, Hercules founded Eclis on the occasion of his wrangle with the thief Cacus, an event that, according to Livy, took place during the rule of Evander (that is, before Aeneas's arrival). The city's name—Eclis—derived from Hercules' own.[50] And although it was eventually renamed Todi, the inclusion in the legend of famous figures from early Roman history (Hercules, Evander, Romulus, and Remus) increased the symbolic value and the recognizability of Todi's early history to all who heard it.

Along with adopting famous Romans, civic foundation legends often align a city's early history with the early history of Rome, claiming close political association (*amicitia*, or "friendship" in the traditional Roman sense of the word) if not actual blood kinship between the two. Of Milan, the grammarian Bonvesin da la Riva (c. 1240–c. 1314) asserted in 1288 that "I have never heard or read that this city ever rebelled against Rome, but rather whenever it was able served as a most faithful comrade and helper. Therefore it was ever called the second Rome."[51] The integration of Milan's more obscure early history with the familiar history of Rome creates a parallel between the two cities. It inserts famous and recognizable events into the early history of Milan, but it also gives that city credit for having contributed to Rome's original success. In the same way, Galvano Fiamma claims that Roman military success was mostly due to the valor and ferocity of Rome's Milanese allies: "In all the wars of the Romans, the citizens of Milan always held the front line. And thus the people of Milan achieved countless victories throughout Italy."[52]

Similarly, Perugia's historical epic, the *Eulistea* (1293), characterizes its citizens not only as descendants of survivors of the Trojan War but also as close allies of the Romans. If Bonvesin characterizes Milan as Rome's younger sibling, Bonifacio da Verona (fl. 1250–1300), author of the *Eulistea*, characterizes Perugia as Rome's older sibling: "sister and relative and friend."[53] Perugia's founder, Eulistes, and his compatriots send aid and fraternal advice to Romulus and his companions, for example, over the matter of the Sabine women. Hence, the success of the nascent Roman state was largely the work of their helpful Perugian mentors. At the same time, the *Eulistea* reminds the citizens of Perugia of their historic *Romanitas*. It describes Romans and Perugians alike as sons of Romulus (*Romulides*),[54] and at one point a Perugian general reminds his troops to be brave because "you are Romans."[55] The cultural implications for medieval Perugians could not be clearer, particularly since the frescoes in the main meeting room in the Perugian city hall (the Palazzo dei Priori, built 1298–1305) contain heraldic shields with Rome's traditional SPQR motif.[56]

Paralleling Bonifacio's story of Perugian aid to Romulus and Remus, the Pisan Chronicler Ranieri Sardo records Pisan aid not only to the Greeks during the Trojan War but also to Aeneas for his battle against Turnus:

> And afterward, the Pisans gave Aeneas help when he fled from Troy and came into Italy to found a new city on the bank of the Roman Tiber; from this people came those who later founded Rome. Having been spurned by Turnus, who was there in the city of King Latinus, Aeneas came to Pisa for help, and he received it from all of Lombardy and all of Tuscany down to the Roman Tiber. And the Pisans sent one thousand knights [*chavalieri*], whose captain was a Pisan named Assila.[57]

In this legend, the city of Pisa is already well established when Aeneas arrives in Italy. Unlike the churlish Turnus, the Pisans welcome the exiles—to their benefit, as the reader would already have known from classical sources like Virgil. Therefore, according to Sardo, the Pisans were on the victorious side in two of the most important conflicts in classical history: the Trojan War and Aeneas's conquest of Italy. By implication, these events might not have had the "right" outcome had it not been for Pisan intervention. Sardo's account elevates his city almost to the level of the divine; Trojan settlement in Italy, the growth of the Roman state, and all that came afterward relied on aid that the Pisans provided to the Romans at crucial historical moments.

Furthermore, Sardo's naming of the otherwise unknown Pisan captain Assila gives his account an aura of authenticity. Such superfluous details were helpful in this regard, but accounts of past renown and alliances were more plausible when supported by physical evidence. Ruins also made the dissemination of Romanizing history easier, since explaining an extant monument was far less complicated than building one from scratch. Consequently, monuments played a significant role in the articulation of Roman civic identity—whether or not those monuments were truly ancient, and whether or not what people said of them was true.

Naturally, when considering the medieval reuse of classical remains, the question of intent must inspire caution. Sheer size and preexistence probably inspired many of those who took over, built on, and inhabited classical remains in the Middle Ages. In some instances, however, historicizing intent is clearly discernible, as when a city adopted a classical object or structure as its civic emblem, like the locally excavated statue that Siena chose to adorn its first public fountain.[58] The ancient statues of a lion and a griffin that the Perugians erected on their town hall complemented the hall's façade of Etruscan and Roman decorative elements copied from the city's ancient arch and city wall (see figures 17 and 20).[59] Although one cannot always locate a particular instance precisely along the spectrum between convenience and choice, the evidence often suggests what medieval builders, historians, artists, and magistrates thought they were doing, or were trying to do, when they embraced a particular classical motif or monument.

For example, ancient monuments, particularly large ones, were often adopted as civic symbols, being the most visible and memorable attributes of specific cities. A large equestrian statue of one of the Antonine emperors, known as the Regisol, served as Pavia's emblem. Some argue that even modern Pavians have never quite forgiven the French for the destruction of the statue during the Napoleonic invasion. It seems clear that the French were making a political gesture designed to crush Pavian independence and reinforce their subjection of the area, rather than, as claimed, attempting to destroy a tyrant's image in the name of republicanism; this suggests the historic depth of the Pavians' attachment to the statue.[60] The Regisol and other well-known monuments appeared on city seals and coinage during the Middle Ages and long after. Further examples include the Augustan arch at Fano, the Nervan arch in Ancona, the Roman arch and bridge at Rimini (figure 2), the Porta Aurea at Ravenna, and the amphitheatre and Roman arcade at Verona.[61]

Communal regimes often co-opted and reinforced the historical associations of these monuments in other media. The Nervan arch in Ancona, for example, consisted of a Roman arch (a gate to the city still used as such in the medieval period) surmounted by a monumental statue of Nerva, by whom it was originally built. The medieval inhabitants of Ancona may or may not have known that the figure was that of Nerva, but they did reproduce it in two key places: on the city seal and in a bas-relief on the podestà's palace in the city's main piazza.[62] Given these choices, one might venture that the medieval inhabitants of Ancona perceived the figure of Nerva to represent not only their entire city but also the maintenance of proper rule and order. Keeping order was a podestà's main charge, and the Romans were famous for it.

Civic chronicles and broader histories often contain elaborate explanations for these monuments. A fourteenth-century Viterbese chronicler named Francesco di Andrea, for example, claims that the city of Viterbo, enclosed by its eleventh-century walls, was originally founded as a fortress by Hercules: "This fortress of Hercules was large and attractive, positioned between two valleys and located on a hill with a bank behind, and it had an attractive village [borgo] in which everyone lodged who wished to travel in the countryside. And he maintained it in prosperity until the time Rome was founded."[63] Francesco cites the entire circuit of the Viterbese walls as a monument supporting his version of the foundation and early history of Viterbo. Not all historiographical references are quite so sweeping; for instance, Giovanni Villani asserts that the early twelfth-century cathedral baptistery in Florence was an ancient temple of Mars.[64] Yet such explanations could be quite elaborate, as in the case of the Porta Aurea in Ravenna. The *Chronica de civitate Ravennae* incorporates the city's Roman gate (the Porta Aurea) and the figure of Caesar into local history as follows: after Caesar crossed the Rubicon, he stopped in Ravenna to reorganize his troops. While he was there, he ordered the elaborate rebuilding of one of the city gates, known as the Asian Gate: "Here he ordered another gate to be built on top of the original gate, with a little house underneath it, which had doors of Arabian gold. . . . Because of this, that gate was called Golden [Aurea] which had previously been known as Asian."[65] This account integrates a number of the methods by which late medieval historians and magistrates incorporated the Roman past into local history. First, it involves a famous Roman figure at a key moment in history; second, it explains a traditional appellation etymologically (the Golden Gate—presumably the gold was long gone); and third, it locates all of those historical claims physically in a monument still extant in Ravenna.

Perhaps the most outlandish type of claim is the adoption of another city's monuments. In the Todese chronicles mentioned earlier, Senna, the son of Remus, conquered most of Umbria to the north of Rome and in so doing came into conflict with both Romans and Tuscans. Senna's wife gave birth to twins named Latinus and Cornelius, and Senna renamed his capital (Eclis) Latina in honor of his elder son.[66] After many years, Latinus and his ally the king of Tuscany defeated the Romans, who began to plead with Latinus that he refrain from destroying their city, which had been constructed with such great labor, and they told him that they would agree to anything he wished [if he would spare the city]. Among other things, Latinus ordered that all of Romulus's heirs should be killed [since Remus had been Latinus's grandfather] and that two gates should be constructed in the city of Rome, one of which should be called Latina in honor of his own name, and the other called Salaria in honor of his wife.[67]

The anonymous chronicler posits not only Todi's victory over early Rome—a rout saved from being a complete sack of the city only by the restraint of the Todese leader—but also a Todese origin and etymology for two of Rome's famous gates (the Porta Latina and the Porta Salaria), despite the fact that the said gates are located on opposite sides of Rome. The Porta Salaria faces north in the general direction of Umbria and Todi, while the Porta Latina, still extant in classical form, provides access to the countryside south of Rome. This story thus extends the trend followed throughout this chapter. Not content to appropriate events and figures from Roman history to fit its city's own historical experience—as, for example, explaining local monuments—the Todese account appropriates both history and monument, for which it posits a previously unknown independent origin. It is perhaps indicative of the poor credibility of this claim even in the Middle Ages that it never appears, as many such do, in a historical work produced outside of the originating city. But the technique of retroactive networking, which the medieval inhabitants of Todi harnessed in their attempt to link the ancient gates of Rome with the history of their city, appears over and over again.

Cultural Appropriations

Historical name-dropping is a fairly easy way to appropriate a past. So far this chapter has demonstrated how Roman names, events, and monuments bestrew the historiographic world of late medieval Italy. But those responsible for promulgating these legends frequently supported their historical explanations with broader social associations, championing Roman traditions and practices as a way of linking the two worlds more closely. This was certainly an ideological maneuver: they manipulated contemporary views of the Roman past to promulgate values that were important to them in influential areas such as law, religion, and ethics.

Classicizing foundation myths were often intended to bolster claims of political autonomy in and for the cities of late medieval Italy. As a result, their presentation frequently emphasized the rights accorded to cities in Roman law or those specifically granted to the city at hand. Perugia seems to have developed the pre-Roman and Roman parts of its civic history to counterbalance the papacy's traditional sovereignty over the city.[68] Communes perceived Roman law as establishing both legal and cultural precedents for their existence, and any privileges a town had gained in the past, however long ago, could be used to justify contemporary independence and self-rule. Riccobaldo da Ferrara, for example, argues that Ferrara was originally constituted in the time of the emperor Constantine as a republic, *unam Rempublicam*. He parses republic as two words (*rem* and *publicam*) but clearly thinks of the term as a single idea referring to a specific type of government. Further, he suggests that because of this founding event, Ferrara has always been, is inherently, and therefore should remain a republican entity.[69] The city as it was first created is its best guide to future development.

Maximizing these parallels, medieval historians, notaries, and other scholars frequently framed medieval concepts in classicizing terms. Roman titles officially adorned certain political systems and municipal offices, but historians and notaries also used classical terminology to describe those systems and offices unofficially. This was true even of medieval offices with no classical cognate. The minutes of the highest Perugian city council were known as the *Annali decemvirali* even though the council regularly comprised many more than ten men and they were not called *decemviri*.[70] Political historians of medieval Italy are used to speaking of "consular" regimes, which were typically the first form of independent government adopted in the rebellious cities of tenth- and eleventh-century Italy.[71] Like their Roman model, these cities were generally ruled by executive magistrates called consuls, in varying numbers and for varying terms.

Even when the consular model was almost universally replaced with the more complex podestarial system, the use of Romanizing terms continued. City councils are frequently referred to as *senatus* (senate) in official documents like council minutes and decrees, as well as in more literary works like civic histories and political treatises. Apart from consul, other Roman titles, such as *magistratus*, *praetor*, and *tribunus*, were revived, some more appropriate than others.[72] One could argue, particularly in the case of a general term like *magistratus*, that writers used these words because they had an uncomplicated meaning in medieval Latin, and not because of their historic significance. Nevertheless, a distinct historical awareness underlies many of these usages. Cola di Rienzo's adoption of the classical term *tribunus* in the context of his reestablishment of the Roman republic in 1347 is the most flamboyant of many such instances.[73]

Medieval scholars and historians even invented fake Roman offices by which to describe, or from which to derive, contemporary medieval offices. The work of Milanese historian Galvano Fiamma is a trove of linguistic improbability; for example, he reports as historical support for the Milanese archbishopric that Milan was the seat of a classical *archiflamen*. The priestly title *flamen* is certainly well documented in Roman religion, but the most prestigious of these priests had names like *flamen dialis*. There was no *archiflamen*. Instead, Galvano has reverse-engineered the Milanese archbishopric in medieval style, most likely to counterbalance the papacy's claim to the title *pontifex maximus* (the traditional, and documentable, head of another group of Roman priests called the *pontifices*). If the papacy based its claims to antiquity on having been the most important of the *pontifices*, Galvano's etymology makes a parallel claim for the derivation of the Milanese archbishopric from the most important of the *flamines*.

Despite their pagan implications, Roman religious terms also appear frequently in the literature of the medieval cities. Sanzanome eulogizes Florence as "built under fortunate auspices" (*haedificata fortunatis auguriis*)—the taking of the auspices being one of the Romans' most important religious rituals.[74] Both Pace da Ferrara (fl. 1300), speaking of Venice, and Bonifacio da Verona, speaking of Perugia, refer to the city's *lares*, or guardian gods.[75] These are rhetorical tropes inherited from classical and postclassical sources, and they certainly do not imply any rebellion against the established medieval church. Nonetheless, I cite them to demonstrate the extent to which classical Roman modes of thought underlay urban consciousness in medieval Italy, both intentionally and unintentionally.

In this way, the Christian Middle Ages embraced pagan Roman traditions and rituals. The role that Roman mythology played in medieval astrology may have mitigated the potentially inflammatory use of pagan gods and ceremonies. Giovanni Villani, for example, explains seriously that Florence's civic problems are the result of the city's foundation under the sign of Mars.[76] The *Florentie urbis et reipublice descriptio* records a prophecy made by the Eritrean sibyl, which had previously been interpreted as referring to the founding of Rome: "It is not true that [the prophecy] speaks of Rome, because this sibyl prophesied long after the city was founded. . . . It should not be overlooked that the Tiburtine sibyl prophesied after the Eritrean sibyl, in the time of Octavian, and, in speaking of some city, said many of the same things. But it is clear from other things she said that she too was referring to the city of Florence."[77] The anonymous work appropriates for Florence not just a prophecy alleged to foretell the destiny of Rome but the entire Roman system of omens, prophecies, and sibyls. We will see the literal embodiment of this cultural appropriation in the next chapter. In 1315, the Paduan commune revived the ancient ceremony of laureation to honor a local poet-notary, Albertino Mussato (1262–1329), and his prorepublican Senecan tragedy *Ecerinis*, thus demonstrating the close kinship of classical and medieval politics and culture.

In fact, medieval Italians perceived Roman society to have been not only well organized and lawful but also fundamentally ethical in a way that was both relevant and useful to Italian cities in the late Middle Ages. Literary works and public art repeatedly emphasize the virtue of Roman principles and historical figures. Villani's medieval Florentines derive from the "noble Romans in their virtue" and the "ancient and worthy Trojans."[78] Some of this may be rhetorical flourish, but art historians have identified a number of Romanizing frescoes in the public art of late medieval Italy. Romans appear as the most numerous figures in a series of historical frescoes, now mostly obliterated, painted in the Loggia dei Cavalieri in Treviso just after the turn of the fourteenth century.[79] The Paduan humanist Lovato Lovati (1241–1309) seems likewise to have overseen the painting of Roman frescoes in Vicenza during his time as podestà of that city. Simone Martini (c. 1280–1344) painted a fresco of Marcus Regulus for the regime of the Nine in Siena, and an early fourteenth-century fresco of the republican hero Marcus Junius Brutus has been attributed to the hall of the Florentine Arte della Lana (the wool guild, the most influential guild in Florence and hence a prominent public place).[80] Public art was didactic above all, and frescoes of Roman subjects emphasized the courage, intellect, and virtue of great Romans as practiced on a public, specifically civic, stage. The inhabitants of late medieval Italy were surrounded by objects and texts that repeated and confirmed the relevance of such moral lessons; they ranged from classical remains to written histories, medieval monuments, frescoes, public terminology, and the oral legends that inevitably accompanied all of these things.

Romanizing legends, however they were articulated—and however farfetched they may seem in hindsight—therefore demonstrate the central role played by the classical past in the construction of late medieval Italian civic identity. Working from the city of Rome's innate prestige and the obvious parallels of experience, republican communes used classical stories and ideas to compare the past and the present, to argue for one city's supremacy over another, and to offer advice on the conduct appropriate to the citizens of a republican city-state. The history of Rome was a yardstick by which every medieval city judged itself and was judged by others.

A classical foundation legend served two notable purposes. First, it added to civic glory. The past was a barometer of present status, with greater prestige going to cities of greater antiquity. Status also accrued to cities associated with famous events or people. As a result, some foundation legends are specifically Roman, but others are Romanizing in the sense of trying to outdo the history of Rome. Thus, we see pre-Roman founders, alternative sets of pagan priests, and alternate genealogies for famous Roman heroes. Second, a foundation legend's emphasis on a joint past encouraged civic unity. Factionalism and self-interest were major dangers to republican city-states, which developed a complex set of rhetorical tools to mitigate these problems. Contemporary political rhetoric stressed the importance of the common good over individual desires, often citing examples from Roman history and Cicero's *De officiis* to support its claims. A foundation legend could have the same effect; it advertised the unitary origin of a city and its people, and it reminded a population of its shared glorious past.

Both of these purposes were essentially didactic, paralleling classical people and situations with medieval ones. Tales of former glory inspired and foretold present glory, and past virtue served as a model for present behavior. Every legend described the ancient glories of its city according to medieval desires and needs, reaching back to associate that city with the people, events, or traditions that its citizens found valuable to contemporary urban experience. Hence the attraction of classical foundation legends in particular: the Romans were famous, their urban way of life was familiar, and their history demonstrated republicanism, both good and bad. The Roman past was a lesson to be learned or ignored at will, and the fate of one's own city hung in the balance.

The Florentine historian Sanzanome uses all of these tactics to explain the importance of Roman and Fiesolan history to his contemporaries: "If we trace our origin from the noble stock of the Romans, and we derive from them our successful advances in virtue, it behooves us to maintain what remains to us of our ancestors, lest we be derided by others as ungrateful. . . . Men, brothers who derive your origin from Italus, from whom all Italy is said to be descended, behold your nobility and the steadfastness of this ancient place."[81] Sanzanome presents the virtuous lives and glorious achievements of the Florentines' classical ancestors as reasons for civic pride and unity, and he suggests them as worthy models for present behavior. This explanation demonstrates why Dante's ideal Florentine woman is a mother who tells her family the legends of Fiesole, Troy, and Rome as she spins. The myths of Florence were considered the key to her family's past, a model for their present identity, and a primer for their future success.

As I have demonstrated, most of these foundation legends reflect common subject material and a similarity of approach. On the other hand, each legend promulgates a unique version of the past. As we have seen, different cities chose different elements of the classical past to adopt or incorporate into their local narratives. Participants may be kings and senators, mythological heroes, or classical authors. The majority are Roman; others are Greek, Trojan, or Italic. Instead of people, some legends champion ancient monuments or religious customs. Each legend emphasizes different aspects of the classical past and promotes a city's chosen past in diverse ways. In the end, a city's choices reflect its unique political and cultural circumstances. Social groups within each city interacted differently, and each city had unique concerns about itself in relation to its neighbors. To demonstrate their similarities as well as their differences, the next four chapters examine in depth the legends adopted by four cities around the turn of the fourteenth century: Padua, Genoa, Siena, and Perugia. I suggest how and why each legend took the specific form it did, given the sociopolitical environment in which a city found itself, and I hope by my choice of cities to demonstrate the wide variability of the classical legend phenomenon.

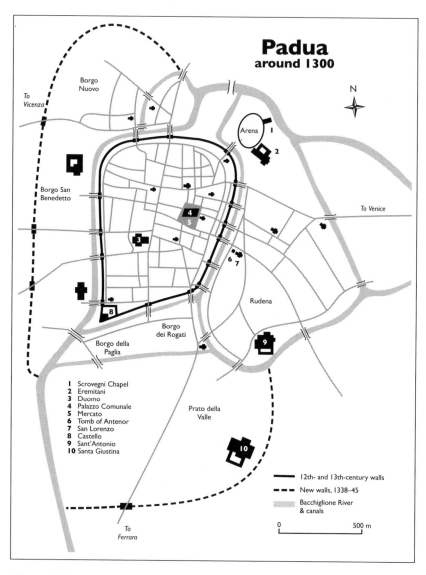

Padua
around 1300

N

To
Vicenza

Borgo
Nuovo

Arena   1

2

Borgo San
Benedetto

To Venice

4
5

3

6   7

Rudena

8

Borgo
dei Rogati

Borgo della
Paglia

9

1   Scrovegni Chapel
2   Eremitani
3   Duomo
4   Palazzo Comunale
5   Mercato
6   Tomb of Antenor
7   San Lorenzo
8   Castello
9   Sant'Antonio
10   Santa Giustina

Prato della
Valle

10

——— 12th- and 13th-century walls
- - - - New walls, 1338–45
     Bacchiglione River
     & canals

0   500 m

To
Ferrara

Map 2   Padua around 1300. Map after Hyde, *Padua in the Age of Dante*, and Kohl, *Padua Under the Carrara.*

PADUA
Rehousing the Relics of Antenor

Antenor was tall, slender, quick-limbed, cunning, and cautious.

—"Dares the Phrygian," *De excidio Troiae historia*

According to the ancient sources—from Virgil and Livy to Solinus and Servius—the northern Italian city of Padua was founded after the Trojan War by Antenor, the only named Trojan survivor of the war aside from Aeneas and his family.[1] Padua's connection with the ancient sources and Rome's renowned ancestor was nonetheless double edged. The version of Trojan history dominant in the Middle Ages, that of Dares and Dictys, asserted that Aeneas and Antenor only escaped with their lives because they were traitors who had betrayed their city to the Greeks, receiving freedom in return for their collaboration.[2] Thus, while Antenor provided Padua with an illustrious heritage traceable to Troy in the most ancient and authoritative sources, he also represented the worst sin known to medieval Christians: betrayal.[3] It cannot have been pleasant to see one's founding father featured as an embodiment of treachery in the lowest circle of hell, namely, Antenora in Dante's *Inferno*.[4]

The figure of Antenor therefore presented a problem, since late thirteenth-century Padua considered itself worthy of a distinguished founder. Its citizens had thrown off the tyranny of Ezzelino da Romano and his family, who had ruled the city from 1236 to 1260; in their place, an autonomous republic was established.[5] Between 1260 and 1328, this commune ruled a prosperous city in the midst of economic and territorial expansion, the construction of a major pilgrimage church, and the development of a university renowned throughout Europe. Considering such public improvements essential to a city-state of Padua's stature, the Paduan commune set out at the same time to rehabilitate the city's classical origins.

Padua's political and economic success in this period is remarkable, as the independent city-republics that had been common to northern and central Italy in the twelfth century were rapidly disappearing—the victims of factionalism, infighting, and/or aggressive expansionism by their neighbors. As the thirteenth century continued, these republican governments were increasingly subsumed into less democratic but more stable signories (hereditary lordships) and petty despotisms. The della Scala family, lords of nearby Verona, were the Paduans' main external threat throughout this period. Indeed, in 1328, the della Scala conquest of the city effectively ended Paduan independence; when the Paduans revolted nine years later, they only replaced della Scala lordship with that of the native Carrara family.[6] But in 1260 these events were far in the future, and at that moment the city's inhabitants rejoiced in their liberation. For almost seventy-five years, they successfully resisted external imperialism, expanded Paduan territorial control, and gradually improved and beautified their city (map 2).

The new Paduan commune was proud but still vulnerable, so it chose its projects carefully. It sought to assert its equality with other nearby regimes ideologically as well as militarily, economically, and diplomatically. By returning to the classical sources for its evidence, Padua's ruling elite bypassed the medieval emphasis on Antenor as a traitor and instead characterized him as a noble Trojan and city founder. Recasting their founder's character in this fashion allowed the Paduans to lay claim to an older and more prestigious past than that of any other neighboring city. The more elements of government and daily life they could somehow connect to ancient Rome, the better. As this chapter will show, the historical material used to accomplish these goals was readily available, thanks to Padua's university and local circle of humanists. The seal of the late thirteenth-century commune even defines the territory of the Paduan city-state in terms of the ancient Roman province: "The Muso [river], the mountain, the Athes [river], and the sea give me definite borders."[7] Reviving the memory of Roman Patavium with its legendary founding by the Trojan Antenor helped to define medieval Padua as a bastion of independent republicanism in a world of encroaching "tyranny," as much for the city's inhabitants as for its external audience.

Growth and Civic Improvement

In the late thirteenth century, republican Padua experienced the sustained growth of its population, economy, and contado (or surrounding territory). The city was a thriving commercial center with an urban population of about thirty-five thousand by 1300.[8] Like many of the northern Italian cities, its chief industries were wool and linen textiles; in 1287, the associations of the cloth and wool merchants were among the most powerful of the city's thirty-six incorporated guilds. Padua maintained close economic ties with the surrounding countryside; in the later thirteenth century, the commune expanded its political control of this territory, including smaller cities and villages. The Paduan chronicles, especially those from between 1280 and 1300, are litanies of towns and rural areas made subject to Paduan control.[9] In a notable example, the Paduans brought the nearby town of Vicenza under their domination in 1266 and held it until Cangrande della Scala of Verona seized it in 1311. At its greatest extent, the Paduan city-state comprised a contado of about two thousand square miles, from the Adige River in the south to Castelfranco and Bassano in the north.[10] The contado held more than twice as many people as the city of Padua itself, bringing the total population of the Paduan territory to about ninety-five thousand people in 1320.

In the midst of expansion, the communal regime sought also to maintain central control. As a result, the government underwent a series of gradual changes designed to clarify and affirm its political rights and responsibilities. New sets of city statutes were promulgated in 1265, 1276, and 1295, while additions and emendations were frequent.[11] The commune's concern with government regulation extended into the contado; for instance, the commune created a policy of assigning Paduan administrators directly to dependent villages and rural areas instead of relying on traditional feudal authorities.

The commune espoused a republican constitution similar to those of other contemporary northern Italian cities. Prime executive power belonged to the podestà, a foreign citizen elected for a term of six or twelve months. The city provided the podestà with a permanent bureaucracy through which to carry out his duties, composed of professional soldiers, notaries, servants, and police. Other divisions of government included a complex judicial system and several different citizen councils, the largest of which was the Consiglio Maggiore (Great Council), whose membership increased dramatically during this period from about four hundred to one thousand members. Supporting the larger council were both a Consiglio Minore of forty to sixty members and a committee of eighteen Anziani, or elders. From 1287 the latter included representatives from the city's thirty-six guilds. As well as encouraging participation in the councils, the commune employed Paduan citizens at every level. A citizen doctor of civil law, representing the podestà, presided in the highest communal court (called the Sigillo, or Seal), and other citizens served as podestà of subject cities, ambassadors, tax collectors, notaries, and bookkeepers. The administration was complex enough to employ as many as one hundred and ten notaries at a time.[12]

In addition to territorial expansion and political reorganization, the commune's third major priority was improving the quality of life in its domain. A new hearth tax levied throughout Paduan territory in 1281 funneled income directly into public works, which included the construction or improvement of roads, bridges, dikes, irrigation canals, and rural fortifications.[13] According to the *Annales Patavini* and the *Liber regiminum Padue*, between 1282 and 1287 the commune replaced seven wooden bridges with stone ones around the contado.[14] The year 1295 saw the construction of a defensive keep across the Adige River from the recently fortified Castrobaldo, as well as an eighth stone bridge.[15]

But public works in the contado paled in comparison to those in and around the city. A second major tax, unusual enough to merit mention in local annals, was assessed for this purpose in 1290–91: "In that time a tax was created in the city of Padua, and an assessment was made in the Paduan villages throughout the district, and tax imposed; and the tax was adjusted for everyone. And at once, therefore, the city was transformed with better buildings."[16] As in the contado, these "better buildings" included gates and bridges: the Altinate gate (one of four major city gates) was rebuilt in 1286–87, followed by the Ognissanti gate and its bridge in 1300.[17] At the same time, the city began a major overhaul of its public buildings. The most famous of these is the Palazzo della Ragione, the hall in which the largest city council met. Begun in 1218 and known familiarly as the Salone, it had been built in the unusual shape of a parallelogram due to space and foundation constraints, and it dominates the two main squares of the city even today. The original building was completed in 1272, but only thirty years later, the commune decided that it required updating. Major remodeling was therefore carried out between 1306 and 1309 by the friar-architect Giovanni degli Eremitani, who restructured the squares on either side of the hall at the same time. Cosmographical frescoes were added by Giotto, fresh from his work on the Arena Chapel, in 1315–17.[18]

Halls for the smaller councils and branches of the Paduan government also underwent renovation during this period. East of the main palazzo, a complex including the Palazzo del Podestà and the Palazzo degli Anziani was completed in 1285–86. The nearby Palazzo del Consiglio was finished in 1285.[19] As these dates demonstrate, a flurry of construction swept the city in the second half of the thirteenth century. It served two purposes: first, to facilitate the smooth running of the newly autonomous Paduan government—a purely practical goal—and second, to provide accommodation appropriate to that government, bearing witness to its status, power, and resources. This goal was more nebulous but no less crucial, given the Paduans' delicate relations with their neighbors.

Correspondingly, the regime sponsored a number of improvements that served this more intangible goal of fostering patriotism, pride, and civic unity. In 1266, for instance, the city paid for the construction of a military *carroccio*, a cart for the Paduan battle standard.[20] The oligarchs in charge clearly recognized the political necessity of presenting the appearance of a strong, growing city-state, as well as being one. A visitor to the city in these years would have encountered construction projects and bustling activity from the time he crossed into Paduan territory to the moment he approached its seat of government—all of it organized and financed by the commune.

As the building of the carroccio suggests, not all of this activity was specifically political, and the commune supervised numerous projects that it did not directly commission. One example of such indirect sponsorship was the commune's support of Padua's new saint, Anthony of Padua (d. 1231), one of Saint Francis's early followers.[21] He was canonized in 1232, only a year after his death, and the basilica dedicated to him was already under construction six years later in 1238. The unfinished church was dedicated in 1248, but work picked up after Ezzelino's death in 1256 as the new republic embraced Anthony as a patron and his cult as a source of local prestige. In 1263, the community installed its saint in his basilica with a citywide feast and procession at Easter, and the commune assumed responsibility for the completion of the church—a massive basilica with circular Byzantine domes and many connected outbuildings. Contemporary sources say that work was mostly finished in 1310 when Anthony's relics were transferred from the nave to the north transept, where they still lie today.[22]

Similarly, the university for which Padua was already famous, having been founded by students from Bologna in 1222, had fallen into disorder during the years of Ezzelino's domination. Communal initiative saw it reestablished in 1262, while papal recognition followed in 1264. The *studium* soon surpassed its previous renown, and students started arriving from across Europe. In exchange for its legal protection and certain privileges for professors and students, the Paduan government claimed considerable control over the schools, and the two entities became closely associated despite a policy maintaining the university's independence from Paduan politics.[23] The connection was a matter of common knowledge: in 1289, Pope Nicholas IV threatened to close Padua's university as a way of punishing its commune for rebellious behavior.[24]

Between 1260 and 1328, therefore, Padua was a growing city with a strong agricultural and commercial base. Its republican government was both engaged with its responsibilities and largely capable of fulfilling them. Several features set it apart from its neighbors and served as sources of local pride. First, it was becoming a major pilgrimage site as penitents arrived to pray at Saint Anthony's shrine. Second, its university brought students and money into the city while spreading the city's fame abroad. Third, the university and the commune together provided the city with an unusually strong pool of legal expertise. Padua's reputation for instruction in law, along with the communal government's employment of large numbers of citizen judges and notaries, made its university a forum for the theory and practice of law. Citizens and members of the university were supposedly forbidden from accepting each other's jobs, but the scope for theoretical exchange and discussion was enormous.[25] Finally, locals took great pride in the fact that these developments had occurred under a republican government that had begun its rule by throwing off the tyranny of Ezzelino da Romano. With these elements added to Padua's territorial gains and economic success, the city could fairly claim to be the equal of any in northern Italy. As the *Annales Patavini* asserts for the year 1310, "At this time, Padua was in the greatest possible state for a commune."[26] Yet the Paduans and their government had good reason to proclaim their wealth and success to anyone who would listen. They faced commercial competition and expansionism from several powerful neighbors, namely Verona, Ferrara, and Venice, the ambitions of whom would give any dedicated Paduan oligarch cause to worry, despite his city's present success.

Antenor and Livy

To a Paduan of the late thirteenth century, invasion and economic eclipse seemed only a distant possibility. Like his neighbors, he was proud both of his city's independence and of all that it had accomplished since overthrowing Ezzelino in 1256. One of the chief ways in which Paduans focused and expressed their civic pride was the commemoration of Padua's classical past. Historians have discussed this phenomenon at length as "Paduan prehumanism" (or protohumanism), in which a small circle of lawyers around and under the aegis of Lovato Lovati (1241–1309) studied classical poetry and drama and also found and recopied lost ancient texts. Their efforts have usually been conceived as precursors to the more established humanist movements of the fourteenth century.[27]

My emphasis here, however, will be on the commitment of the Paduan humanists to the issues and problems of their day. Late thirteenth-century Padua badly
needed a civic self-image that could unify its inhabitants, increase their communal self-respect, and impress neighboring cities. Given the citizens' pride
in having exchanged the tyranny of Ezzelino for a republican commune, the
humanists' expertise in classical matters was undeniably relevant.

Roman myth and history had never been forgotten. Anyone who had ever
read Virgil's *Aeneid*, a basic school text, knew that Antenor was the ancestor of
the Paduans, much as Aeneas was the ancestor of the Romans: "Having escaped
from the midst of the Achaeans, Antenor was able to penetrate the Illyrian
coastline and the innermost realms of the Liburnians, and pass the source of
the Timavus. . . . Here, then, he placed the city of Padua and the home of his
Teucrians; he gave a name to the race and hung up the arms of Troy. Now he
rests, settled in placid peace."[28] Virgil's words were a point of pride, since the
poem states that Antenor founded Padua before Aeneas even arrived in Italy. Paradoxically, the famous first lines of the *Aeneid* assert that Aeneas was the first to
arrive on Italian shores—but Servius notes that Padua at that time was located in
Cisalpine Gaul rather than in Italy, in which case Antenor's earlier arrival did not
count as taking place in Italy.[29] Paduans could also congratulate themselves on
the fact that Antenor founded Padua directly. Aeneas, by contrast, founded Alba
Longa, which produced Romulus and Remus, who founded Rome. Padua's son
Livy expanded on Virgil's comments in the first sentences of the *Ab urbe condita*:

> To begin with, then, it is generally agreed that after Troy was taken,
> while the other Trojans were all massacred, the Greeks spared two of
> them, Aeneas and Antenor, from every penalty of war—owing to old
> claims of hospitality and because they had always advised peace and
> Helen's return. Their experiences afterward were different. Antenor came
> to the innermost curve of the Adriatic Sea with a multitude of Eneti,
> whom a coup had driven from Paphlagonia; they were looking for a
> home and a leader, since their king, Pylaemenes, had fallen at Troy. Hav-
> ing driven out the Euganei, who lived between the sea and the Alps, the
> Eneti and Trojans took possession of those lands.[30]

Aside from these two major authorities, the usual sources that medieval Italian
historians cited on the foundation of Padua were Seneca and Solinus, both of
whom mention the fact without giving further detail.[31] But the classical tradition was clear in its essentials.

Moreover, the surviving evidence suggests that local oral traditions had never lost sight of Padua's classical origins. In a poem written circa 1200, Giovanni da Val di Taro addresses the Paduans as *Antenorides*, sons of Antenor.[32] He presents the Paduans' common descent as a compelling reason to make peace among themselves, the better to resist any external threats: "O sons of Antenor, if you wish to remain safe from the enemy outside the walls, the peace of love must bind you together inside them."[33] The commune publicly endorsed Giovanni's poem in 1210; it was engraved on a plaque and placed on the city's Porta Torricelli, where everyone entering or leaving the city would be able to see it.[34] The choice of a gate was also significant: the reference to Antenorides defined Paduan identity just as the city walls defined Paduan space.

The memorialization of Giovanni's poem in stone suggests that the Paduans were not content to celebrate their forefather in literature alone. They desired a more tangible and more public form of commemoration—so they conveniently discovered his bones and memorialized him with an enormous tomb. Until recently, scholars thought that Antenor's relics were "rediscovered" in 1283–84, when the extant tomb was built.[35] Recent reappraisals suggest that a tomb of Antenor had existed in the city for a number of years before 1283, however, and that 1283 simply saw the renovation of an extant tomb. Brunetto Latini's *Trésor* (composed 1260–66), for instance, identifies Antenor as the founder of Padua and affirms that "his tomb is still there."[36] Similarly, the 1283 entry in the *Chronicon de potestatibus Paduae* says that the tomb was "repaired anew" rather than "discovered."[37] The late thirteenth-century commemoration of Padua's classical origins was, therefore, less a resurrection of something long forgotten than the intensification of a preestablished civic tradition.

The first major statement commending Padua's classical origins to the attention of its medieval descendants comes from the notary Rolandino (1200–1276), a student of the rhetorician Boncompagno da Signa and Padua's greatest thirteenth-century author.[38] His *Liber chronicarum*, a history of northeastern Italy in the time of Ezzelino, asserts that since Padua has now thrown off tyranny, it is worthy of being called a second Rome.[39] Padua even had its own ancient ruins; locals believed that the Paduan suburb of Rudena had been named for its extensive classical remains.[40] As Rolandino writes, "For was not Padua originally founded by Antenor, who left the Trojan city in the same hour as Aeneas, the founder of Rome? Has not it endured many tribulations and wars, like Rome herself? Have not its citizens suffered cruelty, their towers, palaces, houses, and their belongings ruined and cast down? Indeed, if the Roman Curia will pardon me, Padua can now almost be called a second Rome."[41] For Rolandino, Padua's sufferings and perseverance, as much as her successes, qualified the city for comparison with Rome. His civic pride is understandable, since he had lived through Ezzelino's tyranny and helped construct the republican government that succeeded him. As J. K. Hyde explains, "It was his determination to expose [Ezzelino's] evils to future generations which inspired him to write."[42] As such, Rolandino's history is a conscious polemic illustrating the virtues of republican government over signorial tyranny. He explicitly compares medieval Padua with ancient Rome and uses classical examples to drive his points home.

His fellow citizens agreed with his sentiments and his methods. As soon as he finished the *Rolandina* (as his chronicle came to be called) in 1262, the heads of the university and the Paduan government held a public session in the chronicle's honor:

> This book was read and recited in front of the doctors and masters named below, and also in the presence of the worthy society of the graduates and scholars of the liberal arts of the Paduan studium. Also, the venerable men ruling at that time in Padua were there: [list of masters by name and specialty], attentive and valuable professors of grammar and rhetoric. Gathered here specially for the purpose, they solemnly praised, approved, and authenticated the aforesaid book and work, or chronicle, with their professional authority, in the cloister of Saint Urban in Padua, during the 1,262nd year of the Lord, fifth indiction, on the thirteenth day of the month of April.[43]

Scholars debate the extent to which the commune adopted Rolandino's chronicle officially.[44] Nonetheless, the ceremony described above reveals that city leaders were willing to sanction publicly Rolandino's comparison of Padua with Rome—not only in her origins but also in her modern fortunes, in which respect Rolandino sees more to praise in his hometown than in Rome. Only six years after Ezzelino was deposed, therefore, the Paduan commune had already allied itself with a political ideology that was self-consciously republican and Romanizing. Within this paradigm, it placed particular emphasis on the city's classical foundation by Antenor.

Brunetto Latini's *Trésor* attests to the presence of a monument to Antenor in the 1260s, at the same time as Rolandino was writing his chronicle. By 1283, however, whatever had sufficed previously was now "judged inadequate to the importance of the Paduan commune."[45] Under the guidance of the respected

Fig. 5 Tomb of Antenor, Piazza Antenore, Padua, 1283.

intellectual Lovato Lovati, the central figure of the prehumanist movement in Padua, the commune erected a new tomb for its founder (figure 5).[46] According to the 1283 entry of the *Annales Patavini*, "In this year, the stone bridge of San Leonardo was built and the tomb of the noble Antenor, founder of the city of Padua, was made with its capital, next to [the monastery of] San Lorenzo by the gate of Santo Stefano."[47] The *Chronicon de potestatibus Paduae* gives a very similar account: "And the tomb of the most noble Antenor, founder of the city of Padua, was restored anew with its capital."[48]

Lovato's involvement in the project extended to writing a set of verses for Antenor's sepulcher (figure 6), which recalls both Virgil's and Livy's accounts of the founder:

> Noble Antenor, a strong voice, transferred hither a peaceful homeland
> and refugees, the Eneti and the sons of Dardanus;
> cast out the Euganeans; founded the city of Patavium.
> He whom this home, cut from modest marble, holds here.[49]

References to the Eneti, the sons of Dardanus (that is, the Trojans), and the Euganeans indicate that Lovato's verses derive chiefly from Livy, but his phrasing

Fig. 6 Detail of sepulcher, tomb of Antenor, Piazza Antenore, Padua, 1283.

is his own. Using echoes of Virgil (for example, *quietem* and *quiescit*), Lovato emphasizes the act of foundation and its long-term results: *patriam quietem* (peaceful homeland), rhymed with *Patavinam condidit urbem* (founded the city of Patavium). The placement of *condidit* (founded) between *Patavinam* and *urbem* (both referring to Padua) is particularly forceful. Lovato's words equate the values of past and present, uniting them with Antenor's founding act.

The sarcophagus has large "ears," a style popular in the fourth and fifth centuries A.D., but its inscription is written in Lombardic capitals, as was usual in medieval Padua; the classicizing motif does not extend to using classical letterforms or epigraphic formulae. Four brick columns and a roof with a small cupola protect the tomb, which closely resembles the tombs of contemporary jurists like Accursius, Odofredus, and Rolandino Passaggeri in Bologna. The whole stood against the monastery of San Lorenzo in the city center, and Lovato was buried next to it in 1309 (figure 7) as a kind of civic burial *ad sanctos*.[50]

The commemoration of Antenor through his new tomb therefore served as a civic equivalent to the veneration of religious relics; the "cult" of Antenor paralleled that of Saint Anthony in the new basilica across town. Both were famous residents, patrons, and protectors of the city. Their presence added to its consequence in the eyes of both residents and visitors. Hence, the commune's decision to rebuild Antenor's tomb in 1283 fit into its broader program of public improvement throughout Paduan territory at that time.

Several decades after the tomb renovation, a Paduan farmer uncovered a Roman epitaph near the convent of Santa Giustina, which citizens immediately hailed as belonging to Livy, the most famous citizen of Roman Patavium. The inscription, still extant, reads as follows:

V . F

T . LIVIVS

LIVIAE . T . F

QUARTAE . L

HALYS

CONCORDIALIS

PATAVI

SIBI . ET . SVIS

OMNIBVS[51]

Unfortunately, their conclusion was a leap in the wrong direction. The author of the tombstone bears the surname Halys and was a freedman of the Livius

Fig. 7 Tomb of Lovato Lovati, Piazza Antenore, Padua, c. 1310.

family rather than the Augustan historian himself. To fourteenth-century
Paduans unfamiliar with classical epigraphy, however, the inscription T . LIVIVS
seemed self-explanatory. They cleaned off the tombstone and installed it on the
wall of Santa Giustina, where it became one of the sights of the town. Petrarch
wrote his famous letter to Livy while sitting in front of it.[52] The inscription's
influence may echo in the tomb of Lovato's nephew and protégé Rolando da
Piazzola, who died in 1330; the two plinths supporting his sarcophagus read ET

SIBI and ET SUIS, respectively (figure 8), mimicking the SIBI ET SUIS on the mistaken Livy inscription.

Historians have never agreed on the date of this second example of the discovery and translation of civic relics. For a long time, it was thought to have occurred later in the fourteenth century: Petrarch wrote his letter in 1350, a *terminus ante quem*, and several Paduan historians of the mid-fifteenth century

Fig. 8 Tomb of Rolando da Piazzola outside the basilica of Sant'Antonio, Padua, c. 1330.

imply a date from the mid-fourteenth century.[53] In his article "The Post-Mortem Adventures of Livy," B. L. Ullman states simply that the event took place "between 1318 and 1324."[54] He presumably relied on the only record of the event, a *zibaldone* (journal or memorandum book) of Giovanni Boccaccio, which dates from several decades later and is now located in the National Library in Florence:

> In the fourth year of Tiberius Caesar, he [Livy] was removed from the toil of Paduan life. And the citizens wanted him buried there, producing a stone discovered in our days, which was dug up by a farmer of the same city in a field, and on which can be read these letters: [text of inscription].
>
> These carvings are believed to be his epitaph. Moreover, the old stone, cleansed of ancient decay and with letters formed with the greatest elegance, can be seen even today—affixed by order of the noble man Jacopo da Carrara, who was ruling Padua at that time, to the wall of the church porch within the monastery of Santa Giustina the virgin.[55]

Boccaccio's reference to Jacopo da Carrara suggests that the epitaph was found during the rule of Jacopo the Elder as captain general of Padua, that is, between 1318 and 1324.

Recent research on two fronts, however, indicates that the discovery of the epitaph must have occurred earlier. First, Teresa Hankey's work on Riccobaldo da Ferrara demonstrates that the discovery should be dated at least before 1313. Riccobaldo was resident in Padua and teaching at the university between 1293 and 1295, and from 1303 to 1309. The text of the epitaph appears both in Riccobaldo's *Historie* (written at Padua before 1313, probably 1305–8) and in his later *Compendium Romanae historial* (finished in 1318).[56] The text of the *Historie* has only recently reappeared in three late fourteenth-century manuscript copies, but the epitaph's presence in early manuscripts of the *Compendium* is well established. Its citation—probably adapted, like most of the compendium, from the longer *Historie*—reads, "The epitaph written in stone on his sepulcher can be read near the monastery of the blessed Giustina of Padua, written thus: [text of inscription]."[57] Second, Guido Billanovich has published an *accessus* (short biographical introduction) to Livy by Lovato himself, which appears in a fourteenth-century compilation of writings by and relating to the Paduan humanists (Vatican City, Biblioteca Apostolica Vaticana, MS Vat. Lat. 1769). The accessus ends with the inscription much as Boccaccio's and Riccobaldo's do: "And today this stone tomb can be seen in the monastery of Saint Giustina with letters inscribed on the stone in the following fashion. . . . [text of inscription]."[58] Considering that Lovato died in 1309, his accessus and Riccobaldo's witness jointly demonstrate that the epitaph had reappeared by the first decade of the fourteenth century. The event should probably be dated to 1305–9, if not earlier, making it contemporary with the citizens' other classicizing efforts at the turn of the fourteenth century.

The final event publicizing Padua's classicizing ideology in this period also involved a humanist: the crowning of Albertino Mussato (1262–1329) as the first poet laureate since antiquity. Lovato Lovati's nephew Rolando da Piazzola (c. 1260–c. 1330) and his friend and colleague Albertino Mussato were the most prominent humanists of the generation after Lovato, and Mussato has been described alternately as the last luminary of medieval Padua and the first true man of the Renaissance.[59] Born in 1262, two years after the establishment of the republic, he was a notary like most of the humanists, employed throughout his life by the communal government. He was also a prolific historian, poet, and dramatist. In recognition of this last role and in honor of his play *Ecerinis*, the commune bestowed the laurel crown on Mussato in December 1315. A dramatization of the life of Ezzelino da Romano, *Ecerinis* was not only the first Senecan-style tragedy written since antiquity but also a republican polemic in the best tradition of Rolandino fifty years earlier.[60] At the climax of the play, for example, the chorus recites,

> The madness of the cruel tyrant is dead
> and peace returns.
> Together let us all delight in the peace;
> Let every exile safely be recalled—
> He may return to his own home [literally, *lares*]
> secure in the peace.[61]

Mussato contrasts the da Romano regime's chaos (*rabies*) with a republic's natural peace (*pax*), a word that he repeats using the poetic device of anaphora at the beginning of three different lines (*paxque*, line 528; *pace*, lines 529 and 532). By 1315, the Veronese signore Cangrande della Scala's threat to Paduan independence had become acute, and Mussato's tragedy cast Cangrande as a new Ezzelino. In contrasting the dangers of tyranny with the blessings of peace under communal rule, he spoke directly to the city's current situation.

In recognition of Mussato's achievement in writing the play, and acting on the suggestion of Rolando da Piazzola, the commune voted to award Mussato the title of poet laureate. J. K. Hyde has labeled the event the "cultural apogee of the Paduan commune."[62] Like the presentation of Rolandino's chronicle, the ceremony was a citywide event attended by representatives of both the university and communal administrations. A lengthy procession wound its way through the streets of Padua, and the *Ecerinis* was read out publicly.[63] The commune decreed that the reading should be repeated annually for the edification and remembrance of the citizens. The classical theme only went so far, however: the event more closely resembled a medieval academic ceremony, like the awarding of an honorary degree, than a classical laureation. Nonetheless, Padua's government and people understood that they were reviving an ancient tradition that had present-day meaning for them, and that they were doing so in celebration of a poet whose accomplishments promoted the city's classical origins and republican present in both content and style.

Historians have often characterized the Paduan humanists as a small group of intellectuals who used their leisure time to explore a joint interest in classical (particularly Senecan) poetry. Italian scholarship on the subject, for instance, regularly refers to Lovato and his circle of friends as the *cenacolo padovano*, or Paduan literary circle. Certainly many of their activities were private exercises between friends, like a notorious poetic debate about whether one should or should not have children. Nevertheless, their interest in classical literature, objects, and history extended into their public responsibilities, fostering a public, official aspect of Paduan classicism. The communal regime's appropriation of Rolandino's chronicle and Mussato's tragedy, the official rehousing of Antenor's bones, the discovery and display of the pseudo-Livian epitaph—all occurring within the same half century—show that a certain educated and influential sector of Paduan society was eager to equate modern Padua with ancient Rome. The public nature of these events suggests that the stories and principles they evoked already meant or would shortly come to mean something to the Paduan citizenry at large.

Intention and Agency

Who were these men who were so eager to exploit their city's connection with ancient Rome? With whom did the ideas originate? Who decided that they were worthwhile, and who paid for them? The Paduan humanists were certainly at the center of events; they were locally influential, and they knew the classics well. Lovati's expertise is clearly visible in the rebuilding of Antenor's tomb, and both da Piazzola and Mussato played major organizational roles in Mussato's laureation ceremony. Their professional roles demonstrate Paduan humanism's unique public face, but I wish to stress the influence and ubiquity of the legal class as a whole in Padua during this period. All of the members of the *cenacolo padovano* were either lawyers or notaries, as was Rolandino a generation before them. In the late thirteenth century, notaries constituted Padua's most powerful guild, and by 1300 the guild had about five hundred members, of whom (as discussed above) more than one hundred were employed in the communal government at any given time. Notaries and their guild, moreover, were only half the matter. In Padua, unlike many other Italian cities of this period, judges and notaries were not part of the same guild.[64] Instead, judges had their own association, the Collegio dei Giudici del Palazzo (della Ragione). The Collegio had a membership of about one hundred in 1300, which included Paduan citizen judges as well as the university's professors of law.[65]

The university could not employ citizens, and government posts were not available to noncitizens, but the membership of both in the Collegio and a shared profession produced a tightly knit local legal community. The commune not only paid the salaries of the university's law professors—in canon and civil law, as well as in arts and medicine—but also prescribed which textbooks students and professors should use.[66] Judges, notaries, and professors of law therefore dealt regularly with the Paduan commune, which regulated their professional duties while it served as a forum for the theory and practice of law. Albertino Mussato refers easily to Paduan political institutions in classical terms (*Senato* for Consiglio Maggiore, for example; also *senatori, tribuni, plebii,* and *plebiscitii*).[67] In a similar vein, the great theorist Marsilius of Padua, who studied law at the university and whose father was a local notary, designed "ideal" political institutions in his *Defensor pacis* that strongly resembled contemporary Paduan political structures.[68] Judges, professors, and notaries in Padua were trained in Roman law; they were comfortable with its principles and terms of reference, and they dealt with its practical applications on a daily basis.

Lovato Lovati claimed in his letters that his classical interests offered a respite from the pressures of public life.[69] That he did not want his public duties to interfere with his personal interests, however, does not mean that the inverse is also true. Rather, the practical and the theoretical were intimately connected: late medieval Paduan intellectuals and political theorists did not hesitate to apply their classical learning if it could provide some public benefit. Lovati was not just a judge and a humanist interested in Senecan poetic forms; he was also a member of Padua's ruling elite and was therefore personally involved in its politics and public affairs. His personal interest in Roman history and literature proved useful on more than one occasion. For example, the Paduan commune appointed Lovati podestà of Vicenza for 1291, and the annals of the Vicentine Niccolò Smereglo state that he "ruled well and had histories painted and written on the town hall."[70] Manlio Dazzi, along with others, has suggested that *historias* specifically refers to Roman stories, possibly scenes from Livy.[71]

Lovati's action demonstrates, first, that Roman history seemed topical and instructive in a contemporary political setting and, second, that the understanding of politics in Roman terms was confined neither to Padua nor to the small clique of Lovati and his friends—at least two of whom, Benvenuto dei Campesani (1250/55–1323) and Ferreto de' Ferreti (c. 1295–1337), were Vicentines.[72] The impetus for the town hall project may have come from Lovati and his greater familiarity with things classical, but the local council in Vicenza, which would be paying for it, would have to give approval and would want decoration appropriate both to the dignity of the city and to the activities conducted in the town hall. The frescoes would also need to be understandable and instructive for their larger audience—the citizens of Vicenza.

As part of a broad program of public improvements at the turn of the fourteenth century, therefore, the Paduan republic sponsored a series of public events on classical themes: the renovation of a monument for the city's founder (1283); the discovery and monumentalization of the epitaph of its greatest Roman citizen (c. 1305); the crowning of the town's greatest modern poet as "poet laureate," a title unused since antiquity (1315); and the public presentation of both a chronicle (1262) and a play (1315) celebrating the republic's escape from tyranny. These were civic events engineered to glorify Padua and its commune. On an internal level, they were directed at Padua, its citizens, and its subjects in the contado, generating pride in the city and its current regime. Events like these emphasized the city's ancient origins, and that in turn fostered a sense of unity, common descent, and collective purpose among the people. It could also inspire collective resistance to an external threat. Looking beyond Padua, these classicizing events made the same claims to other cities and regimes. Declarations of Trojan ancestry and Roman glory imbued Padua and its republican commune with an aura of antiquity as well as political authority. Such assertions implied that the Paduan government was more important, longer established, and more legitimate than any of its immediate neighbors—and, consequently, that any potential threats to the city-state were doomed to failure.

But this civic program of classicizing projects confronted not only political and military challenges from Padua's neighbors; being itself a means of ideological warfare, it also addressed symbolic threats to the city. Neighboring Venice, for instance, had been founded embarrassingly recently in Paduan terms. Early Venetian chronicles relate how the city's first settlers went out to the lagoon in the sixth century, seeking refuge from the Gothic king Totila's depredations.[73] In search of an older and more illustrious past, late thirteenth-century Venetian historians started laying claim to Antenor in a practice that would continue for several centuries. This first occurs in the chronicle of Marco (1292), who claims that Antenor founded Venice before he founded Padua. Traveling up the Adriatic Sea with his fellow refugees from Troy, Antenor naturally landed first in the lagoon. In fact, Marco's story is more detailed than any of the Paduan accounts of Antenor's arrival:

> And then, the Trojans coming to their boats, they gave their sails continuously to the winds for a long time, until, sailing over the ocean, they came all the way to the place where now the city of the Venetians is built, and . . . they spread out there to build their homes. . . .
>
> And then Romulus and Remus founded Rome. And because of this it is widely known that the first construction of the Rialto preceded the construction of the city of Rome. . . . Trojans came to Antenorida from diverse regions, but when one particular huge crowd arrived there, it could not be housed on the island. Therefore, Antenor departed to occupy dry earth, and in a spot not much distant from the island, he founded a very beautiful city, which he called Altilia. After this he built Patavium, which is today called Padua, and there he lived out his last days, and on his tomb these verses are written:
>
> > Here lies Antenor, founder of the city of the Paduans.
> > He was a good man; everyone followed him.[74]

This is a nice piece of historiographical one-upmanship; it would have horrified any Paduan who heard it, especially given Padua's own efforts to rehabilitate Antenor's image. Unfortunately, it did have the advantage of geographical logic, as a Trojan refugee on his way to Padua would most likely travel through the lagoon to get there. The story appeared in numerous Venetian histories after 1292 and remained popular into the Renaissance.[75]

Direct Paduan responses to the Venetian Antenor legend do not survive, but one example of Paduan retaliation may be the early 1320s *Liber de ludi fortunae*, a multipart work by Paduan judge Giovanni da Nono (c. 1276–1346) that combines a history of Padua with a detailed description of the city in his own time. One section of the *Liber*, known as the *Visio Egidii regis Patavii*, focuses on Egidius, an early king of Padua who has been chased from his city by Attila, "the perfidious pagan king of the Huns."[76] He takes refuge in nearby Rimini, falls asleep, and is favored with a vision in which an angel tells him, "Fear not, king of Padua, for God has placed you among his elect. Being from the noble race of the Altine city, which will never be put into servitude, you will found a city with the name of the Venetians, existing amid the sea water."[77] Contact between the cities of the Veneto was constant, and books and ideas traveled freely. Designating a Paduan king as the founder of Venice may have been da Nono's retaliation against the Venetians' appropriation of Antenor. Far from reflecting a strictly intellectual exercise, therefore, the various manifestations of the classicizing phenomenon in late thirteenth-century Padua served several practical purposes. They could unify the citizens of Padua and focus civic pride, as well as fight off another city's attempt to appropriate their hero.

Such ideological efforts were important because, despite their vaunted prosperity, the Paduans and their government needed every weapon they could muster. For all of the idealism of their republican constitution and their success in deposing Ezzelino, their world was closing in around them. Several threats to their independence loomed, including Venetian economic (and subsequent diplomatic) success to the east; the consolidation of Este power in Ferrara to the south; and, most ominously, della Scala expansion from Verona in the west. Cangrande della Scala's army took Vicenza away from the Paduans in 1311, and Padua itself finally yielded in 1328 after a long and expensive war that ended with a crippling siege of the city. By the turn of the fourteenth century, the proudly independent Paduan commune found itself fighting on two fronts. The first front was military and political, as it struggled to keep its many subject territories out of Cangrande's grasp.[78] The second front was ideological. The image of an Antenor-founded, Roman-strengthened, republican Padua could boost internal morale and intimidate the opposition. In this sense, Antenor's 1283 funerary monument was as much a weapon as the military carroccio commissioned by the Paduan commune in 1266; it was a rallying point, a source of collective identity, and a focus of civic pride.

Virtually everything that the commune concerned itself with in this period—from city statutes to public works, the patronage of learning and religion to city historiography—pointed toward the same end. These endeavors defined what it was to be a Paduan citizen and why being Paduan was a good thing. In most cases, the commune's projects contained both physical and symbolic means of conveying identity. Antenor's tomb was a material focal point in the city center, an impressive structure in its own right, but its presence also reminded local viewers of who they were, where they came from, and where they were going. Their sense of communal identity and common descent unified them, maintaining their resolution and pride in their independence. As Giovanni da Val di Taro had written in 1210, the Antenorides had to unite harmoniously if they wished to fight off external threats.[79] Fuelled by its humanistic legal class, the Paduan commune recognized this principle from the creation of its first constitution after Ezzelino's downfall. The period between that time and Padua's capitulation in 1328 shows the commune's regular efforts to keep Padua's classical origins in the public mind. The promotion of Antenor and Livy in these years was but one facet of the "public improvements" taking place across the Paduan contado, designed to maintain and display the city in the manner that it considered itself to deserve. Antenor, Livy, Saint Anthony, and the university were all instrumental in defining the city's citizens as Paduan rather than Vicentine, Venetian, or even Veronese.

The emphasis that the Paduans placed on their classical origins, and the widespread power of that ideology, was recognized not only by their friends but also by their enemies. As a parting shot, after Padua had finally succumbed to Veronese expansionism in 1328, an anonymous Veronese poet penned a rude mockery of the verses on Antenor's tomb in a poem praising the della Scala regime. Written in 1329, the *Dedizione di Treviso e la morte di Cangrande* turned Lovato Lovati's famous phrases on their head:

> Here lies Antenor, founder of the city of Padua.
> He was a traitor, as is any who follows him.[80]

The Paduans' republican ideology and proud origins fell into subjection along with the regime that had promoted them. The Veronese and their allies saw clearly that to attack the city's founder was to attack its citizens' sense of self.

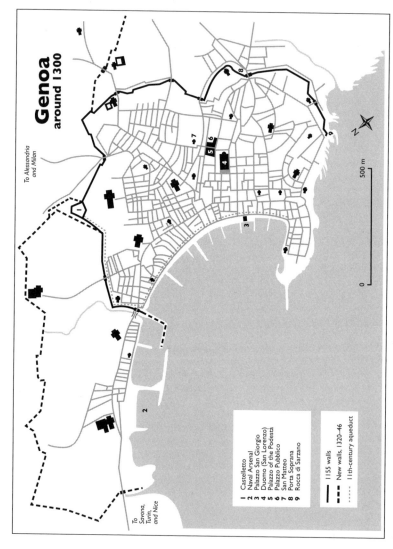

Map 3   Genoa around 1300. Map after Epstein, *Genoa and the Genoese*, and Grossi Bianchi and Poleggi, *Città portuale*.

The following labels appear within the map:

Genoa around 1300

To Alessandria and Milan

To Savona, Turin, and Nice

1   Castelletto
2   Naval Arsenal
3   Palazzo San Giorgio
4   Duomo (San Lorenzo)
5   Palazzo of the Podestà
6   Palazzo Pubblico
7   San Matteo
8   Porta Soprana
9   Rocca di Sarzano

—— 1155 walls
–––– New walls, 1320–46
········ 11th-century aqueduct

0   500 m

GENOA

Many Januses for Civic Unity

> No one should be ignorant of the fact that Janus built Janicula, and that he
> named it after himself. In fact, he did not name it Janua, but Janicula [little Janua],
> using the diminutive on account of its small size—just like Rome, at the time of
> its first construction, when it was small, was called Romula [after its founder,
> Romulus], and afterward, when it grew, it was called Roma. Likewise, our own
> city was very small when it was first constructed, and it was called Janicula;
> and afterward, when it grew, it was called Janua.
>
> —Jacopo da Varagine, *Chronicon Januense*

The Paduans' struggle to preserve their autonomy contrasts markedly with
the fortunes of Genoa, on the other side of the Italian peninsula. While Padua
lost its independence permanently in 1328—in time exchanging the *signoria* of
the della Scala for that of the Carrara before being swallowed by Venetian
expansion on the mainland—the city of Genoa remained an autonomous
republic more or less consistently from the formation of its commune in 1098
until 1797. In 1300, it was one of the largest cities in Christian Europe, with a
population approximately three times that of Padua.[1] It boasted a highly successful maritime economy with trading outposts from the Baltic to the Black
Sea, along with a navy experienced in defending its interests throughout the
Mediterranean.[2] Unlike the Paduans, therefore, the Genoese confronted few
serious external threats to their political and economic autonomy in the later
Middle Ages. Rather, the city suffered from serious internal strife throughout
the thirteenth century and into the fourteenth, and its efforts at community
self-definition and legitimation were accordingly directed inward instead of
outward. This chapter will contextualize the Genoese adoption of the mythical founder Janus in the years commonly considered to be the height of the

medieval Genoese commune, from 1257, the year of Guglielmo Boccanegra's election as *capitano del popolo*,[3] to 1312, when a Genoese government desperate to restore internal order offered control of the city to Emperor Henry VII. Genoese propagation of the cult of Janus, contemporaneous with Padua's revival of the Antenor legend, was one of many communal improvements or advertisements of civic prestige dating from this period of significant urban growth. At the same time, it was a specific ideological attempt by members of the city's ruling class to persuade their compatriots away from internal division by recalling a long-distant but unspoiled joint past.

Growth and Civic Improvement

The medieval city of Genoa was relatively small in area; the twelfth-century city walls, which surround the city center, encompassed less than a square kilometer of land crowded into a hilly space between the sea and the mountains (see map 3). Even today, both of the city's major railway stations are built into steep hillsides. Nonetheless, the city's vast success in the Mediterranean trade economy fostered one of the great population leaps of medieval demography: from a small town of fewer than fifteen thousand people in 1000, Genoa grew to a city of approximately one hundred thousand in 1300.[4] Since available land within the city walls was so scarce, Genoa was a remarkably vertical city in an era of high urban population density. In addition to the towers of the local nobility, omnipresent in medieval Italian urban architecture, tenements of six and seven stories were common throughout the city.[5]

The usual reason—economic opportunity—fueled Genoa's population growth. An important port even in the early Middle Ages, the city rapidly rose to prominence in the Mediterranean trade starting in the eleventh century.[6] In collaboration with the Pisans, the Genoese played a major role in eliminating the threat of Muslim pirates in the western Mediterranean, whose depredations had hampered long-distance trade through the ninth and tenth centuries. In 1087, for instance, the Italian allies made a joint attack on Al-Mahdiyya, a major Muslim capital in North Africa.[7] In the same period, both towns backed the Normans in their quest to reclaim Sicily from the Muslims. Steven Epstein sees these acts as economically, as well as militarily and religiously, motivated: "The Muslim half of the Mediterranean world depended on its coastal shipping from Morocco and Spain to Egypt, and Italian efforts to disrupt this trade and to pillage it . . . could only benefit Genoa and Pisa."[8]

Assisted by their participation in the Crusades and the waning of Muslim sea power, the Genoese developed their maritime network over the course of the next two centuries, so that by 1250 Genoa was the focus of a trading empire stretching from Spain and North Africa to Egypt, the Holy Land, and Constantinople. The city-state expanded its frontiers substantially between 1250 and 1300, benefiting especially from its traditional alliance with the Byzantine Empire. In 1261, the Genoese helped the Byzantines regain their capital from occupying Franks left over from the Fourth Crusade, and although the Byzantines soon reneged on their promise of exclusive trading rights in the Empire, Genoa established important outposts in Greece, Syria, and the Black Sea.[9] Closer to home, the Genoese defeated their chief Italian competitors, Pisa and Venice, in a series of key naval battles (Pisa in 1284 and 1290, Venice in 1298), signing favorable treaties with both in 1299.[10] These far-flung military successes also enabled Genoese merchants to expand their contacts in western Europe, finding markets for their eastern goods in Provence, Champagne, and Flanders.[11] Thus, Genoa gradually assured its position as a hub of the east–west Mediterranean sea trade. Economic development benefited the city on all levels: a mercantile economy provided opportunities for both nobles and entrepreneurial members of the middle class to amass fortunes abroad, and it also supported an internal system of wage employment for poorer native Genoese and increasing numbers of immigrants.

Probably as a result of its early commercial development, Genoa is the first city for which we have direct evidence for the formation of a commune, in the late eleventh century.[12] This occurred on the heels of Genoese triumph during the First Crusade and was contemporaneous with the establishment of an official city chronicle, begun by Andrea Caffaro in 1099.[13] From this point forward, the Genoese government—while technically republican all the way up to 1797, the year of the Napoleonic invasion—fluctuated between several types of regimes, especially during the course of the thirteenth century.[14] Three of the most popular of these political arrangements replaced one another on a more or less regular basis: first, the government of multiple consuls, which was that originally established for the commune and had persisted through the eleventh and twelfth centuries; second, government by capitani del popolo, in which prominent Genoese citizens were elected singly or in pairs to rule over the city; and third, podestarial government like that in Padua, in which trusted foreigners were invited every six months or year to serve as podestà.[15] Between 1257 and 1312, the latter two systems replaced each other regularly as the result of civic revolts that occurred two or three times per decade, except in the quiescent 1280s.[16] Historians have traditionally interpreted these revolts as class struggles between the nobility (being in favor of podestarial government) and the newly influential *popolo*, or wealthy middle class (in favor of government by its representatives, the capitani). The rise of the popolo was a peninsula-wide phenomenon, and the parameters of the struggle varied by city. Recent research on Genoa, however, has emphasized the diverse backgrounds and wealth of members of key factions and the continuity of policy between these two types of government (the Genoese capitani never passed anti-magnate legislation, for example, as many other cities did).[17] The city's factional struggles seem to have been more broadly based than traditional class divisions would suggest.

Genoa's chroniclers chiefly articulate their city's political instability through the traditional opposition of Guelf and Ghibelline allegiances, supportive of papal or imperial claims to Italian sovereignty, respectively. This split had real importance, particularly during Charles of Anjou's southern Italian campaigns on behalf of the papacy in the later thirteenth century and during Emperor Henry VII's struggles to reestablish imperial control in northern Italy in the years after 1300.[18] Genoa's role in supporting or opposing each of these claims depended on which of its chief factions was currently in power. Among the nobility, for example, the Doria and Spinola families were traditionally Ghibelline, while the Grimaldi and Fieschi were traditionally Guelf.[19]

While important in defining Genoa's position within the larger scope of Mediterranean and Italian politics, the nominal factions of Guelf and Ghibelline also served, as elsewhere in Italy, to disguise major power struggles between Genoa's noble families and political factions on a more local level. Medieval Genoese society was unusually territorial, from local district associations called *compagne* to noble *alberghi*, neighborhood enclaves that housed a clan, its relatives, and its clients, and whose barricades could defend the entire *albergo* in times of unrest.[20] Complex social affiliations among Genoa's powerful nobility and *mercatores* as well as its artisans and lower classes exacerbated the city's political disputes, which only increased through the rest of the thirteenth century; one particularly destructive episode (in 1296–97) plays a large role in this chapter.[21]

As mentioned earlier, however, the chief procedures and policies of the late thirteenth-century Genoese commune remained relatively consistent despite frequent changes of regime. The various councils and other offices of the city bureaucracy functioned regardless of which type of leader (capitano or podestà) occupied the main executive position. Despite numerous changes of government, the tradition of sponsoring a municipal chronicle, an official account

of the city's fortunes begun under Andrea Caffaro in 1099, continued unin-
terrupted for almost two hundred years, up to 1294.[22] Between 1257 and 1312,
communal officials appear to have been primarily concerned with improving
urban infrastructure and consolidating Genoese power in the contado. Instead
of establishing Genoese dominance in the region with expensive occupying
troops (of which Genoa, as a maritime power, had very few), they purchased
feudal properties from a debt-ridden territorial nobility, which expanded their
control of Liguria at the same time that it funneled monies back into the local
aristocracy.[23]

Furthermore, starting with Guglielmo Boccanegra's rule as capitano in 1257,
the Genoese commune concentrated its attention on urban improvements,
such as the construction of the Palazzo San Giorgio, the town hall that remains
a chief ornament of the city center today.[24] Its location along the main commercial wharf reflects not only a keen appreciation of the city's mercantile
underpinnings but also an implicit commitment to preserving them in the
future. Boccanegra also arranged for the rebuilding of the harbor jetty and
new wharves along the waterfront. From the 1270s, the capitani Oberto Doria
and Oberto Spinola jointly oversaw the construction of a complex known as
the Palazzo del Comune, which contained both the Palazzo del Podestà for the
chief executive and the Palazzo Pubblico for council meetings.[25] Finally, in
the second half of the thirteenth century, the commune paid for the building
of an aqueduct to bring fresh water to the docks and the western part of the
city.[26] It is perhaps an indication of Genoa's good relations with its neighbors
and the relative concord of its contado that all public improvements taking
place in this period were oriented either toward the Genoese government itself
or toward the sea. Despite significant population growth, the city did not replace its twelfth-century walls, built to resist a besieging Frederick Barbarossa,
until the mid-fourteenth century.

The civic government in its various incarnations enjoyed an unusually close
relationship with the local church—in this case, the archbishopric of Genoa,
which had been established by papal decree in 1133.[27] Church income was high
from special taxes on mercantile endeavors, but in the later thirteenth century
these tax monies were regularly appropriated for public (that is, communal)
works.[28] To confuse the issue further, the commune was in charge of the *Opera
del duomo*, or cathedral works, funded by the same taxes. Major work on the
cathedral of San Lorenzo, such as decorating the cathedral façade, adding on
the chapel of Saint John the Baptist to house relics from the Holy Land, and
frescoing the cathedral canons' cloister, took place sporadically throughout the

early thirteenth century.[29] Communal officials also oversaw the reconstruction and refurbishment of large parts of the cathedral between 1298 and 1312, after a serious fire occurred during the riots of 1296–97.[30]

Despite its size, Genoa did not yet have a university in the mid-thirteenth century, but it was a strong base for the mendicant orders. The Dominican convent in the city taught law, theology, and medicine, and it attained the status of a *studium generale* at the beginning of the fourteenth century.[31] The swift fame across Europe of the *Catholicon* (1286), a comprehensive dictionary by local Dominican Giovanni Balbi (d. c. 1298), testifies to the city's intellectual dynamism.[32] The Dominican intellectual tradition intersected with the long-standing Genoese chronicle tradition in the work of Jacopo da Varagine (c. 1230–1298). Da Varagine is most famous as the author of the *Legenda aurea* (*The Golden Legend*, a popular collection of saints' lives written in the 1260s), but he was also a successful Dominican administrator, an ambassador, a civic historian, and an archbishop of Genoa.[33]

The overlaps of civic and religious bureaucracy may partly explain the persistence of Latin as an official language in Genoa long after other Italian cities had switched to using the vernacular for all but the most formal written documents.[34] Other factors may include the usefulness of Latin as a universal language in long-distance trade and the difficulty of the local Genoese dialect, already considered obscure by other Italians in the thirteenth century. Thus, although Genoa lacked the intellectual brilliance of Bologna or Padua, its complex maritime economy fostered a relatively high educational standard—from the practical necessities of educating successful merchants in training to the broad use of Latin as a bureaucratic language.[35]

Epstein has noted that "this period of Genoese history [1257–1311] is usually depicted as the most brilliant phase of the city's prosperity and influence."[36] Genoa certainly presented a confident image to the outside world—that of a city whose extraordinary growth and broadly based economic success had the backing of a skilled navy and long-standing treaties with both Christian and Muslim Mediterranean powers. Genoese diplomatic skills were also evident in the way that the city's leaders balanced Guelf and Ghibelline partisanship on the Italian peninsula, preserving their political autonomy while at the same time maintaining reasonably good relations with both papacy and empire. The period's many public improvements demonstrate cordial collaboration between church and commune, and literary efforts on both sides (lay and religious) combine scholarly aptitude with a sense of civic responsibility. Above all, the existence of a continuous city chronicle tradition from the years of the First Crusade suggests the value that the Genoese placed first on themselves and second on maintaining an official account of their city's rise to glory.

From the perspective of the later thirteenth century, therefore, Genoa's accomplishments in the Mediterranean were significant militarily and politically as well as economically. At the same time, one historian has observed that Genoese civic unity in the later Middle Ages was inversely proportional to its external success; that is, its serious internal discord became more pressing as the republic neutralized external threats to its survival.[37] Between 1257 and 1312, as Genoa established itself as a dominant force in the Mediterranean, these internal divisions threatened ever more seriously to collapse the city-state from within.

Janus, Janus, and Janus

The publicization of Janus as the founder of Genoa was therefore less a response to external threats, as was the case in Padua, than an attempt to persuade Genoese citizens to put aside their petty factionalism and establish a lasting and productive civic unity. The legend attributing the city's origin to a founder named Janus derives from the fact that Genoa (modern Italian Genova) was known in medieval Latin not as Genua, the Roman name for the city, but as Janua.[38] This variant spelling resulted in a symbolic connection (from at least the twelfth century)[39] with the Latin word *ianua*, meaning door, gate, or threshold. Monumental city gates appear on the city seal and Genoese money from 1139; Petti Balbi argues that this is a conscious portrayal of the city's power and resources in response to the threat of Emperor Frederick Barbarossa, in defense against whom Genoa rebuilt its city walls at the same time.[40] Given the city's appropriation of *ianua* as gate, the logical leap from Janua to the "city of Janus" was minimal, particularly as Janus was the Roman god of *ianuae*. Already in the early thirteenth century, the historian and poet Ursone da Sestri referred to Genoa as "the city of Janus" in his section of the Genoese municipal chronicle.[41]

For local historians, the greatest problem with promoting the classical Janus as the founder of Genoa was that the ancient sources were irritatingly mute on the subject. In fact, the little information they presented implied that there were several different Januses, and no source positively identified any one of these as Genoa's founder. Therefore, medieval Genoese looking for evidence for their supposed founder lacked a unified tradition narrating the actions of a famous person, as there existed in the case of Antenor for Padua. This situation forced the Genoese to employ their own creativity to bridge the gaps.

Solinus and Isidore both address the subject of Janus as founder indirectly rather than directly, dwelling chiefly on his various capacities as a Roman deity. Of cities, for instance, Isidore says merely that "in Italy, moreover, Janiculum was founded by Janus and Saturnia and Latium by Saturn."[42] His statement establishes Janus as a founder, but it does not identify Janiculum with Genoa. Solinus says much the same.[43] Isidore goes on to connect the god Janus with portals, explaining that "doors [ianua] are called after that Janus to whom pagans sanctified every entrance and exit."[44] Isidore mentions Janus twice more in like manner, once in connection to the naming of the month of January and once when discussing the god himself:

> The month of January is called after Janus, to whom it was consecrated among the pagans, or because it is the frontier or portal of the year. And thus Janus is depicted bifrontally, so that he designates both the entrance and the exit of the year.[45]

> They call Janus the door, as it were, of earth and heaven, or of the months; they show him with two faces representing east and west. Indeed, when they depict him four-faced and call him Janus the twin, they are referring to the four regions of the earth or to the four elements or seasons.[46]

Thus, Isidore's description of the Roman god Janus incorporates his usual bifrontal representation, his association with portals and thresholds, and his eponymous link with the month of January. These references provide a good precedent for naming things after Janus, but again, none of them specifically associates him with the city of Genoa/Janua.

The connection between Janus and Saturn goes back to the *Aeneid*, where Virgil makes several references to an ancient *pater* named Janus when relating the background of King Latinus and a pre-Trojan Rome. The bifrontal Janus appears at *Aeneid* 7.180 among a series of statues depicting Latinus's forebears and the early rulers of Italy, but Janus also figures specifically as a founder at 8.355–58: "You see here in these two towns, with their ruined walls, the relics and monuments of men of old. Father Janus built this fortress, Saturn that one; the name of this one was Janiculum, that one Saturnia."[47] Virgil refers to a legend that also appears in the Eusebius-Jerome chronicle tradition: supposedly, Janus was an early king of Italy who founded a city that was called Janiculum after him.[48] Janus, Saturn, and their descendants—Picus, Faunus, and Latinus, whose daughter Lavinia married Aeneas—thus represent the native Italian half of the Roman Aeneas myth. Paul the Deacon's eighth-century *Historia Romana*, which is largely based on the chronicle of Eusebius-Jerome, begins with this legend: "As some say, Janus reigned first in Italy."[49] Paul then goes on to explain Saturn's arrival and his descendants.

The Janus/Saturn myth appears in a number of late Roman sources, such as the anonymous fourth-century *Origo gentis Romanae* once attributed to Aurelius Victor and various chronicles based on Jerome. Macrobius's *Saturnalia* (c. 400) provides the most detailed account:

> Janus held as his realm that region which is now called Italy, as Hyginus relates, following Protarchus of Tralles; he and Cameses, who was also a native, possessed the land in joint sovereignty, so that the region was called Camesene and the town Janiculum. Later the kingdom reverted to Janus alone, who is believed to have had a double face, so that he could see both in front of himself and behind his own back. This doubtless refers to the prudence and ingenuity of a king who both knew the past and could foresee the future; in the same way, Foresight and Hindsight, the most appropriate associates of divination, are worshiped among the Romans. . . .
>
> That [Janus and Saturn] ruled with one accord and built two neighboring towns by their common effort is apparent not only from Virgil, who relates, "The name of this one was Janiculum, that one Saturnia," but also because their descendants called two successive months after them, so that December contains the festival of Saturn and the other, January, contains the name [of Janus].[50]

Like Paul the Deacon, most medieval writers of universal histories and chronicles that begin this far back included the legend of Janus and Saturn, early rulers of Italy, although the sources at their disposal also told the story of a two-faced god worshipped by the Romans. The passage from Macrobius cited above demonstrates that by the late fourth century the two legends sometimes merged. The *Saturnalia* deals chiefly with Janus, the king of Italy, but Macrobius incorporates both traditions: he claims that King Janus's omniscient leadership led to his bifrontal depiction as well as to his veneration by the Romans.

The traditional authorities, therefore, were full of stories about someone (a king, god, and/or hero) named Janus. However, the accumulated evidence was decidedly vague as to his precise accomplishments, how they fit together, and whether they had any link to the founding of Genoa. The only ancient source that clearly deals with Genoa itself is Livy's *Ab urbe condita*, which discusses Roman Genua's role in the Punic Wars but never addresses the city's origins.[51] Thus, when the thirteenth-century Genoese looked for sources about the early history of their city, they found a number of disconnected traditions, all of them frustratingly silent on the subject in which they were most interested, namely, the founding of Genoa.

Although Ursone da Sestri alludes briefly to Janus, as mentioned above, the first Genoese chronicler to deal extensively with the city's origins was the historian Jacopo Doria (1234–c. 1294), who covered the years 1280 to 1293 and was Genoa's last official chronicler.[52] Departing from a tradition in which each official annalist simply picked up where his predecessor had left off, Doria felt it necessary to revisit the city's distant past. As he explains in his preface,

> Before I turn to my proposed material [viz. the years 1280–93], I will relate in these writings what I have found regarding the city of Janua in certain histories and ancient legends, and afterward I will be certain to return to my subject.
>
> For when I did not find anything written before the time of the noble Caffaro, citizen of Genoa, who began the work of the present chronicle in the year of Our Lord 1097 (as is found in the beginning of this chronicle)—nor could I learn of the construction of this city in other books, when nonetheless the founders of many other cities in Italy and other parts of the world are treated in the writings of Isidore and Solinus and other historians—moved by astonishment, I began to think with silent and persistent mind how I could discover anything of ancient times. But up to now I have not been able to discover [Genoa's] founder in any authoritative books, perhaps on account of [the story's] great antiquity.[53]

As Doria relates his vain search to learn more about his city's origins, he expresses his surprise, first, that Caffaro himself did not address the subject and, second, that no other authorities mention the early history of Genoa. Narrowing his search, Doria is particularly put out to find nothing about the *founding* of Genoa, an event that holds a significance for him beyond just "early history." He describes his search specifically as looking for details about the *constructionem huius civitate*, or "building of this city," and complains that tales of the *edificatores*, or founders of other cities, are easily found. *Constructio* and *edificator* refer literally to physical construction. Both terms, however, also allude to the more symbolic establishment of a people by a mythic hero, who founds the city's human community as much as or even more than its physical site.[54] Given his city's contemporary prosperity, Doria is hunting for evidence of an equally brilliant founding hero for the Genoese people, and his failure to find one baffles him, since his sources treat in detail the origins of other cities—which he doubtless regarded as less important. He assumes not only that contemporary fame and success must be the result of an illustrious past, or specifically, an illustrious beginning, but also that having a written history is a significant part of the glorification of a city. For Doria, this is an area in which Genoa is not properly appreciated, and he intends his preface—tangential as it is to the main narrative—to correct the defect as far as possible.

Curiously, the history of the founding of Genoa that Doria then proceeds to tell is not supported by any of the ancient sources. In Doria's legend, Genoa was founded by a Trojan prince fleeing the sack of Troy:

> But common opinion [*opinio vulgaris*] in the city of Genoa holds that after the destruction of Troy a certain noble Trojan by the name of Janus came to these parts and landed in a place now called Sarzano, that is, Janus's landing [*saltus Iani*]. And it is said that he built a fortress in the place now called Castello, where the archiepiscopal palace is today, and he named the city of Genoa after his own name, that is, Janus. And indeed, I found some mention of our city in the book of Titus Livius, who was a great historian of the city of Rome, which partly demonstrates its antiquity; therefore, I will write his words word for word in the present work, followed by similar things which I have found in other ancient writings [*antiquis scripturis*].[55]

Historians have usually understood Doria's use of *vulgo* to be pejorative, that is, to indicate that he is relating a legend popular with the "common herd" to which he himself does not subscribe.[56] On the contrary, it seems more plausible that the phrase *opinio vulgaris* is intended to indicate the widespread dissemination of the Trojan legend in the Genoa of Doria's time. This interpretation makes more sense given his transition to his next point: common opinion holds that a Trojan prince founded Genoa, and indeed (*verum quia*) the city appears in Livy's account of the Punic Wars, so its antiquity is corroborated to at least that period.[57]

Although the Trojan legend of Janus does not appear in the ancient sources, it clearly derives from the legends of Aeneas and Antenor, both of whom were Trojan refugees and founding fathers of Italian cities. Doria's account of the

Trojan Janus repeats many of the same tropes used in the accounts of Aeneas and Antenor, emphasizing his noble descent and his construction of the new city's first fortress on the site-to-be of some prominent medieval edifice—in this case, the archiepiscopal palace. Doria recognizes that nothing in his sources supports this story, so he attributes the legend to as wide a support base as he can (*opinio vulgaris*) and then demonstrates that the ancient sources at least circumstantially support the notion of a Trojan origin.

Finally, after a series of quotations about Genoa from Livy, early medieval chronicles like Paul the Deacon's *Historia Langobardorum*, and local saints' lives, Doria turns to the question of why some ancient sources refer to the city as Genua and others as Janua. His discussion of this subject is unoriginal, being largely based on Isidore's definitions of *genua* (knees) and *ianua* (portals)[58] in *Etymologiae*, book 20, but he does address the various attributes of the Roman god Janus, finally concluding firmly that

> Janua [Genoa] is called after Janus. This Janua, which is a gate, is the first entrance and the first access, because Janus is the god of beginnings, to whom the ancients consecrated every entrance and exit. And therefore, as a gate is the entrance and exit to anyone's house, so too our city is the entrance and exit to all Lombardy. And just as Janua is called after Janus, the god of beginnings, who is depicted as having two faces—namely, forward and back—thus the city of Janua overlooks the sea before and the earth behind. And as he is said to have two *faculas*—that is, two portals— east and west, thus the city of Janua has two gates, namely, a gate to the sea and a gate to the land.[59]

In these few paragraphs, Doria accounts for his city's glorious past in a number of complementary ways. First, the "popular" tale of a noble founder provides the city with a mythic heritage linked to that of Troy and Rome. Written authorities vouch for this legend by attesting to Genoa's prominent role in the Punic Wars (in the third century B.C.) as well as under the Lombards and Carolingians (c. A.D. 400–900). Finally, Doria adduces an etymological explanation of Genoa's Latin names (Genua and Janua), both of which glorify the city. Thus, he approaches the subject from two different directions, the mytho-historical and the etymological. At the same time, he cites evidence from several types of sources: the popular story of the *vulgaris opinio*, the long-standing written authority of the *antiquis scripturis*, and the etymology of the word "Janua" itself.

Doria's wide-ranging account of Genoa's origins serves a number of purposes. The elaboration of Janus as a Trojan prince provides the Genoese with a mythic founder of illustrious lineage—an ideal progenitor both to reassure and to inspire his descendants. The evidence of the *antiquis scripturis* bolsters the Trojan origin myth and proves Genoa's continued importance in the times between its founding and its present. Finally, the idea that its founder, Janus, who was worshiped by the Romans as a god, named the city after himself and for qualities inherent to the name Janua—such as being the gateway to all Lombardy—suggests the inevitability of Genoa's role in human history. Hence, Doria not only provides his city with a glorious early history but also introduces a sense of destiny to its progress, from its beginnings up to its thirteenth-century present. The didactic implications are clear: Doria's fellow citizens have a responsibility, one inherent in their city's very name, to maintain its fame and authority in future years.

As the subscription in the official manuscript asserts, Jacopo Doria presented his portion of the municipal chronicle to the officials of the commune in the summer of 1294, at which time the archbishop of Genoa, Jacopo da Varagine, had already conceived the idea of writing his own history of Genoa.[60] Da Varagine was an experienced Dominican administrator and teacher, as well as an author well known for his *Legenda aurea* (finished c. 1267). He came from a local Ligurian family and had been elected to the Genoese archbishopric in 1292.[61] The preface to his chronicle states that his aim was to write a history of Genoa situated within the larger context of universal history, rather than an annal in the fashion of Caffaro.[62] Da Varagine divides his work into twelve thematic sections, dealing in turn with the foundation of the city, its early history and appearance, and its secular and ecclesiastical governance. He spent the years from 1295 to 1297 working on it and left it mostly completed at his death in 1298.[63]

Like Jacopo Doria, Jacopo da Varagine expresses great surprise and indignation at the absence of any mention of Genoa in the ancient sources and early chronicles: "Thinking, therefore, and considering with careful thought how there are many cities in Italy of which the ancient historians make much mention, we are amazed that so very little can be found written by them on the city of Genoa, as renowned, noble, and powerful as it is."[64] His explanation for this is that Genoa was a smaller city in the days of the early historians, who were only concerned with writing about large and famous cities; nevertheless, he has taken the liberty of collecting all of the references he could find to Genoa's early history.[65] He begins his account not with the founding of Genoa but with the "first founders of cities" (*primi fundatores civitatum*).[66] This not only provides a background to the founding of Genoa but also justifies a focus on cities by explaining their particular significance in human history. Da Varagine points out that "every city, therefore, has two founders: the chief one, namely God himself, and another secondary one, namely a human being."[67] Cities are a work of God just as people are, and he traces civic development through early biblical history. According to da Varagine, for example, Cain built the first city, and it took part in his sin since he retired there to defend himself after having slain his brother Abel; thus were the first walls put around cities.[68] Having explained how Nimrod built the first city after the flood, as well as the city of Babylon, he then describes how civilization spread as people, "one of whom was Janus," set out from the Holy Land to found cities elsewhere.[69] This brings him to the core of the first half of his narrative.

Jacopo da Varagine's treatment of the Janus legend reflects the Dominican penchant for intellectual organization. Instead of trying to combine all of his sources' disparate references to Janus into an account of a single civic founder, thus creating a bit of a mess (as might perhaps be said of Doria), da Varagine sorts them all out and proclaims proudly, "It must be noted that there are supposedly three Januses. The first is Janus, who came from the East to Italy and reigned there first. The second is a certain prince, who was a citizen of Troy, who came to Italy after the destruction of Troy. The third is the king of the Epirotes [from Epirus, in Greece], who came to Rome and after whose death the Romans deified and venerated as a god."[70] He then goes on to tell the story of each of these founders of the city, using them to build on one another. As his chapter titles divide the material, the first Janus founded the city of Genoa (*construxit et hedificavit*), the second made it bigger and better (*ampliavit et melioravit*), and the third was honored in Genoa for his role among the Romans (*in Ianua colebatur*).[71] In this manner, da Varagine constructs a civic myth that combines all three extant Janus traditions into one: Janus the first king of Italy (of the Janus and Saturn myth, as elaborated in Macrobius), Janus the prince of Troy (as told in Jacopo Doria's chronicle), and Janus worshiped by the Romans as a god (as appears in all of the Roman sources, but especially in Isidore and Macrobius).

In the end, da Varagine's explanation is even more comprehensive than that of Doria; he fits three different Januses in neat succession into the early history of Genoa before moving on to the Livian account of the Punic Wars and the conversion of the city to Christianity. His account has the same underlying assumptions as Doria's—the necessity of knowing one's civic origins and the importance of having a written history to elaborate those origins. But da Varagine's account is more systematic, organized, and all-inclusive. He may simply have been trying to be thorough in his use of his sources, but it is also suggestive that all three stories about Janus address the cultural importance of the Genoese in relation to the Romans. Da Varagine's nicely composite civic myth accomplishes three purposes: first, it claims a superiority for Genoa over Rome (and, by extension, over every other Italian city) because the first king of Italy founded it long before the foundation of Rome; second, it equates the history of Genoa with that of Rome by claiming a noble Trojan origin for the city, equivalent to that of Rome (or better, since Aeneas did not actually found Rome itself); and finally, it establishes Genoa's participation in Roman civilization via shared gods and customs. Da Varagine's simultaneous attempts to claim superiority over and close association with Rome may be odd, but he seems to have been more interested in comprehensiveness than consistency.

Da Varagine's reliance on Roman models extends to the rest of his chronicle, suggesting that for him, as for many of his contemporaries, the idea of Rome as *Urbs*, or The City, was not just a figure of speech. Rather, the parallels he draws between Genoa and Rome move from the mythohistorical realm into a more concrete political one. The central core of da Varagine's twelve-part history is parts six through eight, which define and describe the Genoese political system (part six) as well as the qualities appropriate to its rulers (part seven) and to its citizens (part eight). Da Varagine's ideal political system is that of consuls, as in both the Roman republic and the Genoese commune as originally constituted in 1098. His ideal political qualities are essentially Roman with a Christian overlay. For instance, his argument for considering the common good over the individual good points out that "Roman judges and consuls were more concerned with the state than with their own affairs."[72] Although he frequently couches abstract virtues—piety, justice, and mercy—in Christian terms, he sets most of his practical examples in a Roman framework, and in fact most of them come from Roman sources like Cicero, Livy, Vegetius, and Valerius Maximus.[73]

Thus, the favorable comparisons that Jacopo da Varagine draws between Genoa's history and that of Rome support his history's broadest purpose, which, as with Jacopo Doria, is didactic. The ancient Romans stand as a historical example for contemporary citizens of Genoa; further, Genoa's older and more illustrious history should inspire the Genoese to surpass Roman political and economic achievements. Here again is the equation of an illustrious past with an illustrious present, which, as I suggested earlier, is a two-way exchange:

people create illustrious pasts to explain a successful present, while belief in an illustrious past may inspire still greater success in the present and future.

The eloquence of Doria and da Varagine in the 1290s led to the monumentalization of Janus as the official founder of Genoa about a decade later. Genoa's cathedral of San Lorenzo had been badly damaged by fire in a period of rioting in the winter of 1296–97, and the civic officials in charge of the restoration integrated the legend of Janus into the newly reconstructed nave.[74] The introduction of civic propaganda into a sacred space was not unprecedented: in 1226, the commune had commissioned for the cathedral a bronze statue of a griffin—an apt symbol of the city, as it is an uneasy combination of lion and eagle, the symbols, respectively, of the Guelfs (the papal lion) and the Ghibellines (the imperial eagle).[75] Part of the post-1297 reconstruction involved the recommissioning of the griffin in marble rather than bronze, presumably because fire had melted, or at least badly damaged, the bronze statue.[76]

A few streets away, the exterior of the Doria family church of San Matteo hosted a number of inscriptions commemorating recent Genoese naval victories over Pisa and Venice.[77] These were family monuments, since Doria leadership was responsible for each of the victories commemorated, but they were also communal monuments recalling the victories of the Genoese community as a whole. Scholars have observed that Genoa's irregular terrain and population density in the later Middle Ages left few large public spaces for communal monuments.[78] The Genoese had nothing like the two large piazze on either side of Padua's Palazzo della Ragione, for example, and certainly nothing like Siena's famous Campo. As the only large gathering spots and monumental spaces in the city, therefore, Genoa's churches became the repositories of secular memorials as well as religious ones.

The Genoese cathedral renovations included the complete restructuring of the arches on either side of the central nave, and it is here that one finds the monumental commemoration of the Janus legend. The reconstruction of the north side of the nave was completed first, in 1307, and between the two levels of arches, the restorers placed an inscription reading, "1307: Pastono di Negro and Niccolò di Goano had this structure renovated with the legates' tithe" (figure 9).[79] This echoes the ancient Roman practice of inscribing public works with the names of the magistrates in charge.[80] It is certainly related to the medieval practice of putting inscriptions in chapels or on tombs, naming their donors, but differs in that di Goano and di Negro were using the city's funds rather than their own for the cathedral restoration. The inscription thus commemorates their leadership and supervision rather than their financial sponsorship. (Roman magistrates, of course, had to use their own money for public works projects, so di Goano and di Negro were lucky. They received all the credit but incurred none of the personal expense.)

The connection goes further, however. On one of the columns above the inscription, near the front of the nave, the same restorers placed a large sculpted head of Janus above another explanatory inscription. A ridge separating the two halves of his face creates the impression of bifrontality. Both head and inscription (figure 10) are easily visible from the nave; written in contemporary Lombardic capitals, as on the tomb of Antenor in Padua, are the words, "Janus, first king of Italy, of the lineage of giants, who founded Genoa in the time of Abraham."[81] This inscription commemorates the first Janus of Jacopo da Varagine's account, the first king of Italy and a descendant of Noah's grandson Nimrod.[82] The qualification *tempore Abrahe* is particularly suggestive given the inscription's presence in a church, where other images would have reminded the viewer of how long ago "the time of Abraham" was. The carved head, reminiscent of an Old Testament prophet or king, would have provided a similar visual referent. The phrasing also locates a secular civic event within

Fig. 9 North arcade of nave, cathedral of San Lorenzo, Genoa, rebuilt 1307. The head of Janus is at upper right.

Fig. 10 Head of Janus and accompanying inscription, cathedral of San Lorenzo, Genoa, 1307.

Christian chronology, much as Eusebius's chronicle had done in reconciling Roman and Christian historical events.[83] These connections must have evoked pride and piety in any Genoese citizen.

Five years later, in 1312, the same Niccolò di Goano, and another di Negro, Filippo—presumably a relative of Pastono—oversaw the completion of the restoration of the south side of the nave. As before, they inscribed their names and the date, but instead of adding another sculpture, they commemorated Janus by extending their inscription down the nave (figure 11):

> 1312: Filippo di Negro and Niccolò di Goano, restorers of this church, had this structure renovated from the legates' tithe. Janus, a Trojan prince experienced in astrology, sailing in search of a safe, healthy, and defensible place to live, came to Genoa—which had already been founded by Janus, king of Italy, great-grandson of Noah—and seeing it well protected by the mountains and the sea, increased its name and power.[84]

The Janus referred to here is not da Varagine's first Janus but his second, the prince of Troy who improved the previously founded but still very small city of Genoa. As before, the details come from Jacopo da Varagine's chronicle. Furthermore, the inscription on the south side of the church complements that on the north side with its reference to "Genoa, already founded by Janus, king of Italy, great-grandson of Noah."[85] These inscriptions and the head of Janus—high enough to be visually imposing but large enough to be legible from the floor of the nave—are a powerful reminder of the city's illustrious origins: Janus, king of Italy, on the north side, and Janus, prince of Troy, on the south.[86] Janus's regal face looks sternly down on his descendants, admonishing and encouraging them to live up to their heritage.

Thus, the Janus legend's monumentalization in San Lorenzo serves the same purpose as Doria's and da Varagine's texts, but in a more public forum—one which, as a church, was the medieval city's customary arena for providing moral examples and leadership to its people. Conforming to the ancient Roman conception of written history as specifically didactic, each of these three expressions of the Genoese foundation legend was designed to educate the Genoese people about their past and to provide a past worthy of their present late thirteenth-century success. More than that, each sought to present a behavioral standard, simultaneously encouraging individual morality and civic unity. In this way, the Janus legend explicitly addresses the contemporary Genoese problem of internal factionalism. In promoting the illustrious origins of their

Fig. 11 South arcade of nave, cathedral of San Lorenzo, Genoa, 1312.

city, Doria and da Varagine—along with di Goano and the two di Negros—stressed the importance of the common good over the individual good. The myth of Janus reminded the contemporary citizens of Genoa of their shared ancestry and encouraged them to live up to its precedents: two kings, one prince, two city founders, and one savior of Rome, later deified. All were founders dedicated to the civic good; their great fame rested on their service to the city. They were powerful counter-examples to the contemporary Genoese, whose personal rivalries and petty strife threatened to destroy the city. The citizens of Genoa had to consider the common good, the *res publica*, over personal gain or grievance if their city was to achieve its highest potential.

Intention and Agency

The public nature of the media that disseminated the Janus legend in the years around 1300—two well-known literary works and one public monument—does a great deal to demonstrate that Jacopo Doria and Jacopo da Varagine were not two scholars incidentally interested in curious old legends. At the same time, an inquiry into their respective roles in Genoese society and how they saw those roles may clarify the ideological workings of the Genoese city-state. How did the Janus legend go from Doria's *vulgaris opinio* to a personification in stone in the Genoese cathedral, and why did it happen in this period? I have already argued that Genoa's greatest challenges in the years around 1300 were domestic and that the elaboration of the Janus legend was in large part an attempt to address these internal divisions. Who were these men that they were appointed, or appointed themselves, to solve the city's problems?

Jacopo Doria, for his part, filled the same role in the Genoa of the late thirteenth century as did Lovato Lovati or Albertino Mussato in Padua, being a member of the ruling elite who balanced his literary and classicizing interests with his civic responsibilities. The Doria name reveals his membership in one of Genoa's leading Ghibelline families, from a nobility that dominated Genoese history and politics for several hundred years both before and after Jacopo's time.[87] Jacopo himself was never a prominent city official or military leader, but his brother Oberto was one of the more famous capitani del popolo of the thirteenth century; Oberto ruled Genoa jointly with fellow Ghibelline Oberto Spinola for a number of years after the revolt of 1270, and he oversaw the construction of the Palazzo del Comune complex.[88] The Doria family church is also the site of the numerous plaques mentioned earlier that commemorate Genoese naval victories.[89] Hence, the Doria family in general, and Jacopo and Oberto's generation in particular, played a large role both in the workings of the Genoese government and its self-advertisement in the late thirteenth century.

Unlike his brother, Jacopo usually worked out of public view. For most of his adult life, he served as historian and archivist (Latin *custos*) to the Genoese commune, organizing and keeping the city's multitudinous official records; his role in continuing Caffaro's chronicle was a direct result of this employment.[90] Doria also redacted the first volume of the Genoese *Libri iurium*, or books of laws, which recorded laws, treaties, and other official documents.[91] His report in the municipal chronicle of his attempt to document Genoa's historical origins is therefore hardly surprising. A lifetime of dealing with government documents (including international treaties, charters, claims of property rights, and traditional usages) and mercantile investment contracts explains his desire to unearth evidence for Genoa's early history—not to mention his determination to remedy the deficiency if sufficient evidence should not present itself.

But just as Lovati was not only a judge and a humanist, Doria was not only an archivist: he took an active part in public life, if not on the same level as his more famous brother. He served as a representative of the commune on at least two ambassadorial missions (in 1256 and 1271) and at least once held the office of *anziano*, or council member, in the Genoese government.[92] Jacopo Doria was therefore no intellectual dilettante but a member of the ruling class who, together with his friends and relatives, was closely involved in the governance of his city, as well as with its public image both internally and externally—be that via commemorative plaques, municipal histories, or ambassadorial missions. His personal interest in Genoa's classical past and his public persona as an official of the regime were not distinct aspects of his character; rather, the two complemented and built upon each other.

Similarly, Jacopo da Varagine was a prominent Dominican who played a major civic role as archbishop of Genoa. In 1295, he even served as one of the Genoese ambassadors to the pope, a role requiring deft handling to avoid suspicions of conflict of interest.[93] The circumstances in which he wrote his history of Genoa suggest, again, that the work was no academic exercise. Da Varagine began his history in 1295, a year in which, as he narrates, "in the month of January, general and universal peace was made in the city of Genoa between those known as Mascherati, or Ghibellines, and those known as Rampini, or Guelfs."[94] The peace was intended to end a major feud of more than sixty years' duration, and both the commune and the Genoese church welcomed it gratefully. As archbishop, da Varagine played a major role in the reconciliation. He presided over the public declaration of the peace, a mass, and a large communal meal, and blessed the many crowds present. His history expresses all the more regret, then, that the peace so solemnly enacted lasted less than a year: "What sorrow!"[95] The riots that broke out between the Guelfs and Ghibellines in December 1295 resulted in multiple deaths, much damage to property, and, most symbolically, major fire damage to the cathedral of San Lorenzo.[96] Da Varagine was writing his history of Genoa at a highly charged moment when civic harmony and its obstacles were major concerns for Genoa's citizens. These concerns come through clearly in his work, not least in his formulation of the myth of Janus.

Furthermore, the surviving manuscript evidence suggests that da Varagine's readers shared his interests and concerns. At least twelve copies of the work survive from the first hundred years after its dissemination, presumably after da Varagine's death in 1298; most of these are carefully copied and decorated, and some are illustrated or illuminated.[97] More specifically, in his 1941 edition, Giovanni Monleone published an alphabetical list or index found at the back of an important early manuscript of da Varagine's history. The book was copied in Genoa circa 1320 (Monleone's MS B) and served as the archetype for a number of other manuscript copies.[98] The index consists of fifteen *distinctiones, all* associated with ideas of good governance and almost all referring to the Roman examples offered by da Varagine in his text. A representative sampling of these follows:

> Greedy: The consuls of the Romans were not [greedy], and therefore the republic was governed well and grew. Book 7, chap. 4.
>
> Afflicted friends: We ought to assist [them]. For example, the Romans, who rebuilt Genoa after its destruction by the Africans. Book 2, chap. 3.
>
> Trust: Ought also to be extended to enemies. For example, the Romans, who preserved loyalty and trust even with their enemies and never broke treaties, were always victorious and subdued the whole world under them. Book 8, chap. 2.
>
> Modesty: Ought to be sought by every ruler and victor, because his victory ought not to lead him into pride. An example from the Romans. Book 6, chap. 3.
>
> Good: The common good ought to be placed before one's own good. Example of the Roman Marcus Regulus. Book 8, chap. 3.[99]

The list shows its creator's interest not only in civic ideals such as selflessness, magnanimity, trust, modesty, and the common good (as appear above) but also in specific examples linking those ideals with Roman practice.[100] That it was created as a reference tool in a manuscript of da Varagine's history suggests that da Varagine's readers were interested in comparing contemporary Genoa with republican Rome and that at least some of them actively used his text as a handbook, learning how to improve the governing of their city by comparing it with how things were done in ancient Rome. Da Varagine's text provides the Roman model, but the index demonstrates that his contemporaries actually accepted his parallel of contemporary Genoa with ancient Rome and used it on a practical basis.

The trend toward city improvement and civic peace, of which the propagation of the Janus myth formed a large part, was thus a widespread effort with effects on multiple levels. The commune and the Genoese church drove the endeavor, and secular and religious leaders collaborated closely to preserve civic peace; communal officials took charge of cathedral improvements, while the archbishop served as civic ambassador to the pope. All were conscious of the church's role in maintaining peace in the city and uniting its population. Thus, the church, like the Genoese commune, adopted Janus as the city's founder to remind the citizens of their shared ancestry while also serving as an important moral example. In this sense, the monumentalization of the Janus tradition on the arches of San Lorenzo is an appropriate culmination of the civic myth. The foundational text for the sculptural head of Janus and its attendant inscriptions was written by Genoa's own archbishop, Jacopo da Varagine; moreover, the church needed to be restored because of riots that had inspired him to the writing of civic history in the first place. It thus seems fitting that the secular officials overseeing the restoration of the cathedral should have included a monument to the city's founder that both recalled the city's illustrious heritage and reminded its populace of the dangers of factionalism.

Genoa's astronomic success in the late medieval Mediterranean economy and its diplomatic success in balancing between pope and emperor in the slippery world of thirteenth-century Italian politics belied an uneasy tension of partisan politics at home. As the city's prominence among the states of late medieval Italy grew, its domestic situation became ever more fraught. As a result, most of the policies pursued by secular and ecclesiastical authorities in the later thirteenth century aimed to foster a general sense of civic pride and unity, from the successful captaincy of Guglielmo Boccanegra in the late 1250s to the increasingly ineffective and swiftly changing authorities of the early 1300s. Their achievements included a number of new communal palaces and the expansion of the city's waterfront area, all symbols of Genoa's independence and economic success. These structures' prominence in the urban landscape, visible to all, would have vaunted the city's influence and resources, emphasizing its identity as one of the great powers of the late medieval Mediterranean.

Furthermore, the promotion of the classical Janus myth imbued Genoa and its ruling regime with a sense of antiquity and political legitimacy, bolstering the city's ideological claims against such rivals as Pisa and Venice. In these circumstances, however, the more important audience was the Genoese community itself; the founding figure of Janus gave its members a far-reaching civic history, a sense of collective ancestry, and examples of positive civic behavior, all at once. These derive variously from the Bible, early Christian sources, and the legend of Troy—but above all, from republican Rome, which da Varagine's history of Genoa presents as a functional and relevant model of republican life. The monumentalization of the Janus tradition in the cathedral restorations of 1307 and 1312 therefore reveals the success of these efforts at civic unification, as well as their failures. It demonstrates that the Janus legend was influential enough by the turn of the fourteenth century that civic officials included it in their cathedral restoration plans. At the same time, the necessity for the restoration highlights the growing chaos of Genoese life. In fact, 1312—the year that saw the restoration's completion, with its final Janus inscription—was one year after the Genoese had surrendered the city to Emperor Henry VII, in hopes that a foreign emperor could establish order where the civic government could not.

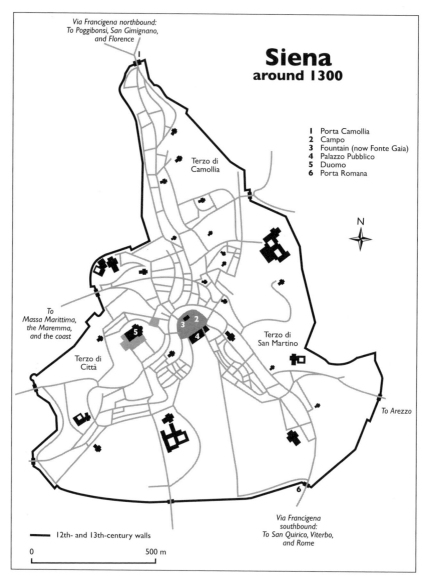

Map 4   Siena around 1300. Map after Waley, *Siena and the Sienese.*

4

SIENA

Romulus and Remus Revisited

Anyone who climbs up to the Campidoglio today [1893] can see the
two live wolves that the City of Rome keeps as a symbol of the Eternal City.
This was also a custom in the Middle Ages. And like neighboring Florence,
which kept a live lion near the gate of their civic palace [in the fifteenth century],
the Sienese started keeping wolves as much as two centuries earlier,
because they symbolized the city's Roman origin.

—Alessandro Lisini, *Miscellanea storica senese*

According to a local legend, the city of Siena was founded by the twins Aschius
and Senius. When they were young, their uncle murdered their father and
usurped his throne, so they fled into the forest on two horses, one white and
one black. There the two boys were suckled by a she-wolf, and when they grew
up, they founded a city called Siena, after Senius. They took the she-wolf as the
symbol of their city and the colors of the horses as their banner.[1] The legend
has proved resilient: the she-wolf is a vivid presence all over Siena even today,
and the half-white, half-black *balzana* takes pride of place as the city's standard during the Palio, the horse race in Siena's main piazza twice every summer. That said, the story will sound eerily, even comically, familiar to readers
acquainted with Roman history, since it closely mimics the famous legend of
the founding of Rome (as narrated, for example, in Livy's *Ab urbe condita*).[2] Only
the horses are lacking in the Roman version: Romulus and Remus, the heirs
of the city of Alba Longa, were hunted from the city by their great-uncle
Amulius, who killed their grandfather Numitor and usurped his throne. Abandoned in the wilderness, they were suckled by a she-wolf, and when they grew
up, they founded the city of Rome. According to the Roman legend, the twins
then quarreled, and Romulus killed Remus. Thus two legends merge, because

according to the Sienese, history repeated itself in the younger pair of twins. Aschius and Senius were the sons of Remus, who were forced to flee because their uncle, Romulus, had killed their father.

The medieval history of Siena lacks the great historiographical tradition of Genoa or Florence. No written version of this strange legend predates the fifteenth century (although its dating has been hotly debated), and only a few scattered fourteenth-century chronicles narrate the earlier history of the city.[3] While much of the evidence for the Genoese legend of Janus is literary, in Siena the overwhelming majority of examples are visual: *lupae* (Latin for "she-wolves") appear in Sienese sculpture, frescoes, city seals, graffiti, and mosaics—not to mention in the flesh. As the Montelupese example in the introduction to this study shows, the she-wolf was sufficiently familiar as a symbol of medieval Siena that the gift of a live wolf could cement a diplomatic alliance with the city. Further, although a written account of the legend is lacking before the fifteenth century, the wolf's appearance in numerous other media testifies to the vivid presence of the *lupa* legend in Siena as far back as the thirteenth century. The regime of the Nine (in Italian, Nove), whose rule lasted from 1287 to 1355, consciously cultivated the Romanizing legend of Aschius and Senius in order to glorify the Sienese state, creating a sense of republican civic identity that persisted long after the fall of the regime itself. During increasingly troubled times on the Italian peninsula—with threats ranging from famine and plague to the attacks of the great lords and mercenary generals—the Nine's actions reveal them to have been extremely aware of the importance of fostering a sense of well-being and unity in the city they ruled.

Growth and Civic Improvement

Siena (map 4) is located in central Tuscany in a hilly area along the Via Francigena, a major medieval trade and pilgrimage route leading from France and northern Italy down to Rome.[4] At the height of the government of the Nine, around 1340, the city claimed a contado reaching approximately thirty miles in every direction from the city, an area of nearly three thousand square miles.[5] The land mostly supported pasturage and crops but also held a number of valuable salt and mineral deposits, especially in the Maremma, the wild marshland west and south of the city.[6] One of the Nine's major objectives was to extend Sienese control throughout the Maremma. At the height of its expansion in the 1340s, the city-state may have contained about one hundred thousand people, approximately half of whom lived in the city itself. This considerable jump from an estimate of about sixty-five thousand people in the 1290s can be attributed to immigration and natural population growth as well as to territorial expansion.[7]

Siena was therefore about half the size of its close neighbor and rival Florence, a fact that its citizens felt keenly. It is probably no coincidence that the Nine declared the border of the Sienese contado to be thirty miles from the city, given that Florence is just over thirty miles from Siena (map 1). Most of the time, the Sienese and the Florentines were allies. Both cities belonged throughout this period to the Tuscan Guelf leagues organized to counterbalance aggression from papal supporters in Rome and imperial claimants in the north, as well as lesser but more immediate threats like the Visconti rulers of Milan.[8] But conflicts did occur; the Sienese defeated the Florentines at Montaperti in 1260, while the Florentines defeated the Sienese at Colle di Val d'Elsa in 1269 and 1357. The cities were close rivals through the thirteenth century, driven as they both were by the twin powerhouses of banking and cloth production. The lack of a convenient water source, however, hampered Sienese development in the latter area, and from the mid-thirteenth century Florence was considerably the more prosperous of the two.[9] Florence sat on the river Arno, which provided the city with fresh water, mill power, and drainage. Siena, by contrast, had no nearby river, as it sat atop three intersecting hilly ridges.[10] Thus, its distance from water was the city's largest problem in this period, affecting both its economy and its quality of life. During their tenure, the Nine addressed this problem from several angles. They countered Siena's exclusion from maritime trade with the purchase of the port of Talamone in 1303, while one of their most celebrated projects of the 1340s was the construction of an aqueduct to supply fresh water to the city.[11]

The government of the Nine Governors and Defenders of the City of Siena was formed in 1287 as a Guelf regime replacing a series of Ghibelline regimes that had been in power earlier in the century. The Ghibelline cause had lost a great deal of ground with the deaths of Frederick II and his heirs (1250–68), and the change of regime in Siena mirrored the changes taking place in a number of central Italian cities in the same period.[12] The Nine were essentially the most powerful citizen council in a podestarial regime similar to those found elsewhere in Italy. Siena's political structure had moved from a consular regime to a podestarial one in the late twelfth century, and the podestà in the early to mid-thirteenth century seems to have had a great deal of power. By the later thirteenth century, an official entourage of judges, notaries, squires, policemen, and a seneschal supported the podestà in his duties. However, his responsibilities had become more circumscribed since the city had acquired two more executive officers: the capitano del popolo and the *maggior sindaco* (chief justice). These were all foreigners, not Sienese citizens, elected every six months.[13]

Effective power, however, lay in the Concistoro, or citizen councils, of whom the Nine were the most important. They were an executive committee of nine men elected every two months from a pool of qualified citizens. Although the qualifications were severely restrictive—rules required candidates to have lived in Siena for a certain number of years, to own a certain amount of property, and not to be known Ghibellines—Siena was more republican than many cities, since up to fifty-four different citizens could sit on its executive council in a given year.[14] For the two months that each group of Nine spent in office, its members were sequestered in quarters in the Palazzo Pubblico to increase their impartiality. Four *provveditori* of the Biccherna (ministers of finance), four consuls of the *mercanzia* (heads of the guilds), and three Captains of the Guelf Party aided their decisions.[15] These officials, including the Nine, were all elected from the city's general council, or Council of the Bell. Yet despite their many advisors, as William Bowsky observes, "there is hardly a conceivable action involving communal government in which the Nine [were] not intimately involved."[16] They served as the first-response group on virtually every issue, internal and external, and the rest of the Sienese government seems to have been more or less auxiliary to them.

If the Nine played a major role in all aspects of communal government, then the commune did likewise for all aspects of Sienese life. After the adoption of the Virgin Mary as the city's patron on the eve of the battle of Montaperti in 1260, the commune took an active part in civic devotion to the Virgin as well as in the maintenance of the Sienese cathedral.[17] Just as civic festivals always had strong religious overtones, the main religious festivals of Siena had strong political overtones. For instance, the Sienese commune required all of its subject territories to participate in the public ceremonies attendant on the feast of the Assumption, Siena's chief festival in honor of the Virgin.[18] Similarly, the Palio was also strongly politicized. Referring to both of these festivals, Bowsky notes, "That the celebrations increased in size and splendor throughout the rule of the Nine despite famines, wars, and rising government expenses, suggests that the ruling oligarchy recognized that these religio-political festivals served to affirm the power of the commune."[19] At the same time, the Nine managed a number of civic institutions that in other cities were run chiefly or entirely by the church. They ran the town's chief hospital for the elderly, poor, and infirm, and they actively supported the city's studium by funding professorial salaries, providing housing, and offering a number of privileges designed to attract professors and students from nearby Bologna.[20]

As Randolph Starn and Loren Partridge have pointed out in their book on halls of power, the Sienese were acutely aware of the necessity for observable as well as functional urban improvements. The Nine aimed to beautify the city, improve its amenities, and expand the visible authority of the Sienese state both in and around the city. Over the course of their seventy-year rule, the Nine encouraged land reclamation and improvement, particularly in the Maremma; they authorized the building of new towns and villages in the contado, and new suburbs for the city itself. Alert to the crucial role of trade in the city's economy, they oversaw the improvement of water and road systems, including canals, bridges, and highways. They required the lords and communities who owned the land to build and maintain many of these, but the Nine themselves paid for the maintenance of all major bridges.[21] They also appointed at least two officials to oversee these works. In 1292, a "judge of the roads" was created to oversee the commune's investments and the works' completion. Similarly, in 1308 the commune eliminated the single office of the *scorridore*, or scourer of the roads, and reassigned the job of ensuring that roads were safe to a larger group of the podestà's knights.[22] These actions increased the regime's profile throughout the contado while ensuring the security of trade and the easy provisioning of the city.

Like the communes of Padua and Genoa, the Nine pursued improvements within the city while extending Sienese control in the contado. Most unrealistically, in 1322 they sponsored a notorious plan to improve the Sienese cathedral by turning the existing nave into the transept of a much larger cathedral, which when completed would have been the largest church in Western Christendom.[23] Daniel Waley has observed that this decision was almost certainly a reaction to the beginning of construction in the late thirteenth century on new cathedrals in Florence and Orvieto.[24] Work began in 1339, but only one wall of the larger church was completed before structural defects, inferior workmanship, and a lack of workers and funds dating from the 1348 plague caused the abandonment of the project in 1356.[25] Most of the plans formulated by the Nine were more successful, however. The gates to the city were all rebuilt in the 1310s and 1320s.[26] The commune also commissioned an immense altarpiece of the Virgin and Child from painter Duccio di Buoninsegna in 1308, which was installed in the cathedral with great pomp in 1311.[27]

Closer to the commune's own quarters, the Nine oversaw the renovation of the secular heart of the city—the main piazza, or Campo. They approved the construction of the Palazzo Pubblico in 1288 "for the honor and glory of the city," as the statute says; work began in 1297, and the main section was completed in 1310.[28] Construction of its bell tower, the famous Torre del Mangia, was finished in 1344. Not by accident, its imposing height of 102 meters, or 334 feet, made it just slightly higher than both the campanile (1313) of the Sienese cathedral and the campanile (1314) of the Palazzo Vecchio in Florence.[29] The Campo was paved in its idiosyncratic semicircular shell shape,[30] with a monumental public fountain as an outlet to the new city aqueduct, which was completed in 1343.[31] Together, the designs of the Palazzo Pubblico and Campo explicitly sought to display the grandeur and power of the ruling regime: the palazzo had nine merlons to each side of its central battlement,[32] while the Campo has nine sections to its shell, all converging on the palazzo's entrance (figure 12).

To complement the architecture of their new hall, the Nine commissioned the most famous artists of the day to decorate its interior.[33] The two painters whose work is best represented are Simone Martini (c. 1280–1344) and Ambrogio Lorenzetti (c. 1290–1348). Martini's *Maestà* (1315) adorns the wall of the palazzo's main council chamber; portraying the Virgin and Child with the city's four patron saints, the fresco addresses its political audience with the words of the Virgin, who advises, "Love justice, all you who rule the earth."[34] Between 1337 and 1340, Lorenzetti painted his *Good and Bad Government* frescoes in the Sala della Pace (Hall of Peace), the council chamber of the Nine.[35] The frescoes depict the diverse effects of good and bad government on an idealized city and its contado; the landscape portrayed, however, is clearly that of Siena, adding immediacy to the frescoes' message.[36] Other frescoes in the palazzo included Lorenzetti's *Mappamondo* (a map of the Sienese state, no longer extant), illustrations of conquered territories, and Martini's depiction of the condottiere Guidoriccio da Fogliano, all of which added to the grandeur and consequence of the Nine and, by extension, of Siena itself.[37] Yet the artistic commissions did not stop with frescoes. The official accounts kept by the Gabella and Biccherna all have painted wooden covers, as does the *Caleffo d'Assunta*, the official book of the city's rights and privileges; these covers show the city of Siena in various forms, or the Sienese bureaucracy at work.[38]

Efforts by the Nine to improve Siena's physical fabric and appearance paralleled less visible but equally valuable attempts to define the authority and rights of the Sienese commune. The legal tradition in Siena is extensive and well documented. The century following the year 1250 saw the production of the *Breves* of 1250, the Constitutions of 1262, and the vernacular statutes of 1309–10 and 1337–39, while codified council deliberations survive for almost the entire period.[39] The documents display the concern of the Nine with their city's well-being on virtually every level; in addition to making weighty decisions on domestic and foreign policy, they issued decrees on the maximum width of overhanging balconies in city streets and on the places in which prostitutes could and could not do business.[40] They appointed officials to enforce sumptuary laws and rules of public hygiene, and they mandated that the palazzi in and around the Campo conform architecturally to the Palazzo Pubblico and the

Fig. 12 Palazzo Pubblico as it might have appeared in 1350 (with the exception of the clock on the Torre del Mangia, which was added in 1360), Siena.

Campo, to create a uniform visual effect.[41] These "quality of life" issues were regarded so highly that the lapsed office of praetor, an official in charge of public order and city beautification, was revived in 1346.[42]

In the same vein, the Nine focused on expanding the city's studium, which, after its genesis in the early thirteenth century, had remained essentially a local institution, unlike that of Padua or Bologna. The commune offered huge publicly funded salaries and perquisites to attract scholars during the Bolognese emigration of 1321.[43] Starting in 1338, it also devoted both funds and energy to gaining the privileges of a *studium generale* from the pope, a desire not fulfilled until 1357, two years after the fall of the Nine. Even then, the privilege came from the emperor rather than the pope.[44]

Thus, the Nine ruled over a relatively peaceful and prosperous city; the Sienese never showed the penchant for killing one another that the Genoese did, and their political position was at least theoretically more secure than that of the Paduans in the same period. When the regime took shape in 1287, the Sienese were still exhilarated from their defeat of the Florentines at Montaperti in 1260, even though the Florentines had retaliated by defeating them in 1269. But despite relative economic success and population growth, the city's geographical position and resources (or lack thereof, as with water) hampered the substantial growth that occurred in Florence in the same period. Not without cause, the Nine feared that their city was losing its competitive edge; they were thus hypersensitive to issues touching the "honor and glory of the commune." Despite the policies of the Nine, Florentine competitors had almost entirely replaced the Sienese bankers at the papal court in Avignon by the 1320s, after the Sienese banking industry was badly hurt by bankruptcies during the first two decades of the century.[45] Political threats also troubled them. Siena suffered considerably from the Guelf wars with Castruccio Castracani of Lucca in the 1320s, while domestically the Nine put down a rebellion in 1318 and a conspiracy in 1346. The city's population was then more than halved by the Black Death in 1348.[46] Arguably, Siena never recovered from that disaster and the public disorder attendant on it. Much more so than Florence, Siena's smaller size and more limited resources made it a target for military takeover and signorial expansionism. Following the fall of the Nine in 1355, the Sienese suffered a decisive defeat at the hands of the Florentines in 1357; several different governments were formed and dissolved in rapid succession, and in 1399 the city lost its independence entirely, to the Visconti *signori* of Milan.[47]

Siena was very similar to its neighbors in its economic base, its worries about its political position in the rapidly changing world of central Italy around 1300, and its desire to maintain its independence and self-sufficiency. Several factors make it unique for the purposes of this study, however. First is the level of control wielded by the ruling class from which each group of Nine was elected; the Nine issued decrees on every aspect of Sienese life, from politics and economics to religion, education, urban design, and public health. Second, William Bowsky has observed that one major difference between Siena and Florence in this period was that in Siena display and luxury chiefly took public forms—improvements to the cathedral, the Palazzo Pubblico, the Campo, the streets, the aqueduct, and the studium—while in Florence more of that money and effort went into private forms of display: "By the period of the cultural efflorescence of the late thirteenth and early fourteenth centuries . . . the Sienese had a greater tradition than their neighbors of cultural investment through government and civic rather than private display."[48] For example, fourteenth-century Siena had no elaborate private chapels belonging to the nobility or merchant families, such as those that decorate Florentine churches.[49] Part of the reason for this may be, as Bowsky goes on to argue, that the Sienese government was more inclusive of major social groups than the Florentine government was; not only did it involve more citizens per year, but it also gave high positions to members of the nobility, who were excluded from office in Florence. Hence, a larger number of Siena's citizens had a personal stake in the regime.

Finally, and most important, the decrees of the Nine explicitly equate the physical and conceptual aspects of Siena—following the idea that a city's physical appearance mirrors its inner harmony or disharmony, and vice versa—more than those of any other city in Italy in this period.[50] The Nine chose their civic improvement projects to embody their abstract ideals about what a city should be. Thus, they ordered the newly subject territory of Giuncarico painted on the wall of the main council chamber; the painted reality inside the Palazzo Pubblico was intended to mirror the actual reality outside it. As Starn and Partridge point out, the frescoes in the palazzo reflect the reality of the Sienese state while simultaneously prescribing an ideal, and in so doing they force a mental comparison between the way things are and the way they ought to be.[51]

Romulus and Remus, Aschius and Senius

The medieval mythographers of Padua and Genoa had ample classical source material to work with when formulating their classical foundation legends. By contrast, there is no ancient evidence for the myth of Aschius and Senius. The story of Romulus and Remus was widespread, of course, but no ancient writer ever suggested that Remus fathered sons, much less sons who were suckled by a she-wolf.[52] Local custom assumed an early origin for the city, and inscriptions on local coins often refer to it as *Sena vetus*, or ancient Siena.[53] But the area held no ancient ruins as elsewhere (for example, Padua), and the classical sources are strangely mute on the city's early history.

Unfortunately for the Sienese, the most widely known story of the foundation of Siena came from the twelfth-century *Policraticus* by John of Salisbury. It linked the Sienese not to the Romans or any other native Italic people, but to the French and the British. John claimed that Siena received its name from a group of ancient Gauls called the Galli Senones:[54]

> In his twentieth book, Pompeius Trogus recounts that when the Senonese Gauls, soldiers of Brennus, came into Italy, they exiled the Tuscans from their homes and founded grand cities there: Milan, Corneto, Brescia, Verona, Bergamo, Trent, and Vicenza. And they built the city of the Sienese for those that were old or weak, and for their herdsmen. The truth of this is not only in the histories but in a well-known tradition (which is therefore more reliable) that the Sienese seem more similar in the proportions of their limbs, the beauty of their faces, the fairness of their coloring, and their customs to the Gauls and Britons, from whom they can trace their origin.[55]

John's sources remain unclear, since the story does not appear in any of the usual late antique or early medieval histories. In the end, it may not have mattered a great deal to John, as an Englishman, whether the Sienese were descended from Romans or from Gauls, but in an Italy where most cities could name at least one classical founder, including those cities on John's list, to be descended from Gauls—that is, from the French—may have been less than desirable.

The creation of a Roman origin for Siena was therefore a greater task than that faced by either the Paduans or the Genoese. The Sienese could not merely appropriate and promote an extant classical source; rather, they were forced to overcome an established but undesirable foundation legend, replacing it with one more becoming to their consequence. John of Salisbury's story was especially damning because it did not just affirm, as with Milan or any of the others, that the Galli Senones had founded the city; John adds that they founded it specifically for their elderly, invalids, and herdsmen.[56] Furthermore, he argues that the fair coloring and the customs of the Sienese—characteristics integral to Sienese identity—corroborate his story. Such perceived insults provided ammunition for those who might wish to denigrate the Sienese—such as the Florentines, as I will demonstrate below.

On the other hand, Siena's connection with wolves reaches back to at least the mid-thirteenth century. A statute of 1262, for instance, offers a reward to anyone who captures a live wolf.[37] Likewise, an artist was fined in 1264 for painting a graffito showing a lion (the symbol of the popolo rather than the ruling regime, but also the symbol of nearby Florence) fighting and defeating a wolf.[58] As I mentioned earlier, no written account of the Aschius and Senius legend exists from before the fifteenth century, but the popularity of the wolf as a symbol implies that the story predates its first written version (as, for instance, Jacopo Doria asserted of the Trojan founding of Genoa).[59] Furthermore, the contemporary popularity of classical history, law, and art in Siena suggests that the wolf symbols championed by the Nine refer specifically to a Roman foundation legend.

The 1262 bounty on wolves appears to have been effective, since the eighteenth-century Sienese diarist Girolamo Gigli recounts how the Sienese kept a live wolf (or wolves) in the Palazzo Pubblico starting in the early thirteenth century: "You can see a torn remnant on the walls of a great map of the Sienese state, put there for demonstrations of what was happening in subject territories, and it is said that it was badly treated in some way and harmed by a certain domesticated wolf which at one point was kept in that room."[60] Mascots like these were not unusual; both the Florentines and the Venetians kept lions as civic mascots in the later Middle Ages.[61] Siena's penchant for keeping live animals probably became well known over time, as the commune of Montelupo would hardly have sent the Sienese a wolf without reason to believe that they would welcome it as a gift.[62] Most likely, the practice was not continuous in Siena but rather depended on the availability of appropriate animals. Nevertheless, the likelihood that live wolves were present in the palazzo from the early thirteenth century reinforces the wolf's role as a Sienese symbol. A live wolf provided a physical reality to which the symbolic wolf could be connected; the Sienese wolf would have been real and meaningful rather than a randomly chosen heraldic symbol.

In particular, the presence of real wolves emphasized Roman over Gallic origins. It is notable that the Palazzo Pubblico, the very design of which glorified the regime of the Nine, housed the live mascots as well as the Nine themselves. An integral part of that building's design was its drainspouts, each of which was fashioned as a wolf nursing two infants. Two wolves appear on the main wing of the palazzo, and eight more decorate corners of the Torre del Mangia (figure 13). The drainspouts currently visible on the palazzo are eighteenth-century copies, but two of the original drainspouts, much damaged by centuries of exposure, are kept on the ground floor of the building. These wolves are unusually naturalistic for the style of the period, and art historians have attached them to the workshop of the classicizing sculptor Giovanni Pisano (c. 1250–1314), who was in Siena at the time acting as *capomaestro* for the cathedral's new façade.[63] Iconographically, the Sienese drainspouts (*lupe-doccioni*, as one historian has called them) are some of the earliest from the postclassical period to depict the she-wolf suckling the twins.[64] They are made of local stone and loom above the ground with wide toothy jaws from which the rain ran in standard gargoyle fashion. But the menacing appearance of each wolf is tempered by a row of teats from which it suckles two infants, one on either side. Thus, the Nine incorporated the legend of the she-wolf and twins into their largest civic projects from the beginning of their regime. The appearance of this motif on the façade of the Palazzo Pubblico is as much a political statement as the division of the Campo into nine sections; it emphasizes the Roman origins of Siena and posits the Nine as the legitimate successors to Roman rule.

Fig. 13 She-wolves on the Palazzo Pubblico, after originals, Siena, c. 1295.

The image of the wolf and twins is not limited to the Palazzo Pubblico, however. It was incorporated into a number of projects sponsored by the Nine between 1300 and 1350. The same sculpture, without the drainspout, appears on the Sienese Porta Romana (Roman Gate), so called because it guarded the road to Rome, which led out of Siena at the southeast corner of the city walls (map 4 and figure 14). As part of the Via Francigena, the Porta Romana was one of the two most important gates to the city. The commune rebuilt the gate in 1327 as a large walled entry space and a monumental gatehouse built into the city wall. Travelers arriving in Siena and waiting for admittance in the entry space would thus have been confronted with the sight of two stone she-wolves, each complete with a pair of twins, guarding the gate to the city from above.[65] Furthermore, as a recognizable local monument, the Porta Romana appears as one of two identifying landmarks in Ambrogio Lorenzetti's fresco of the *Allegory of Good Government* (1337–40) in the Palazzo Pubblico (figure 15).[66] That Siena is the "ideal" city depicted is clear from the striped cathedral and campanile in the upper-left corner of the fresco. Likewise, the gate dividing the city from its contado in the middle of the fresco is clearly the Porta Romana, with its gatehouse, entry space, and guardian wolf with twins.[67]

Fig. 14 Porta Romana, Siena, rebuilt 1337–40.

Still, the sculpture on the Porta Romana is not the only appearance of the wolf and twins in Lorenzetti's fresco. An authoritative male figure dominates the allegorical political tableau at the center of the work both symbolically and spatially. At his feet lies a she-wolf nursing two curly-haired infants, one of whom she carefully licks with her tongue (figure 16).[68] Precisely what the figure represents has been much debated by scholars; suffice it to say that he is certainly meant to personify and idealize the regime of the Nine.[69] His accessories reinforce this attribution; in particular, his black robe and white mantle present him in half white and half black, a combination already used in the banner of Siena. Four letters surround his head like a halo: CSCV, an acronym usually interpreted as *Commune Senarum, Civitas Virginis*, or the Commune of the

Fig. 15 Porta Romana, detail of Ambrogio Lorenzetti, *Effects of Good Government*, in the Sala della Pace, Palazzo Pubblico, Siena, 1337–40.

Fig. 16 The Good Commune/Common Good with the Sienese wolf and twins, detail of Ambrogio Lorenzetti, *Allegory of Good Government*, in the Sala della Pace, Palazzo Pubblico, Siena, 1337–40.

Sienese, City of the Virgin.[70] The Nine had adopted this as the city's official description, and Sienese coins from 1350 onward bear a similar acronym.[71] The figure's gold shield, now mostly blank, contained an image of the Virgin Mary.[72] Along with the other words and images associated with this magisterial figure, Lorenzetti presents the wolf and twins at his feet as a major emblem of the city. On another level, their presence echoes the parallel Roman legend from which the Sienese story supposedly derives.[73] In this sense, the Roman wolf and twins, appearing below the allegorical symbols of Siena, are the literal as well as the symbolic foundation on which the city was built. Here more than anywhere, it is clear that the wolf and twins were semiotically useful to the Nine, since they symbolized simultaneously the Sienese commune and its Roman roots.

This particular representation of the Sienese commune, showing the seated male figure with the city's civic symbols, appears a second time on the cover of one of the books of the Biccherna for 1344.[74] As Siena's official account books, their wooden covers usually featured images related to the work of the Biccherna: Sienese symbols, tax collection, or images of banking and trade. The reproduction of the image from the Sala della Pace on the 1344 Biccherna cover shows, first, that the image functioned as a successful symbolic whole; all of the elements that contributed to the allegorical portrayal of Siena in Lorenzetti's fresco are present on the book cover. Second, the image's reproduction confirms that it symbolized the city-state of Siena in some official capacity, since the Nine approved not only its appearance in the fresco but also its reuse on the Biccherna cover.

Also in 1344, after a century of using wolves as mascots, the Sienese commune finally adopted the wolf and twins on its official seal.[75] An entry in the account book of the *Camarlingo* of the Biccherna for December 20, 1344, reads, "Item, to Micchele ser Memmo, goldsmith, nine pounds, for the price of one silver seal which he made for the Lords Nine, on which is carved a wolf; this [was done] by order of the Lords Nine . . . £9."[76] The seal combines the two major symbols or patrons of the city, secular and religious. The top half shows the *Madonna della misericordia*, the Virgin Mary as intercessor and protector, spreading her cloak to protect her people. The bottom half shows the Sienese wolf suckling the two infants. The seal thus balances the city's secular and religious patrons; moreover, because the depictions of both emphasize their protective and nurturing role for the Sienese *civitas*, they reinforce each other. The seal's creation, which made the wolf and twins an official symbol of the city, was the culmination of a trend begun more than a century earlier: Siena, and the regime of the Nine in particular, gradually adopted the image as an emblem of their particular version of Sienese reality. The figures' ubiquity in the city—as statues, drainspouts, live wolves, frescoes, and seals—would only have reinforced the city's claims to a Roman past.

Spurring the proliferation of wolves and twins throughout Siena was not the only means by which the Sienese ruling class asserted a Roman rather than a Gallic origin. Latin literacy was high in Siena, and more than one Sienese citizen was engaged in this period in translating the Latin classics into the Italian vernacular for wider consumption.[77] This relatively widespread knowledge of Roman history created an audience for Romanizing efforts during the tenure of the Nine. In his 1958 book on Ambrogio Lorenzetti, George Rowley debunked the incredulity of earlier historians regarding the level of classical awareness in the fourteenth century:

> Under the year 1337 the chronicler Agnolo di Tura reports that Ambrogio painted Roman stories. This sounded so incredible that previous writers under the spell of the word Renaissance have doubted the chronicler's veracity. However . . . the description is too specific to leave doubt that these frescoes were painted on an outside wall and for a new palace and not the Palazzo Pubblico, which was completed in 1310. The passage reads: "After the Sienese had made the palace with the new prison, they made above the Council Hall the offices of the Signori and other officers in the hall of the middle of the palace, and they had the offices painted on the outside with Roman stories by the hand of Master Ambrogio Lorenzetti." From the records we know that this palace, identified by the prison, was begun in 1327 and finished in 1342.[78]

As Rowley then notes, frescoes were discovered in the twentieth century in a village called Asciano, not too far from Siena, which appear to have been based on Lorenzetti's "Roman" frescoes. They depict famous men of antiquity, such as Priam, Agamemnon, Scipio Aemilianus, and Cyrus.[79] The fact that only one of the men depicted was technically Roman, yet Agnolo di Tura identifies them as "Roman stories," may suggest the degree to which the late Middle Ages identified with and valued classical history primarily for its "Romanness"—even the parts that were not Roman.

Like Giovanni Pisano, Lorenzetti used Roman models in his frescoes for the Sala della Pace; art historians have discussed at length the stylistic precedents for the classicizing figures of Peace, Security, Dialectic, and Summer.[80] In fact, scholars have identified in the frescoes a dependence on Roman models at a number of different levels, from artistic style to conceptual program. Quentin Skinner, for instance, argues that the worldview presented by Lorenzetti is more Ciceronian than Aristotelian,[81] while Randolph Starn and Loren Partridge have analyzed the texts associated with the frescoes for a decidedly Romanizing rhetoric.[82] In another case, the *Camarlingo di Biccherna* for February 20, 1330, records Simone Martini's payment for a fresco of the Roman patriot Marcus Attilius Regulus in the Palazzo Pubblico.[83] Hence, the commissions of the Nine show Romanizing tendencies on multiple levels. They valued not only Roman subjects but also a Romanizing artistic style and broader conceptual programs based on Roman virtues and civic values. Considered together, these projects were designed to create a clear philosophical parallel between Siena's Roman past and its modern adoption of Roman civic values. As in Jacopo da Varagine's Genoa, classical Rome—and specifically the Roman republic—stood for justice, longevity of regime, and the pursuit of the common good.

The strange story of the Lysippan Venus may best demonstrate the extent to which the Nine modeled their rule after Roman precedents. At some point during excavations for civic improvements in the 1320s or 1330s, a statue of the classical goddess Venus was discovered, labeled with the name of the great Greek sculptor Lysippus.[84] The citizens admired the statue greatly; a century later, Lorenzo Ghiberti would even claim to have seen a treasured scrap of paper belonging to a very old Sienese monk, on which was a drawing of the Venus by Ambrogio Lorenzetti himself.[85] Therefore, during the final stages of the project to bring water to the Sienese Campo in 1342 or 1343, the Nine decided to dedicate Siena's new fountain at its outlet to the Virgin Mary and to put this statue of Venus at the fountain's head.[86] As far as can be determined, the design of the fountain specifically accommodated the statue since it lacked the full canopy typical of contemporary designs.[87] When the work was completed and water arrived in the city, the Nine sponsored a vast civic festival.[88] The statue presided over the Sienese Campo and its fountain for about ten years; however, in 1357, after an embarrassing rout by the Florentines, Siena's new regime concluded that their city's defeat was punishment for publicly displaying an idolatrous and immodest figure. They ordered the Lysippan Venus pulled down, broken up, and its pieces buried in Florentine territory.[89] Both the pride with which the statue was originally erected and the fierce superstition that led to its destruction and burial in enemy soil indicate the Sienese people's intense regard for their civic symbols. They may also indicate the extent to which the Sienese use of the classical past was linked specifically with the regime of the Nine.

Intention and Agency

Over the course of their seventy-year rule, therefore, the Nine consciously promoted Roman civic ideas, values, and symbols in support of their regime. They
adopted a Roman symbol that equated their history with that of ancient Rome
while simultaneously linking the two via the Sienese legend of the sons of
Remus.[90] One unique feature of the Nine's civic improvements—distinguishing them, for instance, from those of the Paduan commune—is the integration
of their classicizing efforts with their public works. In Padua, the reconstruction of the monument to Antenor was a different project than the building of
the Palazzo della Ragione or the repairing of the city gates.[91] By contrast, Siena
had no major projects specifically intended to glorify its founders. Instead, the
symbol of the wolf and twins featured in the commune's major projects in
smaller but more ubiquitous ways, appearing on the façade of the Porta Romana,
the drainspouts of the Palazzo Pubblico, the frescoes of the Sala della Pace, and
similar places. Even the keeping of live wolves was a matter of everyday experience; they were housed on the ground floor of the Palazzo Pubblico instead of
having special quarters built for them.

The reader may be surprised that an oligarchic regime could maintain the
same policies across decades when the chief magistrates changed every two
months. But, as already discussed, each group of Nine was elected from a small
ruling class whose members were unusually invested in the public fortunes of
their city. Thanks to a robust tradition of Latin literacy and the growing
strength of the Sienese studium (a trend cultivated by the Nine themselves),
these men were increasingly aware of the sources for Roman history and their
relevance to Siena's political position. Translations such as those by Ciampolo
di Meo degli Ugurgieri (c. 1290–after 1347) broadened the availability of these
sources even to those without a Latin education. On the other hand, the men
who served on the Nine were more likely to be composing the translation than
reading the end product. The nobility, along with "known Ghibellines," were
eligible for public office, although they were excluded from serving on the
Nine. However, even those rules were not strictly enforced; most of Siena's
prominent families had members on the Nine at one point or another, including a number of nobles. They had similar goals for the commune of Siena and
seem to have identified in the Roman past a means of reaching the idealized
state portrayed on two walls of their council room.

Luckily, the Nine could rely on men who not only knew their Roman history but also were capable of depicting it in the ways they desired. The Nine

could instruct any sculptor to fashion a wolf nursing a pair of twins, but Giovanni Pisano produced a result that closely imitated Roman models. The same is true of Ambrogio Lorenzetti; anyone could have created an "allegory of good government," but only someone with the desire to study Roman artistic styles and the ability to reproduce them could have painted his frescoes in the Sala della Pace. Lorenzetti was a Sienese citizen and participated in local government in addition to painting commissions for the regime. His contemporaries attest that he was a scholarly and learned man, and some historians have attributed to him either or both the complex internal program of the Sala della Pace and its associated inscriptions.[92] While Siena may not have had a home-grown circle of professional humanists, it did have an educated and engaged ruling class who knew where to find talent and how best to use it in the service of the commune.

The choice of projects, no less than the choice of artists, is revealing. Presumably the Nine were involved in planning the public works on which they were going to spend the city's money, and the projects chosen reflect an acute awareness of the use of public imagery. Starn and Partridge point out that Lorenzetti's allegorical representation of the idealized commune, with the various figures of Justice, Charity, Mercy, Wisdom, and so forth, was painted on the far wall of the Sala della Pace, against which the Nine would sit.[93] The members of the council would almost seem to be part of the fresco in the eyes of a petitioner or ambassador standing before them. The wolf and twins would appear over their heads with the other symbols of the city—arguably the most meaningful place in the entire Sienese state. Faced with this tableau, the observer might be inclined to reflect on other instances of the same symbol; after all, the frescoed she-wolf and twins appear in a room on the second floor of a palazzo protected by menacing stone *lupae*, in the center of a city protected at its gates by more *lupae*. The depiction of the Porta Romana in Lorenzetti's fresco reminds the viewer of that fact in an almost circular fashion. Similarly, the choice to depict both the Virgin Mary and the wolf and twins on the city seal, as well as to erect a classical statue on a fountain dedicated to the Virgin, proclaimed that the ruling regime saw no contradiction between its Roman past and its Christian present. Instead, both saint and mascot act as ideals that encourage—and symbolize in two different ways—the achievement of the Sienese state's highest possible good. The Nine chose their projects, and the political messages they contained, carefully.

These projects had the city's inhabitants as their first audience. On a practical level, they improved the standard of life in Siena, providing a peaceful and extensive contado, roads safe for travel, protective city walls, a convenient public water source, clean and wide streets, and a grand seat of government fronting an aesthetically unified central piazza. On a more theoretical level, these projects increased the citizens' pride in their city for supplying such amenities and looking after its people. The most public of these improvements focused that civic pride into a form chosen by the Nine—one based on Sienese descent from a Roman foundation. The myth of Aschius and Senius promoted an illustrious Roman heritage in place of an embarrassing Gallic one. The substitution not only increased civic pride but also provided a way to compare the ancient Roman state with the modern Sienese state. On account of the inherent ambiguity as to whether the wolf and twins refer to the legend of Romulus and Remus or Aschius and Senius, the symbol inspired the parallel of early Rome with contemporary Siena.

The activities of the Nine imply that this was their goal: their cultivation of the she-wolf image, their similar cultivation of other Romanizing projects like Lorenzetti's Roman stories and Martini's Marcus Regulus, and their concern with providing a public standard by which the city's success could be judged. Lorenzetti's frescoes in the Sala della Pace are the pictorial equivalent of the legal constitutions promulgated by the Nine; both provide guidelines for assessing the success of the Sienese state and, by extension, its government. The adoption of the wolf and twins as the city's chief symbol cemented this conception of Sienese identity.

The effects of the Aschius and Senius legend reached beyond the city walls, however. Foundation by the sons of a founder of Rome was a decidedly nobler past than foundation by elderly Gauls, so the Romanizing legend would have imbued the city with greater legitimacy in the world of Italian politics. Sienese diplomats could finally feel themselves the equals of men from Florence, Genoa, Milan, and other cities, each of which could point to a significant native Italian foundation as a reason for its political predominance in late medieval Italy. A city's antiquity and illustrious past were significant factors in political maneuverings even among the Guelf cities of Tuscany; they were nominally allies, but the political arena was cutthroat enough that any one of them would leap at the opportunity to gain an advantage over its neighbors. Siena's Romanizing origin legend linked its foundation with that of Rome, providing a direct line of descent from the classic Roman origin myth. As in Padua, the legend proposed not only Siena but also its government (in this case, the Nine) as the heirs of the Romans, legitimizing both city and regime in the eyes of its citizens and neighbors.

Such legitimation was crucial at the turn of the fourteenth century, since the Sienese were fighting a losing battle with Florence, their larger and dominant neighbor. Despite the two cities' nominal alliance in the Guelf League, the Nine could sense even at the beginning of their tenure that they were rapidly losing political and economic ground to the Florentines. Furthermore, it was all too obvious from the fortunes of other cities in central Tuscany, such as Pistoia, that Florentine ascendancy led to Florentine hegemony, if not outright takeover.[94]

The promulgation of the wolf and twins as the chief symbol of Siena, and by implication the promulgation of the Romanizing myth of Aschius and Senius as the "true" history of Siena, extended the diplomatic struggle between the two cities into ideological territory, eliciting Florentine response. Dino Compagni's chronicle of Florentine factionalism, for example, includes a reference to the *lupa puttaneggia, ciò è Siena*, or "whorish she-wolf, that is, Siena," in his account for 1303.[95] The modern reader may see in this reference the success of the Sienese attempts to associate their city with the emblem of the wolf, but the Florentine Compagni is clearly trying to present the analogy in the worst possible light.

Perhaps the most ignominious portrayal of Sienese history in these years comes from Giovanni Villani. Having dated the foundations of Florence and its sister-city Fiesole to the earliest years of Italian history, Villani devotes about ten chapters of his chronicle to discussing the early histories of the other chief cities in his part of Italy.[96] On the whole, these accounts are not especially pejorative, repeating Trojan or Roman legends popular in Villani's day. None of them is as illustrious or ancient as the legends Villani tells of Florence, but that is to be expected. It is only when Villani comes to chapter 2.19, "on the city of Siena," that he becomes truly offensive. He writes,

> The city of Siena is a relatively new city, which was founded around the year of Christ 670, when Charles Martel, father of King Pippin of France, came with the French into the region of Apulia in service to the Holy Church, to fight a people who called themselves Lombards. . . . And the said host of the French and other ultramontanes [*oltramontani*: people from beyond the Alps], finding themselves in the place which is today Siena, left there all the old people, and those who were unwell, and those who were not able to bear arms, so as not to take them along into Apulia. And those remaining at rest in the aforesaid place settled there . . . and the one dwelling with another was called Sena, from those who stayed behind on account of their old age.[97]

Villani's chief source for what the Sienese would have viewed as scurrilous lies is clearly John of Salisbury, but Villani has taken each of John's points and exaggerated it to make it more insulting. John, for instance, wrote that Siena was founded by the soldiers of the Gallic leader Brennus, which would set it during the time of the Romans. Villani extrapolates this scenario into the soldiers of the French king Charles Martel in the seventh century A.D., thus making the Sienese not just Gallic but French[98] and moving the foundation of the city forward by nearly a thousand years. This would naturally destroy any Sienese claim to antiquity among a group of cities—in Tuscany, or throughout Italy—founded by the Romans or their predecessors. Moreover, those other cities' founders were native Italians or classical Trojans rather than the French, whom Villani differentiates with his phrase "the French and other ultramontanes"; everyone not from Italy is a breed apart and by implication inferior.

In the same fashion, Villani extrapolates John of Salisbury's statement on the founders of Siena from "the elderly, the weak, and the herdsmen" into "the elderly, the unwell, and the weak"—a fairly subtle change, but one that causes the tone of the sentence to take a turn for the worse.[99] Conspicuous by their absence are wolves, infants, and Romans; leaving them out would necessarily have been a conscious decision, since by the late 1330s the wolf and twins were well known as the symbol of Siena.

Thus, the Sienese promotion of their she-wolf symbol and its associated legends was doubly important in the face of Florentine aggression, both political and mythographical. The Florentines had a political stake in arguing that the French had founded Siena only seven or eight centuries earlier. The Sienese likewise had clear political reasons for arguing that their city was more than three times that old and that it had been founded by the sons of a founder of Rome itself. The ubiquity of the wolf symbol in the civic projects sponsored by the Nine seems to have stemmed from their understanding that they would have to replace John of Salisbury's embarrassing French origin legend with their own Romanizing myth—and that the Florentines would do whatever they could to prevent that.

In conclusion, the chief goals of the Sienese state under the Nine were the expansion, clear definition, and improvement of the state. The Nine accomplished these goals through a variety of methods, from legislation to public works, military and diplomatic negotiation, the patronage of education, and, finally, the adroit use of mythography and symbolism. In its own way, each of these projects defined Sienese identity. They increased Sienese citizens' pride in their city, as is apparent from the citywide events celebrating the completion of several of these projects, including Duccio's *Maestà* and the city aqueduct. Everyone could take part in the city's achievements, especially since the Nine's projects tended to merge ancient glory with modern technology, as in the case of the Lysippan Venus and the aqueduct.

At the same time, Siena's civic improvements increased the city's prestige in the eyes of its allies and enemies. The image of the she-wolf and twins played a major part in this physical and mental renovation of the city. As the city's symbol, it focused and directed the way that the outside world viewed Siena. Dino Compagni's reference to the "whorish she-wolf" may have been insulting, but his comment nevertheless perpetuated Siena's connection with the she-wolf. Similarly, the image of the wolf and twins unified the citizenry by reminding them not only of their shared past and present but also of the ideal common good toward which they were all supposed to be striving. The ferocious animal nursing the two infants proposed a historical—that is, Roman—standard by which to assess civic behavior, and it imparted a useful dual personality to the city's rulers: nurturing toward their own progeny but fierce in their defense. It was a vision of unexpected harmony in a harsh world. In the broadest sense, providing that harmony was the chief goal of the Nine; in their view, it was to be consciously sought on the model of Siena's Roman ancestors. The wolf and twins were thus the cornerstone of every civic good sought by the Nine during the seventy years of their rule.

The centrality of the wolf and twins to the regime of the Nine, and the equation of the two in the eyes of the Sienese population as well as the other cities of Italy, may account for the symbol's disappearance in the years after the fall of the Nine in 1355. After a proliferation of civic projects in the first half of the fourteenth century, many of which had Romanizing tendencies or included the image of the wolf and twins, later fourteenth-century Siena seems bare of ideological pretensions. Its difficult political position may explain this change; rather than claiming an equal place among a number of cities in Guelf Tuscany, Siena was increasingly caught between the powerhouses of Florence and Milan. In the chaotic years after the fall of the Nine, the city faced a new battle for survival, void of intellectual posturing. Siena allied itself with Milan in 1389 for protection against Florence and officially lost its independence in 1399 after ten years of Visconti domination.

The Sienese fortuitously regained their independence in 1404, however, after the unexpected death of Giangaleazzo Visconti. With independence came a revitalized celebration of the city's Roman roots. The most famous examples of the Aschius and Senius legend date from these years. The sculptor Jacopo della Quercia was commissioned to rebuild the fountain in the Campo, bare since the scapegoating of the Lysippan Venus in the 1350s. He decorated the new fountain with multiple she-wolves and two female figures similar to the Lysippan Venus, who probably represent Rhea Silvia and Acca Larentia, the mother and foster-mother of Romulus and Remus.[100] Each woman holds an infant in her arms, referring both to the founding of Rome by the grown-up Romulus and Remus and to the parallel destiny of Aschius and Senius. Inside the Palazzo Pubblico, Taddeo di Bartolo was commissioned to paint Roman heroes in the chapel, and the wolf and twins appear everywhere— carved on chests, sculpted in relief onto ceremonial dishes, and cast in bronze.[101] Most visibly, the commune commissioned Giovanni di Turino to cast a great bronze wolf in imitation of its Roman ancestor, which took pride of place on a Roman column in front of the Palazzo Pubblico.[102] Not least, the Aschius and Senius legend was finally written down.[103]

It is no coincidence that the legend of Siena's Roman origins reappeared in these years of regained civic independence. Between 1287 and 1355, the Nine had constructed a world in which an independent Sienese republic based its collective understanding of its own identity on its founding by the twin sons of Remus. Half a century later, after the Sienese had thrown off Milanese domination and were once again free to rule themselves, they simply picked up where the Nine had left off.

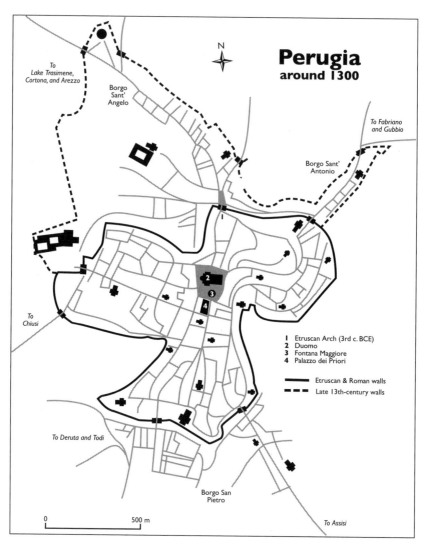

Map 5   Perugia around 1300. Map after Grohmann, *Città e territorio.*

5

PERUGIA
Adopting a New Aeneas

Boniface of Verona, master of astrology and poetry, has come to the city
of Perugia and wishes to make a solemn work, a book of the ancient history
and concerns of the Commune of Perugia, and to recall these antiquities to
memory for the honor of the Commune of Perugia.

—*Annali decemvirali* (Perugian council minutes), June 1293

The Umbrian town of Perugia does not usually spring to mind as one of the
great city-states of medieval Italy. Its secondary status may be the result of a relative lack of great writers and artists, exclusion from the long-distance trade
that sustained Florence, Genoa, and Venice, or the city's questionable status
as a republic due to its location within the Papal States. Yet as Sarah Blanshei
has pointed out, early fourteenth-century Perugia was "one of the leading city-
states dominating the political, economic, and cultural life of late medieval
Italy."[1] In the Middle Ages, this medium-sized university town dominated
Umbria, chiefly by developing an economy based on industry and trade in a
region that was still overwhelmingly agricultural. Like the other oligarchies
discussed in this book, the thirteenth-century rulers of Perugia worked to extend the city's economic preeminence into the political sphere. Accordingly,
the commune funded many of the same public improvements seen elsewhere,
materially asserting its power and benevolence in both city and contado.

Although these projects consolidated and demonstrated the city's control
of its territory, the most important ones provided a narrative background to
that control: the commune also invested in the legend of Eulistes, Perugia's
supposed classical founder. The mysterious figure of Eulistes is related, but not
identical, to the more famous Odysseus or Ulysses of Greek epic. He seems to
have been invented for the benefit of the medieval commune and relegated to

obscurity after its dominance had ended. Unlike Padua, Genoa, and Siena, late thirteenth-century Perugia faced no major threats, internal or external, to its sense of community. Nonetheless, its rulers were determined to establish a public image for Perugia commensurate with its cultural and political stature. Like its counterparts in other cities, Perugia's commune seized upon classical ideas and legends as a valuable way to accomplish that goal. This chapter contextualizes the myth of Eulistes in the period from the creation of the office of the capitano del popolo (1255) to the formation of the new executive committee of the Priori (1301). A rich assortment of contemporary sources suggests that during this relatively stable half century of Perugian history, the commune considered the promulgation of a classical foundation legend a natural part of its efforts to define Perugian identity.

Growth and Civic Improvement

Perugia, like Siena, is a landlocked city built at the intersection of several hills (map 5). The city's commercial success may seem surprising since Perugia lacks Siena's location along a major trade and pilgrimage route. However, the city's siting may have worked to its advantage. Perugia perched high on a ridge between the major north–south highways of the Via Cassia (from Rome north to Florence and the Po Valley) and the Via Flaminia (from Rome northeast to Rimini and the Adriatic coast), and between the major river valleys of the Tiber and the Chiana. Hence, the city was the nexus of a regional road system directing communication and trade throughout upper Umbria.[2]

At its greatest extent shortly after 1300, the Perugian contado occupied about five hundred square miles to the north and west of the city, including Lakes Trasimene and Chiusi.[3] It was significantly smaller in area than most of the cities in this study; Padua's contado, for example, was approximately four thousand square miles in area in the same period. The relatively small size of Perugia's contado, however, conceals an unusually high population density. In 1300, about thirty-five thousand people lived in the city itself (equivalent to the population of Padua or Siena), and the hills around the city were heavily settled.[4] Perugia's regional influence was therefore considerable; in 1351, thirty-three subject communes participated in the annual ceremonies in honor of Perugia's patron saint Herculanus.[5]

The city's commercial success and territorial expansion both began in the twelfth century, reaching their peaks in the late thirteenth century. As in other commercial centers, merchants and bankers dominated civic policy from an early date, but later more traditionally industrial guilds challenged their economic and political power. The area's many rivers and lakes provided industrial power as well as fresh water and food, fueling the expansion of industries in leather working and metallurgy along with more familiar activities like wool working.[6] By the mid-thirteenth century, the city's most influential guild, after that of the merchants and bankers, was that of the shoemakers.

The significance of industry in the regional economy resulted in Perugia's development as more of a "guild republic" than the other cities considered in this study. Local guilds dominated the commune's ruling councils, and political representation was strongly slanted in favor of the artisanal middle classes.[7] This was true even in the twelfth century, when Perugia had a consular regime like many other Italian cities, but it became more true during the thirteenth century. By 1265, four citizen councils made most of the city's decisions. Largest and least active were the two major assemblies—the Consiglio Maggiore, which had about six hundred members, and the smaller Consiglio del Popolo, which had only about four hundred members but included the Rettori delle Arti, or heads of the guilds. Further adjustments between 1300 and 1305 increased the guilds' control of these large councils.

At a higher level of government, both large councils incorporated the Consiglio Speciale e Generale (henceforward the CSG), which met regularly and made most of the commune's everyday decisions. The CSG was technically two councils (the Speciale and the Generale) consisting of about fifty and a hundred members, respectively, but it usually functioned as a single body. After 1270, this group's activities were directed by the city's smallest and most powerful council, the Consoli delle Arti (consuls of the guilds), a group of five elected by the Rettori delle Arti. In addition to supervising the CSG, the Consoli advised the executive branch of both podestà and capitano del popolo. Foreigners with terms of a year, these two magistrates shared many duties, but—following the same trend seen in the councils—the capitano, as representative of the middle-class popolo, gradually assumed most of the responsibilities originally allotted to the podestà.[8]

Perugia's late medieval development parallels similar changes highlighted elsewhere in this study. Urban expansion began in the eleventh and twelfth centuries, reaching its highest point in the later thirteenth century. Meanwhile, the city used its economic resources and geographic position to extend its influence over a sizable contado. Although the city nominally owed fealty to the papacy as one of the foremost cities in the Papal States, it was essentially autonomous. Effigies of unpopular popes and cardinals were occasionally burned in the city's main square, while the taxes due Rome were more often negotiated than paid readily.[9] Among themselves, Perugia's citizens gradually refined the contours of a republic dominated by the city's most influential guilds.[10]

The tasks of preserving the property and honor of the commune were originally delegated to the podestà, and when the office of the capitano was invented in 1255, the oversight of public works shifted to both officials together. Their tasks included defensive projects like the construction of a castle at Torciano in 1274 and the maintenance of public bridges and roads important to Perugia's central position in the Umbrian trade network.[11] The commune built seven new bridges in different areas of the contado between 1270 and 1300, while also repairing several extant bridges. In 1298, it established a special commission to oversee the upkeep of the contado's various *castelli*, like that at Torciano, as well as the city's more immediate defenses of gates and walls.[12]

Parallel efforts aimed to improve the city itself. The Perugian commune never went as far as the Sienese in mandating the appearance of building façades, but it did arrange for street paving, starting in 1255 with the main piazza between the cathedral and the city hall, continuing to the two main thoroughfares, and by 1294 extending to every street in town. Medieval Perugia was not a large place, but having paved streets instead of the more common packed earth would have made a substantial difference in the everyday experience of living and working in the city.[13]

Since Perugia sat at the top of a hill, like Siena, its rulers were similarly concerned with the public water supply. In 1254, a year before the decision was made to pave the main piazza, the council commissioned one Fra Plenario to design an aqueduct that would bring water from Monte Pacciano, three miles out of town, to a monumental public fountain to be built in the main piazza. Unconvinced by Fra Plenario's plan, the councils discussed a number of different options from 1260 onward, including the construction of new fountains and sinking wells. In 1276, however, the commune contracted with the local Franciscan friars to execute the original aqueduct plan, and the new fountain (the Fontana Maggiore; figure 17) was in use by the end of 1278.[14] It had been overseen by a friar named Fra Bevignate and sculpted by Nicola and Giovanni Pisano (Nicola c. 1220–c. 1284; Giovanni c. 1250–1314). The renovation of aging fountains and the construction of new ones in other parts of the city complemented this major addition to the city center.

In addition to these practical improvements, the commune sponsored projects more strictly aimed at the glorification of the city and its ruling regime.

Probably spurred by similar decisions in Florence, Orvieto, and Siena, the Perugians decided in 1300 that they needed a new cathedral to replace their small Romanesque building. However, the cathedral was not started until 1345, as other needs took precedence. One of these projects was a new city hall, plans for which were being discussed as early as the 1270s. Construction on the Palazzo Nuovo (now Palazzo dei Priori; figure 17) began in 1292, and work went

Fig. 17 Fontana Maggiore and Palazzo dei Priori, Perugia, c. 1275–1300.

quickly; the palazzo's earliest frescoes date from 1297 to 1300.[15] The speed with which the hall was completed suggests that it was one of the commune's highest priorities in those years.

At the same time that it renovated and improved Perugia's external appearance, the commune reorganized the city's internal structure. Perugia's first unified set of statutes dates from 1279, and archives of council minutes and tax records from the mid-thirteenth century onward attest to a system of permanent written records from at least that time.[16] This growth in record keeping was a deliberate effort to establish and preserve the commune's rights, privileges, and authority—as much an attempt to define the city's scope and possessions as the delineation of geographical bounds and the construction of castles in the contado. The year 1255 also saw the establishment of a city mint and the striking of the first Perugian money, which served as a statement of the city's wealth, independence, and resources.[17] In the intellectual sphere, the gathering of scholars from nearby Bologna and the same trends in political awareness resulted in the acquisition of a charter for a studium generale from Pope Boniface VIII in 1301.[18]

Thus, between the establishment of both the office of capitano and the city mint in 1255 and the formal commissioning of the city's university in 1301, the Perugian commune systematically set about enlarging its contado, consolidating its authority, beautifying the city, and making the improvements it considered necessary for an important and successful city-state. The city's inhabitants were closely involved in these efforts; they sat on city councils, but they were also responsible for numerous independent acts of patronage, such as the building and restoration of churches.[19] In the same period, Perugia gained prestige as a papal city, since the popes were often in residence there. Pope Martin IV died in Perugia in 1294, so the city hosted the conclave that elected Pope Celestine V (r. 1294–96). Although Perugia's economic wealth gave its commune considerable leverage with the papacy, papal patronage also increased the city's political consequence.[20]

These years were the heyday of the Perugian commune. As the fourteenth century unfolded, the lack of a major water source would hamper Perugia's industrial development as much as it did Siena's, and the removal of the popes to Avignon naturally reduced the effects of their patronage. In the second half of the thirteenth century, however, Perugia was regionally influential, prosperous, and growing. The surviving decrees and council minutes of the late thirteenth-century Perugian commune provide a unique perspective on how the regime and the city handled this growth—and where they directed it.

Heulixstes, Eulistes, and Ulixes

Antiquarians and scholars have been understandably quick to link Eulistes, the legendary founder of Perugia, with the Homeric hero Ulysses or Odysseus. Some have simply observed that Eulistes' name may derive from that of the more famous Greek, while others have theorized that "Eulistes" is just a vernacular medieval spelling for Ulysses, who was therefore thought to have founded Perugia at some point during his years of wandering.[21] The name's variable spelling complicates matters; Perugia's mythical founder appears in contemporary sources as "Eulistes," "Heulixstes," and several variations in between.[22] It would be only a small step to assume that the intended word was "Ulixes," as Ulysses' name was commonly spelled. Unfortunately, there is little documentary support for this theory; nothing else in the classical tradition connects the Greek hero with the town of Perugia, and what little we know of the medieval Eulistes legend indicates that he was more often believed to be Trojan than Greek.

Luckily, a better solution presents itself. Perugia appears widely in classical literature because of its status as one of the *Etruriae capita*, the chief Etruscan cities allied against Roman expansion during the Samnite Wars, as well as because of its sack by Octavian in 40 B.C. during the civil wars.[23] Beyond references to the Etruscans in the works of authors such as Livy, medieval readers generally encountered only one other early history for the city. Without mentioning Ulysses or the Trojan War, Justinus's epitome of Pompeius Trogus asserts that the city was founded by Greeks: "The Perugians take their origin from the Achaeans [Greeks]."[24] Neither legend goes into any detail or deals with the early history of the city.

Servius's commentary on the *Aeneid* provides one fleeting reference. Twice in the *Aeneid* (10.207 and 12.290), Virgil refers to one Aulestes, a native Tuscan king who allies with Aeneas against Turnus. Virgil does not expand on Aulestes' family or affiliations, but Servius's commentary on *Aeneid* 10.198–200—speaking of Ocnus, son of Manto (another of Aeneas's local allies)—asserts that some "claim that Ocnus was the son (or brother) of Aulestes, who founded Perugia."[25] As Anna Imelde Galletti notes, the name "Eulistes" more likely derives from the Virgilian-Servian Aulestes, founder of Perugia, than from the more famous but unrelated Greek hero. Her view is that "probably the figure of the hero is a result of adapting the Servian mention of Aulestes . . . to the general characteristics of Ulysses."[26] Together, the Livian account of Etruscan Perugia and the Virgilian tradition of Perugia's foundation by the Tuscan Aulestes provide considerable material for a medieval foundation legend for the city, even before bringing Ulysses into the matter.

Although the legend of Eulistes probably existed in oral tradition before Perugia commemorated him in a more permanent fashion, the first document-able time Eulistes appears in the medieval landscape is as "Heulixstes," one of twenty-four sculptural figures framing the top basin of the Fontana Maggiore, central Perugia's monumental fountain (figure 18).[27] I have already mentioned the Fontana Maggiore as a public improvement that brought water to the city center while ornamenting the newly paved main piazza. Yet the fountain's role in the formation and expression of civic identity was as important as its role as a water source. The fountain's iconographical program is wide-ranging; art historian John White has called it "a Perugian encyclopedia in stone."[28] In fact, it shows many of the same encyclopedic qualities as the Lorenzetti frescoes in Siena's Palazzo Pubblico, representing the desires, ideals, role models, and prin-ciples of the regime that commissioned it.[29] Alberto Grohmann comments that the fountain "represents one of the most significant examples of inter-national Gothic culture, where one perceives in tangible form the ideologies and models of a society at one of the greatest peaks of its development, neatly combining new political, economic, and social exigencies with the teachings of memory."[30] The aqueduct project began in 1254, but the fountain was not built until 1276–78.[31] It consists of two sculptural basins topped by a third bronze basin with a central group of three caryatids. The upper sculptural level features twenty-four figures from history, myth, and allegory, including Eulistes, while reliefs on the lower level depict historical scenes along with characters from Aesop's fables and the months of the year. The fountain has been restored sev-eral times over the centuries, but a number of clues have enabled modern schol-ars to reconstruct its original appearance with some certainty.[32]

In particular, the choice and arrangement of figures reveals the designers' intent. An inscribed label identifies each figure on the fountain, and despite a wide range of topics, two concerns are clear: first, law, especially as applied in Perugia, and second, Roman history, especially as related to Perugia. White's reconstruction anchors the fountain's main axes with four key figures: "Eulistes, founder of the Perugian city" (north), "August Perugia" (south), "Rome, head of the world" (west), and Saint John the Baptist (east).[33] The north–south axis, with Eulistes on one side and Perugia on the other, faced the cathedral and the future city hall, respectively. Twenty other figures appear between these four, including Old Testament kings and prophets, Perugia's two patron saints, and the com-mune's two executive officials for 1278 (Hermanno da Sassoferrato, capitano,

Fig. 18 Eulistes ("Heulixtes Perusine conditor urbis"), sculpted by Nicola and Giovanni Pisano on the Fontana Maggiore, Perugia, 1278.

Fig. 19 Matteo da Correggio (podestà in 1278), sculpted by Nicola and Giovanni Pisano on the Fontana Maggiore, Perugia, 1278.

and Matteo da Correggio, podestà). Their arrangement is precise. Perugia's founder, Eulistes, looks like an Old Testament prophet and legislator.[34] He is flanked on the fountain's nearest points by the two contemporary officials; the depictions and their proximity encourage the comparison of biblical legislators, the legislator who founded the city, and the legislators who were maintaining it centuries later (figures 18 and 19).

On the other side of the fountain, August Perugia appears with her traditional Roman epithet; the name *Augusta Perusia* had been inscribed on the Etruscan arch in the city walls during the first century A.D. Perugia's appearance derives from classical personifications of abundance, and she holds a cornucopia.[35] She closely resembles the figure of Rome on the fountain, and she is flanked by the city's two patron saints, Lawrence and Herculanus. This portrayal of the personified city emphasizes Perugia's self-sufficiency; the figure's label reads, "August Perugia, fertile in all these things."[36] Continuing the trend, the minor figures between Perugia and the city's protecting saints are the Lady of the Lake (*Domina Laci*, referring to Trasimene) and the Lady of Chiusi (*Domina Clusii*), which together signify the Perugian contado and its wealth in fish and grain.[37] Meanwhile, saints and prophets emphasize the main religious differences between ancient and contemporary Perugia. The patron saints on either side of August Perugia parallel the figures of Saints Peter and Paul placed on either side of the figure of Rome. Personifications of Theology and the Roman Church further emphasize the rise of Christian Rome at the expense of classical Rome.

Thus, the twelve figures on the fountain's main level, including the four axial figures, embody medieval Perugia through references to its religion, history, government, and economy. Twelve minor figures support the twelve major ones, much as Perugia is flanked by the figures representing her contado. As a whole, they suggest that, like Rome, Perugia is an amalgam of her classical and Christian roots.

The lower tier of the fountain consists of a series of fifty reliefs complementing the sculpted figures above. Their subjects expand on the statues in the upper tier, representing encyclopedic themes like the seven liberal arts, the months, scenes from Aesop's fables and the Old Testament, and Romulus and Remus. These reliefs serve two purposes. First, they reinforce the iconography in the upper tier; for instance, Romulus and Remus (here Remulus), the founders of Rome, appear under the figure of Rome. The reliefs are organized in pairs, so both Romulus and Remus appear on one panel; they are depicted as well-dressed noble youths, each with a bird of prey. Furthermore, the set of panels to the right of Romulus and Remus shows the Roman she-wolf with the twins, and Rhea Silvia, labeled as the *mater Romuli*.[38] Thus, the proximity of scenes depicting the young founders of Rome and the statue of the personified city emphasizes the boys' act of foundation as a parallel to the founding of Perugia, whose founder appears on the other side of the fountain.

Second, the broader scope of the scenes on the lower tier of the fountain contextualizes the more focused message of the figures on the upper tier. The scenes of the seven liberal arts that appear on the fountain below the figure of Eulistes, for instance, suggest the broad knowledge necessary for good governance. The liberal arts, months, and Aesopic scenes provide a panoramic view of the world in which the viewer can situate Eulistes, August Perugia, and their companions. The two creation scenes on the lower tier reinforce this point, since they portray the creation of the world with Adam and Eve, and the creation of Rome—the archetypical urban community—with Romulus and Remus. The scenes on the lower tier depict the world as a whole, and the statues on the upper tier depict the figures in that world who are important specifically to Perugia. The most important of these, of course, are the axial figures of August Perugia and the city's founder, Eulistes.

The Fontana Maggiore gives no account of Eulistes' foundation of Perugia; its inscription merely describes him as "Eulistes, founder of the Perugian city." For his story and the early history of Perugia, we must turn to a poem written for the commune in 1293 by the poet Bonifacio da Verona (fl. 1250–1300). In the space of six months, he produced a long poem on Perugia's history, followed by a prose version of the same text. The poem is now known as the *Eulistea* after its chief hero, but contemporary records refer to it as the *Liber antiquitatum comunis Perusii* (Book of antiquities of the commune of Perugia).[39] In nine books it narrates the history of the city from its founding after the Trojan War up to the thirteenth century. In so doing, it evokes themes similar to those on the Fontana Maggiore, as one might expect of two works commissioned by the same municipal government. Galletti notes that "the poem caps a process of the construction of civic identity which has already seen the consolidation of a patron saint's cult; the creation of the two great heraldic symbols of the city, the gryphon and the lion; the completion of the Fontana Maggiore. Other media have already established the parameters for a synthesis of civic and political sentiment."[40]

The poem begins with a brief prose prologue, which moves quickly from the usual reminders of the value of history and literature to Bonifacio's introduction of the poem's protagonist: "[This book] will begin with the coming of

Eulistes, august founder of the city of Perugia; it will recite his victories and his distinguished titles and offices."[41] Bonifacio's Latin is turgid, but he shows a certain linguistic dexterity and a desire to highlight the classical and Roman elements of his material. His pun on the word august (*augusto*) is typical; the reader expects it to modify *Perusia* on account of its position in the sentence and local tradition (as "August Perugia" on the Fontana Maggiore). Instead, *augusto* modifies *fundatore*, creating "Eulistes, august founder of the city of Perugia." A change of ending thus suggests that Perugia's traditional epithet originated with Eulistes himself. Here and throughout the prologue, Bonifacio uses terms associated with Rome, and the prologue ends with a prayer in which Romulus appears as a kind of patron saint: "Let us all remain sheep in Christ, and let the people of Romulus, together with their rulers, be worthy to enter into his sanctuary."[42] The poem's historical approach is already apparent: the epic will praise and commemorate Eulistes as founder while linking Perugian history as closely as it can with Roman history.

The main text of the poem continues this approach. When Eulistes enters the narrative in book one, Bonifacio immediately compares him to Aeneas, the Romans' founding father:

> There came a king from the Greeks, knightly and innately noble,
> His tongue no less brilliant than Ulysses of Ithaca,
> And likewise in his lineage, having been born from ancient origins.
> Eulistes was his name. A long time after the sack of
> Dardanian Troy, a good while after—
> Many years later, after the rule of Saturn—
> He came to Italy, driven by the fates,
> When powerful Aeneas had arrived—before Rome had been founded,
> And his [Aeneas's] gods were established, and his walls were standing.
> Here [was] the first builder of the city, the Perugian fatherland;
> He was its founder, and the reason it was called that.
> Thus the city began: so much [Cassius] Dio tells us.[43]

Like Aeneas and Antenor, the exiled Eulistes arrived in Italy driven by the fates (*fatis agitantibus illum*), where he founded a city. The double reference to Aeneas and Saturn, city founders and early kings of Italy, stresses the pre-Roman origins of that city.[44] Whether Eulistes was a Trojan fleeing from the Greeks (fleeing *ex Daneis*) or a Greek king (descended *ex Daneis*) is unclear. Nonetheless, the passage establishes that Eulistes was of ancient lineage and that he lived in the years just following the Trojan War, before Rome was founded.[45] Bonifacio's description goes beyond these two facts, however; he recounts not only Eulistes' ancient lineage but also his character and rank. Noble both in birth ("a king") and in breeding ("knightly and innately noble"), Eulistes is everything the founder of a city should be, and he thus provides Perugia with a moral example as well as an illustrious ancestry. Furthermore, in addition to mentioning Aeneas and Saturn, Bonifacio compares Eulistes with Ulysses of Ithaca (*Ytacensis Ulixes*). The gesture flatters Eulistes while distinguishing him from Ulysses, as if Bonifacio wants to ensure early in the poem that none of his readers confuse the two heroes.

The rest of Bonifacio's discussion of Eulistes focuses on the two basic actions of his founding: the choice of a location and a name for the city, and the city's actual construction. First, Bonifacio narrates Eulistes' hunting of a female bear (*ursa*), an act that explains the name and location of the future city: "For this great triumph / Eulistes ordered that the city be called thus, *Perusina* . . . // Hence Eulistes took the name for the city from a bear, / as befits your stature and your greatness."[46] Deriving *Perusia* from *per ursa*, Bonifacio rationalizes why—unlike other cities, including Genoa and Siena—Perugia was not simply named after its founder. Rather, in a gesture reminiscent of Aeneas's experience with the white sow,[47] Eulistes decides that he will found his city on the site where he killed the bear and that its name should recall the event. Having established its location and pretext, Bonifacio discusses the actual building of the city: "As these words have shown, Eulistes undertook to found / the city here, and to connect the works of the walls in circuit, / and thus were built the walls of this great city."[48] Since the topoi of medieval law and literature defined a city by its walls, it is fitting that Eulistes' founding of Perugia is essentially an act of wall building. Thus, Perugia came into existence on more than one level: its people acquired a genealogy reaching back to the Trojan War, the city acquired a purpose, and the city's very walls were imbued with an illustrious history.

The beginning of book one reminds the reader that Perugia, because it dates to the time of Aeneas, was founded before Rome. Bonifacio structurally reinforces this point by devoting the entirety of book one to the founding of Perugia, so that only in book two does the reader encounter Romulus, Remus, and the she-wolf. Book two, which focuses on Perugia's role in early Roman history, begins,

But as the Perugian city was built according to its laws
and in this order—as the earliest writings recall
and the stories relate—twin brothers were

suckled and fed by a she-wolf, and then, as the tale tells,
the Romuli then speedily built up their walls.[49]

Here, the story of Romulus and Remus follows the same pattern the reader has
just encountered with Eulistes and his city in book one. Bonifacio carefully uses
the same diction, such as *condere muros*, to describe both acts of foundation. This
strengthens the parallel between the two cities and again points out that Perugia
came first. Furthermore, throughout book two Bonifacio casts Eulistes as Romulus and Remus's figurative elder brother: they appeal to him for help when
they encounter trouble with the Sabines over the matter of female companion-
ship, and the assistance that Eulistes and his followers provide establishes "love
between the Romans and the Perugian camps."[50] Further shared experiences
reinforce these familial relations, as when the Perugians help the Romans fight
off the Gallic invasion under Brennus (traditionally identified as that of 390 B.C.):

> From today the thriving cities of the Romans and Perugians
> shall be sister and relative and friend, to the end of days.
> The glory of the Romans and their nursling was always allied to
> [Perugia]:
> One's strength was given to the other, and they often called upon
> their pact of friendship, with their names connected throughout the
> world.[51]

The grammar does not specify whether the dominant party in these relationships is Perugia or Rome. One would normally identify Rome as the parent and
Perugia as the offspring, but Bonifacio's narrative suggests the reverse. His words
merge the two populations, implying that the Perugians and the Romans were
on such close terms that it was barely possible to tell them apart. He reiterates
this point so many times that by the middle of book three, a Perugian leader
inspires his fellow citizens by saying,

> . . . So trust in Rome;
> You are all Romans, risen again after a long time.
> This fact the gates of the city and sculpted panels attest.
> And these preserve ancient Trojan models here.[52]

This passage merges the pasts of Rome and Perugia. Riding on the Eternal
City's coattails, Bonifacio argues that while his contemporaries know Roman

history well, no one has yet properly recognized the crucial role played by Perugia in its more famous events. Even as it recounts contemporary Perugian events, Bonifacio's epic reinforces this thematic conflation of the two cities with a vocabulary that specifically evokes ancient and Roman history. He refers to Perugia and Perugian things as ancient (*antiquus*); he also uses Roman terms like *Romulides, Quirites,* and *lares,* while he regularly refers to Perugian history in terms that are generally applicable but also specifically meaningful in the context of Roman history, like *urbs, civis, lex, vates, provincia, fides,* and *patria.*[53]

In the end, Bonifacio's main goal is to make a connection with classical Rome that reinforces Perugia's claim of having preceded it and helped foster its achievements. He does this even at the expense of internal consistency, the most glaring example of which is Eulistes' ambiguous heritage. As mentioned above, Bonifacio's introduction of Eulistes states that he came to Italy *ex Daneis,* "from the Greeks," confounding the reader as to whether Eulistes was Greek or Trojan. This ambiguity continues throughout the epic. In some places the poem implies that Eulistes was Trojan like his counterpart Aeneas, and the inhabitants of his city are therefore, like the Romans, descendants of the Trojans. The speech quoted above, for example, visualizes contemporary Perugia as preserving ancient Troy, even though other passages refer to Eulistes as Greek. For example, the poem's epilogue recalls how "noble Eulistes, founder of the Perugian city, / Waged many wars against the Trojans," which naturally suggests that Eulistes was Greek.[54]

It is remotely possible that Bonifacio was simply being sloppy and did not bother to check his details, but this seems unlikely, since he had six months to write the poem and knew that his work would be examined by the commune's representatives once he was done. Consequently, Bonifacio must have known what he was doing and simply did not care. Not having to choose between Greek and Trojan origins meant that he could use both sides in his epic. Furthermore, as with Jacopo da Varagine, comprehensiveness may have counted for more than consistency. At one point in book six, Bonifacio suggests that Eulistes' parentage is unknown:

> Here they say that Eulistes, who was a great king
> And terrible in war, founder of his fatherland and city . . .
>
> . . . .
>
> Possibly because he came entirely from Trojan blood.
> Others suppose that he came originally from Athens.[55]

Bonifacio admits the existence of some debate on the subject of Eulistes' origin, but it fails to worry him. The important facts are these: like Aeneas, Eulistes came from the eastern Mediterranean in the years of the Trojan War, and therefore Perugia was founded long before Rome. Anything else in the epic that permitted him, first, to flaunt his knowledge of classical history and, second, to conflate Perugian history with classical history was an additional benefit. Bonifacio's official history of Perugia thus provided it with a pre-Roman classical foundation, explanations for the city's name and location, and an early history closely linked to that of Rome. This allowed Perugian history to bask in the reflected glory of the Roman past while claiming a certain superiority, since Perugia had been founded first and—at least in Bonifacio's formulation— had taken the senior role in fraternal relations between the two. Bonifacio solidifies these historical links through his regular use of classicizing terminology and his frequent reference in all contexts to the griffin, the city's chief heraldic symbol.

Despite Eulistes' indeterminate origin, the Perugian commune deemed Bonifacio's work acceptable. In fact, the judges appointed to assess it decided that it was worth the significant sum of twenty-five gold florins and that Bonifacio should be paid the same sum again to produce a prose version of his poem. It is not clear whether the commune played a large role in determining the events of the epic in the first place, or whether they simply approved it after it was already finished. In either case, the city's main council formally endorsed the "ancient history" that Bonifacio constructed. The Fontana Maggiore had been the commune's first foray into promoting Perugia's classical origin, and Bonifacio's *Eulistea* developed these trends further.

However, the commune did not limit its shaping of civic memory to these two large endeavors; the legend of Perugia's classical foundation filtered into its other projects as well. At the same time that Bonifacio was writing his *Eulistea*, the commune was in the early stages of overseeing the construction of its new city hall—another step in the monumentalization of the main city piazza that had begun with street paving half a century earlier. The Palazzo Nuovo, now known as the Palazzo dei Priori, was built in the mid-1290s on the south edge of the piazza, facing the figure of August Perugia on the Fontana Maggiore. Aspects of the palazzo's decoration, both external and internal, suggest that the commune wished to promote publicly the historical "facts" narrated by Bonifacio's epic. The carved molding along the front of the palazzo between its first and second floors, for instance, echoes similar molding on the city's famous Etruscan arch (figure 20). The arch was the city's largest and best-known

Fig. 20 Etruscan gate in the city wall, Perugia, third century B.C.

remnant of classical antiquity, and it had been prominently incorporated into the medieval city wall. Neither the designers of the palazzo nor the council members who approved the design could identify it as specifically Etruscan. Nonetheless, the visual similarity suggests that they wished to link the contemporary seat of government to Perugia's largest and oldest monument, thereby reminding observers of the city's long and illustrious history. The effect must have been augmented by the scenes on the fountain opposite.

Frescoes inside the palazzo continue this trend. The monumental main doors open into the Sala dei Notai (Hall of the Notaries), the palazzo's biggest meeting hall. Eight massive elliptical arches span the hall, and every surface is painted. These anonymous frescoes have been much restored and supplemented over the years, but the earliest were originally painted in the years of the palazzo's completion, about 1297 to 1301. Like the lower tier of the Fontana Maggiore, the frescoes depict scenes from the Bible, astronomy and astrology, and Aesop's fables.[56] Jonathan Riess describes them as "a summa of the themes in [late medieval] communal art."[57] He also emphasizes their underlying program, which promotes the commune's political ideals just as the Fontana Maggiore and the *Eulistea* do.[58]

My concern, however, is less with the main painted scenes than the heraldic shields that complement them. One scene appears on each spandrel (left and right) of each Romanesque arch, and to the inside of each narrative scene, as the available space on the spandrel shrinks rapidly, appears a roundel with a shield. The room contains about thirty of these roundels. Most depict the arms of prominent local families, but these mingle with roundels displaying the medieval coat of arms of Rome—that is, a red field crossed diagonally with the letters SPQR in gold (figure 21).[59] On a strictly political level, these shields would have identified the city of Perugia as a Guelf city allied with Rome, the traditional seat of the popes. However, considered together with the external decoration of the palazzo and the sculpture on the Fontana Maggiore, the letters identify Perugia not only with contemporary Rome but also with ancient, classical Rome—and everything for which it was traditionally imagined to stand.

The various projects sponsored by the Perugian commune in the last quarter of the thirteenth century—fountain, civic epic, palazzo—were all directed at the same end. They established and elaborated an ancient origin for Perugia based on the city's pre-Roman foundation by Eulistes. They emphasized the historical parallels between the ancient cities of Rome and Perugia, as well as Perugia's crucial role in well-known events of early Roman history. Most of all, through the broad scope of these projects, the commune sought not only to promote an "appropriate" origin for Perugia but also to articulate the city's role in the larger context of world history.

Intention and Agency

Thanks to the preservation of the late thirteenth-century minutes of the Perugian councils and the scrupulousness with which the city's scribes recorded their deliberations and arrangements, the details of the commune's projects are clearer than for any of the other cities in this study.[60] This makes Perugia a valuable witness in the attempt to uncover the identities and motivations of those who promoted the classical past. The first point that the institutional sources reveal is the large number of Perugian citizens making decisions about their city's public appearance. Major projects such as the Fontana Maggiore were supervised by the Consiglio Speciale e Generale (CSG), the city's largest council that met regularly. It consisted of roughly one hundred fifty to two hundred citizens led by the consuls of the guilds. Rather than appointing a committee to supervise public works generally, or even one for each project, the CSG

Fig. 21 Frescoed SPQR shield in the Palazzo dei Priori, Perugia, 1297.

administered such works itself. It heard proposals, arranged the hiring of staff, and even approved reimbursements and the price of materials on a case-by-case basis.[61] Roughly two hundred people would therefore have voted on whether to commission Bonifacio da Verona to write the *Eulistea*.

Additionally, among those two hundred were many educated men, who would have been conscious of the political implications and benefits of such projects. Noblemen, notaries, and judges all appear on the CSG's contemporary membership lists.[62] Guido de Corgnia, for example, was one of the judges appointed to examine Bonifacio's poem. He was a wealthy member of the local nobility who held a seat in the CSG in both 1277 and 1285, despite anti-magnate legislation. Local tax assessments reveal that he was one of the five wealthiest members of the CSG; in 1285, he was ordered to pay £2,500, when the median assessment was £500 and the most commonly occurring assessment £100.[63] The presence of men like Guido in the highest levels of the Perugian government, and their involvement in communal projects like the Fontana Maggiore or the *Eulistea*, suggests a sophisticated awareness of the workings of civic ideology among Perugian citizens in this period. It also indicates that civic history and the city's public image had a certain universal appeal. Perugia's classicizing public improvements involved not only the city's wealthy intellectuals but also its middle-class guildsmen and artisans; tax assessments in the membership of the CSG ranged from £25 to £8,000.[64] The Perugian council and tax records thus reveal the extent to which these ideological and humanistic concerns were of general public interest.

For example, the documents recording the construction of the Fontana Maggiore and its aqueduct demonstrate the CSG's strong desire to get the best possible value for its investment. Beginning in 1276, when it decided to make the water supply a priority, the council periodically hired experts to advise it. On May 5, 1276, it solicited opinions on the aqueduct plan from the local heads of the Franciscan and Dominican orders.[65] Nine months later, on February 16, 1277, Fra Alberico (a Franciscan), Master Guido from Città di Castello, Master Coppo from Florence, and Don Ristoro from Santa Giuliana all appeared before the council with different proposals for the fountain.[66] These ranged from building an aqueduct out of lead piping to replacing the small cistern already on the site. Apparently unsatisfied with these suggestions, that same session of the CSG decided that advice should also be sought from the Venetian master currently working on a fountain at Orvieto.[67] These experts were all paid for their travel, time, and advice—such as the £6 "paid to Master Guido of Città di Castello, for the nineteen days in which he stayed in the city of Perugia to give his opinion on and examine the aqueduct."[68] Thus, the CSG spent significant time and money consulting with experts from all over central Italy before construction began. The commune's priorities are also evident in the speed with which the project was executed once the technical details had been settled. Boninsegna da Venezia, the hydraulics expert then working in Orvieto, was appointed to design and execute the project on February 26, 1277, and both aqueduct and fountain were finished by the end of 1278.[69]

Since the fountain was to be the centerpiece of the main piazza, directly between the city's seats of secular and spiritual authority, the council also wanted to employ the best available artisans and artists. The superintendent, a Benedictine named Fra Bevignate, was regularly employed by the commune; he came to the fountain project fresh from overseeing the construction of a bridge over the Tiber at Deruta in the Perugian contado.[70] In succeeding years, he would oversee the improvement of the local road system, among other similar projects. The commune hired Boninsegna da Venezia straight from his work in Orvieto. Rosso, the smith responsible for the massive bronze bowl that crowns the fountain, had likewise worked in both Siena and Orvieto.[71]

Finally, Nicola and Giovanni Pisano, the father-and-son team who sculpted the fountain's stone panels, were at the time among the most famous sculptors in central Italy. Nicola was at the height of his professional renown, having just completed his famous pulpit for the baptistery in Pisa, and his son Giovanni (aged about twenty when they received the Perugian commission) was just starting an equally illustrious career. The two worked together all over central Italy—not only in Perugia but also in Bologna, Siena, and Pistoia.[72] Art historians from Vasari onward have often characterized their style as prehumanistic, that is, prefiguring the art of the Renaissance in the realism of their modeling and their dependence on classical models.[73] Given the classical ideals espoused by north-central Italy's republican cities, the popularity of a classicizing style of sculpture in which to express those ideals is hardly surprising, and the Perugian commune's desire to hire artists with that reputation even less so. The Pisani are typical examples of the Perugians' hiring practices; the artisans who built the fountain were all recognized experts working at the top of their professions. Their work supported the Perugian commune's joint desires for the city's material improvement and a classicizing self-image. At about the same time, the commune wrote to Charles of Anjou, the papal vicar in Rome, to request the services of Arnolfo di Cambio (c. 1245–c. 1310), a student of Nicola Pisano also known for his avant-garde classicizing style, for another fountain (since demolished).[74] Clearly, the citizens on the Perugian council preferred the best and most famous contemporary artists, working in the newest styles.

The archival entries recording Bonifacio's commission to write a Perugian *Aeneid* reveal similar circumstances and motivations. A native of Verona driven into exile during the *signoria* of Ezzelino da Romano, he supported himself on the strength of his literary training like a little-known Dante or Petrarch. Two other epic poems by Bonifacio survive—the *Veronica* and the *Annayde*—and both are dedicated to cardinals (Ottaviano degli Ubaldini and Guillaume de Braye) who presumably helped to support him.[75] The Perugian records suggest that the idea for the poem was Bonifacio's own, but that the commune embraced the idea quickly. The two relevant entries in the minutes of the CSG read,

> Tuesday, the last day of June [1293]: . . . Master Bonifacius of Verona, a master in astrology and poetry, has come to Perugia and wishes solemnly to create a work, a book of the ancient history and concerns of the Commune of Perugia, and to recall these antiquities to memory for the honor of the Commune of Perugia, if it pleases the council that while he stays in the city of Perugia to assemble and complete the said work, he should have his expenses paid by the Commune, and, once the said work is finished, [some amount] shall be provided to him, as will seem appropriate to the Consuls for the time in question and as the Council of the People recommends.[76]

> [Upon the reconvening of the council . . . it was decided and passed] that expenses for Master Bonifacius and his son should come from the monies of the Commune of Perugia, while he remains [here] and is working on the book of antiquities of the Commune of Perugia. And the Consuls of the Arts will cause the aforesaid expenses to be paid as will seem appropriate to them, and once the aforesaid work is finished, payment for his effort will be provided to Master Bonifacius as will seem appropriate.[77]

Upon his arrival in Perugia, Bonifacio appeared before the CSG to make his proposal. The council welcomed the opportunity that Bonifacio provided and agreed to all of his proposed terms; it may have gone beyond the original terms in agreeing to support his son as well.[78] Although we do not know of any other civic histories from Bonifacio's pen, it is indicative of a general mood in Italian cities of this period that Bonifacio saw any likelihood of success in pitching his poem idea—the *librum antiquitatum et negotiorum Comunis Perusii*—to the Perugian council. To put this in modern terms, he had reason to think that there was a market for his product. Furthermore, the classicizing diction notable in the finished work appears in the council minutes arranging its commission. The repetition of the word "antiquities" (*antiquitates*) stresses the city's ancient origins, and its combination with the phrase "business of the Commune of Perugia" (*negotiorum Comunis Perusii*) implies strong historical continuity between the city's classical past and the current Perugian government.

The council minutes also emphasize the importance of history to contemporary public life. Bonifacio proposed "solemnly . . . to recall these antiquities to memory for the honor of the Commune of Perugia" (*solempne antiquitates reducere ad memoriam pro honore Comunis Perusii*), thereby articulating his belief that a city's present consequence is inextricably linked to its past. To produce the desired effect, a city's noble past must be publicly known and appropriately presented—by Bonifacio's own poem. At the same time, the diction suggests that Perugia and its present regime are interchangeable; the poem will increase not only the honor of the city in general but also the honor of its commune. The two reinforce and complement each other, since the commune is the custodian of the city's honor. The speed with which the CSG adopted Bonifacio's proposal suggests its agreement with these premises—that a poem about its *antiquitates* would enhance Perugia's honor, glory, and consequence.

The agreement was made at the end of June 1293, and Bonifacio's poem was finished by mid-November, at which point another spate of notices appears in the council minutes regarding the author's payment. The first item notes that the work is done and payment must be decided on; the second announces the appointment of two doctors of law, Guido de Corgnia and Tribaldo di Forte, to inspect the work and determine appropriate remuneration; and the third contains the results of the examination. According to the account, Guido and Tribaldo studied the poem and consulted with seven other "men wise in the law," several of whom also held seats on Perugian councils:

These men wise in the law, together with the others, have decided that Master Bonifacius, for the work which he versified about the deeds of the Commune of Perugia, should have from the credit of the Commune of Perugia, and from the Perugian Commune itself, twenty-five gold florins. . . . And that Master Bonifacius himself ought to divide and organize and compose that work in prose. For writing and organizing said prose work, when it is done, he should have for himself from the credit of the Commune of Perugia twenty-five gold florins, and let them be paid to him from the credit of the Commune as payment for his effort and the aforesaid work, if it is done by him and organized as agreed. And he should give the said books to the Commune.[79]

Perhaps the most surprising fact for a modern reader is that the commune assigned lawyers to assess the poem. The act suggests that men trained in Roman law were generally considered the best educated in the community, especially on matters concerning the classics. It thereby parallels the combined political and academic roles played by judges and notaries in Padua. Also notable is that Guido, Tribaldo, and their advisors commissioned Bonifacio to write a prose version of his epic for another twenty-five gold florins. The second commission suggests that they approved of Bonifacio's work and, furthermore, that they thought a more accessible version of the work would be useful to the commune and therefore worth the expense.[80]

Finally, the negotiations for Bonifacio's literary efforts closely resemble those for the construction of the Palazzo Nuovo and the Fontana Maggiore. He was treated like any other craftsman whose work was valuable to the "honor of the Perugian commune." The council minutes refer frequently to his work (*opus*) and effort (*labor*), using phrases such as "payment for his effort and the aforesaid work" (*mercede laboris et opere supradicto*).[81] Elsewhere the minutes refer to him as a *mercenarius*—literally, a hired worker or employee.[82] Rather than seeing Bonifacio as a superior academic mind, the Perugian commune regarded him as one of the many technical experts hired to enhance the glory of the city, from the engineer who designed its aqueduct to a citizen's servant who carried a statue from one place to another. In a parallel case on November 2, 1277, the commune paid Master Coppo, a Florentine, "for the work he did on the pipes and his effort on our aqueduct."[83] Work (*opus*) and effort (*laborerio*) are the same words used to describe Bonifacio's epic. The commune perceived the *Eulistea* in the same light as the Fontana Maggiore, the Palazzo Nuovo, and even street paving. It was a public improvement that used words and stories rather than brick or stone.

In the late thirteenth century, construction and city beautification projects surrounded Perugia's citizens, many of whom would have been involved in their creation. Maintenance of the regional road system, construction of bridges and churches, street paving, improvement of the water supply, and the monumentalization of the city's main piazza all improved the lives of the city's inhabitants in practical and aesthetic ways. Such projects would have fostered a sense of civic consciousness and unity, as well as pride and patriotic support for the regime responsible for them. They would have bolstered the city's public image among outsiders, demonstrating that Perugia had the resources and good governance to accomplish such goals.

Conceptually, these improvements defined Perugian civic identity and history on a deeper level. They not only taught the city's inhabitants about their own origins but also provided them with relevant ethical and political models. The reliefs on the Fontana Maggiore and the frescoes in the Palazzo Nuovo defined the cosmos and human history, locating Perugia in these broader spheres. Their encyclopedic nature provides a context for Perugian geography, history, and knowledge. Thus, the contemporary rulers of medieval Perugia flank Eulistes on the Fontana Maggiore, implying that the actions and principles of the figures portrayed there are eternally relevant. Like Lorenzetti's frescoes in the Sienese Palazzo Pubblico, the Fontana Maggiore mirrors contemporary Perugia while simultaneously prescribing a civic ideal for it.[84] The *Eulistea*, for its part, narrates an unbroken chronicle of events from the city's foundation in the days of Troy up to the year of the poem's composition, implying continuity between the past and the present, and the presence of universal values and principles. The overarching emphasis on Roman figures and events, often in parallel to Perugian ones, provided the contemporary audience with a strong set of ethical principles based in historical experience.

To an external audience, Perugia's new classical self-image would have increased its consequence, matching every other city in Italy with an illustrious heritage. Bonifacio's *Eulistea* claims that a close and exclusive relationship existed between Perugia and Rome from both cities' earliest days, subconsciously if not explicitly denying other cities' similar claims. This assertion and the parallels between ancient and contemporary Perugia emphasize Perugia's antiquity and historical significance while imbuing its current regime with an aura of legitimacy as the direct heirs of Eulistes himself. Perugia's claim to an ancient past may have been especially useful in its relations with the papacy. The city's councilors, being laymen, probably welcomed the suggestion that their city was not defined solely by its status as an important papal city, although this was indeed a matter of considerable prestige. Moreover, a pre-Christian foundation and Roman political principles may have served Perugia well as a way of balancing its political relations with the papacy, asserting as it did that its association with the Roman church was voluntary rather than compelled.

The civic projects sponsored by the Perugian commune in the later thirteenth century were part of a larger program designed to improve and define Perugian and common experience. Each project embodied different ways of defining civic identity, but all together created a unified whole. Civic constitutions, public improvements, and the sponsorship of learning, art, and historiography drew attention to Perugia's glorious past and even more glorious present. As Alberto Grohmann points out, "They become unified symbols of communal reality, 'public monuments' representative of what has been, what is, and what should be; they continually recreate both past and present, the imaginary and the actual, myth and reality."[85] They served both as ideals for the city's populace and as a way of impressing outsiders.

The constant maneuvering to define insiders and outsiders reveals the fluidity of late medieval Italian culture and its civic myth making. People and ideas moved easily from place to place. The Pisani, for example, worked in most of Italy's major cities over the course of their joint lives; in this case, they came to Perugia from Pisa and left there to go to Siena.[86] This propensity for travel highlights the existence of a common culture with similar values and suggests that classical legends were relatively well known even outside intellectual circles. Perugia is a particularly telling case because—in contrast to Genoa, for example—none of the experts whom the Perugian council commissioned to create their Romanizing self-image were actually Perugian. Nicola and Giovanni were Apulian and Pisan, Bonifacio was Veronese, and the engineer Boninsegna was Venetian. Several other experts the council consulted were Florentine, including Arnolfo di Cambio, although he was requisitioned from work in Rome. This array displays unusual mobility as well as the wide dissemination of classicizing themes. Even a city with no local expert—no Lovato Lovati or Jacopo Doria—could recognize the benefits of having a well-known classical founder, and it could hire people to do the work of creating or promoting one.

The cutthroat civic competition, or *campanilismo*, for which Italian cities are so famous is clearly at work here.[87] Maintaining a place in the delicate balance of republican city-states and dynastic lordships was a constant concern in historiography as in architecture. Like the Sienese, who determined the height of their Torre del Mangia by the height of the new tower in Florence plus a few inches, late thirteenth-century Perugians were driven by a desire to keep up appearances, to ensure that their city's public image appropriately reflected their sense of its political and economic stature. When Boninsegna da Venezia arrived from Orvieto to give his opinion on plans for the Perugian aqueduct, what earned him the commission was his assertion that he could build the Perugians a bigger and better fountain than the one in Orvieto.[88] The classicizing themes that would appear on that fountain, and in so many other contemporary communal works, were part of a major effort to improve Perugia's prestige at its neighbors' expense. Perugia was a prosperous medium-sized city dominated by middle-class guildsmen, its political regime was reasonably well established, and it had a nascent university but no humanist circle. Far from manifesting the historiographical curiosity of a few wealthy intellectuals, therefore, the Perugian commune's adoption and promulgation of the classicizing story of Eulistes was an obvious and well-established means of publicly defining Perugian identity in a world of other cities doing exactly the same thing.

CLASSICAL SCHOLARSHIP AND PUBLIC SERVICE

[Cicero] was master and inventor of the great science of rhetoric, that is, of
speaking well . . . which advances all the other sciences because of the constant
need to speak of important things, whether in making laws, and in deciding civil and
criminal cases, and in civic affairs; or in waging war and organizing battle lines and
encouraging knights in the service of the empire, realm, or princedom; in governing
peoples and realms and villages and strange and diverse races; or in coming into contact
with the great circular map of the world. . . . And I, Fra Guidotto of Bologna,
perceiving his great virtues, conceived the idea of translating some parts of the *Flower of
Rhetoric* from Latin into our language, since they pertain generally to the public.

—Guidotto da Bologna, introducing his translation of the *Rhetorica ad Herennium*

This study has focused on the pursuit of a broad civic classicism in the republican communes of Padua, Genoa, Siena, and Perugia. In the years around 1300, each formally adopted the legend of a classical founder or founders, which reinforced and promoted communal virtues such as civic unity, fortitude in the face of aggression, fairness and justice in legal matters, and the pursuit of the common good. Such values were crucial for the survival of all republican city-states. Hence, these four cities provide a representative sample of a much broader trend. The presence of a classicizing ideology is well documented in fourteenth-century Florence, Venice, and Rome, but as I discussed in chapter 1, small communes like Todi in Umbria and Asti in the Po Valley also advertised their foundation by classical heroes and used classicizing themes as part of their self-images. The phenomenon was prevalent among republican communes across the northern half of the Italian peninsula.

These communes' efforts at classicizing self-presentation display a remarkable unity of purpose. Using the same classical sources, they identify with the same kinds of heroes—such as Trojan refugees and Roman military leaders—and cite the same episodes in Roman history as examples of good and bad political behavior for their citizens. The reader is therefore justified in wondering about the transmission of Romanizing ideas between cities. What was their appeal, and how did they spread? The first half of this chapter will address the substantial influence and relative coherence of a group I call the educated elite: a complex network of civil servants, merchants, scholars, teachers, judges, notaries, members of religious orders, and others, who were educated in the Latin classics and interested in issues touching contemporary republican politics. Their extensive travel and common interests meant that books, ideas, and policies spread quickly from one part of the Italian peninsula to another.

Consideration of the interactions of people within cities is equally crucial. Clearly, the creation or promulgation of a Romanizing identity required the collaboration of various types of people; the person who wrote an official civic chronicle was not necessarily the same person or people who commissioned it. Not all of these were members of the educated elite, so the second part of this chapter considers how those who could read Latin shared their ideas and values about the proper administration of a republic with the rest of the urban community. Not wishing to assume that classicizing identity was invented from scratch in the highest levels of government and then imposed on an indifferent or gullible populace, I investigate the processes by which members of the entire urban community took part in shaping a particular sense of civic self.

The classicizing phenomenon therefore depended on the regular exchange of ideas among scholars and civic servants across Italy, as well as the dynamic circulation of ideas within and between communities. Its success hinged on a widespread agreement that Roman matters were relevant and useful to life in a medieval commune. In the epigraph to this chapter, Guidotto da Bologna explains in his translation (c. 1280) of the pseudo-Ciceronian *Rhetorica ad Herennium* that Cicero's work can help people in every profession—from legislation, judicial affairs, and government to diplomacy and commerce. He assumes the existence of people in those fields who are unable to read the original Latin text; his purpose is therefore to present it to an audience who will benefit from its wisdom but who would not otherwise be exposed to it. As a Latin-literate university professor and member of a mendicant order, Guidotto was one of the educated elite, but his *Fiore di rettorica* was aimed at those who were not, particularly the growing number of citizens who participated in civic affairs without a classical education. This chapter seeks to untangle the social and intellectual networks that enabled such broadly based classicism, asking why, for example, Cicero should have been considered important for merchants and politicians. In an attempt to answer by whom, how, and why classical ideas were propagated, this chapter explores the middle ground between famous intellectuals like Jacopo da Varagine and Petrarch and the less educated and often undifferentiated populace of the medieval Italian cities—in the end explicating the complex social webs that constituted Italian life in the late Middle Ages.

The Educated Elite

The prominent figures in this study, those who were most responsible for the promulgation of classicizing foundation legends in medieval Italian cities, were men with both the knowledge and the influence to promote classicizing ideas within the urban community. Such men—for they were always men—were part of an educated elite who dominated the religious, social, political, and economic life of their respective cities. They came from the mercantile and artisanal classes as well as the landed nobility, and they held high ecclesiastical as well as civic offices; nevertheless, they shared a dedication to the urban community and the common good. Their lives and their works demonstrate their conviction of the relevance of classical scholarship to public life.

The legal profession formed the backbone of the civic elite due to its vocational training and its members' experience.[1] Judges and notaries staffed the communal governments. The poet Albertino Mussato (1262–1339) seems to have played a number of different roles at various times within the Paduan commune, ranging from "official notary" to ambassador, diplomat, and captain of the militia. Some of these were more formal appointments than others; most but not all of them involved his professional legal skills. For example, the writing and official adoption of his republican tragedy *Ecerinis* was a political gesture beyond the capacity of most notaries. Somewhat higher up the political ladder, Albertino's mentor Lovato Lovati (1241–1309) was a judge of the Paduan commune who also served as podestà of Vicenza.[2] Members of the legal profession played a crucial role in communal politics, not only by providing the commune with most of its staff but also by applying their professional expertise and classical knowledge in their roles as citizens.

In addition to judges and notaries, writers, artists, and philosophers with classical training and interests used their professional skills in the service of the commune. Sometimes this connection was direct, as with political theorists like Remigio de' Girolami (1240s–1319) and Ptolemy of Lucca (c. 1236–1327), whose works illustrate the close parallels between the events of classical history and medieval principles of republican governance. In other cases, educated people simply applied their knowledge to local politics. The friar-poet Guittone d'Arezzo (1235–1294) has been credited with inventing the *dolce stil nuovo*, but his Guelf politics resulted in his exile from Arezzo in 1256.[3] The same fate befell the poet Dante, exiled from Florence in 1302.[4] As detailed in earlier chapters, the painter Ambrogio Lorenzetti (c. 1290–1348) participated in the Sienese government, and the well-known author Jacopo da Varagine (c. 1230–1298) played a major role in Genoese politics as the local archbishop, using his Dominican training not only in service to the church but also to the benefit of the Genoese commune.[5] None of these men was a lawyer professionally, but each moved in the same intellectual circles and contributed to local political discourse.

Some contemporary writers were actually trained in Roman law. In his "Letter to Posterity," Petrarch explains that he took pleasure in his legal studies as a young man because he enjoyed the numerous references to Roman antiquity.[6] Despite his abandonment of law for poetry at age nineteen and his vituperations against the legal profession in general, Petrarch spent much of his adult life as a diplomat.[7] Guido delle Colonne (c. 1210–after 1287), author of vernacular poetry as well as the immensely popular Latin romance *Historia destructionis Troiae*, was a judge by profession, a point that both his *Historia* and its various contemporary translations take pains to make clear. One 1324 translation identifies the author as *Io Giudice Guido de le Colonne di Messina* (I, Judge Guido delle Colonne of Messina).[8]

This close link between legal knowledge and rhetorical skill resulted in part from contemporary educational practices. Local notaries usually provided elementary education, while jurists and judges doubled as professors, political advisors, and social theorists.[9] The judge Cino da Pistoia (c. 1270–1337), a friend of both Dante and Petrarch and an advisor to the Holy Roman Emperor Henry VII, taught civil law at several universities, including Bologna; he wrote a number of acclaimed legal commentaries as well as poetry in the *dolce stil nuovo*.[10] Notaries and judges often combined their professional skills to educate their fellow citizens in correct civic behavior. The Bolognese notary Rolandino Passaggeri (1215–c. 1300), a famous jurist who seems to have run the Bolognese commune for most of the later thirteenth century—even when he held no official position—wrote one of the most famous notarial guides of the late Middle Ages (the *Summa totius artis notarie*, or *Encyclopedia of the Entire Notarial Art*).[11] Such manuals were a popular genre, consisting of model letters, contracts, and speeches for every situation that might arise in communal life. Through his manual, the author put his own training in grammar, rhetoric, and official formulae at the disposal of the commune and anyone seeking to participate in municipal politics. Matteo dei Libri's *Arringhe* (Bologna, c. 1250) and Filippo Ceffi's *Dicerie* (Florence, c. 1320), both written in the vernacular rather than in Passaggeri's learned Latin, are two similar manuals that survive in numerous manuscript copies.[12]

A small number of diligent polymaths embraced all of these fields. The notary Brunetto Latini (c. 1220–1294), for instance, is best known as one of Dante's early mentors and chancellor of the city of Florence between 1272 and 1274, but he was also an accomplished poet and historian in his own right; his *Trésor* combines universal history with rhetorical advice for the practice of politics.[13] Similarly, Andrea Dandolo (1306–1354) studied law at Padua before embarking on a life of public service in Venice, culminating with his election as doge at the unusually young age of thirty-seven in 1343. Over the course of his public life, he patronized a number of poets, such as Albertino Mussato, in addition to writing two chronicles of Venice and a treatise on Venetian law.[14] As prominent members of society who spanned the worlds of municipal politics, literature, and education, Latini and Dandolo are especially good examples of medieval Italy's overlap of professional interests.

Extensive social networks and frequent travel facilitated intellectual community and the transmission of ideas. Through their families, studies, and professions, members of the educated class regularly met and corresponded with one another. Family tradition, for example, frequently dictated one's occupation and professional associations. The notary-poet Albertino Mussato and the political theorist Marsilius of Padua both came from families of Paduan notaries, while the father of Florentine jurist Bono Giamboni (c. 1240–after 1292) had been a judge in Orvieto and Florence.[15] Nicola Pisano (c. 1220–1278) trained his son Giovanni (c. 1250–1314) in sculpture; together they were responsible for many of northern Italy's works of monumental art at the turn of the fourteenth century, such as the Perugian Fontana Maggiore.[16] To cite an extreme example, four different men named Matteo da Correggio—all of them related and all judges by trade—earned a living as professional podestà between 1250 and 1320. One of these four (c. 1230–after 1329) appears on the Fontana Maggiore in Perugia, as he was podestà of the city in 1278 when it was completed.[17] Whether in law or sculpture, occupational knowledge passed from one practitioner to another, and family ties reinforced the natural links between men in the same profession.

On the other hand, the tradition of family diversification contributed to a strong sense of community. One member of the family might go into the family business, another into law, and a third into the church. By these means, leading merchant or noble families maintained both voice and ear in diverse areas of influence. As shown in chapter 3, the aristocratic Doria family of Genoa included both Oberto (before 1230–1306), a renowned naval commander and capitano del popolo, and his brother Jacopo (1233–c. 1300), a civic historian and archivist; other members of the family served prominently in the church and in Genoese trade in the Mediterranean.[18] Similarly, Ciampolo di Meo degli Ugurgieri (c. 1290–after 1347), a member of the noble Sienese Ugurgieri family, was a professor at the university in Siena and a well-known translator of Virgil's *Aeneid*, while the political theorist Ptolemy of Lucca came from the noble Lucchese family of the Fiadoni.[19]

Family diversification occurred in the educated middle classes as well as the nobility. Ranieri Granchi (fl. 1300–1342), a Pisan responsible for a long historical poem urging Roman civic virtue on his compatriots, spent much of his professional life as a Dominican administrator.[20] One of his near relatives, Andrea di Marco Granchi, appears in numerous Pisan documents as a banker, while both Andrea and another relative (possibly a brother), Giovanni, served in the Pisan government as *anziani* (council members)—Andrea in 1290 and 1297, and Giovanni in 1324, 1327, and 1330. The interests of the Granchi family covered trade, politics, and the church, with members of the family holding local high ecclesiastical and secular posts.[21]

The many levels of contemporary education cultivated close social ties among students and teachers, from a young boy's first grammar teacher to a judge-in-training's university tutor. Convenevole da Prato (c. 1270–1338) taught both Petrarch and Cardinal Niccolò da Prato as boys, while the Dominican scholar Remigio de' Girolami and the Florentine chancellor Brunetto Latini each mentored a young Dante Alighieri in the 1290s.[22] The university in Bologna fostered the Paduan notary Rolandino's studies under the rhetorician Boncompagno da Signa (c. 1170–after 1240),[23] as well as Cino da Pistoia's lectures in law to the poet Giovanni Boccaccio and Bartolus of Sassoferrato, possibly the greatest jurist of the late Middle Ages.[24] Looking at the same influence in art, Nicola Pisano passed his particular style of classicizing sculpture on to his apprentices, including his son, Giovanni, and Arnolfo da Cambio.[25]

Finally, ties of professional employment and patronage connected men of similar backgrounds and interests. Galvano Fiamma (1283–after 1344) came from a family of secular notaries but joined the Dominican order and spent his life as a clerical notary attached to the Visconti family of Milan; he was a prolific historian and used the substantial Visconti library as his main source of material.[26] Benzo d'Alessandria began his career as a notary in the entourage of the bishop of Como but later became chancellor to Cangrande della Scala, lord

of Verona. In the same period, Cangrande supported a sizable court of notaries, writers, lawyers, and assorted hangers-on, including Ferreto de' Ferreti
(c. 1295–1337), Guglielmo da Pastrengo, and Dante Alighieri, as well as Dante's
sons Pietro and Jacopo.[27] Cardinal Guillaume de Braye (d. 1282) patronized
both the poetry of Bonifacio da Verona (who wrote the *Eulistea* for the commune of Perugia; fl. 1263–94) and the sculpture of Arnolfo di Cambio; de Braye's
tomb by Arnolfo still stands in the church of San Domenico in Orvieto.[28]
Connections between patrons and clients, several patrons of the same writer
or artist, and the many clients of a great lord all facilitated the dynamic exchange of ideas.

Such networks—familial and intellectual as well as professional—remained
close-knit across significant distances on account of the constant movement
of people up and down the Italian peninsula. The political volatility of many
Italian city-states was one factor. Citizen embassies were common, and the
practice of electing noncitizen podestà meant that lawyers and judges traveled
constantly, amassing wide personal contacts. The Matteo da Correggio mentioned above, who appears on Perugia's Fontana Maggiore (figure 19), was
podestà of at least thirteen different cities in north-central Italy over the forty
years between 1250 and 1290.[29] The practice of exiling political figures with
every change of regime contributed to this peripatetic tendency; Dante,
Brunetto Latini, and Petrarch's father, Ser Petracco, are three of the best-known
victims of this practice, but others who appear elsewhere in this study include
Riccobaldo da Ferrara, Bonifacio da Verona, Albertino Mussato, and Cino da
Pistoia. Exiled or not, professional commitments obliged members of numer-
ous professions to travel extensively. The church required its administrators to
make regular journeys both within Italy and to and from the Curia in Avignon.
Scholarly figures such as Dante and Petrarch traveled to gain patronage, and
also on diplomatic missions. Arnolfo di Cambio, who studied under Nicola
Pisano, was born c. 1245 near Siena (in Colle di Val d'Elsa) and died c. 1310 in
Florence, but completed major commissions over the course of his life in Rome,
Viterbo, Orvieto, Perugia, and Florence.[30]

Professors and teachers may have been some of the best-traveled men of
their day. Boncompagno da Signa, author of a notarial manual called the *Rhetorica novissima*, taught rhetoric at the universities in Bologna, Venice, and Padua.
Petrarch's teacher Convenevole da Prato taught in both Pisa and Avignon
before retiring to his hometown of Prato to teach Ciceronian Latin with the
title of "official professor of the commune."[31] Cino da Pistoia was a jurist in Pisa,
Avignon, and Rome before becoming a professor at age forty-four, after which

he taught not only at Bologna but also at Treviso, Siena, Florence, and Perugia.[32] On the religious side, although Ranieri Granchi was regularly affiliated with the convent of Santa Caterina in Pisa, he studied and taught at the Dominican schools in Arezzo, San Gimignano, Florence (San Miniato), Perugia, and Lucca.[33] His compatriot Bartolomeo da San Concordio studied in Pisa, Bologna, and Paris, and afterward taught logic, philosophy, and canon law in Todi, Rome, Florence, Arezzo, Pistoia, and Pisa itself.[34] The internal organization of the religious orders, as well as competitive hiring practices among the peninsula's schools and universities, encouraged travel all over Italy and beyond.

The peripatetic existence of teachers and students, in particular, emphasizes the fluid nature of intellectual exchange in this period. On the one hand, common educational norms united teachers and students across Italy, including those from relatively small towns like Prato and Vicenza. On the other hand, certain institutions, like the Dominican convent of Santa Maria Novella in Florence, acted as nodes in the wider network, demonstrating extraordinary concentrations of intellect and professional skill. Along with renowned local Dominicans—including Bartolomeo da San Concordio, Ptolemy of Lucca, and Remigio de' Girolami—the English commentator Nicholas Trevet (c. 1265–after 1334) and the artists Duccio di Buoninsegna and Giotto di Bondone, as well as Dante, all lived, worked, or studied at Santa Maria Novella around the turn of the fourteenth century.[35]

Ties of blood, profession, patronage, and intellectual interest therefore all combined to create a network of educated men with similar interests, which extended across the Italian peninsula and beyond. This network was the means by which its members made introductions; arranged promotions, commissions, and appointments; and disseminated or gathered new information. Even relatively obscure figures like the papal notary Simone d'Arezzo (c. 1280–1338) can bring to light important details about this network and its functioning. Simone spent much of his life at the papal court in Avignon, although, as his name suggests, Arezzo was his hometown. From 1316 until his death in 1338, he also held a canonry with the cathedral in Verona; this appears to have been more a source of income than anything else, as he traveled here and there on clerical and diplomatic errands. He was a member of the *familia* of Cardinal Niccolò da Prato, whose will he executed in Avignon in 1321.[36] Tracing Simone's friends and colleagues, scholars have surmised that Simone made Niccolò's acquaintance originally through Petrarch's father, Ser Petracco, who moved his family from Arezzo to Avignon via Pisa in the years 1310–13 and knew Niccolò quite well.[37] As mentioned above, Petracco had entrusted the early education of his son Francesco (better known as Petrarch), first in Pisa and then in Avignon, to Convenevole da Prato, Niccolò da Prato's own former tutor.[38] Simone's personal and professional connections—like those of Niccolò da Prato, Petracco, and later Petrarch—therefore stretched between southern France and northern Italy. Paradoxically, local pride may have strengthened ties between Italians who were traveling in distant areas; the thirty miles separating Prato (Niccolò), Florence (Petracco), and Arezzo (Simone), which were so divisive for locals, might well have seemed insignificant at the papal court on the other side of the Alps.

Simone's personal and professional connections to the higher church bureaucracy and the family of one of Italy's greatest poets supported his own intellectual interests; his will attests to the fact that his relationships were scholarly as well as pragmatic, personal as well as official. At his death in 1338, Simone bequeathed the books that he had collected over the course of his life to the Dominican and Franciscan friars of Arezzo.[39] The booklist contains many classical authors such as Livy, Sallust, Seneca, and Terence, including a codex containing the rather rarer works of Pliny the Younger and Apuleius.[40] Among his volumes was a copy that Simone made around 1328 of the Veronese Livy, an important manuscript of the first decade; this may have been one of the manuscripts whose variants Petrarch later copied into his own copy of Livy.[41] The booklist also contains commentaries on Seneca, Livy, Boethius, and the book of Job by Nicholas Trevet, the English Dominican who, like Simone, was a client of Niccolò da Prato, as well as a sometime resident of Santa Maria Novella in Florence; Trevet had composed his commentary on the tragedies of Seneca at Cardinal Niccolò's request. Based on the presence of Trevet's commentaries in Simone's collection, Ruth Dean has suggested that Simone acquired some of his books from Niccolò da Prato, perhaps as payment for his notarial services.[42] Along with encompassing numerous cities on both sides of the Alps, therefore, Simone's acquaintances spanned both civic and ecclesiastical affairs and involved much exchange of books and intellectual information.

This easy movement of books and people thus facilitated the exchange of ideas among artists, friars, notaries, professors, and civic officials up and down the peninsula, while ties of friendship, family, profession, and common interest linked the educated and influential citizens of medieval Italy across disciplines. Given this complex web of interpersonal connections, it is hardly surprising that a sculptor in Orvieto should display many of the same cultural concerns as a Dominican notary in Milan, a prominent merchant in Florence, and a professor of rhetoric in Padua. The same factors—common ideals and a similar education—that encouraged their commitment to republican politics gave cultural prominence to men with a close knowledge of and respect for the Roman past. The educated elite had a vested interest in the practical aspects of Roman history and exerted themselves to increase its accessibility.

Beyond the Elite

Accessibility to Roman history would have been important because even by the mid-thirteenth century a significant number of people in the ruling class might well have lacked a Latin education. The Florentine chronicler Giovanni Villani was a prominent merchant and banker who held several offices in the local government, but he chose to write his Florentine chronicle in Italian rather than in Latin. Most of the relatives of the Latin authors treated in this study would have known no more than basic Latin, if that. The "educated elite," in other words, was only a part of a much larger set of people who drove local commerce and government. It was therefore crucial that those who could engage directly with the classical sources would be able to discuss their ideas and priorities with those who did not have the same education. Such avenues of communication included political participation, civic festivals and public works, and popular literature.

Each city-state had its own ways of encouraging and structuring citizen participation in communal politics. Despite their republican rhetoric, the communes were oligarchies, which comprised the following groups in differing proportions: the local hereditary nobility, the *popolo grasso* (broadly invested bankers and merchants), and the *popolo minuto* (artisans and other small businessmen).[43] Around 1300, only the first two of these would have likely had any but the most rudimentary formal education.[44] Each city's ruling class thus included an unusually high percentage of the civic population; the largest civic councils were occasionally as large as one thousand members in cities where the total population cannot have been more than thirty or forty thousand people.[45] These large civic assemblies, however, rarely met more than once or twice a year; rather, the political structures of most republican cities provided for a number of smaller councils with various qualification requirements and electoral procedures. Perugia had at least five such councils, ranging from several hundred members to an elite council of five representatives elected by the rectors of the city's guilds from among themselves. The council that made most of the city's decisions could be any of these. In Siena, it was the high council of the Nine; in Perugia, it was a regularly meeting council of two or three hundred men. Hence, the

extent to which a citizen was directly involved with his city's legislative decisions varied widely from city to city—but each city's mechanisms for involving
large numbers of citizens varied as well. Membership on the Nine, for example, changed every two months, so that in a given year up to fifty-four citizens
could take part; in Perugia, the general council was larger, but its membership
changed less often.[46]

Legislation generally belonged to the citizen councils, while judicial powers
lay chiefly with the foreign (that is, noncitizen) podestà. This system struck a
useful balance between peripatetic professional magistrates and local citizen
councils; the councils retained most practical power, but the fact that any
prominent citizen with legal experience might expect an invitation to act as
podestà in some other city at some point in his life ensured the circulation of
magistrates and intellectuals among the Italian cities. The regular presence of
foreigners in the city and the frequent use of citizen ambassadors ensured not
only that political and intellectual ideas circulated quickly but also that the citizenry at large was exposed to such ideas fairly regularly due to membership
on one council or another. Particularly in the thirteenth century, very few ruling councils were ever able to maintain a closed oligarchy, and those that did
were quickly replaced with a regime more sympathetic to the demands of the
more broadly based popolo.[47] Even cities famous for the limited nature of their
citizenship were generally still open to new blood and broad participation;
membership in the Venetian aristocracy, for instance, only closed with the
institution of the Golden Book in 1297.[48]

Thus, the ruling class—literally, those taking an active part in communal
politics—was relatively large, sometimes encompassing up to 10 percent of a
city's total population. Considering that half of that population was ineligible
because it was female (yet may have exerted its influence through male relatives),
this was a relatively high proportion. A local shoemaker would not have had the
same political influence and level of involvement as a university-educated lawyer
or wealthy merchant, but he would at least have had considerable exposure to
matters concerning the commune and the opportunity to express his opinion.
Furthermore, such citizens and the councils on which they sat displayed a surprising unity of purpose throughout this period. Factionalism and disputes over
who ought to run the government presented serious (and in many cases bloody)
difficulties, but actual policies regarding civic affairs frequently carried over from
one regime to the next. As outlined in the previous chapters, ruling regimes
sought to increase and maintain the political and economic privileges that had
been granted to them by pope, emperor, or both over the course of the preceding

centuries—exemption from (or the reduction of) papal taxation, for example, or the right to try judicial cases in a municipal court. They regulated trade both inside the city and with neighboring competitors and maintained order within the city walls. In larger cities, the commune frequently agitated for the establishment of a studium, or university, passing laws designed to entice masters and students but also sending ambassadors to the pope or the emperor to negotiate the granting of an official charter for that institution. Magistrates also spent vast amounts of money building and improving urban amenities, including aqueducts, paved streets, grand cathedrals, and urban fortifications.

In short, the urban communes were concerned with keeping order, boosting their political status, advancing their citizens' commercial success, and advertising their progress in those areas with more cosmetic improvements such as new buildings, public works projects, and civic art and literature. Like anything else on which the commune could spend its money, projects that developed or publicized a particular classical foundation myth—in fresco, mosaic, written history, or city seal—would have required the knowledge and approval of some proportion of the civic population at their outset. Accordingly, the opinions of local judges, notaries, authors, and professors were highly respected owing to their education and training. Men like Brunetto Latini and Jacopo da Varagine were not just intellectuals but used their interest in ancient history to the public benefit; the ways in which such men combined their political and historical interests suggest a remarkably organic connection between the two. They saw the two realms—political and historical, practical and academic—as vitally interdependent, and their duty as scholars was to educate those lacking similar knowledge.

As the communes' financial commitment to matters of art and literature suggests, discussions of civic history and good governance were not limited to the political arena. A vibrant oral culture incorporating public rituals, art, and architecture extended these matters beyond the literate and politically active members of the community, allowing the city's entire population to participate. In fact, the adoption of a classicizing civic identity was a two-directional process. On the one hand, indirect evidence suggests that many of these legends existed in oral form before becoming enshrined as political iconography via art or literature. In his Genoese chronicle, Jacopo Doria cites the "opinion of the common people" (*opinio vulgaris*) when introducing the story of Genoa's founding by Janus, a prince of Troy.[49] This naturally suggests that Janus was an established figure in Genoese folklore before Doria recorded the legend. Local historians have made similar arguments for the foundation legends of Siena and

Perugia, especially since Eulistes, the legendary founder of Perugia, appeared on the Fontana Maggiore in 1278 (figure 18), fifteen years before the elaborate poem that officially records his exploits was commissioned in 1293.[50] Eulistes' presence on the fountain suggests that the legend was already established in oral folklore before 1278, and that the actions of the Perugian government between 1278 and 1301 merely made his story official and authoritative.

That the definition of civic identity was indeed a phenomenon involving the entire population is also suggested by the public celebrations that attended the completion of classicizing public projects. These resembled the observance of a major religious festival or patron saint's day. The ceremonies usually involved representatives from all of the city's guilds, confraternities, and dependent territories walking in a procession that encompassed some large portion of the downtown area. Shops were ordered to remain closed; music, games, and elaborate public speeches were de rigueur. In this fashion Siena celebrated the completion of both Duccio's *Maestà* altarpiece and the public fountain in the Campo. Agnolo di Tura's record of the day the fountain was finished emphasizes the magnificence of the festivities:

> The water for the fountain in the Campo came to the Campo on the __ day of June, ___ ; it is impossible to write and relate the wonderful things that were provided for everyone. For the Nine as well as for magnates, "ordinary people" and artisans of all kinds . . . [there were] new games and infinite variety, with great expense of candles, favors, solemn wines and foods, and meals, without any sense of shame—all of which was so constantly accompanied by songs, dances, and festive rejoicing for men, women, and children, as well as the religious and country folk, that it would be impossible to describe.[51]

Agnolo stresses the inclusion of the entire Sienese population in the celebrations: rich and poor, religious and lay, male and female, city dwellers and "country folk."[52] Padua celebrated the coronation of Albertino Mussato as the world's first poet laureate since antiquity in the same manner, with a grand procession and a public reading of Mussato's *Ecerinis*.[53] Since spectacles like these were the late medieval Italian cities' chief form of public entertainment, even those members of the community who did not have a family member participating would have turned up simply to enjoy the sight.

Art and architecture were likewise important conduits for civic identity. The previous chapters have discussed Antenor's tomb in Padua, the head of Janus in

Genoa's cathedral of San Lorenzo, the wolves in Sienese painting and sculpture, and the Etruscan-style ornamentation of the Palazzo Nuovo and the many statues on the Fontana Maggiore in Perugia. Some of these depictions make their points visually—for example, Janus's resemblance to an Old Testament prophet, or the similarities between the Fontana Maggiore's *Augusta Perusia* and *Roma capud mundi*. These visual elements were reinforced by the explanatory inscriptions common to later medieval art and architecture. The tomb of Antenor in Padua and the head of Janus in the Genoese cathedral have accompanying inscriptions similar to that describing the statue of Eulistes on the Fontana Maggiore in Perugia. The transmission of meaning from the literate to the illiterate was a well-established route; as with the biblical scenes depicted in stained-glass windows, those who could read the scene were expected to explain it to those who could not.[54]

Numerous avenues thus existed for both literate and nonliterate members of the community to participate in the adoption of a classical founder. Council meetings and public festivals alike served as forums for the negotiation and proclamation of communal identity. Gradations in contemporary levels of literacy, however, provided one further venue by which classical ideas filtered from their original Latin sources down into the general population. As I mentioned earlier, many of the politically active "new men" of the communal governments were not Latin literate. Accordingly, the early fourteenth century saw the first major translations of the Latin classics into the Italian vernacular.[55] As the epigraph to this chapter suggests, such translations were generally made for legal, moral, and historical purposes as well as for entertainment. They aimed to make the classical past more accessible because it was relevant to practical experience, not because it was amusing or inherently superior.[56] A few of these translations are anonymous, such as the 1313 Italian translation of the French *Faits des Romains* and the translation of Livy's first decade, written about 1320.[57] But in most cases we know or can deduce the authors, many of whom were closely involved in communal politics and civic life. The Florentine judge Bono Giamboni, a friend of Brunetto Latini, produced the first Italian translations of Orosius and Vegetius in the late thirteenth century.[58] Several decades later, his compatriot Andrea Lancia wrote an early translation of Virgil's *Aeneid*.[59] Along with a number of Florentine statutes, Lancia has been identified with contemporary translations of Palladius, Quintilian, Ovid, and certain Senecan epistles.[60]

In some cases, there are clear parallels between a specific translation and the circumstances that inspired it. Brunetto Latini, for instance, translated a number of Cicero's orations and *De inventione* into Italian; the choice of rhetorical works is logical for a civic chancellor. On a more poignant note, the notary Alberto della Piagentina translated Boethius's *Consolatio philosophiae* while a political prisoner in Venice between 1322 and 1332. Given that he died while still imprisoned in 1332, the parallel between his situation and that of Boethius illumines his choice of base text.[61] These works integrate the classical interests of the educated ruling class with its political and civic commitments. The Florentine notary Filippo Ceffi wrote the first Italian translation of Ovid's *Heroides*, the first Italian version of Guido delle Colonne's *Historia destructionis Troiae*, and at least one well-known podestarial tract called the *Dicerie*, a collection of model letters and speeches for public life.[62] Ceffi thus illustrates the congruence of interests; his *Dicerie* are based on classical models just as his more literal translations are.

Those who concerned themselves with translation work were not just notaries but many of the period's professional intellectuals—men whom one might expect to have considered the vernacular beneath their notice. Ciampolo di Meo degli Ugurgieri, a master in the Sienese *studium*, undertook another early translation of the *Aeneid* in the 1320s, while his university colleague Guidotto da Bologna wrote a vernacular treatise called the *Fiore della rettorica*, a loose translation of the pseudo-Ciceronian *Rhetorica ad Herennium*.[63] Guidotto was a friar, like the Dominican Bartolomeo da San Concordio and the Carmelite Guido da Pisa (before 1290–1337), both of whom also translated Latin authors: Bartolomeo was responsible for Sallust's monographs and Cicero's first Catilinarian oration, while Guido wrote a long vernacular history called the *Fiore d'Italia*. The *Fiore*'s second book, a loose translation of the *Aeneid*, enjoyed wide circulation separate from the rest of the work as the *Fatti d'Enea*.[64] Some of Giovanni Boccaccio's earliest works seem to have been translations of Valerius Maximus and Livy, specifically the third and fourth decades of the *Ab urbe condita*; if the recent attribution is correct, these date to the 1330s and early 1340s, at least in part while he was pursuing legal studies in Bologna and Paris.[65]

The activity of translation thus concerned men in various occupations—both professional scholars such as university professors and more practical users of classical materials such as notaries and magistrates. They were all Latin literate, so their works were not intended for a small clique of educated peers but rather for an audience less educated in the classics than themselves. Brunetto Latini's *Trésor* includes a history of the world and an account of the founding of Florence as well as model letters for the use of public officials, while, in addition to his *De magnalibus Mediolani*, Bonvesin da la Riva wrote an Italian translation of the *Distichs* of Cato, a basic Latin school text.[66] There was clearly an increasing sense among those who could read Latin that classical materials were useful even to those without the benefit of a Latin education.

Tellingly, the usual dedicatees of such works are merchants, bankers, and holders of public office. Bono Giamboni, for example, dedicated both of his translations to members of prominent Florentine families; the introduction to his Orosius explains its genesis at the request of one Lamberto, of the prominent Abati family,[67] and he dedicated his Vegetius to the banker Manetto Scali, a member of the noble Cerchi clan and a leader of the White Guelf party.[68] Half a century later, Coppo di Borghese Migliorato Domenichi (fl. 1308–53), a wealthy Florentine merchant and a prominent public official, sponsored Andrea Lancia's translation of the *Aeneid.* Coppo held the public offices of prior and gonfalonier (standard bearer) multiple times and served on an emergency provisions committee known as the Six during the famine of 1328–29.[69] His friend Boccaccio refers to him in one of his *zibaldoni* as "Coppo di Borghese Domenichi: Florentine, most fervent lover of the republic [*amantissimus reipublice*], and father of [our] traditions [*morum pater*]."[70]

Bartolomeo da San Concordio, although a Dominican, seems to have had similar social connections. He dedicated his *Ammaestramenti degli antichi*, a rhetorical tract based on classical models, to the prominent banker and politician Geri Spini, a political opponent of the Manetto Scali mentioned above.[71] Furthermore, Bartolomeo made translations of Sallust for Nero Cambi (c. 1250–c. 1320), the Spini family's agent at the papal court.[72] All of these dedicatees, except Lamberto degli Abati, played major roles in Florence's factional politics during the early years of the fourteenth century, and at least one of them, Cambi, did not know Latin.[73] These facts suggest that such dedications were sometimes a matter of practical use rather than, or in addition to, political flattery; Scali may have been able to read Vegetius in the original, but Cambi needed Sallust in translation.

In many cases, the authors' comments concerning their works explicitly state their desire to increase the accessibility of classical materials. Riccobaldo da Ferrara's *Compendium Romanae historiae* folds multiple classical sources into a prose history in two modern volumes, and his medieval Latin is much easier to follow than the complex syntax of Livy or Virgil.[74] His prologue explains his rationale: "Indeed, I confess that you have persuaded me with logic that I should make an effort to reduce the bulk of this work and to put it into a popular style [*stillum plebeium*]; for indeed, many people avoid larger tomes on account of the expense of the copying and because of their lofty style, which is not

unsuitable for the educated."[75] His intent to make the material more appeal-
ing to people unaccustomed to reading classical Latin is clear; he mentions a
"lofty style" as well as the "expense of writing" such "huge tomes" as reasons
why potential readers might lose interest.[76] Riccobaldo's *Compilatio chronologica*
reveals his determination that such superficial problems should not hinder
access to useful material. Having related his discovery of an old manuscript of
the Eusebius-Jerome chronicle, he comments in the prologue, "I was saddened
that a thing so worthy of the knowledge of good men should have been con-
cealed and lost like buried treasure. So I decided to arrange this chronicle for
public use [*ad publicam utilitatem*], as a work that is not difficult to understand
and whose text has been kept brief."[77]

Riccobaldo was essentially a compiler, but translators of ancient authors
frequently express the same desire for their work to reach the general public.
Guidotto da Bologna's translation of the pseudo-Ciceronian *Rhetorica ad Herennium*, cited in the epigraph at the beginning of this chapter, rhapsodizes at
length on Cicero's genius and the value of rhetoric even to those who cannot
read Cicero in Latin, stressing that Cicero's lessons "pertain generally to the
public [*laici*]." [78] Likewise, the fourteenth-century chronicle of Florence attributed to Ricordano Malispini begins by stating the book's purpose: "In honor
and reverence to God the Father, from whom comes the highest good, and to
the benefit and use of all who read this, whether educated or lay [*degli alletterati
come de' laici*]. . . ."[79] Guidotto and Malispini do not intend the terms "lay" and
"laity" to distinguish those with religious vocations from those without, as in
the modern distinction between clergy and laity, although that is doubtless
their origin. Rather, the words suggest two ends of an educational spectrum.
Literatus implies not just someone who could read but someone with extensive
Latin training. *Laicus* signifies the opposite—someone lacking the education
expected in a priest.[80] Nero Cambi was *laicus* and *illiteratus*, despite his influential position at the papal court; he and the growing number of men like him—
socially influential but non-Latinate—formed the chief intended audience for
such translations.

Bartolomeo da San Concordio articulates this purpose in the introduction to
his translations of Sallust: "Both of these books [on the Catilinarian conspiracy and the Jugurthine War] are written in extremely subtle language, such that
common people [*gl' uomini volgari*] cannot appreciate or make use of them. Therefore, I have exerted myself to put them into the vernacular."[81] Bartolomeo's use
of *uomini volgari*, referring to people who knew only the *volgare*—the vernacular—parallels the terms *laicus* and *illiteratus*. Yet he considered Sallust's works

instructive for the proper conduct of civic life. The rubric introducing Bartolomeo's translation of the *Coniuratio Catilinae* in early manuscripts explains that "in this prologue Sallust intends to urge the minds of men to the practice of virtue," and the rubric introducing the *Bellum Jugurthinum* likewise announces, "Here begins the prologue to the 'Jugurthine [War]' of Sallust, which is intended to demonstrate how one acquires honor and glory through effort or purity of heart, and especially how useful the study of true stories is."[82] To men like Bartolomeo, history was a moral lesson, especially when it was as relevant to civic experience as the history of the Romans. As such, it applied not only to intellectuals but also to the public at large. The practice of translation sought to broaden the audience who could appreciate the relevance and utility of such histories.

The physical form that many of these vernacular works took supports the idea that they functioned as a bridge between the intellectual culture of the universities and the everyday culture of commerce. Extant manuscripts appear to have been written carefully and at some expense. For example, MS Gaddi rel. 71 in Florence's Biblioteca Medicea-Laurenziana is essentially a schoolbook, dating from the early fourteenth century; it contains Filippo Ceffi's translation of Ovid's *Heroides*, part of Andrea Lancia's translation of the *Aeneid*, and two other lesser-known medieval Troy poems.[83] Although its contents are all in the vernacular, they are written in a careful *mercantesca* bookhand on parchment and extensively glossed in the margins like an authoritative text.[84] This particularly stands out in Ceffi's *Heroides* translation, which looks like a cross between an early copy of Dante's *Divina commedia* because of its mercantesca script and a glossed copy of Gratian because of its layout. Thus even the physical book bridges the worlds of the merchant and the university.

In the same way, the earliest copy of Ciampolo di Meo Ugurgieri's translation of the *Aeneid* (now MS S.IV.11 in Siena's Biblioteca Comunale degli Intronati) is not only elaborately illustrated but also glossed in the same fashion as the Gaddi manuscript.[85] Its first page (figure 22) is a careful balance between miniature (Ciampolo, or possibly Virgil, at his desk), vernacular text, and gloss. The appearance of Ciampolo's work is even more formal than that of the Gaddi manuscript because it is written in Bolognese textura, the formal script of medieval Italian law books. The preparer of the manuscript equated the works of Virgil and Ovid with those of major legal authorities such as Gratian. Both the format and the contents of the manuscript reflect the status attributed to the base text: its extensive and intricate gloss suggests that Ciampolo's translation is worthy of serious study, while the manuscript's formal qualities—size, script, and decoration—show that it was created for important and wealthy people.

Fig. 22 Opening page of Ciampolo di Meo Ugurgieri's glossed Italian translation of the *Aeneid*, mid-fourteenth century. Biblioteca Comunale degli Intronati, Siena (MS S.IV.11, fol. 1r).

In other words, the *Aeneid* enjoyed a prominent status as a literary work even though its language was no longer Latin but rather the vernacular, traditionally considered to deserve a less formal presentation. The manuscript therefore generates the image of a wealthy reader who valued Virgil's poem as a didactic work but could not read its original Latin form.

As both the content and the form of these literary works demonstrate, this kind of cultural dissemination—of translated exempla, glossed epic poems, and condensed classical histories—occurred because the experiences of the Romans were seen as directly pertinent to those living in the medieval city-states. Like their medieval descendants, the Romans subscribed to a specifically didactic vision of history and addressed forthrightly the moral and political complications of living in an urban republic. In words reminiscent of Livy's prologue to the *Ab urbe condita*, the rhetorician Boncompagno da Signa explains in his *Liber de obsidione Ancone* that "the deeds of the ancients have been put into writing so that their human heirs may benefit from their series of examples, so that when they hear what glory the victors reaped, they may grow from virtue to virtue, and when they understand with what scorn criminals and villains are bespattered, they may beware the same lest they thereafter incur equal infamy."[86] Medieval scholars reading Roman history would have found plenty of examples of both vice and virtue in a civic milieu, as we saw with Jacopo da Varagine and the Roman exempla in his history of Genoa. In particular, compendia of moralizing stories and excerpts from the Latin classics such as those by Valerius Maximus (*Factorum et dictorum memorabilium*, first century A.D.) and Solinus (*Collectanea rerum memorabilium*, third century A.D.) were widely copied in this period, both in Latin and in the vernacular.[87] I previously mentioned that the earliest translation of Valerius Maximus dates to the 1330s; that period also saw several new collections in the same pattern, like the Paduan judge Geremia da Montagnone's *Compendium moralium notabilium*.[88] These collections brought together moral and instructive stories that could be used either singly or *in toto* to educate the ignorant about the behavior appropriate to a republican commune.

Some of the lessons provided by classical sources were purely moral, dealing with individual instances of vice and virtue. Most of them, however, focused on the individual's role in politics and society. (Like Aristotle, they tended to see the two as essentially the same: a community of people is necessarily a political body.) In recent years, for example, historians have analyzed the influence of Roman stoicism on medieval Italian political thought.[89] Medieval professors often lectured on Cicero's *De officiis*, which discusses questions of honor and good citizenship, for legal studies at the university level.[90] Cary Nederman has stressed the collectively consensual nature of Cicero's Aristotelianism as understood by theorists in medieval Italy, who believed that "entry into human society is at the same time renunciation of the primacy of one's private and individual interests. Thereafter the common welfare and benefit take precedence over the needs and desires of particular members of the community."[91] Civic virtue in the medieval community was chiefly viewed as a renunciation of self-interest with the goal of maintaining collective *libertas*, or the free life as led under a republican government.[92] Cicero says in the *De officiis*, "Those who would take charge of the affairs of government should remember two of Plato's rules: first, to keep the good of the people so much in view that they connect it to whatever they do, forgetful of their own interests; second, to care for the welfare of the whole body politic and not in serving the interests of some one party to abandon the rest."[93] As Quentin Skinner has shown, medieval political theorists and civic magistrates believed that only under such harmonious conditions could the urban community attain its proper end: civic honor, glory, power, and wealth.[94]

Self-interest and greed, on the other hand, gave rise to factionalism and strife, which hampered the community's proper functioning and growth. Cicero had attributed to factionalism the civil wars in Athens and in the Rome of his own time, citing "not only dissensions but disastrous civil wars in our own republic."[95] Lucan's *Pharsalia*, a later poem on the civil wars of the late republic, provided medieval readers with an even more cynical view of them. Medieval writers on politics frequently quoted one passage from Sallust's *Jugurtha*, which read, "It is by way of concord that small communities rise to greatness; it is as a result of discord that even the greatest communities fall into collapse."[96] This was a common trope for the urban historiographers of medieval Italy, who usually attributed all social ills, more or less accurately, to civic discord, or faction. The Florentine historians Giovanni Villani and Dino Compagni are only two of the most famous to have done so. Compagni's introduction to his account of Florence's civic struggles between 1280 and 1312 blames its citizens' selfishness for the city's woes: "By their pride and ill will and competition for office, they have undone so noble a city, and abused its laws, and sold off in a moment the honors which their ancestors had acquired with great effort over many years."[97] Not coincidentally, the sentiments are the same. Cicero, Sallust, and Lucan addressed issues crucial to the urban classes of medieval Italy: the preservation of civic peace, the administration of justice, and the maintenance of equitable social order. One anonymous fourteenth-century chronicle of Ravenna asserts that the city "will never be destroyed by anyone unless it is divided within itself."[98]

In truth, the medieval republican system paralleled that of the Romans at the end of their republic. Republican oligarchies grappled with dense populations, factionalism, and intense socioeconomic competition; speeches and assemblies played a large part in political life; and major civic figures led very public lives whose proper display frequently involved the spending of large amounts of their own money.[99] Classical works on ethics and governance therefore provided a secular model of civic virtue that accorded with the medieval urban experience in ways that traditional Christian doctrine could not. For instance, the medieval church taught that it was always more virtuous to contemplate heavenly things (Saint Augustine's *civitas dei*) than to become embroiled in the vanities of the material world (the *civitas mundi*). Monks, who renounced the world, were by definition more virtuous than merchants. This was acceptable as an abstract principle, but it was not pragmatically useful; the economic and political success of the Italian city-states depended directly on their citizens' commitment to the material world. Roman authors mitigated this tension by providing a secular model of virtue. The first book of Cicero's *De officiis*, for example, lays out principles of *honestas*, or moral rectitude, which assume that the virtuous man will take a public part in society. While not specifically antithetical to Christian teaching—being mostly concerned with virtues like honesty, generosity, and kindness—Cicero's views and examples spoke more directly to the everyday lives of the urban community than, for instance, most Christian saints' lives did.[100] In short, texts like the *De officiis* presented the possibility of leading a virtuous life without renouncing society. Already in 1230, the Florentine author Sanzanome asserted that "honor is not gained by sitting passively" (*honor non acquiritur quiescendo*).[101]

Beyond the City Walls

A relatively small group of wealthy, Latin-literate, and politically influential people may thus have driven the adoption of classical ideals—and thereby classical heroes and founding fathers—in the medieval communes, but awareness of such ideals was not limited to that class. The broader civic community shared its enthusiasm for the classical past, and the expertise of men such as Brunetto Latini, Bartolomeo da San Concordio, and Albertino Mussato—educated in the classics and skilled in conveying the lessons of Roman history to their fellow citizens—was valued highly. Literature, politics, art, and public ritual all facilitated the dissemination of these ideas. Ultimately, the articulation of a classical civic identity benefited from the participation of all citizens—educated and illiterate, rich and poor, franchised and unfranchised. The cities of medieval Italy were sites of seething public debates over the proper conduct of communal affairs; given the parallels that their inhabitants saw between contemporary and classical politics, it would be surprising if their discussions of history and the classical past should be otherwise.

In his introduction to the *De magnalibus Mediolani* (1288), however, Bonvesin da la Riva explains that he is directing his work to two separate audiences:

> Since I address myself not only to foreigners but also to my compatriots who sleep in the desert of ignorance—that is to say, unknowing of the marvels of Milan—I have decided to aid and counsel their opinions, so that in opening their eyes, they may see, and in seeing, they may understand why and how greatly our city is worthy of admiration. . . .
>
> [Thus] all the foreigners who come to know the nobility and dignity of the Milanese will respect, honor, love, and defend them everywhere and above all men, [and] my fellow citizens, seeing themselves in this mirror and considering the fatherland of which they are sons, will not diminish its nobility in any way, nor will they pollute or defame their fatherland with dishonorable behavior.[102]

Bonvesin intends his book not only for the general population of Milan, so that his fellow citizens can properly appreciate the virtues of their own city, but also for foreigners, "to know the nobility and dignity of the Milanese." He phrases this politely, but he is as comfortable with civic one-upmanship as with more traditional notions of Christian charity. Civic foundation legends functioned as weapons of civic competition as well as weapons of civic unity. This is evident in the insults and boasts exchanged between particularly fierce competitors— this study has considered Padua's rivalry with Venice, and Siena's with Florence— and in civic records that insist on the maintenance of the honor of the commune in the eyes of "all foreigners." Foreigners were common in the city, given contemporary political structures and frequent professional travel. Competition between cities was therefore a major motivating factor in questions of public appropriations; recall that the engineer Boninsegna da Venezia received the commission for the Fontana Maggiore in Perugia because he claimed that he could build a fountain bigger and better than the one he was just finishing in Orvieto.[103]

The articulation of a particular classicizing civic identity involved a complex encounter between educated intellectuals and their books, oligarchs and the urban populace, one city and another. Each community elaborated on its chosen theme in a slightly different way, since it was shaping its self-image to address its specific social and political circumstances. Accordingly, the evidence for classicism in each city also varies; the surviving evidence for Siena's origin legend is almost entirely visual, whereas that for Genoa is overwhelmingly literary. Genoa's legend was intended to address the city's internal problems with factionalism, while Padua's sought to fend off the expansionist ambitions of neighboring city-states. Local humanists spearheaded Padua's efforts to promulgate its classical roots, while Perugia had to import scholars specifically for the task. Each city-state did what it could to present its civic past as it wished to be seen, and most had to deal with others' criticisms of their claims. The result was a rich and widespread engagement with the classical past. Rather than being set in stone, civic foundation legends were part of a constantly changing cultural discourse, both inside and outside the city walls.

Conclusion

Si fabulas quaeris, easque aniles, haec lege.
[If you are looking for legends and old wives' tales, read this.]

—Ludovico Muratori's 1725 footnote to a medieval chronicle of Ravenna

Presented with preposterous stories of duplicate wolf-nursings, multiple founders with the same name, and legions of previously unknown Trojan princes, the
reader may begin to wonder whether any of the citizens of the cities discussed
in this study believed in the pasts recounted by their chronicles, frescoes, and
statuary. Did anyone in fourteenth-century Todi actually think that two of the
gates of Rome were named after primeval Todese conquerors of Rome? How
likely is it that Remus had twin sons who were also suckled by a she-wolf?
Post-Enlightenment scholars, tourists, and others have traditionally laughed
off such ideas as typical "Dark Ages" credulity, assuming that a medieval legend's
promulgator, his audience, or both together couldn't tell the difference between
fact and legend. As I hope this study has shown, however, the circumstances
that produced and promoted such legends in medieval Italy were more complex than manipulation on the one hand and credulity on the other; the construction of history in any period is never a matter of simple truth and falsity.[1]
We live in a world that is hardly less concerned with facts and their "spin"—
and matters of personal, ethnic, religious, and national identity are still rich in
sensitivity, disagreement, and insult.

In 2003, for example, Mayor Gerald Sherratt of Cedar City, Utah, ran a series
of faux-scholarly paid advertisements in a local newspaper.[2] Attempting to
improve tourism in the area, he reported the discovery of ancient Viking artifacts documenting a previously unknown medieval settlement called the kingdom of Himmelsk, founded by one Prince Knut Blodoks in the tenth century
A.D. Despite the almost complete absence of ethnic Scandinavians in Cedar
City, the articles created a buzz and rumors began to fly out of control. To

extract himself, the mayor published a further notice announcing that the artifacts had been claimed for the Smithsonian Institution in Washington, D.C. Immediately, Cedar City's town hall was deluged with phone calls from locals anxious to retain important fragments of their heritage. Some claimed personal ownership of the artifacts on territorial or family grounds, while others blamed the Smithsonian intervention on a vast government conspiracy. All rejected the mayor's admission that he had made the entire story up, and insisted that such important evidence of the town's ancient heritage should remain in Cedar City. Rather than seeing this episode as medieval credulity extrapolated forward to the present day, I see the story of Cedar City's Viking heritage as an object lesson of the eagerness with which people have always incorporated their surroundings and their sense of the past into their own personal and collective identities. Such legends are invaluable for how they reveal the complex political, intellectual, and social networks that connect the events, people, and places in which they originated.

The preceding pages have attempted to characterize the proliferation of classical foundation legends in the cities of northern and central Italy between 1250 and 1350 A.D. I have tried to delineate not only the historical phenomenon but also why it developed as it did—why so many civic leaders were interested in the classical past and what role they saw it playing in the life of the late medieval *civitas*. Ultimately, when the Italian republics looked for ways to inspire their citizens and increase the "honor of the commune," the ancient Romans loomed large. All around them were the inescapable reminders of a great empire that had dominated the known world—an achievement that medieval rulers consistently tried and failed to reproduce. Although the Romans had been pagans, their skills in architecture, military conquest, literary composition, and political administration could not be gainsaid. Beryl Smalley has commented that medieval people, "knew perfectly well that the Roman people had flourished and had won their most striking victories in the good old days of early Roman tradition."[3] In their efforts to claim a classical past, however, Italians had the advantage of immediacy over the French or the English, both of whose royal families claimed descent from Trojan exiles in this period. Later medieval Italians were increasingly aware that the history of Rome was their history; its remains surrounded them, and their cities often featured in the pages of Roman historians.

More important, however, were the examples that the history of the Roman republic provided to communities similarly engaged in republican self-rule. When communes first appeared in the late eleventh and twelfth centuries, they almost invariably adopted two rotating annual executive magistracies called consuls, just as had existed in the Roman republic.[4] City councils frequently appear in official documents as *senatus*.[5] The pages of Cicero, Sallust, Lucan, and other classical authors—often in translation for the first time—provided both models for republican governance and dramatic evidence for what happens when such governance goes disastrously wrong: civil war. Jacopo da Varagine's Roman glossary denounces ambition, factionalism, and personal greed on the same page that it praises magistrates who work for the common good.

A considerable overlap of political, financial, and intellectual spheres facilitated the use and manipulation of classical materials for ideological purposes. Merchants, magistrates, and professors came from the same leading families and formed an educated elite whose participation in civil society benefited the entire urban population. Lovato Lovati, Jacopo da Varagine, Ambrogio Lorenzetti, and Bonifacio da Verona all held official appointments in communal government, while Brunetto Latini, Andrea Dandolo, and Albertino Mussato combined the personae of teacher, civil servant, poet, and historian into a single career. They were in a prime position not only to appreciate the relevance of Roman history to the circumstances in which they found themselves but also to pass that knowledge on to others.

Given the labyrinthine networks of kinship, partisanship, civic allegiance, and feudal obligation that characterized Italian politics in the late Middle Ages, every city—no matter how small—had a stake in the communal pot of civic honor. Cities the size and influence of Genoa and Venice, with populations of about one hundred thousand in 1300, participated, but so did much smaller towns like Todi, with populations of fewer than five thousand. The adoption of civic foundation legends was widespread and extremely variable; it was not unique to "culturally developed" cities like Florence and Venice, nor specific to a certain type of regime. In the interest of brevity and coherence, I have limited my study to republican city-states, but I think it crucial to stress that similar analyses could be done for imperial or aristocratic ideologies in the same time period. Florence may have proclaimed its foundation by Julius Caesar, but so did the Colonna family in Rome, while the Este of Ferrara based their claim to the March of Ancona (which included Padua) in part on descent from their Trojan ancestor Ateste.

Likewise, I have limited this study to a specific span of one hundred years. The propagation of Roman foundation legends is not limited to these years; there are fascinating examples from the eleventh as well as the sixteenth centuries. Rather, this century was a crucial turning point for the republican cities on which I have focused—a period of rapid growth, fierce competition, and near-cataclysmic political upheaval. By 1400, the political landscape had changed considerably. Instead of numerous independent city-states connected by regional and partisan alliances, a few large powers like Florence and Milan faced off against a backdrop of subject and dependent territories. The high-pressure politics of the century between 1250 and 1350 therefore produced particularly eloquent examples of civic ideology in central and northern Italy. The republican city-states promulgated classical foundation legends that are carefully articulated, like the myth of Janus in Genoa, as well as broadly disseminated, like the imagery of the she-wolf in Siena. Whether written, painted, or built, they are conscious monuments to civic pride, honor, and glory, and as such have the same cultural function as other contemporary civic improvements.

Each of the four cities discussed in detail here engaged in the same projects at approximately the same time: city walls and gates to protect its citizens, aqueducts to provide convenient running water, statutes to define the city's privileges and improve communal life, a university or studium for the education of future leaders, and a town hall that appropriately reflected the "honor and glory of the commune." As the Perugian council minutes demonstrate clearly, the same research, imagination, and attention went into the formulation of a civic foundation legend as into more concrete civic infrastructure. Art and literature were considered as crucial to the commune's success as utilities, architecture, and public institutions.

Civic competition and questions of honor were particularly vital not only because the political sphere was so volatile but also because the urban network was so closely woven. Within the city, population density was extremely high, with much of everyday life taking place in public, while outside city walls, merchants, magistrates, intellectuals, ambassadors, artists, and clerics moved about constantly, up and down the peninsula as well as further afield. As attested by the various histories that collect lists of civic foundation legends, municipal improvements were certain to be seen and spoken of, and most legends were well known outside their city walls.

The articulation of such a legend was an engagement with the outside world as well as among a city's various groups and leaders, and in many cases these legends illustrate the transmission of certain images, ideas, and ideologies from city to city. The ideological dialogues between Padua and Venice, and Florence and Siena, are conspicuous examples; each city formulated its own civic myth not only for itself but also against its rival, bolstering its civic honor at the other's expense. Yet the intersecting accounts traced by this study have shown that cultural transmission is rarely so tidy. Historical figures, symbolic images, and even physical monuments usually have a richly intricate afterlife not apparent to the casual viewer.[6]

Most visitors to the Capitoline Hill in Rome today visit not the Roman commune's pet wolves, as they might have done in 1893, but the famous bronze Capitoline wolf and twins.[7] The twins were added to the wolf after its transfer to the Capitoline in the 1470s; in the thirteenth century, the famous *lupa* was standing with other classical trophies outside the Lateran palace in Rome. As a she-wolf, the bronze sculpture was already connected with the Romulus and Remus legend, but it lacked twins. Medieval representations of Romulus and Remus from the ninth century on usually focus on the twins themselves, relegating the she-wolf to secondary importance.[8] To my knowledge, the earliest medieval representations of the wolf with the twins that appear in a public venue are Nicola and Giovanni Pisano's reliefs for the Fontana Maggiore in Perugia, from 1278, and the drainspouts on the Palazzo Pubblico in Siena, from 1300–1310. It is tempting to theorize that the Pisani and their associates were the first to reuse the iconography of the wolf and twins in their work in Perugia and Siena, and that the Romans reclaimed the idea to add the infants to the Capitoline wolf in the fifteenth century from them. The development of these respective foundation legends may have been more culturally interdependent than historians have generally recognized and may in fact reveal more about the historic relations between these cities than mere "urban legends" are usually expected to do.

Biographical Appendix

The following entries are intended to orient the reader by identifying the main characters in this study, without being collectively or individually exhaustive.

Albertino Mussato (1262–1329)

Paduan notary; friend and colleague of Lovato Lovati, Benzo d'Alessandria, and Rolando da Piazzola. Albertino was knighted by the commune in 1296 and served as a civic ambassador to Pope Boniface VIII (1302) and Emperor Henry VII (1311). He was a prisoner of war in Verona in 1314–15. On his return to Padua in 1315, the Paduan commune awarded him the laurel crown for his anti-tyrannical drama *Ecerinis*, an event that inspired Petrarch's ambition for the same. In 1325, he led an uprising against the Veronese-friendly Marsiglio da Carrara, an act for which he was banished to Chioggia until his death in 1329.

Works include *Ecerinis*, a Senecan tragedy; a dialogue on Seneca's metrical scheme; several Latin summaries of Seneca's tragedies; and several works of history, including the Livian *De gestis italicorum*, dedicated to Paduan bishop Pagano della Torre.

Bibliography: Dazzi, *Mussato preumanista*, and Witt, *Footsteps of the Ancients*, 117–73.

Alberto della Piagentina (d. 1332)

Notary, probably Florentine; acquaintance of the Sienese poet Bindo Bonichi. Alberto was a prisoner in Venice from 1322 until his death in 1332.

Works include a translation of Boethius's *Consolatio philosophiae* into Tuscan, written during his imprisonment in Venice. He may also have translated certain works of Ovid.

Bibliography: Marti, *DBI*, 1:747–48, and Battaglia, *Boezio e l'Arrighetto*.

Ambrogio Lorenzetti (c. 1290–1348)

Florentine painter; younger brother of the painter Pietro Lorenzetti and colleague of Giovanni Pisano and Simone Martini. Ambrogio moved away from
Florence sometime after 1321 and returned there late in life after spending most
of his working years in Siena; Vasari records his active participation in Sienese
political life. He and his brother Pietro probably died in the 1348 plague.

Works include *Saint Dorothy* (Siena, 1326), two Franciscan frescoes (San
Francesco, Siena, 1329 and 1336), *Maestà* (Palazzo Pubblico, Massa Marittima,
1330), frescoes for the Ospedale della Scala (with his brother Pietro, Siena, 1335),
Saint Nicholas Altarpiece (San Procolo, Florence, 1332), "Roman frescoes" (Palazzo
Pubblico, Siena, c. 1337), *Allegories and Effects of Good and Bad Government* (Sala
della Pace, Palazzo Pubblico, Siena, 1337–40), and *Presentation in the Temple* (Siena,
1342).

Bibliography: Becchis, *DBI*, 65:792–99; Frugoni, Donato, and Monciatti,
Pietro and Ambrogio Lorenzetti; and Starn, *Ambrogio Lorenzetti*.

Andrea Dandolo (1306–1354)

Jurist and doge of Venice (1343–54); friend and correspondent of Petrarch. The
Dandolo were an established family of the Venetian nobility that produced several doges, admirals, and other prominent citizens; Andrea's brother Simone
was also a judge and Venetian podestà of Treviso. Andrea studied law at the
university of Padua and later served as a professor of jurisprudence there. He
was named a procurator of the basilica of San Marco at the unusually young age
of twenty-two in 1328 and held numerous communal posts after that. After his
election as doge in 1343, he oversaw the reorganization of the Venetian statutes,
sponsored the renovation of the *Pala d'oro* (the great altarpiece of San Marco),
subdued several revolts on the Istrian (Croatian) mainland, especially at Zara,
and led the fleet that defeated the Genoese at the Battle of Lojera in 1353.

Works include the *Summula statutorum floridorum Veneciarum* (c. 1342), a compilation of Venetian law; he also composed two chronicles of Venetian history,
the *Chronica brevis* (c. 1342) and the *Chronica extensa* (c. 1346).

Bibliography: Ravegnani, *DBI*, 32:433–40; Arnaldi, "Andrea Dandolo, Doge-
cronista"; Lazzarini, "*Dux ille Danduleus*"; and Pincus, "Andrea Dandolo and Visible History."

Andrea Lancia (c. 1280–after 1355)

Florentine notary and public official; acquaintance of Dante Alighieri, friend of
Giovanni Villani and Zanobi da Strada, neighbor and colleague of Giovanni

Boccaccio. Andrea appears regularly in Florentine notarial acts between 1315 and 1357; his father and son Filippo were also notaries. He held numerous positions, such as notary to the executors of the Ordinances of Justice, archivist of the Camera del Comune, and consul of the guild of judges and notaries, and he made numerous diplomatic trips for the commune of Florence—to Avignon and the Veneto as well as closer destinations like Pisa, Pistoia, and San Miniato. He also worked for a time in Volterra during the Florentine *signoria* of Walter de Brienne, duke of Athens (1342–43).

Works include a loose, abbreviated early translation of the *Aeneid* into Tuscan (c. 1316), which he wrote at the behest of prominent citizen Coppo Domenichi, a friend of Boccaccio's. He is the author of the *Ottimo commento* (c. 1343), an early commentary on the *Divina commedia* of Dante, whom Andrea met on a trip to the Veneto around 1318; he also authored the Florentine sumptuary laws of 1355. Andrea may have translated certain Senecan epistles, Palladius's *De agricultura*, Ovid's *Ars amatoria* and *Remedia amoris*, and possibly Valerius Maximus.

Bibliography: Cerroni, *DBI*, 63:317–20; Azzetta, "Per la biografia di Andrea Lancia"; and Bruni, "Between Oral Memory and Written Tradition."

Armannino Giudice (before 1260–after 1325)

Bolognese judge, also known as Armannino da Bologna; friend of Bosone Novello da Gubbio. Armannino lived throughout the course of his life in Bologna, Viterbo, and Fabriano, where he held various legal posts from notary to judge. His father was Tommasino di Armannino, a Bolognese judge and author of a treatise on the *ars dictaminis* called the *Microcosmus*.

Works include *Fiorità* (c. 1325), a universal history dedicated to Bosone Novello that emphasizes classical history and civic origins.

Bibliography: Ghinassi, *DBI*, 4:224–25; Mazzatinti, "*Fiorità*"; and Sassi, *Armannino Giudice*.

Arnolfo di Cambio (c. 1245–c. 1310)

Artist, architect, and sculptor, born in Colle di Val d'Elsa, near Siena; colleague of Nicola and Giovanni Pisano. Arnolfo spent a number of years working as Nicola's assistant, most famously on the tomb of Saint Dominic in Bologna and the pulpit of the cathedral in Siena; thereafter he operated independently, as, for example, on a fountain in Perugia (no longer extant) commissioned shortly after the Fontana Maggiore. He died in Florence.

Works include statues of Charles of Anjou (marble, Rome, 1266–67) and Saint Peter (bronze, Rome, c. 1296); the tombs of Cardinal Annibaldi (Rome,

1276), Pope Adrian V (Viterbo, 1276), Cardinal Guillaume de Braye (Orvieto, 1282), and Pope Boniface VIII (Florence, c. 1300); and the ciboria of San Paolo fuori le Mura (Rome, 1283) and Santa Cecilia (Rome, 1293). In 1296, he was in charge of construction of the cathedral in Florence. He is said to have had a hand in designing other major buildings in Florence, including the baptistery, the Franciscan basilica of Santa Croce, and the Palazzo Vecchio.

Bibliography: Bottari, *DBI*, 4:285–90; Moskowitz, *Italian Gothic Sculpture*, 44–67; and Napoli, *Arnolfo di Cambio*.

Bartolomeo da San Concordio (c. 1262–1347)

Dominican friar, born in San Concordio, near Pisa. Bartolomeo studied in Pisa, Bologna, and Paris before returning to Italy to teach logic, philosophy, and canon law; he was most often in Pisa but also spent time teaching in Todi, Rome, Florence, Arezzo, and Pistoia. Chiefly a historian, translator, and compiler, Bartolomeo was well connected and very interested in classical history and literature. He dedicated his *Ammaestramenti degli antichi* to Geri Spini, a banker and one of the leaders of the Black Guelfs in Florence between 1302 and 1308. His translations of Sallust were done at the request of Nero Cambi, the Spini agent in Rome.

Works include the rhetorical handbook *Documenta antiquorum*, which Bartolomeo translated into Italian as the *Ammaestramenti degli antichi* (ed. Colombi); a *Summa casuum conscientiae*, translated as *Pisanella* or *Maestruzzo*; various sermons; part of the chronicle of the convent of Santa Caterina in Pisa; and several works on grammar, meter, and spelling based largely on the late antique grammarian Priscian. Intriguingly, he expresses a strong preference for classical over medieval orthography. He also translated several major classical works, including Sallust's *Catilina* and *Jugurtha* (both ed. Puoti). Several of Bartolomeo's works are no longer extant, including the treatises *De virtutibus et vitiis* and *De memoria*; commentaries on Virgil and the tragedies of Seneca; and a *Tabula ad inveniendum Pascha*.

Bibliography: Segre, *DBI*, 6:768–70, and Colombi's introduction to Bartolomeo da San Concordio, *Ammaestramenti degli antichi*.

Benzo d'Alessandria (fl. 1311–29)

Probably born in Alessandria, near Milan, as his name implies; friend of Guglielmo da Pastrengo, Albertino Mussato, and other Paduan and Veronese humanists. Virtually nothing is known of his early life except that he studied law at Bologna. In 1311, he appears in Milan, serving as notary to the imperial vicar Cione delle Bellaste of Pistoia. From 1313 to 1320, he served as notary to Bishop Leone Lambertenghi at Como. By 1325, he had joined the court of

Cangrande della Scala in Verona, and by 1328, he was chancellor to the della Scala family (first to Cangrande and then to his nephews Alberto II and Mastino II), a post he held until his death in 1333. Benzo received praise from Guglielmo da Pastrengo and was a dedicatee of Albertino Mussato.

Works include an immense *Chronica* (unedited), which follows history from the beginning of the world to the death of Emperor Henry VII in 1313. In compiling the *Chronicon*, Benzo used a vast array of classical sources, most of them from the capitular library in Verona.

Bibliography: Ragni, *DBI*, 8:723–26; Ferrai, "Benzo d'Alessandria"; and Berrigan, "Benzo d'Alessandria."

Bonifacio da Verona (fl. 1250–1300)

Poet and historian, born in Verona but exiled with numerous compatriots by Ezzelino in 1253. Bonifacio may have been in service to the church, as he is the author of two poems in honor of cardinals. In the 1270s and 1280s, he may have been a client of Rudolf of Hapsburg. He wrote the Latin epic *Eulistea* for the commune of Perugia in 1293; Perugian records speak also of a son who was living with him at the time.

Works include two poems—the *Veronica*, written for Cardinal Ottaviano degli Ubaldini (1245–1272), and the *Annayde*, written for Cardinal Guillaume de Braye (also the patron of Arnolfo di Cambio, 1263–1282). He also authored the *Eulistea*, upon the completion of which the Perugian commune also commissioned him to write a vernacular translation of the work.

Bibliography: Arnaldi, *DBI*, 12:191–92; Mazzatinti, "Bonifacio da Verona"; and Galletti, "Materiali per una storia."

Boncompagno da Signa (c. 1170–after 1240)

Professor of grammar and rhetoric, born in Signa, near Florence. Boncompagno studied at Florence and Bologna, attaining the status of master at a very young age. He taught the *ars dictaminis* thereafter at Bologna, Venice, and Padua, where he may have participated in the secession of scholars from Bologna that established the university in Padua (1222); the historian Rolandino of Padua was among his students. He also spent time in Ancona, Vicenza, and Rome, where he made several unsuccessful attempts to gain a position in the curia. Several of his contemporaries mention him with admiration, including Rolandino, Boto da Vigevano, and Salimbene de Adam.

Works include numerous rhetorical tracts advocating a plain direct style, such as the *Oliva, Cedrus, Palma, Breviloquium, Ysagoge,* and *Rethorica novissima;* his masterwork was *Boncompagnus*. These engaged particularly with rhetoric as it pertained to law. Boncompagno also wrote goliardic poetry and the historical work *Liber de obsidione Ancone*, about Frederick Barbarossa's siege of Ancona in 1173; it was dedicated to Ugolino Gosia, a professor of law at Bologna and podestà at Ancona.

Bibliography: Pini, *DBI*, 11:720–25; Witt, "Boncompagno and the Defense of Rhetoric"; and Stone's introduction to Boncompagno da Signa, *History of the Siege of Ancona*.

Bono Giamboni (c. 1240–after 1292)

Florentine judge and scholar; colleague of Brunetto Latini. His father, a judge, was originally from Orvieto but moved to Florence around the time of Bono's birth; Bono adopted his father's judicial profession and appears regularly in Florentine records as a procurator and witness between 1260 and 1292. He was also a judge of the commune for the Sestiere di Por S. Pietro. As a scholar, he is chiefly known for his translations of classical texts dedicated to prominent Florentines of the day; for example, his translation of Vegetius is dedicated to Manetto Scali, a leader of the White Guelf party. He may also have translated Brunetto Latini's *Trésor* into Italian, but recent scholars have argued that Latini wrote his own translation.

Works include translations of Vegetius, *De re militari*, and Orosius, *Historiae adversus paganos*, and one original work, *Libro dei vizi e delle virtudi*. One redaction of the *Fiore della rettorica* (a vernacular translation of the *Rhetorica ad Herennium*) attributes its translation to him.

Bibliography: Foà, *DBI*, 54:302–4, and Holloway, *Twice-Told Tales*, 8–10 and 359–62.

Bonvesin da la Riva (c. 1240–c. 1314)

Milanese poet and grammar teacher. Bonvesin was a member of the Umiliati, an order that collected taxes in Milan and controlled the communal treasury.

Works include extensive amounts of poetry in both Latin and Italian; several religious and hagiographical tracts; a treatise on table manners, the *De quinque-ginta curialitatibus ad mensam*; and the *De magnalibus Mediolani* (1288), a poem in praise of his native city notable for its precise statistics and details (including Milan's 120 bell towers, 120 lawyers, and 6 communal trumpeters).

Bibliography: Avalle, *DBI*, 12:465–69, and Chiesa's introduction to Bonvesin da la Riva, *De magnalibus Mediolani*.

Brunetto Latini (c. 1220–1293/94)

Florentine notary; friend of Bono Giamboni and mentor of a young Dante Alighieri. After a period of study in Bologna, Brunetto appears in official Florentine documents from 1254. In 1260, he was sent as Florentine ambassador to Alfonso X ("el Sabio") of Castile to request assistance against the Sienese, who were then allied with Frederick II's illegitimate son Manfred. On the return journey, he heard about the Florentine defeat at the Battle of Montaperti and his resultant exile, so he settled in Avignon between 1260 and 1267. On his return to Florence, he became a teacher of grammar and (from 1272) chancellor to the Florentine government. His death is mentioned in an act of December 1293. He appears among the sodomites in Dante's *Inferno* (15.82–87).

Works include Italian translations of a number of Ciceronian orations and the *De inventione*, the encyclopedic *Livres dou Trésor* (in French), and the Italian *Tesoretto*—all completed during his exile. He also wrote a *Favolello* dedicated to Rustico di Filippo, vernacular poetry, and other moral tracts. The vernacular chronicle and translation of Aristotle's *Nicomachean Ethics* often attributed to Brunetto are probably not his.

Bibliography: Inglese, *DBI*, 64:4–12, and Holloway, *Brunetto Latini* and *Twice-Told Tales*.

Ciampolo di Meo degli Ugurgieri (c. 1290–after 1347)

Sienese professor and poet. From a prominent Sienese noble family, Ciampolo first appears in a contract of 1324. By 1347, he was a professor and official of the Sienese studium.

Works include one of the first Italian translations of Virgil's *Aeneid* (c. 1315) and a brief commentary on Dante's *Divina commedia*.

Bibliography: P. Nardi, *Insegnamento superiore a Siena*, and Prunai, "Studio senese dalla 'migratio'."

Cino da Pistoia (c. 1270–1337)

Pistoiese poet and jurist (full name Guittoncino dei Sinibaldi); friend of Dante, Petrarch, and Bosone da Gubbio. Cino studied law at Bologna under Accursius. He was exiled from Pistoia as a Ghibelline in 1307, spending time in France and Rome, where he acted as an official of Henry VII shortly before Henry's death in 1313. After filling several high judicial offices, he became a doctor of civil law at Bologna, and he subsequently taught at Treviso, Siena, Florence, Perugia, and Bologna. The great jurist Bartolus of Sassoferrato and the poet Giovanni Boccaccio were his students. On his death, he was honored with a large monument in the nave of the cathedral in Pistoia.

Works include several famous commentaries on the statutes of Pistoia and the Codex (*Lectura super Codice*), and numerous lyrics and sonnets (*Rime*) in the *dolce stil nuovo*.

Bibliography: Chiappelli, *Vita e opere giuridiche*, and Gagliardi, *Cino da Pistoia*.

Convenevole da Prato (c. 1270–1338)

Teacher of the *trivium* in Pisa and Avignon, originally from Prato. Convenevole's students included the future cardinal Niccolò da Prato and a young Francesco Petrarca. His father and brother were both notaries, and his maternal uncle a noted jurist. On his return to Prato in 1336, he was named "official professor of the commune," but died shortly thereafter. He was buried with much pomp in the crypt of the cathedral in Prato.

Works include no major compositions but numerous small works, such as poems and introductions to longer scholarly works.

Bibliography: Pasquini, *DBI*, 28:563–68, and Giuseppe Billanovich, "Ser Convenevole."

Dante Alighieri (1265–1321)

Florentine poet; student (probably informally) of Brunetto Latini and possibly Remigio de' Girolami, and acquaintance of Cino da Pistoia, Francesco Petrarca, Benzo d'Alessandria, and others. Dante was the renowned author of works in both Italian and Latin. He remained active in politics until his exile from Florence in 1302; thereafter he was peripatetic, often a member of the della Scala court in Verona. He died in Ravenna in 1321.

Two of Dante's sons accompanied him to Verona and settled there: Jacopo (before 1300–1348), a canon of the Veronese cathedral, and Pietro (before 1300–1364), a judge in the employ of Cangrande della Scala. Pietro was a friend of Petrarch, whom he may have met while both men were studying civil law at Bologna sometime around 1327.

Works include the *Divina commedia*, *Vita nuova*, *Monarchia*, *Convivio*, and *De vulgari eloquentia*. As for his sons, along with certain minor works of poetry, both Pietro and Jacopo wrote commentaries on the *Divina commedia*. Jacopo's commentary was one of the earliest, a relatively conventional work, probably written around 1322. Pietro's commentary was written around 1337–40 and shows both a decided command of classical materials and a humanist view of literature.

Bibliography: Chimenz, *DBI*, 2:385–451 (Dante); D'Addario, *DBI*, 2:452–53 (Jacopo); and D'Addario, *DBI*, 2:453–54 (Pietro). Also Jacoff, *Cambridge Companion to Dante*, Caesar, *Dante: The Critical Heritage*, and Pietro Alighieri, *Comentum super poema*.

Dino Compagni (1246/47–1324)

Florentine merchant, political leader, and historian; Manetto Scali was his maternal uncle. Compagni was a consul six times between 1282 and 1299; prior in 1289 and 1301; and gonfalonier of justice in 1293, during which time he supported the popular reforms of Giano della Bella. He narrowly escaped exile with the fall of the White Guelfs in 1302, and died in Florence in 1324.

Works include *Cronica delle cose occorrenti né tempi suoi* (written 1310–12 and covering political events in Florence between 1280 and 1302) and some minor verses.

Bibliography: Arnaldi, *DBI*, 27:629–47, and Bornstein's introduction to Dino Compagni, *Dino Compagni's Chronicle of Florence.*

Duccio di Buoninsegna (1246/47–c. 1319)

Sienese painter; mentor of Pietro and Ambrogio Lorenzetti and Simone Martini. Duccio first appears in 1278, working for the commune of Siena. He spent most of his time there, although he did travel, perhaps even as far as Paris. In 1308, he was commissioned to paint the main altarpiece to the Virgin for the cathedral of Siena; his *Maestà* was finished in 1311 and installed in the cathedral after a lengthy procession and a grand civic festival. Along with his numerous religious works, he painted several official wooden chests and at least one Biccherna (account book) cover for the Sienese commune.

Works include, among many other smaller works, the *Rucellai Madonna* for Santa Maria Novella, Florence (1285); a crucifix for San Francesco, Grosseto (1289); a *Maestà* for the cathedral in Massa Marittima; and the Sienese *Maestà* (1311).

Bibliography: Bologna, *DBI*, 41:742–49, and Satkowski and Maginnis, *Duccio di Buoninsegna.*

Ferreto de' Ferreti (c. 1295–1337)

Notary of Vicenza and official for Cangrande della Scala. His grandfather, father, and brother were also notaries. Ferreto was a student of the Vicentine poet Benvenuto dei Campesani (whose work celebrated the contemporary rediscovery of the works of Catullus) and friend of Albertino Mussato of Padua and Moggio de' Moggi of Parma (tutor to Petrarch's son Giovanni).

Works include the classicizing *De Scaligerorum origine*, written for Cangrande in 1328, along with some minor Latin poetry and a Latin history of Italy.

Bibliography: Bortolami, *DBI*, 47:57–60, and Cipolla, introduction to the *Opere.*

Filippo Ceffi (fl. 1310–30)

Florentine notary. Little is known of his life, but manuscript evidence suggests that his father was also a notary.

Works include the *Dicerie*, a tract on political rhetoric (1324–28), and Italian translations of Ovid's *Heroides* (c. 1320) and Guido delle Colonne's *Historia destructionis Troiae* (c. 1324).

Bibliography: Palma, *DBI*, 23:320; Palma, "Redazione autografo delle *Dicerie*"; and Buonocore, "*Heroides* di Filippo Ceffi."

Francesco Petrarca (1304–1374)

Scholar and poet known in English as Petrarch. He was of Florentine origin but spent most of his life elsewhere. His father, a notary, was exiled from Florence at the same time as Dante in 1302, so Francesco was born in Arezzo. He spent most of his early life in Florence, Pisa, Avignon, and nearby Carpentras, where his father was a notary in the papal court. Although Francesco studied law at Montpellier and Bologna, he gave it up in favor of clerical offices that allowed him to devote more time to his writing. He traveled widely, often as an ambassador, but became best known for his literary works, for which he was crowned poet laureate in Rome in 1341 by Charles of Anjou. He expended much effort collecting, copying, and collating rare manuscripts, especially of classical texts, and often corresponded with Guglielmo da Pastrengo of Verona, Giovanni Boccaccio, and others on the subject. By his death in 1374 (at Arquà, near Padua), he had amassed a large and valuable library, which he attempted without success to bequeath to the city of Venice.

Works include, in Italian, the *Trionfi* and numerous revisions of his Italian poetry (*Rime disperse*, or *Canzoniere*); in Latin, the epic *Africa*, the unfinished *De viris illustribus*, the Augustinian dialogue *Secretum*, and numerous moral treatises. He also left several books of correspondence, including famous letters to classical figures such as Cicero and Livy.

Bibliography: Mazzotta, *Worlds of Petrarch*; Dotti, *Vita di Petrarca*; and Stierle, *Francesco Petrarca*.

Galvano Fiamma (1283–after 1344)

Milanese Dominican from a family of notaries. Galvano entered the Dominican convent of Sant'Eustorgio (site of an active studium) in 1298. He taught in Pavia between 1308 and 1313 but spent most of his life in Milan. He was appointed as clerk to the archbishop of Milan (Giovanni Visconti) in 1339, which gave him access to the large Visconti library. He used the library to compile a series of chronicles with strong Milanese, Dominican, and Viscontean biases; these often consist of entire works strung together so that they advance Galvano's particular agenda, an activity for which historian J. K. Hyde dismissed him as a "nasty plagiarist" ("Medieval Descriptions of Cities," 336).

Works include *Chronica parva* (1333), *Manipulus florum* (1335), *Chronica Galvagnana* (1337?), *Chronica maior Ordinis Predicatorum* (1344), *Chronica extravagans, Chronicon maius/maior, Politia novella,* and *Chronica pontificum Mediolanensium.*

Bibliography: Tomea, *DBI,* 47:331–38, and "Per Galvano Fiamma"; and Ferrai, "Cronache di Galvano Fiamma."

Geremia (Hieremias) da Montagnone (c. 1250–1321)

Paduan judge; friend and colleague of Lovato Lovati, Albertino Mussato, and Rolando da Piazzola.

Works include *Compendium moralium notabilium* (1295–1300), a didactic florilegium or collection of moral quotations, many of them from classical sources such as Catullus, Martial, Horace, Seneca, Virgil, and Ovid.

Bibliography: Milan, *DBI,* 53:400–403; Folena, *Storia della cultura veneta,* 31–32; and Ullman, "Hieremias de Montagnone."

Giotto di Bondone (c. 1266–1337)

Florentine painter and architect, born in the village of Vespignano, near Florence; student of the painter Cimabue. Throughout his prominent career he worked not only in Florence but also in Padua, Rome, Naples, and possibly Assisi. In 1334, the city of Florence honored Giotto with the title of *magnus magister* (great master) and appointed him city architect and superintendent of public works; in this capacity he designed the famous campanile of the cathedral. He died in 1337, before the work was finished.

Works include, in Padua, the frescoes in both the Arena Chapel and the Palazzo della Ragione in Padua (1303–6); in Rome, the *Navicella* mosaic (1305–13) and *Stefaneschi Altarpiece* (c. 1330); in Naples, several works (no longer extant) for Robert of Anjou; in Florence, a large crucifix for Santa Maria Novella (1290–1300), the *Ognissanti Madonna* (c. 1310), the Bardi and Peruzzi chapels in Santa Croce (1320–25), and the *Baroncelli Polyptych* (c. 1334). His authorship of the Saint Francis cycle (1290s) in the upper church of San Francesco in Assisi—and much else—is disputed.

Bibliography: Boskovits, *DBI,* 55:401–23, and Derbes and Sandona, *Cambridge Companion to Giotto.*

Giovanni Balbi (d. c. 1298)

Genoese grammarian and Dominican. Little is known of him, but he appears to have become a Dominican at a relatively advanced age. According to a local legend, he upset his family by giving all of his wealth away before he entered the order.

Works include a grammatical treatise and encyclopedic work, *Summa prosodiae*, better known as the *Catholicon* (1286), and two minor theological tracts.

Bibliography: Pratesi, *DBI*, 5:369–70.

Giovanni Boccaccio (1313–1375)

Florentine writer and poet; friend of Petrarch. Giovanni grew up in Florence, where his father worked for the Bardi bank; they moved to Naples when his father was appointed to head the bank's Neapolitan branch. Giovanni was apprenticed to the bank but eventually persuaded his father to let him study law at the Naples studium. He spent much of his later life in Florence, Certaldo, and Ravenna; he was often called on as a citizen ambassador, spent many letters and long hours discussing literature and manuscripts with Petrarch, and advocated for the study of Greek in Florence. He may have taken minor orders in 1359.

Works include, in Italian, *Filocolo, Teseida, Filostrato, Ninfale fiesolano*, the *Decameron*, assorted poetry (*Rime*), the *Vita di Dante*, and a commentary on the *Divina commedia*; in Latin, *De casibus virorum illustrium* (1355–74), *Genealogia deorum gentilium* (1360), and *De mulieribus claris* (1361–75). He also left several *zibaldoni* of notes and recollections.

Bibliography: Sapegno, *DBI*, 10:838–56; Consoli, *Giovanni Boccaccio*; and Zaccaria, *Boccaccio*.

Giovanni da Nono (c. 1276–1346)

Paduan judge from a prominent local family. He entered the Paduan college of judges in 1306 and served on the tribunals of the commune from 1310 until his death in 1346.

Works include a tripartite historical work, the *De ludi fortunae* (early 1320s), which comprises the *De aedificatione urbis Patavie*, the *Visio Egidii regis Patavie*, and the *Liber de generatione aliquorum civium urbis Padue*.

Bibliography: Zabbia, *DBI*, 56:114–17, and Fabris's introduction to Giovanni da Nono, *Liber de ludi fortunae*.

Giovanni Pisano (c. 1250–1314)

Sculptor and architect, possibly from an Apulian family but largely peripatetic; son of the sculptor Nicola Pisano and colleague of Arnolfo di Cambio (who also studied with Nicola), Duccio di Buoninsegna, the Lorenzetti brothers, and Simone Martini. Giovanni trained in his father's workshop, and they worked together on the pulpit in the Siena cathedral (1265–68) and the Fontana Maggiore in Perugia (1275–78); he then worked mostly in Pisa and Siena. He was eventually granted Sienese citizenship and immunity from taxation for his work as *capomaestro* (chief architect) on the cathedral there.

Works include architectural design for the exterior of the baptistery in Pisa (1277–84), sculptures and architectural design for the facade of the cathedral in Siena (1284–98), the pulpit for the church of Sant'Andrea in Pistoia (1297–1301), the cathedral pulpit in Pisa (1302–11), the tomb of Margaret of Luxembourg (wife of Henry VII) in Genoa (1313), and various Madonnas for churches in Padua and Prato.

Bibliography: Carli, *Giovanni Pisano*, and Moskowitz, *Italian Gothic Sculpture*, 21–93.

Giovanni Villani (c. 1276–1348)

Florentine merchant, public servant, and historian from a prominent local family. Giovanni was a partner in the Peruzzi company between 1300 and 1309, making trips to Rome (1301) and Siena (1309), and staying for an extended time in Bruges (1302–7). He was one of two general directors of the Bonaccorsi company between 1310 and 1342. From 1316 on, Giovanni played an active role in Florentine public life, holding the office of prior three times; he was also one of eight *sapientes* who directed Florence's war with Lucca in 1323. He was superintendent of the mint in 1316 and 1327, as well as one of several officials in charge of food rationing during the famine of 1328. Giovanni was jailed briefly in 1345 as a result of the failure of the Bonaccorsi and Bardi banks, and he died in 1348, probably of plague.

Works include the famous *Nuova cronica*, which he probably began around 1315 after being inspired by his pilgrimage to Rome during the Jubilee of 1300. After his death in 1348, the work was continued by two relatives in succession (his son Matteo and nephew Filippo).

Bibliography: C. Frugoni, *Villani illustrato*; Porta's introduction to Giovanni Villani, *Nuova cronica*; and Clarke, "Villani Chronicles."

Guglielmo da Pastrengo (c. 1290–1362)

Veronese jurist employed by the della Scala court; friend of Petrarch, Benzo d'Alessandria, and others in the Veronese and Paduan humanist circles. After studying at Bologna, he had settled in Verona by 1323. In 1324–25, he served as judge and vicar for Cangrande della Scala in Vicenza, and by 1337, he was a judge of the Veronese commune. Guglielmo later became chancellor to Mastino II della Scala and frequently traveled on diplomatic missions for Mastino and his brother Alberto. He first met Petrarch at Avignon in 1339; the two corresponded frequently thereafter, especially on matters concerning the discovery and copying of classical texts.

Works include two encyclopedic works, *De originibus rerum* and *De viris illustribus*, the latter of which was more comprehensive and less narrative than the *De viris* by his friend Petrarch. One section of the *De originibus* is dedicated to the origins of cities.

Bibliography: Cerroni, *DBI*, 61:17–22; Folena, *Storia della cultura veneta*, 2:126–29; and Bottari's introduction to Guglielmo da Pastrengo, *De viris illustribus*.

Guido da Pisa (c. 1290–c. 1340)

Pisan Carmelite. Little is known of his life, but the evidence of his works (as, for example, the dedication of his commentary on Dante) suggests that he probably spent time in at least Rome and Genoa.

Works include *Fiore d'Italia*, a wide-ranging vernacular history in seven books, of which the entirety is unpublished. The second book, however, is a loosely paraphrased translation of the *Aeneid* and was often disseminated independently (and has since been published) as the *Fatti d'Enea*. Guido also wrote an *Expositiones et glose super Comediam Dantis* dedicated to the Genoese aristocrat Luciano Spinola (fl. 1323–47).

Bibliography: Terzi, *DBI*, 61:411–17; and Canal, *Mondo morale* and "Venti anni di studi."

Guido delle Colonne (c. 1215–c. 1290)

Sicilian, probably Messinese, judge; associated with the Sicilian School of vernacular poetry and the courts of Frederick II and his son Manfred. Dante praises Guido's work in the *De vulgari eloquentia*. His *Historia destructionis Troiae* (c. 1287), a Latin prose adaptation of Benoît de Sainte-Maure's *Roman de Troie* was immensely popular in late medieval Italy and survives in numerous manuscripts, in several Italian translations as well as its original Latin.

Works include several histories, including the *Historia destructionis Troiae*, as well as a small amount of vernacular poetry.

Bibliography: Beretta Spampinato, *DBI*, 38:32–36; Antonelli, di Girolamo, and Coluccia, *Poeti della scuola siciliana*; and Griffin's introduction to Guido delle Colonne, *Historia*.

Guidotto da Bologna (*fl. 1255–80*)

Friar of uncertain affiliation or origin. He may have taught rhetoric in Siena in the late 1270s and early 1280s. Guidotto's name is affiliated with one of four recensions of the *Fiore di rettorica*, a loose translation of the pseudo-Ciceronian *Rhetorica ad Herennium*; the version attributed to Guidotto is dedicated to Frederick II's son Manfred.

Bibliography: Gentili, *DBI*, 61:466–70, and Bruni, "Documenti senesi per fra Guidotto da Bologna."

Guittone d'Arezzo (*c. 1235–1294*)

Poet of Arezzo, where his father was a communal official. Guittone was exiled from Arezzo for his Guelf sympathies in 1256. He took orders after a midlife religious conversion and died in Florence in 1294.

Works include poetry in the *dolce stil nuovo*, a style of Tuscan poetry that Guittone helped initiate, inspired by that of the Sicilian School. He became known as a secular poet but wrote chiefly religious poetry after his conversion.

Bibliography: Cerroni, *DBI*, 61:545–51; Picone, *Guittone d'Arezzo*; and Borra, *Guittone d'Arezzo*.

Jacopo da Varagine (*c. 1230–1298*)

Genoese Dominican, archbishop, and historian. Jacopo joined the Dominican order in 1244 and became famous as a preacher and professor. He was provincial of Lombardy from 1267 to 1286, attending chapter meetings at Lucca in 1288 and another at Ferrara in 1290. Jacopo was proposed as archbishop in 1286, but he refused to take the position and Obizzo Fieschi was elected instead. In 1288, Pope Nicholas IV (r. 1288–92) commissioned him to free the Genoese from the interdict they had incurred for assisting the Sicilians in their 1282 revolt against the King of Naples. When Fieschi died in 1292, Jacopo was elected to succeed him. He spent his tenure trying to restore peace between different factions in Genoa, on the whole unsuccessfully.

Works include the famous *Legenda aurea* (sometimes called the *Legenda sanctorum*), a collection of saints' lives; the *Chronicon Januense* (or *Cronaca della città di Genova*), a Latin history of the city; a collection of over three hundred sermons; and several moral and theological tracts.

Bibliography: Casagrande, *DBI*, 62:92–102; Monleone's introduction to Jacopo Varagine, *Chronicon Januense*, 1:1–196; Airaldi, *Jacopo da Varagine*; and Bertini Guidetti, *Paradiso e la terra*.

Jacopo Doria (1234–c. 1294)

Genoese historian, diplomat, and archivist from a prominent family. His brothers Oberto and Lamba played major roles in the Genoese government and military, but Jacopo seems to have preferred research and administration to a position in the public eye. He was a historian and archivist for the Genoese commune, appointed to continue the official chronicle begun by Caffaro in 1199; he presented his portion of the chronicle (covering 1280–93) to the commune in 1294, shortly before his death. He represented the commune on at least two ambassadorial missions, in 1256 and 1271, and at least once held the office of *anziano*, or council member, in the Genoese government.

Works include *Annales Januenses*, the official chronicle of Genoa for 1280–93.

Bibliography: Nuti, *DBI*, 41:391–96, and Imperiale di Sant'Angelo, *Jacopo d'Oria*.

Lovato Lovati (1241–1309)

Paduan judge; uncle to Rolando da Piazzola and friend of Albertino Mussato, Geremia da Montagnone, and other early humanists. Lovato was the son of a notary. He began his legal career as early as 1257 and joined the Paduan college of judges in 1267. He held a number of communal appointments, including that of podestà of Vicenza in 1291–92. Lovato was the central figure of the humanist movement in Padua and oversaw the construction of the new tomb of Antenor in 1283–84. He also expended much effort searching out copies of classical texts from the ancient libraries around Padua—for example, at the abbey of Pomposa and in the capitular library in Verona.

Works include a collection of poems in classicizing style, chiefly on the model of Seneca.

Bibliography: Kohl, *DBI*, 66:215–20; Weiss, "Lovato Lovati"; and Witt, *Footsteps of the Ancients*, 81–116.

Marsilius of Padua (c. 1275–1342)

Paduan political theorist (full name Marsiglio de' Mainardini). He was the son of a Paduan notary and probably attended university at Padua before going on to a notorious career at the University of Paris (of which he was a rector in 1313), where he was associated with Pietro d'Abano and leading Averroists of the time. Marsilius is best known as the author of the *Defensor pacis*, a treatise arguing for the exclusion of the church from politics, published in 1324 during a particularly vicious struggle between Pope John XXII and Ludwig of Bavaria (later Emperor Ludwig IV); unsurprisingly, John XXII condemned the work in 1326. Marsilius spent the rest of his life under Ludwig's protection, accompanying him to Italy in 1327–28 and then settling in Nuremberg.

Works include *Defensor pacis* (1324); *Defensor minor* (1342), a condensation and restatement of Marsilius's chief arguments in the *Defensor pacis*; and the *De translatione imperii* (c. 1342), an adaptation of an earlier work by Landolfo Colonna.

Bibliography: Dolcini and Lambertini, *DBI*, 67:569–76, and Moreno-Riaño, *World of Marsilius of Padua*.

Matteo da Correggio (c. 1225–after 1288)

Lawyer and podestà, born near Parma to a political family. Matteo's father was podestà of Genoa in 1250, and Matteo himself served as podestà in Piacenza (1250); Gubbio (1252); Jesi (1255); Florence (1257); Padua (1258–59, 1263–64, 1269, and 1280); Bologna (1261 and 1282); Treviso (subject to Paduan control, 1265–66); Mantua (1269–72 with his brother Guido, and 1274); Cremona (1271–72); Perugia (1278); Modena (1283); Pistoia (1286); and Parma (1288). He was commended by the chronicler Rolandino of Padua for having organized Padua's rout of the forces of Ezzelino da Romano while podestà in 1258–59. He also oversaw the completion of the Fontana Maggiore while podestà of Perugia in 1278 and appears as one of the sculpted figures decorating the fountain. Matteo should not be confused with his three contemporaries by the same name and with similar careers, two of whom were his relatives.

No works by him are known.

Bibliography: Montecchi, *DBI*, 29:462–64.

Matteo dei Libri (1214–1275)

Bolognese notary active in his profession from 1232 until about 1265.

Works include four manuals on the *ars dictaminis*, three in Latin and one in the vernacular. He is most famous for the last, the *Arringhe* (c. 1250), a podestarial advice manual much like Filippo Ceffi's *Dicerie*.

Bibliography: Tamba, *DBI*, 65:64–65, and Kristeller, "Matteo de' Libri."

Niccolò da Prato (c. 1250–1321)

Pratese Dominican and cardinal (full name Niccolò Albertini). He entered the order in 1266, where he studied with Convenevole da Prato at Santa Maria Novella in Florence; he then continued his studies in Paris and Rome. He was named Dominican procurator at the papal court in 1296, and provincial general in 1297. Boniface VIII named him bishop of Spoleto in 1299, and Benedict XI named him cardinal bishop of Ostia in 1303. In these capacities, Niccolò frequently acted as papal legate on diplomatic missions to France and various Italian city-states. He was a great patron of the arts; he commissioned Giovanni Pisano to create both Benedict XI's tomb in the Dominican church in Perugia and certain decorations in the Dominican church in Prato. In Avignon, he was a patron of the Petrarca family, Simone d'Arezzo, Nicholas Trevet, and others. He commissioned Nicholas Trevet's commentary on the tragedies of Seneca; Giuseppe Billanovich has postulated that he became interested in Seneca after meeting Albertino Mussato and Rolando da Piazzola at the court of Henry VII in Italy. Niccolò acted as dean and vote counter for the conclave that elected John XXII in Avignon in 1316. He died there in 1321 and was buried in the local Dominican church, which he had earlier had restored; Simone d'Arezzo executed his will.

Works include two treatises, *De Paradiso* and *De pontificalium comitiorum habendorum ratione* (both now lost).

Bibliography: Redigonda, *DBI*, 1:734–36; R. Dean, "Cultural Relations in the Middle Ages"; and Giuseppe Billanovich, "Tra Dante e Petrarca," 8–10.

Nicholas Trevet (c. 1258–c. 1334)

English Dominican. Nicholas was the son of a judge, who studied at Oxford and Paris, taught at Oxford, and was prior of his order in London. He also appears to have spent some time in Avignon and Italy, where he was affiliated with the school of Santa Maria Novella in Florence. While there, he probably wrote his commentary on Boethius, which he dedicated to a former teacher of his in Pisa. Cardinal Niccolò da Prato, whom he probably met in Avignon, commissioned his commentary on Seneca's tragedies.

Works include the earliest known medieval commentary on Livy, as well as commentaries on Cicero (now lost), Juvenal, Boethius, the tragedies of Seneca, Aristotle, and several books of the Old Testament. He wrote independent works on astronomy, theology, and history.

Bibliography: R. Dean, "Cultural Relations in the Middle Ages" and "Dedication of Nicholas Trevet's Commentary"; Ziolkowski and Putnam, *Virgilian Tradition*, 750–53.

Nicola Pisano (c. 1220–c. 1284)

Sculptor, probably from a Puglian family; father of Giovanni Pisano. Giovanni, Arnolfo di Cambio, and several others trained in his workshop. Nicola led the late medieval Italian trend of using classical styles for medieval purposes; for example, he based his sculpture of Fortitude on a classical naked Hercules. Arnolfo and Giovanni both adopted this practice in their own works.

Works include the baptistery pulpit in Pisa (1255–59), the cathedral pulpit in Siena (1265–68), the tomb of Saint Dominic in Bologna (1265–71, with Arnolfo di Cambio), and the Fontana Maggiore in Perugia (1271–78, with his son Giovanni).

Bibliography: Moskowitz, *Nicola and Giovanni Pisano* and *Nicola Pisano's Arca di San Domenico*, and White, "Nicola Pisano's Perugia Fountain."

Pace da Ferrara (fl. 1300)

Professor of grammar and logic at Padua, originally from Ferrara (formerly and incorrectly called Pace dal Friuli); colleague of Pietro d'Abano and friend of Albertino Mussato.

Works include a poem in praise of Venice dedicated to Doge Pietro Gradenigo, *Descriptio festi gloriosissime Virginis Marie* (c. 1300), and another (c. 1302–4) in praise of Pagano della Torre, who had been appointed bishop of Padua in 1302 (Pagano was also the dedicatee of Albertino Mussato's *De gestis italicorum*). Pace also wrote both a commentary on Geoffrey of Vinsauf's *Poetria nova* and the *Evidentia Ecerinidis* (1316–17), a short grammatical preface to Mussato's *Ecerinis*.

Bibliography: Stadter, "Planudes, Plutarch, and Pace da Ferrara," and Cicogna's introduction to Pace da Ferrara, *Festa delle Marie*.

Pietro Lorenzetti (c. 1280–1348)

Florentine painter; elder brother of the painter Ambrogio Lorenzetti and colleague of Simone Martini. Pietro was the more peripatetic of the Lorenzetti brothers, executing commissions across Tuscany and Umbria. He and his brother Ambrogio probably died in the 1348 plague.

Works include the *Tarlati Polyptych* (Santa Maria della Pieve, Arezzo, 1320), an altarpiece for the Carmelite church in Siena (1329), scenes from the life of Christ in the lower church of San Francesco in Assisi (1315–30), and a *Birth of the Virgin* for the Sienese cathedral (1342).

Bibliography: Becchis, *DBI*, 65:803–11, and Frugoni, Donato, and Monciatti, *Pietro and Ambrogio Lorenzetti*.

Ptolemy of Lucca (c. 1236–c. 1327)

Dominican (full name Bartolomeo Fiadoni) from a prominent Lucchese family; student of Thomas Aquinas and colleague of Remigio de' Girolami and others. Ptolemy studied under Aquinas in Paris (1261–68) and later traveled with him in Italy. He occupied a number of prominent posts in the Dominican order, including prior of San Romano in Lucca in 1288 and of Santa Maria Novella in Florence in 1301, and spent most of the first two decades of the fourteenth century at the papal court in Avignon. John XXII appointed him bishop of Torcello, near Venice; after a dispute with the patriarch of Grado, during which he was briefly imprisoned, he died in Torcello at about age ninety. Ptolemy was a civic and ecclesiastical historian as well as a political theorist; the principles and examples in his work were echoed by both Remigio de' Girolami and Dante.

Works include the *Annales*; *Historia ecclesiastica*; a commentary on Genesis; *Determinatio compendiosa de juribus imperii*, a treatise on the Roman Empire; and his most famous work, the *De regimine principum* (c. 1301), a continuation of Aquinas's work by the same name.

Bibliography: Blythe's introduction to Ptolemy of Lucca, *De regimine*; Davis, "Ptolemy of Lucca and the Roman Republic" and "Roman Patriotism and Republican Propaganda"; and Nederman and Sullivan, "Reading Aristotle Through Rome."

Ranieri Granchi (fl. 1300–1342)

Pisan Dominican. His grandfather was a banker and merchant in Pisa, and his father a communal administrator. His relatives Giovanni (possibly a brother) and Andrea di Marco (possibly a cousin) served the Pisan commune as *anziani*. Ranieri became a Dominican sometime before 1326; he was twice the regional head of the Dominican order in Pisa and appears often as a witness for deeds drawn up at the monastery of Santa Caterina in Pisa. Nonetheless, he was well traveled, having studied and/or taught at the Dominican convents in Arezzo, San Gimignano, San Miniato (Florence), Perugia, Lucca, and Pisa.

Works include the classicizing historical poem *De proeliis Tusciae*.
Bibliography: Ronzani, *DBI*, 58:450–52.

Remigio de' Girolami (d. 1319)

Florentine Dominican from a family active in the Florentine wool guild; colleague of Ptolemy of Lucca. He studied several times in Paris, including under Thomas Aquinas in 1269–72, and then spent over forty years teaching theology in the school of Santa Maria Novella. He also taught in Perugia and visited Rome to petition for the granting of a studium generale to Florence. He was a well-known preacher and teacher, author of numerous moral and civic treatises, and may have been a mentor to the young Dante Alighieri.

Works include several treatises applying Aristotelian political theory to the problems of the medieval city-state, including *De bono communi* and *De bono pacis*; the treatise *Contra falsos ecclesie professores*; numerous sermons; and a commentary on the Song of Songs.

Bibliography: Gentili, *DBI*, 56:531–41; Davis, "Early Florentine Political Theorist" and "Remigio de' Girolami"; and Panella, "Nuova cronologia Remigiana."

Riccobaldo da Ferrara (c. 1245–1318)

Ferrarese notary and professor. Riccobaldo began his career as a notary in Ferrara for Obizzo II d'Este between about 1275 and 1290. He left Ferrara, probably as an exile, and was teaching in Padua about 1293–95. He is next found practicing as a notary in Ravenna in 1297, remaining there until about 1302 and then returning to the university in Padua for 1303–9. After visits to Verona and Rome, Riccobaldo returned to Ferrara between 1309 and 1313. He died around 1318, probably in Verona.

Works include numerous classicizing compilations of history: *Pomerium Ravennatis* (1297–1300), a continuation of Jerome's continuation of Eusebius's universal history; *Historie* (1305–8); and *Compendium Romanae historiae* (finished 1313). Other works are *De septem etatibus*, *Chronica parva Ferrariensis*, *Chronica extracta*, and *Compilatio chronologica*. The last of these includes an appendix of city foundations in Italy.

Bibliography: Berrigan, "Riccobaldo and Giovanni Mansionario"; Hankey, *Riccobaldo of Ferrara*; and Zanella, *Riccobaldo e dintorni*.

Rolandino of Padua (1200–1276)

Paduan notary. Rolandino was the son of a Paduan notary and studied at Bologna under Boncompagno da Signa. On his return to Padua, he combined notarial practice with teaching in the city's new university (established in 1222). His chronicle, the *Liber chronicarum*, is a history celebrating the 1256 overthrow of the da Romano signoria in Padua; it was formally read before, and approved by, the commune and university masters in 1262, and was considered a kind of "official" chronicle of the independent commune.

Works include *Liber chronicarum*, familiarly known as the *Rolandina* (c. 1260–62); it later served as inspiration for Albertino Mussato's *Ecerinis*.

Bibliography: Arnaldi, *Rolandino di Padova*, and Andrews, "Albertano of Brescia."

Rolandino Passaggeri *(c. 1215–c. 1300)*

Bolognese notary. Rolandino was the son of an innkeeper and tax collector. He joined the Bolognese guild of notaries in 1234 and had become a communal notary by 1238. He acted as notary of the bankers' guild between 1245 and 1262. From about 1270, he became increasingly involved in Bolognese politics; by 1278, he had formed, and was in charge of, the pro-*popolo* Company of the Cross, a confraternity/civic militia. After the company prevented a pro-magnate coup, Rolandino was elected a rector of the commune in 1279, and he helped revise the communal statutes in 1284. He also taught the notarial arts from about 1284. Upon his death, he was buried in a large tomb just outside the church of San Domenico in Bologna.

Works include his most famous text, *Summa totius artis notarie* (1255–56), and an important legal treatise on wills and inheritance, *Flos ultimatum voluntatum*.

Bibliography: Palmieri, *Rolandino Passaggeri*, and Tamba, *Rolandino e l'ars notaria*.

Rolando da Piazzola *(c. 1260–c. 1330)*

Paduan judge; nephew of Lovato Lovati and friend of Albertino Mussato. Rolando was deeply involved in Paduan politics of the late republican period, holding judgeships and other official posts; he served as Paduan ambassador to Rome in 1303 and suggested that the commune offer Mussato the laurel crown. He served as vicar to the podestà of Bologna in 1322. Rolando joined Lovati and Mussato in searching for and imitating ancient texts; his copy of Seneca's tragedies (now Vatican City, Biblioteca Apostolica Vaticana, MS Vat. Lat. 1769) is one of the most important witnesses to the text and bears inscriptions by all three humanists. He retired from public life in 1323 and died sometime between 1324 and 1333. He is buried in a classicizing tomb just outside the basilica of San Antonio in Padua.

Works include a short treatise, *De regibus*; numerous other works have been attributed to him, but most have been discredited.

Bibliography: Girardi, *Rolando da Piazzola*; Prosdocimi, "Arca di Rolando di Piazzola"; and Guido Billanovich, "Cicerone di Rolando."

Simone d'Arezzo *(c. 1280–1338)*

Notary, originally from Arezzo. Before 1316, he was connected with the papal court in Avignon, probably as a clerk in the household of Cardinal Niccolò da

Prato, whose will he executed in Avignon in 1321. (On Cardinal Niccolò, see also Nicholas Trevet.) He was named a canon of the cathedral in Verona in 1316, a post that he held until his death in 1338; the canonry was probably little more than a source of income, since Simone appears to have traveled regularly back and forth between Verona and Avignon. It has been surmised that he made the acquaintance of Niccolò da Prato originally through Petrarch's father, Ser Petracco, who moved his family from Arezzo to Avignon in 1313 and knew Niccolò quite well. At his death in 1338, Simone bequeathed his books (including copies of Nicholas Trevet's five commentaries) to the Dominican and Franciscan friars of his hometown of Arezzo. That he owned Trevet's works suggests that Simon inherited some of Cardinal Niccolò's books, perhaps in payment for his notarial services.

No works by him are known.

Bibliography: R. Dean, "Cultural Relations in the Middle Ages"; Muttoni, "Simone d'Arezzo"; Giuseppe Billanovich, "Dal Livio di Raterio," 136–50; and Pasqui, "Biblioteca d'un notaro aretino."

Simone Martini (c. 1280–1344)

Sienese painter; a student of Duccio and colleague of the Lorenzetti brothers and Giovanni Pisano. His first major work was the large fresco of the *Maestà* (1315–21) commissioned by the commune of Siena as a counterpart to the altarpiece by Duccio recently installed in the cathedral. He traveled extensively thereafter, working in Naples, Pisa, and Assisi; in 1340, he made a trip to the curia at Avignon, seemingly on church business rather than as a painter. In Avignon he met Petrarch and illustrated his Virgil. He died in 1344.

Works include the *Maestà* for the Palazzo Pubblico in Siena (1315–21); *St. Louis of Toulouse Altarpiece*, for Robert of Anjou in Naples (1317); a fresco of Guidoriccio da Fogliano, again in the Palazzo Pubblico in Siena (1328–33); the *Cycle of St. Martin of Tours* in the lower church of San Francesco in Assisi; the *Uffizi Annunciation* (1333, with his brother-in-law Lippo Memmi). In Avignon, he completed *Christ Returning to His Parents* (1342); Petrarch's Virgil illustration; and frescoes for both Notre-Dame des Doms and the Palais des Papes.

Bibliography: Becchis, *DBI*, 71:254–61; Hoch, "Antique Origins of an Emperor"; and Leone de Castris, *Simone Martini*.

Notes

Abbreviations

AP1 *Annales Patavini* (First Redaction). Edited by Antonio Bonardi. Rerum italicarum scriptores, n.s., 8.1. Città di Castello: Zanichelli, 1905.

AP2 *Annales Patavini* (Second Redaction). Edited by Antonio Bonardi. Rerum italicarum scriptores, n.s., 8.1. Città di Castello: Zanichelli, 1905.

CIL *Corpus inscriptionum Latinarum.* 17 vols. Berlin: Akademie der Wissenschaften, 1862–.

CPP *Chronicon de potestatibus Paduae.* Edited by Sante Bortolami, as "Per la storia della storiografia comunale: Il *Chronicon de Potestatibus Paduae.*" *Archivio Veneto* 105 (1975): 69–121.

CTC Brown, Virginia, and Paul Oskar Kristeller, eds. *Catalogus translationum et commentariorum: Mediaeval and Renaissance Latin Translations and Commentaries: Annotated Lists and Guides.* 8 vols. Washington, D.C.: Catholic University of America Press, 1960–.

DBI *Dizionario biografico degli Italiani.* Edited by Alberto Maria Ghisalberti. 72 vols. Rome: Istituto della Enciclopedia italiana, 1960–.

LRP *Liber regiminum Padue.* Edited by Antonio Bonardi. Rerum italicarum scriptores, n.s., 8.1. Città di Castello: Zanichelli, 1905.

Introduction

The epigraph is drawn from Petrarch, *Invectiva contra eum qui maledixit Italie* 60, in *Invectives*, 416. "Quid est enim aliud omnis historia quam Romana laus?"

1. "Magnifici et potentes domini honorandi. Per Nannem Matthei Lapetti terrigenam nostram mittimus Magnificentie Vestre, quam semper amavimus, quendam lupum. Et quamvis hoc animal ex sui natura ferox et immane sit, nichilominus lupus iste plusquam catulus mansuetus et domesticus est. Nam ipsum ab uberibus matris abstractum, nostri filii nutriverunt. Ad honores et beneplacita vestra parati. Datum in terra Montis lupi. Dis vij Maij, xv Indictione Mccccxxij. Servitores vestri Consilium et terre Montis lupi / Comune comitatus Florentie." Lisini, "Lupa," 28.

2. Hahn, *Tower Menagerie*, 23–28. See Matthew Paris, *Chronica maiora* for 1241 (Cambridge, Corpus Christi College, MS 16 II, fol. 152v) and 1255 (MS 16 I, fol. iir/ivr; other versions are London, British Library, Cotton MS Nero D.1, fol. 169v, and Cotton MS Julius D.VII, fol. 114). Paris's drawings in the Corpus Christi manuscript are reproduced in de Hamel, *Parker Library*, 74–75.

3. Pluskowski, *Wolves and Wilderness*; Algazi, Groebner, and Jussen, *Negotiating the Gift.*

4. Rondoni, *Tradizioni popolari e leggende*, 28.

5. Chapter 4 of this study discusses Siena and its foundation legend in detail.

6. On Reims, see Wiseman, *Remus: A Roman Myth*, 150, and Flodoard of Reims, *Historia Remensis ecclesiae*, 62–63. On the two forged charters of the University of Bologna (both purporting to have been issued by Theodosius II in 433, but actually dating to the early thirteenth century), see Rashdall, *Universities of Europe*, 1:142–43. For Henry II and the British Trojan legend, see Wace, *Roman de Brut*, 2–33.

7. Graf, *Roma nella memoria e nelle immaginazioni*, 18–23. Along with Wace on London's Roman myth, see his source, Geoffrey of Monmouth, *History of the Kings of Britain*, 53–74, as well as William Fitzstephen, *Norman London*, 55. On Paris's Roman myth, see Levine's translation of the *Grandes chroniques de France* in *France Before Charlemagne*, 12–16, as well as Beaune, *Birth of an Ideology*, as cited in note 32 below. On Cologne, see *Anno-Lied*, 10.

8. See the works cited in note 42 below.

9. For an overview of this period in medieval Italian history, see Hyde, *Society and Politics in Medieval Italy*; Larner, *Italy in the Age of Dante and Petrarch*; Bordone, *Società urbana*; Waley, *Italian City-Republics*; or Ascheri, *Città-stato*.

10. On the early communes, see Jones, *Italian City-State*, 130–51.

11. Nicholas, *Growth of the Medieval City*, 41–50, and Lilley, *Urban Life*, 44–54.

12. France and England, for example, had strong monarchies that supported urban development while extending royal authority within their realms; cf. S. Reynolds, *English Medieval Towns*, esp. chapters 2, 6, and 8.

13. The traditional designations of Guelf and Ghibelline, which date from the thirteenth century, refer to the political opposition of pope and emperor, respectively, on the Italian peninsula. A city (or a specific faction within it) could be Guelf or Ghibelline depending on which overlord it supported, but these alliances were more often based on immediate and local political expediency than any broader sense of loyalty; see the discussion in Waley, *Italian City-Republics*, 200–218.

14. Following the practice of recent scholars, I use the term "republic" in this book to refer to polities that conceived of themselves as such. Degrees of popular representation varied widely from city to city. I consider the implications of popular participation in government in chapter 6, but see also the discussions in Witt, "Republican Liberty"; Mundy, "In Praise of Italy"; Jones, *Italian City-State*; and Maire Vigueur, *Cavaliers et citoyens*.

15. Cammarosano, *Italia medievale*, 39–111, and Petrucci, *Medioevo da leggere*.

16. See, for example, Gehl, *Moral Art*; Petrucci, "Reading and Writing *Volgare*"; Witt, "What Did Giovannino Read and Write?"; and Steinberg, *Accounting for Dante*. On the concept of pragmatic literacy generally, see Britnell, *Pragmatic Literacy*.

17. Generally, Witt, "Origins of Humanism," and Albini, *Scritture del comune*. Studies dealing with specific cities are Costamagna, *Notaio a Genova*, and, on Bologna, Giansante, *Retorica e politica nel Duecento*, and Tamba, *Rolandino e l'ars notaria*.

18. Gehl, *Moral Art*, 16, and Martines, *Power and Imagination*, 64.

19. I use "Renaissance" here in the traditional sense, to mean the intellectual and artistic movement of fifteenth- and sixteenth-century Italy that was largely based on classical models; see Burke, *Italian Renaissance*, 8–10 and 27–39, as well as Burckhardt, *Civilization of the Renaissance in Italy*. Kohl and Smith, *Major Problems*, document some of the major recent debates on the concept and characterizations of the Italian Renaissance.

20. Weiss, *Renaissance Discovery*, and Sabbadini, *Scoperte dei codici latini e greci*; more recently, Alessio and Villa, "Nuovo fascino degli autori antichi."

21. Benzo d'Alessandria discusses the Veronese amphitheatre in the universal chronicle he wrote in Milan around 1316; see Berrigan, "Benzo d'Alessandria," 178–79. On the Regisol, see Sòriga, "Statua del 'Regisole.'"

22. See the biographies of Petrarch by de Nolhac, *Petrarch and the Ancient World*; Wilkins, *Life and Works of Petrarch* and *Life of Petrarch*; and Foster, *Petrarch: Poet and Humanist*. Scholarly portraits of Dante tend to take a similar approach; examples of his classical interests (in the *Commedia*, the *Monarchia*, and elsewhere) are generally cited as evidence of how unusual Dante was for his own time.

23. See the discussions in Giuseppe Billanovich, *Primi umanisti*; Folena, *Storia della cultura veneta*; Weiss, *Spread of Italian Humanism* and *Renaissance Discovery*; and Witt, *Footsteps of the Ancients*, as well as

the works cited in chapter 2 of this study. For a broader approach, see Leonardi and Munk Olsen, *Classical Tradition*, and Petitmengin and Munk Olsen, "Bibliographie de la réception."

24. See, for example, Burke, "History as Social Memory," as well as Eco and Marmo, *Medieval Theory of Signs.*

25. Le Goff, *History and Memory*; Fentress and Wickham, *Social Memory*; and Burke, "History as Social Memory," esp. 45–46.

26. Lowenthal, *The Past Is a Foreign Country*, 213.

27. Boynton, *Shaping a Monastic Identity*, and Herrick, *Imagining the Sacred Past*. Classic works on this subject include Farmer, *Communities of Saint Martin*, and Remensnyder, *Remembering Kings Past.*

28. Spiegel, *Romancing the Past* and *Past as Text*; Lifshitz, *Norman Conquest of Pious Neustria*; Shopkow, *History and Community*; and Geary, *Myth of Nations*, esp. 1–14. For recent surveys of work in this area, see Hen and Innes, *Uses of the Past*; Althoff, Fried, and Geary, *Medieval Concepts of the Past*; and Deliyannis, *Historiography in the Middle Ages*. On medieval memories more specifically, see Yates, *Art of Memory*; Carruthers, *Book of Memory*; Coleman, *Ancient and Medieval Memories*; and van Houts, *Medieval Memories.*

29. For a classic political approach, see Brezzi, *Comuni medioevali*, or Artifoni, "Podestà professionali." Burke, *Italian Renaissance*; Larner, *Culture and Society*; Martines, *Power and Imagination*; and Rubinstein, "Political Ideas in Sienese Art," have all considered the importance of art and ideology to the sociopolitical instability of the late medieval period in Italy, while art historians like Baxandall, *Painting and Experience*, and Greenhalgh, *Survival of Roman Antiquities*, have stressed the economic and political implications of classicizing tendencies in fourteenth- and fifteenth-century Italian art. The classic article on this topic is Wieruszowksi, "Art and the Commune"; see also the recent collections *Roma antica nel medioevo*; Norman, *Siena, Florence, and Padua*; and Cannon and Williamson, *Art, Politics, and Civic Religion.*

30. Starn and Partridge, *Arts of Power*; Skinner, "Ambrogio Lorenzetti"; and Norman, *Siena and the Virgin.*

31. *Coscienza cittadina*; *Senso della storia*; and Boone and Stabel, *Shaping Urban Identity*. Many of these historians have emphasized the role played by patron saint cults in the formation of civic identity; a city's patron saint (like Saint Mark, in Venice) was venerated alongside its classical founder, serving a parallel purpose but in a religious context. See, for instance, Galletti, "Sant'Ercolano, il grifo, e le lasche" and "Motivations, modalités," on Perugia; Golinelli, *Città e culto dei santi*; Webb, *Patrons and Defenders*; and Thompson, *Cities of God*, esp. 103–40.

32. For a similar study focused on a kingdom, see Beaune, *Birth of an Ideology*. Recent works on the mechanics of self-promotion in other historical eras are illuminating as paradigms of a similar process—for example, Peter Burke's work on the construction of Louis XIV's public persona in seventeenth-century France, *Fabrication of Louis XIV*, or Paul Zanker's exposition of propaganda imagery in the early Roman empire, *Power of Images in the Age of Augustus*. The works of Mary Jaeger, *Livy's Written Rome*, and Catherine Edwards, *Writing Rome*, are also significant insofar as they address the construction of public memory in Rome, both in literary and in physical form.

33. See the discussion in chapter 6.

34. Paul Veyne, *Pain et le cirque*, has described how, during the republic, wealthy Romans spent money on public works and games to ensure their place in the public memory—and how this function was later usurped by the emperor and his family.

35. On Frederick, see Kantorowicz, *Frederick the Second*; Abulafia, "Kantorowicz and Frederick II" and *Frederick II*; Shepard, *Courting Power*; and *Federico II e l'antico*. On Henry and Ludwig, see Bowsky, *Henry VII in Italy*; Thomas, *Ludwig der Bayer*; and Pauler, *Deutschen Könige und Italien.*

36. Baron, *Crisis of the Early Italian Renaissance* and *In Search of Florentine Civic Humanism*, as well as Hankins, *Renaissance Civic Humanism*. For medievalists' responses to the Baron thesis, see the recent Blythe, "'Civic Humanism' and Medieval Political Thought," along with Davis, "Ptolemy of Lucca and the Roman Republic," and Skinner, "Rediscovery of Roman Values."

37. Cassidy, *Politics, Civic Ideals, and Sculpture.*

38. On the della Scala, see Varanini, *Scaligeri*, and the works cited in chapter 2 of this study. On the Este in Ferrara, see T. Dean, *Late Medieval Ferrara*; Visser Travagli, *Ferrara nel medioevo*; and Iotti, *Estensi.*

39. See note 35, above, on Frederick. See also Powell, *"Liber Augustalis,"* on Frederick's law code, and Hersey, *Aragonese Arch at Naples*; Meredith, "Revival of the Augustan Age" and "Arch at Capua"; and De Robertis, *Federico II di Svevia*, on Frederick's patronage of classicizing art and architecture.

40. See, for example, Hale, *Renaissance Venice*; Pincus, "Venice and the Two Romes"; and P. F. Brown, *Venice and Antiquity*, as well as Becker, *Florence in Transition*; Weinstein, "Myth of Florence"; and Brucker, *Renaissance Florence* and *Florence: The Golden Age*.

41. I have generally used Bairoch, Batou, and Chèvre, *Population des villes*, for my population estimates, noting the few occasions on which their estimates differ significantly from those recorded by historians of a given city. I should note that all premodern population estimates are extremely approximate; the estimates by Russell, *Medieval Regions and Their Cities*, another frequently cited source, are usually one-third to one-half lower than those in Bairoch, Batou, and Chèvre. For the cities cited here, see *Population des villes*, pages 49, 43, 47, and 40, respectively.

42. Examples include Armannino Giudice's *Fiorita* (unedited); Guglielmo da Pastrengo, *De viris illustribus et de originibus*; and Riccobaldo da Ferrara, *Compilatio chronologica*. I compare these and other such lists of civic foundations in a forthcoming article, Beneš, "Ancient and Most Noble."

43. See Benson, "Political *Renovatio*," and Baron, *Crisis of the Early Italian Renaissance*, for early and late examples, but Starn and Partridge, *Arts of Power*, is the best study encompassing a broad period of time.

44. Although, see recent work on the *Regno*—for example, S. Kelly, *New Solomon*, on the *Cronaca di Partenope*, and Oldfield, *City and Community in Norman Italy*, on civic identity in southern Italian towns.

45. Skinner, *Foundations of Modern Political Thought*, 1:6.

Chapter 1

The epigraph is drawn from *Paradiso* 15.124–26. "Traendo a la rocca la chioma, / favoleggiava con la sua famiglia / d'i Troiani, di Fiesole, e di Roma."

1. Giovanni Villani, *Nuova cronica* 9.36, ed. Porta, 2:58. Villani's chronicle has been partly translated by Selfe and Wicksteed in *Villani's Chronicle*; for the textual tradition, see Clarke, "Villani Chronicles," and Porta, "Censimento dei mss." More generally, see Galletti, "Mitografie della memoria urbana."

2. The best article on this subject is still Hammer, "New or Second Rome," but see also Jacks, *Antiquarian and the Myth of Antiquity*, chapter 1. See also Boje Martenson, "Diffusion of Roman Histories."

3. The Genoese kept a single authorized copy of the official chronicle of their city in their municipal archives, and they also erected a large sculpted head in the nave of their cathedral, which contemporary inscriptions identify as Janus, the legendary founder of Genoa. See chapter 3 for both of these examples.

4. "Considerando che la nostra città di Firenze, figliuola e fattura di Roma, era nel suo montare e a seguire grandi cose, sì come Roma nel suo calare, mi parve convenevole di recare in questo volume e nuova cronica tutti i fatti e cominciamenti della città di Firenze." Giovanni Villani, *Nuova cronica* 9.36, ed. Porta, 2:58.

5. "Figliuola e fattura di Roma." Ibid.

6. A *podestà* (from the Latin *potestas*, meaning "power") was an executive official with judicial powers, elected for a term of six months or a year. He was usually required to be a foreigner—i.e., a citizen of another city—on the grounds that a foreigner could be impartial in judging civic affairs. He was usually paid well, and a number of men made careers out of being the podestà of one city after another; see the discussion in chapter 3.

7. "And may Christ favour and preserve their city in a covenant of peace, because Florence abounds in riches. She defeated her enemies in war and a great uprising; she enjoys prosperity and distinctions as well as a masterful citizenry. She acquires and affirms, and now impulsively extends her battle camps in safety; she rules the land, she rules the sea, she rules the whole world. Thus, by her domination, all of Tuscany becomes prosperous—and like Rome continues to lead the triumphs in wisely restraining all under her firm law." Modesto, "Il Primo Popolo," n. 2. Recent scholarship has

debated the traditional attribution of the inscription to Dante's mentor Brunetto Latini, chancellor of Florence between 1255 and 1260; Modesto provides a good review of the debate, as well as a photograph, a transcription, and an English translation of the inscription.

8. "Tutta fatta e edificata al modo di Roma . . . a similitudine di quegli di Roma, . . . come quello di Roma." Ricordano Malispini, *Storia fiorentina*, 16. The chronicle purports to have been written in the 1280s by one Ricordano, a member of the prominent Florentine Malispini family, but recent scholarship has shown that the chronicle is more likely a mid-fourteenth-century compilation based on Dante and Giovanni Villani, among others. See Davis, "Recent Work on the Malispini Question," and Porta, "Villani e Malispini." As the puzzle has never been resolved definitely, I cite the chronicle as Ricordano's in this study for ease of reference.

9. In which case, unlike Rome, Florence was "built in a day." The proverb as relating to Rome is first documented in a twelfth-century vernacular French text, so awareness of it in medieval Italy is at least possible.

10. See, for example, Ricordano Malispini, *Storia fiorentina*, 17, and Sanzanome, *Gesta Florentinorum*, 2.

11. "Fu popolata della migliore gente di Roma, e de' più sofficienti, mandati per gli sanatori di ciascuno rione di Roma per rata, come toccò per sorte che l'abitassono." Giovanni Villani, *Nuova cronica* 2.1, ed. Porta, 1:62.

12. The chronicle of Sanzanome, *Gesta Florentinorum*, c. 1230; the account given by Brunetto Latini in his *Trésor*, c. 1260–65; the *Chronica de origine civitatis* and its contemporary Italian translation, the *Libro fiesolano*, both c. 1265; the chronicle of Giovanni Villani, c. 1330–37; and the *Storia fiorentina* attributed to Ricordano Malispini, probably after 1340.

13. Dino Compagni, *Cronica*, 2. The work has been translated by Bornstein as *Dino Compagni's Chronicle of Florence*.

14. "Producti de genere Romanorum." *Florentie urbis*, 122.

15. "Hec fuit ex primis gens Rome florida civis. / Nam fuit ex binis vetus urbs renovata ruinis, / Quam spata Ponpeia monuit laudare trophea." *De laude civitatis Laude*, 8, lines 9–11. The text is problematic, especially in line 11, and my translation is conjectural.

16. "Due gentil scudieri, / Silvio et Mutio del popul Romano, / Discesi e nati di pro' cavalieri." Matteo Ciaccheri, *Cronachetta di S. Gemignano*, 1, lines 4–6. Pro' is most likely a short form of either *prode*, meaning valiant, or *probo*, which can mean anything generally positive, from good and honest to virtuous.

17. Ciaccheri's "knights" do not correspond to the Roman class of the *equites*; in this case, the term refers to the nobility, and therefore the Roman patrician, or senatorial class.

18. Livy, *Ab urbe condita* 5.35–42.

19. Benzo d'Alessandria's *Chronicon* repeats a number of these myths; see Berrigan, "Benzo d'Alessandria."

20. See chapter 2.

21. Beaune, *Birth of an Ideology*, and Federico, *New Troy*; Brunetto Latini, *Livres dou Trésor* 35, ed. Barrette and Baldwin, 25–26. An English translation, *Book of the Treasure*, is also by Barrette and Baldwin.

22. Riccobaldo da Ferrara, *Compilatio chronologica*, 244, and Guglielmo da Pastrengo, *De viris illustribus et de originibus*, 282 and 286.

23. Bartolomeo da San Concordio, *De origine civitatis Pisanae*, col. 163.

24. "Et trovasi chome i Pisani dectono aiutorio a Greci quando erano a chanpo sopra a Troya et distrussola." Ranieri Sardo, *Cronaca di Pisa*, 8. Sardo's chronicle dates to the later fourteenth century, but he adopted his material on the early history of Pisa nearly verbatim from older thirteenth-century texts; cf. Banti, "Testi cronistici pisani," as well as his introduction to Sardo's text.

25. Ranieri Sardo, *Cronaca di Pisa*, 7.

26. "De tempore autem, quo aedificata fuit, certum est, longo tempore ante Urbe Romanam conditam." Bartolomeo da San Concordio, *De origine civitatis Pisanae*, col. 163.

27. "Roma fu edifichata nella quarta etade, overo nella quinta, chorente nel quatro mila cinquantasei dal cominciamento del mondo. . . . Et Pisa si fu innanzi che Roma 268 anni." Ranieri Sardo, *Cronaca di Pisa*, 9.

28. "Ergo antiquissimo tempore ante Romam constructa fuit." Galvano Fiamma, *Chronica Mediolani*, col. 542.

29. "E nota ch'ella fu la prima città edificata nella detta terza parte del mondo chiamata Europia, e però fu nominata *Fia sola*, cioè *prima*, sanza altra città abitata nella detta parte." Giovanni Villani, *Nuova cronica* 1.7, ed. Porta, 1:13.

30. Ricordano Malispini, *Storia fiorentina*, 2.

31. "Di lui nacquero grandi signori che apresso di lui signoreggiaro non solamente la città di Fiesole e la provincia intorno, ma quasi tutta Italia, e molte città v'edificaro; e la detta città di Fiesole montò in grande potenzia e signoria, infino che·lla grande città di Roma nonn-ebbe stato e signoria." Giovanni Villani, *Nuova cronica* 1.9, ed. Porta, 1:15.

32. Isidore of Seville, *Etymologiae* 9.2.26–30; English translation by Barney et al. On Isidore and etymological interpretation, see Del Bello, *Forgotten Paths*, 95–115, and Galletti, "Mitografie della memoria urbana."

33. For example, *Chronica de civitate Ravennae*, col. 574, along with several other chronicles edited by Muratori in the same volume.

34. "Et floruit Civitas Ravennae longo tempore. . . . Et Ravenna erat Sedes Regni, in qua Barones, et Milites, et Nobiles commorabantur, et ei tota Italia deserviebat usque ad tempora Romanorum." *Chronica de civitate Ravennae*, cols. 574–75.

35. Eusebius of Caesarea, *Chronicorum libri duo*. See also Burgess and Witakowski, *Studies in Eusebian and Post-Eusebian Chronography*; Deliyannis, *Historiography in the Middle Ages*; and Kretschmer, *Rewriting Roman History in the Middle Ages*.

36. Brunetto Latini, *Livres dou Trésor* 34, ed. Barrette and Baldwin, 24.

37. Ricordano Malispini, *Storia fiorentina*, 7.

38. The chronicle of Jacopo da Varagine, discussed in chapter 3.

39. See Campana, "*Cippo riminese.*"

40. "Lapis, me puero, ostendebatur fori medio, ubi Caesar concionatus ferebatur." Petrarch, *Vita Julii Caesaris*, ed. Razzolini, 2:464. Only a small portion of the *De viris illustribus* has been edited, by Martellotti; Razzolini gives Petrarch's Latin life of Caesar along with a facing-page contemporary translation by Donato degli Albanzati. See also Campana, "*Cippo riminese*," 10.

41. "E di questo Catellina nobilissimo re di Roma, nacque uno figliuolo, lo quale ebbe nome Uberto Cesare, lo quale fue uomo savio e di grande prodezza. . . . E quando quest'Uberto fue grando di xv anni si tornò in Roma e fue ribandita, e perdonatoli dal Comune e dalli Consoli: e fulli fatto grand'onore da tutti i Romani, e fue rimesso sopra lo suo patrimonio . . . e andovi e sinoreggiò Firenze con .vii. compagni tra di Romani e di Fiesolani: ed elli era signore in tutto, e teneali per lo comune di Roma. Sicchè avvenne che Uberto Cesare prese moglie di Fiesole ed ebbe .xvi. figliuoli, i quali multiplicarono molto in lore nazione come piacque a Dio." *Libro fiesolano*, 64.

42. Catiline is an ambiguous figure in medieval Italian legend. He was one of the better-known traitors in Roman literature, and medieval scholars knew about his crimes from reading Cicero and Sallust. The Pistoiesi were regularly taunted by neighbors like the Florentines for having Catiline as a founding father. There is some evidence, however, that the inhabitants of Pistoia embraced rather than disowned their disreputable ancestor: a late medieval stone tower standing just off the main square of Pistoia is still known as Catiline's Tower (Torre di Catilina); it abuts the *via della tomba di Catilina*, or "street of Catiline's tomb." These bear witness to a medieval legend in which, after his defeat, Catiline was reputedly buried in or beneath the tower. Presumably, for the Pistoiesi, even notoriety was preferable to obscurity. See Osmond, "Catiline in Florence."

43. *Historia Tudertine civitatis*, 82.

44. B. Nardi, *Mantuanitas Vergiliana*; Ziolkowski and Putnam, *Virgilian Tradition*, 446–48; and Gramaccini, *Mirabilia*, 218–22. Signorini, "Two Notes from Mantua," reproduces both statues. See also note 48 below.

45. De Nino, "Ovidio nella tradizione popolare."

46. A. Mancini, "Macrobio Parmense," and the discussion in Weiss, *Renaissance Discovery*, 121–23.

47. On the importance of grammar and rhetoric, see especially Gehl, *Moral Art*, and Witt, *Footsteps*

of the Ancients; on education more generally, see Grendler, *Schooling in Renaissance Italy*, and Black, *Humanism and Education*.

48. On Virgil in the Middle Ages, see Comparetti's dated but classic text, *Vergil in the Middle Ages*, as well as Ziolkowski and Putnam's anthology, *Virgilian Tradition*. Dante's choice of Virgil as his guide through the *Inferno* was probably not entirely based on the latter's reputation as a classical author; see Kallendorf, "Virgil, Dante, and Empire," and Jacoff, *Cambridge Companion to Dante*, 107–24 and 181–200.

49. Here the Todese story of Senna parallels the Sienese legend of Aschius and Senius, who were also supposedly the sons of Remus, a legend discussed at length in chapter 4. According to the *Historia Tudertine civitatis*, Senna went to Tuscany and founded Siena only after he had conquered most of Umbria and established his capital, Eclis.

50. As these details may suggest, the early history of Todi according to these chronicles is rather convoluted. The basic story goes as follows: Senna, chased out of Rome by the army of his uncle Romulus, travels north, founding first Narni and then a city he calls Eristo. He gets into a dispute over the ownership of the land on which Eristo sits with the nearby city of Eclis (founded many years earlier by Hercules). This dispute leads to a war, which Senna wins, and he marries the Eclesian priest's daughter, taking Eclis as his capital. Battles with both Romans and Tuscans ensue, all of which the Eclenses naturally win until they are finally subdued by the Romans for supporting the rebels during the Catilinarian conspiracy.

51. Bonvesin da la Riva, *De magnalibus Mediolani*, 162.

52. "In omnia pugna Romanorum semper Cives Mediolanenses primam aciem haberent. Et sic populus Mediolanensis infinitas victorias per Italiam faciebat." Galvano Fiamma, *Chronica Mediolani*, col. 553.

53. "Soror atque parens et amica in fine dierum." Bonifacio da Verona, *Eulistea* 2.91, MS p. 14.

54. See chapter 2 of this study on Paduans as *Antenorides*.

55. Bonifacio da Verona, *Eulistea* 3.225, MS p. 27; ed. Bonaini, Fabretti, and Polidori, 13.

56. I discuss all of these features at greater length in chapter 5, but it is worth noting here that the Roman commune had resuscitated the SPQR abbreviation as a political symbol in the twelfth century. In this period, its political connotations were clear enough, but knowledge of the acronym's original meaning was rare; see Beneš, "Whose SPQR?"

57. "Et dipoi y Pisani dectono aiutorio a Enea quando si fugì di troya et venne in Talia presso al Tevero di Roma per fondare nuova cittade; della quale giente uscirono poi [coloro che] edifichorono Roma. Essendo chontradiato da Turno che era nella città del re Latino, Enea venne a Pisa per aiuto et per tucto Lonbardia et per tucto Toschana, (insino al Tevero di Roma) [ed] ebbe socchorso. Et da Pisani ebbe mille chavalieri et si nne fu chapitano uno Pisano chiamato Assila." Ranieri Sardo, *Cronaca di Pisa*, 8.

58. On the story of the Lysippan Venus, see chapter 4.

59. Riess, *Political Ideals in Medieval Art*, 15–23; see also Caputo, "Tradizione etrusca del grifo."

60. Sòriga, "Statua del 'Regisole,'" refers to the French as "foreign barbarians" and to their explanation for the statue's destruction as a "specious pretext" (36–37). Pavia was the site of considerable resistance to the French invasion.

61. Bascapè, "Sigilli dei comuni italiani," categorizes and illustrates a number of these.

62. Ibid., 79–80.

63. "Era el dicto castello di Hercule grande e bello, posto tra doi valloni et riterrato in uno poggio con ripe dintorno, et haviva uno bel borgo, per lo quale albergavano tutti quelli, che volevano andare in compagnia. Et cui se mantenne in prosperita, in sino che Roma fu edificata." Francesco di Andrea, *Croniche di Viterbo*, 688. White, *Art and Architecture*, 63 and 264, notes that Viterbo was well known for its magnificent walls and that architecturally significant additions to the walls, such as the tower of San Biele, show that the city was continually concerned with their maintenance and improvement.

64. Giovanni Villani, *Nuova cronica* 2.5, ed. Porta, 1:67–68.

65. "Hic mandavit fieri supra Portam Auream quamdam [*sic*] Portam de auro, et subtus eam domunculam, quae habebat ostia de auro de Arabia. . . . Ex tunc illa Porta vocata est Aurea, quae prius dicebatur Asiana." *Chronica de civitate Ravennae*, col. 575.

66. The story parallels numerous others: the twins Cornelius and Latinus are most likely derived from Romulus and Remus, and the name Latinus is that of Aeneas's father-in-law, as given both in the *Aeneid* and in Eusebius (on which see note 35 above).

67. "Romani . . . ceperunt rogare Latinum, ne destrueret civitatem eorum edificatam multo labore. Illi autem dicebant esse facturi quicquid imperare vellet. Latinus inter cetera iubet interficere omnes heredes Romuli et iubet construi duas portas in urbe Romana, unam quarum fecit vocare Latinam in honore sui nominis, altera vocata Salaria in honore sui cognati." *Historia Tudertine civitatis,* 80.

68. See the discussion in chapter 5.

69. Riccobaldo da Ferrara, *Chronica parva,* 106. As an idea referring to "the State," the word "republic" usually appears in the classical sources as two words, *res publica,* which literally means "the public thing" and is probably best translated by the modern English "commonwealth," implying both a system of government and an abstract concept referring to the common good. The word was occasionally used in the early and high Middle Ages (e.g., in some Carolingian cartularies—cf. du Cange, *Glossarium*—to mean, very generally, "the realm" or "the fisc"), but when used by Riccobaldo in the fourteenth century, it clearly referred to a specific type of representative government first practiced under the ancient Romans.

70. Mazzatinti, "Bonifacio da Verona."

71. See Jones, *Italian City-State,* 32, 90, and 140–50.

72. For specific examples, see Mazzatinti, "Bonifacio da Verona," 559–60; Dazzi, *Mussato preumanista,* 47; Fisher, "Awakening of Historical Interest," 172–73; Remigio de' Girolami, *De bono communi,* 140ff.; and Bowsky, *Siena Under the Nine,* 295. More generally, see Davis, "Ptolemy of Lucca and the Roman Republic," and Mundy, "In Praise of Italy."

73. Discussed in Wright, *Life of Cola di Rienzo;* Beneš, "Cola di Rienzo"; and several recent books, including Collins, *Greater than Emperor,* Carpegna Falconieri, *Cola di Rienzo;* and Musto, *Apocalypse in Rome.*

74. Sanzanome, *Gesta Florentinorum,* 30.

75. Pace da Ferrara, *Festa delle Marie,* 20, and Bonifacio da Verona, *Eulistea* 1.84, MS p. 5.

76. Giovanni Villani, *Nuova cronica* 4.1, ed. Porta, 1:46.

77. "Etsi dicatur, quod loqui potest de Roma, non est verum, quia hec Sybilla claruit diu post urbem conditam. . . . Sed hoc non omittitur, quod post Erithream tempore Octaviani claruit Tabertina sybilla, que tractans de quadam civitate, ponit quasi similia, sed per alia verba, cuius dicta per multos ad civitatem Florentiam verisimiliter reducuntur." *Florentie urbis,* 123.

78. "Gli antichi buoni Troiani, e' valenti e nobili Romani." Giovanni Villani, *Nuova cronica* 1.1, ed. Porta, 1:4.

79. Coletti, *Treviso,* 32–36.

80. Ruck, "Brutus als Modell des guten Richters." See Wieruszowksi, "Art and the Commune," 495–98, on Marcus Regulus, and chapter 2 of this study on Lovati in Vicenza.

81. "Si de nobili Romanorum prosapia originem duximus sumpsimus, et ab eisdem victoriosa incrementa virtutum, decet nos patrum adherere vestigiis, ne tamquam ingrati simus gentibus in derisum. . . . Viri fratres qui ab ytalo sumpsistis originem, a quo tota ytalia esse dicitur derivata, nobilitatem vestram respicite et antiqui loci constantiam." Sanzanome, *Gesta Florentinorum,* 3.

Chapter 2

The epigraph is drawn from Meister, *Über Dares von Phrygien,* 15; English translation by Frazer, *Trojan War,* 143. "Antenorem longum gracilem velocibus membris versutum cautum."

1. Virgil, *Aeneid* 1.242–49; Livy, *Ab urbe condita* 1.1; Solinus, *Collectanea rerum memorabilium* 2.10; and Servius, *In Vergilii carmina commentarii,* commentaries on *Aeneid* 1.1, 1.242, and 1.601.

2. These were Latin translations of Greek texts originally written in the first or second centuries A.D. Medieval scholars preferred their "eyewitness" accounts—Dares on the Trojan side, Dictys on the Greek—to the texts derived from Homer; see Griffin, "Unhomeric Elements" and *Dares and Dictys,* and Frazer, *Trojan War.* Western Europeans preferred Dares to Dictys for having been on the correct, albeit losing, side—a nice example of the pro-Trojan bias of the Latin Middle Ages as a whole. See Beschorner, *Untersuchungen zu Dares Phrygius.*

3. See Braccesi, *Leggenda di Antenore*, and Cimegotto, "Figura di Antenore."

4. Dante Alighieri, *Inferno* 23.88.

5. Ezzelino was killed in battle in 1256, but it took until 1260 for all of his relatives and would-be successors to either be killed as well or expelled from Padua. On the years of da Romano dominance, see Cracco, *Nuovi studi ezzeliniani*; Polizzi, *Ezzelino da Romano*; and Rapisarda, *Signoria di Ezzelino da Romano*.

6. On relations with Verona, see Berrigan, "Tale of Two Cities"; on the growth of Carrara influence, see Kohl, *Padua Under the Carrara*.

7. "Muson, Mons, Athes, Mare certos dant michi fines." Kohl, *Padua Under the Carrara*, 3. Since the text is a fully metrical dactylic hexameter, it most likely derives directly from a classical source. The municipal seal with this motto is reproduced as plate 1 of Hyde, *Padua in the Age of Dante*.

8. Bairoch, Batou, and Chèvre, *Population des villes*, 47. Hyde, *Padua in the Age of Dante*, 48, gives a population estimate of thirty thousand for 1320. On the medieval history of Padua generally, see also Simioni, *Storia di Padova*, and Collodo, *Società in trasformazione*.

9. Arnaldi, *Cronisti della Marca Trevigiana*. Chronicles in annalistic form include the *Annales Patavini* (*AP1* and *AP2*), the *Liber regiminum Padue* (*LRP*), and the *Chronicon de potestatibus Padue* (*CPP*).

10. See the foldout map at the back of Hyde, *Padua in the Age of Dante*.

11. The statutes of 1265 and their amendments have been published in Gloria, *Statuti*; some of the later amendments appear in Zorzi, "Ordinamento comunale padovano."

12. Hyde, *Padua in the Age of Dante*, 48. Many of these ninety to one hundred and ten offices would not have been full-time positions. Membership in the guild of notaries was probably about six hundred in the late thirteenth century, but this (along with employment by the municipal government) was restricted to Paduan citizens. Many notaries who were neither citizens nor members of the guild probably also worked in Padua.

13. Ibid.

14. *AP1*, 204–5; *AP2*, 230; and *LRP*, 336–39.

15. *AP1*, 205 and 207; *AP2*, 230–31; and *LRP*, 343.

16. "Eo tempore factum fuit extimum in civitate Padue, et facta fuit impositio in villis paduanis districtus, et imposita datia; omnibusque fuit damnum emendatum; et ideo fuit statim civitas melioribus aedificiis reformata." *LRP*, 340.

17. *AP2*, 230–32. See Lucianetti, "Sviluppo della città medievale," on the city's urban development.

18. Mor, *Palazzo della ragione*, and Fantelli and Pellegrini, *Palazzo della Ragione*; on the frescoes, see *L'Uomo, la terra e gli astri*. Giotto's work in the Palazzo is not much discussed by art historians since it was destroyed by a fire in 1420, but see the discussion and bibliography in Norman, *Siena, Florence, and Padua*, 1:141–44 and 201–2.

19. *AP1*, 187; *AP2*, 230; and *LRP*, 338–39.

20. *AP2*, 227, and *LRP*, 328. On the Paduan carroccio, see Rolandino of Padua, *Liber chronicarum*, 124–25; on carrocci in general, see Tucci, "Il carroccio nella vita comunale italiana," esp. 95–104.

21. On the life and works of Saint Anthony of Padua, see Bertazzo, *Vite e vita*; Raffard de Brienne, *Saint Antoine de Padoue*; and Rigon, *Dal libro alla folla*. On his cult in Padua, see *S. Antonio, 1231–1981*.

22. Lorenzoni and Bresciani Alvarez, *Edificio del Santo*.

23. Siraisi, *Arts and Sciences at Padua*; chapter 1 deals extensively with university-commune relations. See also Arnaldi, "Primo secolo dello studio"; Marangon, *Ad cognitionem scientiae festinare*; and the numerous municipal decrees in Gloria, *Statuti*.

24. Siraisi, *Arts and Sciences at Padua*, 27.

25. Hyde, *Padua in the Age of Dante*, 121–53, esp. 124ff. and 146ff.

26. "Hoc tempore Padua erat in communi statu excelso." *AP1*, 209. English misses the dual meaning of *commune* in Italian and Latin; it can be translated alternately as "commune" or "community." See my discussion in chapter 1 of this study.

27. Mann, "Origins of Humanism," gives a general overview of humanism's development from the Middle Ages to the fifteenth century, including Padua's place in it. Important studies considering Paduan humanism in its larger intellectual context are Weiss, *Spread of Italian Humanism* and *Renaissance*

Discovery, 16–24, and Sabbadini, *Scoperte dei codici latini e greci*, 2:106–21. On Paduan humanism specifically, the best recent studies are Witt, *Footsteps of the Ancients*, 81–173, and Folena, *Storia della cultura veneta*, especially Guido Billanovich's long chapter on Paduan humanism, "Preumanesimo padovano," 2:19–110. But see also Giuseppe Billanovich, *Primi umanisti*; Guido Billanovich, "*Veterum vestigia vatum*"; and Kristeller, "Umanesimo e scolastica a Padova."

28. "Antenor potuit, mediis elapsus Achivis, / Illyricos penetrare sinus, atque intima tutus / regna Liburnorum, et fontem superare Timavi . . . // Hic tamen ille urbem Patavi sedesque locavit / Teucrorum, et genti nomen dedit, armaque fixit / Troia; nunc placida compostus pace quiescit." Virgil, *Aeneid* 1.242–44 and 247–49.

29. Virgil's poem begins, "Arma virumque cano, Trojae qui primus ab oris / Italiam, fato profugus, / Laviniaque venit / litora." (I sing of arms and the man who, exiled by fate, first came from the coasts of Troy to Italy and the Lavinian shores.) Virgil, *Aeneid* 1.1–3. Servius's commentary reads, "Qui primus: Quaerunt multi, cur Aeneam primum ad Italiam venisse dixerit, cum paulo post dicat Antenorem ante adventum Aeneae fundasse civitatem. Constat quidem, sed habita temporum ratione peritissime Vergilius dixit. Namque illo tempore, quo Aeneass ad Italiam venit, finis erat Italiae usque ad Rubiconem fluvium: cuius rei meminit Lucanus. . . . Unde apparet Antenorem non ad Italiam venisse, sed ad Galliam cisalpinam." ([On the words "qui primus":] Many people ask why [Virgil] says that Aeneas arrived in Italy first, when just after that he says that Antenor founded his city before the arrival of Aeneas. In fact, this is consistent, since Virgil, with his rational logic, spoke according to the habit of his time. For when Aeneas came to Italy, Italy ended at the Rubicon River: this fact is attested by Lucan. . . . Thus it becomes apparent that Antenor did not arrive in Italy, but rather in Cisalpine Gaul.) Servius, *In Vergilii carmina commentarii*, commentary on *Aeneid* 1.1.

30. "Iam primum omnium satis constat Troia capta in ceteros saeuitum esse Troianos, duobus, Aeneae Antenorique, et uetusti iure hospitii et quia pacis reddendaeque Helenae semper auctores fuerant, omne ius belli Achiuos abstinuisse; casibus deinde uariis Antenorem cum multitudine Enetum, qui seditione ex Paphlagonia pulsi et sedes et ducem rege Pylaemene ad Troiam amisso quaerebant, uenisse in intimum maris Hadriatici sinum, Euganeisque qui inter mare Alpesque incolebant pulsis Enetos Troianosque eas tenuisse terras." Livy, *Ab urbe condita* 1.1.

31. Seneca, *Ad Helviam de consolatione* 7.6, and Solinus, *Collectanea rerum memorabilium* 2.10. Solinus includes Antenor in a long abbreviated list of founders, in the middle of which is "Padua, ab Antenore" (Padua, [founded] by Antenor). Neither Dares nor Dictys discusses the fortunes of Aeneas and Antenor after the war: in both accounts, the two men have a disagreement that causes Aeneas to leave Troy (and disappear from the narrative), while Antenor remains as ruler in Troy.

32. The descriptor "son of Antenor," or "Antenorite," seems to have been reasonably well known: Dante describes Paduan territory as *in grembo a li Antenori* (in the bosom of the Antenori) in *Purgatorio* 5.75, while Marsilius of Padua describes himself as an *Antenoridis* at the beginning of the *Defensor pacis*, 6. The difference between the two references is that Dante's reference contains definite overtones of treachery, echoing the familiar medieval story of Antenor (Dante's story is that of Jacopo del Cassero, who was mistaken in thinking that he would be safe in Paduan territory), while Marsilius's use of the term is clearly positive, reflecting his sense of personal and civic identity.

33. "Vos Antenorides, si tuti vultis ab hoste / Esse foris muro, pax vos liget intus amoris." Gasparotto, "Origine del mito," 7. The poem's emphasis on the evils of factionalism echoes the contemporary and classical texts discussed in chapter 1 of this study.

34. Ronchi, "Padova che si rinnova" and "Vecchia Padova."

35. Weiss, *Renaissance Discovery*, 18; Ullman, "Post-Mortem Adventures of Livy," 40; Jenkyns, *Legacy of Rome*, 64; and others, all of whom relate that a skeleton was dug up during construction in 1283 and that Lovati identified it as that of Antenor.

36. "Encor i est son sepulture." Brunetto Latini, *Livres dou Trésor* 39, ed. Barrette and Baldwin, 28.

37. "De novo reparata fuit" (*CPP*) for the former; "inventa fuit" (*APi*) for the latter.

38. See Andrews, "Albertano of Brescia," and Arnaldi, *Cronisti della Marca Trevigiana* and *Rolandino di Padova*, as well as the related but more general Arnaldi, "Notaio-cronista"; Fabris, *Cronache e cronisti padovani*; and Bortolami, "Da Rolandino al Mussato."

39. Rolandino of Padua, *Liber chronicarum*, 159. The work has been translated by Berrigan as *Chronicles of the Trevisan March*. On the motif of the "second Rome" more generally, see chapter 1.

40. Rolandino of Padua, *Liber chronicarum*, 124.

41. "Numquid Padua condam [*sic*] est ab Antenore constituta, egresso civitatem troianam eadem hora cum Enea, conditore romano? Numquid passa est multas tribulaciones et werras, ut ipsa Roma? Numquid in suis civibus est offensa crudeliter, turris et palaciis, domibus et decoribus suis dirutis et prostratis? Nempe, si michi parcat romana Curia, iam Padua dici potest quasi secunda Roma." Ibid., 159.

42. Hyde, *Padua in the Age of Dante*, 287.

43. "Perlectus est hic liber et recitatus coram infra scriptis doctoribus et magistris, presente eciam societate laudabili bazallariorum et scollarium liberalium arcium de Studio paduano. Erant quoque tunc temporis regentes in Padua viri venerabiles: [list of masters] in gramatica et rethorica vigiles et utiles professores. Qui ad hoc specialiter congregati predictum librum et opus sive cronicam sua magistrali auctoritate laudaverunt, approbaverunt et autenticaverunt solempniter in claustro sancti Urbani in Padua, currente anno Domini millesimo duecentesimo sexagesimo secundo, indictione quinta, die tercia decima intrante mense aprilis." Rolandino of Padua, *Liber chronicarum*, 173–74.

44. Arnaldi, *Cronisti della Marca Trevigiana*, 138–40, argues that the *Rolandina* became Padua's official city chronicle, but Hyde, *Padua in the Age of Dante*, states only that it "became a part of the city's political tradition, serving at a more sophisticated level the same function as the songs and verses of the Ezzelino legend among the populace in maintaining the political ethos of the restored commune" (288). The quoted description indirectly supports Arnaldi's view, since its notarial phrasing of *laudaverunt, approbaverunt, et autenticaverunt* (praised, approved, and authenticated) derives directly from that used in official contracts and decrees. I am indebted to Simon Teuscher for this point.

45. Gasparotto, "Origine del mito."

46. On Lovati, see Weiss, "Lovato Lovati," and Witt, *Footsteps of the Ancients*, 87–116. On the tomb of Antenor, see Fabris, "Tomba di Antenore" and "Demolizioni di S. Lorenzo," and Lazzarini, "Tomba di Antenore." Two of these sources date from 1937, when local scholars lobbied successfully against a municipal proposal to demolish or move the monument. The tomb's restoration in 1989 also provided the occasion for a fascinating collection of articles (Zampieri, *Padova per Antenore*) ranging from analyses of the wood and pollen found inside the tomb to considerations of the legend's classical iconography.

47. "Factus fuit pons lapideus sancti Leonardi hoc anno et inventa arca nobilis Antenoris, conditoris urbis Paduae, cum capitello, penes Sanctum Laurentium a porta sancti Stephani." *AP2*, 262. *Inventa*, from the Latin *invenire* (to find or discover), would seem to contradict the entry in *CPP* claiming that the tomb was renovated in that year, but medieval uses of *invenire* sometimes have overtones of "to devise or build" rather than simply "to discover." That the tomb was rebuilt rather than built in 1283 is corroborated, for instance, by the reference to it in Brunetto Latini's *Trésor*; see note 36 above.

48. "Et de novo reparata fuit archa nobilissimi Antenoris urbis Paduae conditoris cum capitello." *CPP*, 104.

49. "Inclitus Antenor patriam vox nisa [*sic*] quietem / transtulit huc Enetum Dardanidumque fugas / expulit Euganeos patavinam condidit urbem / quem tenet hic humili marmore cesa domus."

50. After the demolition of the monastery and the clearing of the area around the sarcophagus in the nineteenth century, the resultant piazza became known as the Piazza Antenore. The Bar Antenore is one current tenant.

51. *CIL* 5:2865. An approximate expansion and translation might be, "V(ivus) f(ecit), T(itus) Livius, Liviae T(iti) f(ilia) Quartae l(ibertus) Halys Concordialis Patavi sibi et suis omnibus" (Titus Livius Halys of Padua, freedman of Livia T. F. Quarta and priest of Concordia, made this while alive for himself and his family). See M. P. Billanovich, "Miniera di epigrafi e di antichità," and Guido Billanovich, "Primi umanisti padovani."

52. Petrarch, *Rerum familiarium libri* 24.8, trans. Bernardo, 3:332–33.

53. See the text accompanying *CIL* 5:2865, and Ullman, "Post-Mortem Adventures of Livy," as cited in the following note.

54. Ullman, "Post-Mortem Adventures of Livy," 55. As detailed in Ullman's article, the discovery of the Livyesque inscription in early fourteenth-century Padua was only the beginning of the city's romance with its historian ancestor: the Paduans claimed to have dug up Livy's bones in Santa Giustina in 1413, and his so-labeled mortal remains had a long and exciting afterlife. In discussing the later discovery of the bones, chroniclers of the early fifteenth century—such as Giacomo Cavacio, the chronicler of Santa Giustina, and Sicco Polenton, a humanist friend of Niccolò Niccoli—mention the epitaph as having been uncovered about fifty (Cavacio) or eighty (Polenton) years earlier. This would indicate a date of 1333 or 1363 for the earlier discovery, both of which are clearly too late. On attitudes toward Livy in the Renaissance, see also Bodon, "Immagine di Tito Livio a Padova."

55. "Anno Tiberij caesaris .iiij. pataui vitae ac labori subtractus est: et ibidem cives sui sepultum volunt: producentes lapidem unum ab agricultore agrum secus ciuitatem altius solito fodiente, diebus nostris compertum, in quo hae leguntur litterae: V. F. T. LIVIVS. LIVIAE. T. F. QVARTAE. L. HALYS. CONCORDIALIS PATAVI SIBI ET SUIS OMNIBVS. Quas in suum epitaphium sculptas credunt. Is autem lapis vetusta purgatus carie et litteris in primam formositatem redactis iussu inclyti viri Jacobi de carraria tunc pataui imperantis apud monasterium Sanctae Justinae virginis in pariete uestibuli ecclesiae affixus in hodiernum usque videtur." Hortis, *Cenni di Giovanni Boccacci*, 100–101. The National Library zibaldone is commonly known from its provenance as the Zibaldone Magliabechiano, to distinguish it from Boccaccio's other zibaldone, now in the Biblioteca Medicea-Laurenziana in Florence. The Zibaldone Laurenziana is available in facsimile as Biagi, *Zibaldone Boccaccesco*; the Livy inscription occurs there at fol. 59v. See also Picone and Cazalé-Bérard, *Zibaldoni di Boccaccio*.

56. Hankey, "Riccobaldo of Ferrara, Boccaccio, and Domenico," 218–19, and Hankey, *Riccobaldo of Ferrara*, 129. See also Zanella, "Riccobaldo e Livio."

57. "Eius sepulture epytaphium scriptum in saxo legitur Padue apud monasterium beate Iustine sic scriptum: [text of inscription]." Riccobaldo da Ferrara, *Compendium Romanae historiae* 8.23, ed. Hankey, 2:488.

58. "Et hodie Patavi cernitur eius saxeus tumulus in monasterio Sancte Iustine cum huiusmodi saxo incisis litteris . . . [text of inscription]." Guido Billanovich, "Preumanesimo padovano," 104.

59. Witt, *Footsteps of the Ancients*, 117–73, and Dazzi, *Mussato preumanista*, as well as Feo, "The 'Pagan Beyond' of Albertino Mussato," and Guido Billanovich, "Preumanesimo padovano," 41–85. On Rolando da Piazzola, see Girardi, *Rolando da Piazzola*, and Prosdocimi, "Arca di Rolando di Piazzola."

60. The most recent edition of the *Ecerinis* is *Écérinide*, a French-Latin facing-page translation edited by Chevalier; English translations by Carruba and Berrigan are also available. See also the recent analysis by Locati, *Rinascita del genere tragico*.

61. "Occidit seui rabies tyramni / Paxque reuixit. / Pace nunc omnes pariter fruamur; / Omnis et tutus reuocetur exul, / Ad lares possit proprios reuerti / Pace potitus." Albertino Mussato, *Ecerinis*, lines 527–32, ed. Chevalier, 24–25.

62. Hyde, *Padua in the Age of Dante*, 302.

63. Mussato's letter describing these events is edited in the appendix to Dazzi, *Mussato preumanista*, 188–90.

64. Hyde, *Padua in the Age of Dante*, 110–75, analyzes the legal structure of the Paduan government in detail.

65. See also Gloria, *Monumenti della Università*.

66. Siraisi, *Arts and Sciences at Padua*, 27.

67. Dazzi, *Mussato preumanista*, 47.

68. See Nederman's afterword to Marsilius of Padua, *Defensor pacis*, 447, as well as Hyde, *Society and Politics in Medieval Italy*, 187–95.

69. Padrin, *Carmina quaedam*, and Bolisani, "Poesia preumanistica latina."

70. "In MCCLXXXXI fuit D. Lovatus Iudex potestas Vincentiae, qui fecit bonum regimen et fecit depingi et scribi historias de palacio." Niccolò Smereglo, *Annales civitatis Vincentiae*, 16.

71. Dazzi, *Mussato preumanista*, 22–23. Ambrogio Lorenzetti painted "Roman scenes" at Siena in the 1320s; see chapter 4. As discussed in Mommsen, "Decoration of the Sala Virorum Illustrium," similar scenes of Roman heroes, to a scheme devised by Petrarch, were painted for the Carrara signori in Padua in the second half of the fourteenth century.

72. On Vicentine and Veronese scholarship in this period, see Folena, *Storia della cultura veneta*, vol. 2, esp. chapters 2 and 3.

73. *Origo civitatum Italie*, 30–31, 31; Carile, "Aspetti della cronachistica veneziana"; and P. F. Brown, *Venice and Antiquity*, 11–25. On Totila versus Attila, see note 76 below.

74. "Itaque accedentes Troiani ad eorum vassella, dederunt continuo vela ventis, tam diu per equora navigantes quo<u>sque pervenerunt al quandam [*sic*] tu<n>bam, ubi nunc Venetiarum civitas est constructa, et . . . disposuerunt ibi ipsorum construere mansiones. . . .

"Et tunc Romam Romulus et Remus condiderunt. Et propter hoc scitur aperte quod prima constructio Rivoalti, precessit constructioni Romane<civitatis>. . . . Quid dicam? Troiani ex diversis partibus ad Antenoridam accesserunt sed quidem moltitudo maxima illuc perveniens, in insula non potuit hospitari. Antenor, inde recedens, occupavit siccam terram et in loco parum distanti ab insula fundavit pulcerimam civitatem, quam Altiliam appellavit. Postea vero edifficavit Pataviam, que hodie Padua appellatur, ibique diem clausit extremum, in cuius tumulo scripti sunt hii versus: *Hic iacet Antenor, Paduane conditor urbis. | Vir bonus ille fuit, omnes secuntur eum.*" Marco, *Prima edificacio civitatis Venetorum*, 12.1–22.

75. Pertusi, *Storiografia veneziana*; Carile, "Problema delle origini di Venezia"; Carile and Fedalto, *Origini di Venezia*; T. S. Brown, "History as Myth"; and P. F. Brown, *Venice and Antiquity*. An intriguing recent addition to this collection—unfortunately beyond the scope of this study, since it deals with an eleventh-century text—is Berto, *Vocabolario politico e sociale*.

76. "Perfido pagano Athilla ungarorum rege." Giovanni da Nono, *Liber de ludi fortunae* 10–11.1. Unlike most medieval Italian sources—Villani, for instance, in book 2.1—Giovanni manages not to confuse the sixth-century Ostrogothic king Totila (r. A.D. 541–52) with the fifth-century Hun Attila (c. A.D. 406–453), whose pillaging of Italy only halted outside the gates of Rome due to the mysterious intervention of Pope Leo I. More often Totila is (probably incorrectly) cited as the great source of urban destruction. Early Venetian sources disagree as to whose pillaging forced their first flight to refuge in the lagoon. That both Goths and Huns tend to appear in sources like this as *ungari*, Hungarians, only aggravates the confusion.

77. "Non timeas, rex Padue, quoniam Deus in sede suorum electorum posuit te. Ex Altine civitatis nobiliore gente, que nunquam in servitute posita erit, civitatem unam Veneciarum nomine, existentem intra marinam aquam, hedificabis." Giovanni da Nono, *Liber de ludi fortunae* 10–11.2.

78. On Veronese expansion and the rule of Cangrande della Scala, see *Verona e il suo territorio*.

79. See note 33 above.

80. "Hic iacet Antenor Patavine conditor urbis. / Proditor ille fuit quique sequuntur eum." Padrin, *Dedizione di Treviso*. The Vicentine poet Ferreto de' Ferreti, a friend of Mussato, sidesteps the question of what comes after the first line in his 1328 *De Scaligerorum origine*, written for Cangrande, by tactfully giving only the first line—"Here lies Antenor, founder of the city of Padua"—and leaving completion of the distich, either pro- or anti-Paduan, to the mind of his reader. Ferreto de' Ferreti, *De Scaligerorum origine* 5.291, ed. Cipolla, 3:94.

Chapter 3

The epigraph is drawn from Jacopo da Varagine, *Cronaca della città di Genova*, 343. "Nullus debet hoc ignorare quin Ianus Ianiculam construxerit et quin a suo nomine eam appellaverit. Vocavit autem non Ianuam, sed Ianiculam in diminuto propter eius parvitatem, sicut enim Roma a principio sue constructionis, quando adhuc erat parva, vocabatur Romula; postquam autem crevit, dicta est Roma. Sic civitas nostra a principio sue edificationis fuit multum parva et vocabatur Ianicula; postquam autem crevit, dicta est Ianua." This study cites the text of Jacopo's chronicle from the Latin-Italian facing-page translation by Bertini Guidetti, which reprints the standard Latin edition of Monleone, *Jacopo da Varagine e la sua cronaca*.

1. Bairoch, Batou, and Chèvre, *Population des villes*, 43 and 46.

2. On Genoese maritime history, see Ortalli and Puncuh, *Genova, Venezia, il Levante*; Caro, *Genua und die Mächte*; and Hattendorf and Unger, *War at Sea*, esp. 119–36 and 137–50.

3. Capitani del popolo were executive magistrates like consuls and podestà. Sometimes they ruled singly and sometimes in pairs; occasionally they shared power with a podestà. Unlike a podestà, however, capitani were usually citizens. The popolo whose interests they supposedly protected were the nonaristocratic but increasingly wealthy middle classes; their demands for greater representation in municipal government complicate later medieval Italian politics considerably. See the discussion in Jones, *Italian City-State*, 505–19 and 586–94, as well as Maire Vigueur, *Cavaliers et citoyens*, 349–87.

4. Bairoch, Batou, and Chèvre, *Population des villes*, 43. De Negri, *Storia di Genova*, 209–99, provides a good account of this growth.

5. Mazzino, de Negri, and von Matt, *Centro storico*, 18.

6. On Genoa in the early Middle Ages, see especially Origone, *Bisanzio e Genova*; Pavoni, *Liguria medievale*; and Kedar, "Incursione musulmana."

7. See Cowdrey, "Mahdia Campaign of 1087." There are no contemporary Genoese accounts, but the 1088 *Carmen in victoriam Pisanorum* tells the story from the Pisan side.

8. Epstein, *Genoa and the Genoese*, 23.

9. Assisting the Byzantines gained the Genoese six years' excommunication by the pope for conspiring with schismatics. See Manfroni, *Genova, l'impero bizantino, e i turchi*; Origone, *Bisanzio e Genova*; and Geanakoplos, *Michael Palaeologus and the West*. On Genoese trade in the East, see Day, *Genoa's Response to Byzantium*, and Balard, *Mer Noire*.

10. After Genoa and Pisa's early collaboration against the Muslims, economic tensions had always been higher between them than between either city and Venice, on account of their relative proximity. See Boscolo, *Sardegna, Pisa e Genova*, and Ortalli and Puncuh, *Genova, Venezia, il Levante*, as well as the other works cited in note 2 above.

11. Fischer and Pedrotti, *Città italiane*, 38, provide a map comparing Genoese, Pisan, and Venetian trade routes and outposts in the Mediterranean and the Black Sea. Liagre-de Sturler, *Relations commerciales*, contains Genoese notarial documents relating to both Flanders and the Levant.

12. Jones, *Italian City-State*, 134, and Epstein, *Genoa and the Genoese*, 33–38.

13. See Andrea Caffaro, *Annales Januenses*. The best general study is Petti Balbi, *Caffaro e la cronachistica genovese*. For its focus on the chroniclers' sense of history (*senso della storia*), see also Petti Balbi, "Presente e il senso della storia," and Dotson, "Genoese Civic Annals." Caffaro (c. 1080–1166) was an eight-time consul of the city and a participant in the Genoese siege of Caesarea in 1101, during the First Crusade; see *DBI*, 16:256–60, and Airaldi, "Caffaro."

14. I say "technically republican" not least because the city underwent several periods of more (and less) transparent *signoria* through the years.

15. See Vitale, *Comune del podestà*, on the podestarial system in Genoa.

16. According to the appendix to Epstein, *Genoa and the Genoese*, 325–27, revolts occurred in 1257, 1259, 1262, 1265, 1270, 1278, 1291, 1295–96, 1300, 1306, and 1310; half of these resulted in a change of regime.

17. See the discussion in Jones, *Italian City-State*, 505–19 and 586–94, as well as Maire Vigueur, *Cavaliers et citoyens*, 349–87.

18. See, for example, Macconi, *Grifo e l'aquila*, for Genoa's relations with the Holy Roman Empire, and Bowsky, *Henry VII in Italy*, on Henry VII.

19. Guelf or Ghibelline affiliations were hardly monolithic. The civil war into which the city fell after the death of Henry VII in 1313, for example, chiefly consisted of fighting between Doria and Spinola, both traditionally Ghibelline families. On the convoluted relations between Guelf and Ghibelline, see the introduction to this book.

The Fieschi family's Guelf connections were so close that they produced several late thirteenth-century popes: Sinibaldo Fieschi became Pope Innocent IV (r. 1243–54), and his nephew Ottobuono became Pope Adrian V (r. 1276). Dante's pilgrim encounters Adrian V in *Purgatorio* 19.88–145, where the prelate is atoning for the sins of avarice and worldly ambition.

20. The Genoese commune of 1098 may have been a newly formalized union of the older neighborhood compagne into a citywide *compagna comunitatis*. On territoriality, see Hughes, "Kinsmen and

Neighbors." Grossi Bianchi and Poleggi, *Città portuale*, present an interesting socio-architectural study of the side-by-side alberghi of the Spinola and Grimaldi families in the neighborhood of San Luca.

21. Epstein, *Genoa and the Genoese*, 133–52. Jacopo da Varagine, *Cronaca della città di Genova*, describes how "general and universal peace was made in the city of Genoa between those known as Mascherati, or Ghibellines, and those known as Rampini, or Guelfs" (502). The Ghibelline Mascherati were the Doria and Spinola factions, and the Guelf Rampini were the Grimaldi and Fieschi factions; the peace to which Jacopo refers lasted less than a year.

22. See note 13 above.

23. Epstein, *Genoa and the Genoese*, 133–37; more generally, see Airaldi, *Genova e la Liguria*.

24. See Cabona, *Palazzo San Giorgio*, and Ferrando Cabona and Lagomaggiore, *Palazzo San Giorgio*.

25. Grossi Bianchi and Poleggi, *Città portuale*, 106–9.

26. Ibid., 104 and 129 n. 39.

27. On the church in Genoa and Liguria generally during this period, see Polonio, *Istituzioni ecclesiastiche*.

28. Di Fabio and Besta, *Cattedrale di Genova*, 223.

29. Di Fabio, "'Mito delle origini,'" 97–107, and Bozzo and Bartolozzi, *Cattedrale e chiostro*, 20–25, 43–44, and 60–62. On the use of classical *spolia*, see also Müller, *Sic hostes Ianua frangit*.

30. This reconstruction will be discussed in greater detail below.

31. Petti Balbi, "Società e cultura," 133. On young Jacopo's education, see the introduction by Imperiale di Sant'Angelo to Jacopo Doria, *Annales Januenses*, xxxv.

32. Epstein, *Genoa and the Genoese*, 162–63. The 1971 edition of Giovanni Balbi's *Catholicon* is a facsimile of the work's earliest printed edition (Mainz, 1460). See also Needham, "Johann Gutenberg and the Catholicon Press."

33. Jacopo da Varagine, *Legenda aurea*, translated by Ryan as *Golden Legend*.

34. Epstein, *Genoa and the Genoese*, 161–62 and 176; see also Borlandi, "Formazione culturale del mercante," and Petti Balbi, *Insegnamento*. On the position of Genoese notaries "between prestige and power," see Costamagna, *Notaio a Genova*.

35. The extensive fourteenth-century booklist of the cathedral of San Lorenzo features a number of classical authors, such as Caesar, Cicero, Sallust, and Vegetius, as well as historical sources like Eusebius and Isidore; Pistarino, *Libri e cultura*.

36. Epstein, *Genoa and the Genoese*, 140.

37. Ibid., 138.

38. Medieval sources usually refer to the city as Ianua, but I have chosen throughout this chapter to use a J for the Latin consonantal I, substituting Janua for Ianua to accord better with the English Janus. Printed sources are cited as written; the manuscripts do not distinguish between the two.

39. Di Fabio, "Mito delle origini," 37–41, and Petti Balbi, *Città e il suo mare*, 315, are the best analyses of Genoese mythmaking and ideology; the chapter in *Città e il suo mare* on "the civic myth," 311–26, repeats much of the material in Petti Balbi, "Mito nella memoria genovese," but provides a better overview.

40. Petti Balbi, *Città e il suo mare*, 315, and Pavoni, "Simboli di Genova." The Porta Soprana, a monumental gate built in the twelfth century as part of the defenses against Barbarossa, is still a major city landmark; see Dufour Bozzo, *Porta urbana nel medioevo*.

41. Petti Balbi, *Caffaro e la cronachistica genovese*, 57–58. For a general account of local foundation legends, including those of Janus, see Scovazzi, *Origini, miti, e leggende liguri*.

42. "In Italia autem a Iano Ianiculum, a Saturno Saturnia atque Latium conditum." Isidore of Seville, *Etymologiae* 15.1.50. Isidore takes this from Virgil, *Aeneid* 8.355–58; see notes 47 and 48 below.

43. "Nam quis ignorat vel dicta vel condita a Iano Ianiculum, a Saturno Latium atque Saturniam." (For who does not know that Janiculum was founded and named by Janus, and Latium and Saturnia by Saturn?) Solinus, *Collectanea rerum memorabilium* 2.5.

44. "Ianua a Iano quodam appellatur, cui gentiles omne introitum vel exitum sacraverunt." Isidore of Seville, *Etymologiae* 15.7.4.

45. "Ianuarius mensis a Iano dictus, cuius fuit a gentilibus consecratus; vel quia limes et ianua sit anni. Vnde et bifrons idem Ianus pingitur, ut introitus anni et exitus demonstraretur." Ibid., 5.33.3.

46. "Ianum dicunt quasi mundi vel caeli vel mensuum ianuam: duas Iani facies faciunt, propter orientem et occidentem. Cum vero faciunt eum quadrifrontem et Ianum geminum appellant, ad quattuor mundi partes hoc referunt, vel ad quattuor elementa sive tempora." Ibid., 8.11.37.

47. "Haec duo praeterea disiectis oppida muris, / reliquias veterumque vides monumenta virorum. / Hanc Ianus pater, hanc Saturnus condidit arcem; / Ianiculum huic, illi fuerat Saturnia nomen." Virgil, *Aeneid* 8.355–58.

48. This Janiculum, as mentioned in the ancient sources, is most likely the Janiculan hill in Rome, above Trastevere on the south side of the river. As the epigraph to this chapter indicates, however, Roman Janiculum and Ligurian Janua were frequently conflated in the Middle Ages, either as two cities both founded by Janus or as a single city with various appellations, as is implied by Jacopo da Varagine's explanation that Janicula is merely a diminutive for Janua.

49. "Primus in Italia, ut quibusdam placet, regnavit Ianus." Paulus Diaconus, *Historia Romana*, 5.

50. "Regionem istam, quae nunc vocatur Italia, regno Ianus optinuit, qui, ut Hyginus Protarchum Trallianum secutus tradit, cum Camese aeque indigena terram hanc ita participata potentia possidebant, ut regio Camesene, oppidum Ianiculum vocitaretur. Post ad Ianum solum regnum redactum est, qui creditur geminam faciem praetulisse, ut quae ante quaeque post tergum essent intueretur: quod procul dubio ad prudentiam regis sollertiam que referendum est, qui et praeterita nosset et futura prospiceret; sicut Antevorta et Postvorta, divinitatis scilicet aptissimae comites, apud Romanos coluntur . . . hos una concordesque regnasse vicinaque oppida communi opera condidisse praeter Maronem, qui refert: *Ianiculum huic, illi fuerat Saturnia nomen etiam illud* in promptu est quod posteri quoque duos eis continuos menses dicarunt, ut December sacrum Saturni, Ianuarius alterius vocabulum possideret." Macrobius, *Saturnalia* 1.7.19–20 and 23; see also the English translation by Davies.

51. Livy, *Ab urbe condita* 21.32 and 28.46.

52. As detailed above (note 13), Andrea Caffaro began the Genoese annalistic tradition in 1099. His account does not address the origins of the city but plunges into contemporary events with the participation of the Genoese in the First Crusade (1095–99); see Caffarus, *Annales Januenses*. For reasons that remain unclear, the annalistic tradition begun by Caffaro ended with Jacopo Doria in 1294. Doria presented his work to the commune shortly before his death, and no other chronicler was appointed.

53. "Antequam ad propositam accedam materiam, redigam in scriptis quedam que inveni de civitate Ianue in quibusdam ystoriis et legendis antiquis, et postea ad meam materiam redire curabo.

"Nam cum non inuenirem aliquid scriptum ante tempus Caphari nobilis ciuis Ianue, qui opus presentis cronice incepit anno Domini .mlxxxxvii., prout in principio huius cronice inuenitur, nec constructionem huius ciuitatis in libris aliquibus reperirem, cum tamen de multis aliis ciuitatibus Ytalie et aliarum partium mundi per Ysidorum et Solinum et alios ystoriographos edificatores ipsarum scriptum inueniatur, admiratione motus cepi tacita ac vigili mente pensare, qualiter ab antiquo tempore possem aliquid inuenire; set constructorem ipsius in libris aliquibus autenticis non potui usque nunc inuenire, forte propter antiquitatem ipsius." Jacopo Doria, *Annales Januenses*, 3–4.

54. Cf. chapter 1. Giovanni Villani's account of the building and early settlement of Florence encompasses precisely these two aspects: the new city's composition with respect to both buildings and people.

55. "Set vulgaris tenet opinio in ciuitate Ianue, quod post destructionem urbis Troiane quidam nobilis Troianus nomine Ianus applicuit ad has partes, et in loco ubi nunc dicitur Sarçanum, id est saltus Iani, descendit, castrumque in loco ubi nunc Castellum dicitur, ubi est domus archiepiscopalis modo, hedificauit, et ciuitatem Ianue a suo nomine scilicet Iano denominauit. Uerum quia in libro Titi Livi, qui fuit magnus ystoriographus urbis Rome, quedam de ciuitate nostra inueni, que antiquitatem ipsius in parte demonstrant, ideo verba ipsius de uerbo ad uerbum in presente opere scribam, et postmodum similiter que inueni in aliis antiquis scripturis." Jacopo Doria, *Annales Januenses*, 4.

56. See, for example, Imperiale di Sant'Angelo's introduction to Jacopo Doria, *Annales Januenses*, xxxv. Epstein, *Genoa and the Genoese*, translates *vulgo* as "'vulgar opinion,' an unreliable source" (165).

57. Livy, *Ab urbe condita* 21.32 and 28.46.

58. Isidore of Seville, *Etymologiae* 11.1.108 and 15.7.4.

59. "Ianua a Iano dicitur. Hec Ianua, id est porta, primus ingressus, primus introitus, quia Ianus est deus principiorum, cui antiqui omnem exitum et introitum consecravuerunt. Unde sicut porta est introitus et exitus cuiuslibet domus, ita ciuitas nostra est introitus et exitus totius Lonbardie. Vel dicitur Ianua a Iano deo principiorum, qui pingitur habere duas faties, scilicet ante et retro, sic ciuitas Ianue prospicit ante mare, et retro terram; et dicitur, habere duas faculas, id est duas portas, oriens et occidens, sic ciuitas Ianue habet duas portas, uidelicet portam maris, et portam terre." Jacopo Doria, *Annales Januenses*, 8.

60. Doria's presentation copy is Paris, Bibliothèque Nationale, MS Lat. 10136; the subscription is on fol. 27v.

61. See Bertini Guidetti's introduction to Jacopo da Varagine, *Cronaca della città di Genova*, 9–30, as well as Airaldi, *Jacopo da Varagine*, and Bertini Guidetti, *Paradiso e la terra*.

62. Jacopo da Varagine, *Cronaca della città di Genova*, 337–38. On da Varagine's chronicle, see Bertini, "Mito di Genova," and Bertini Guidetti, "Contrastare la crisi," "Iacopo da Varagine e le *Ystorie antique*," and *Potere e propaganda a Genova*.

63. On the history and its composition, see Bertini Guidetti's introduction to Jacopo da Varagine, *Cronaca della città di Genova*, 19–74, as well as Monleone's discussion in Jacopo da Varagine, *Chronicon Januense*, 197–237.

64. "Cogitantes igitur et sedula meditatione volventes quod multe civitates in Ytalia sunt de quibus antiqui ystoriographi magnam faciunt mentionem, mirati sumus quod de civitate Ianuensi tam inclita, tam nobili, tam potenti, satis modica ab ipsis invenientur expressa." Jacopo da Varagine, *Cronaca della città di Genova*, 337.

65. Ibid., 337–38.

66. Ibid., 340.

67. "Habet igitur civitas quelibet duplicem constructorem: unum principalem, scilicet ipsum Deum; alium secundarium, scilicet aliquem hominem terrenum." Ibid., 341.

68. Ibid.

69. "De quorum numero fuit Ianus." Ibid., 342.

70. "Notandum est quod tres fuisse Iani dicuntur. Primus est Ianus, qui de partibus Orientis in Ytaliam venit et ibi primo regnavit. Secundus est quidam princeps, qui fuit civis Troie, qui post destrutionem Troie ad Ytaliam venit. Tertius est rex Epyrotarum, qui Romam venit et post mortem suam Romani ipsum deificaverunt et tanquam deum coluerunt." Ibid., 342.

71. Ibid., 338.

72. "Romani iudices et consules plus rem publicam quam propriam zelabant." Ibid., 402. This precisely echoes Cicero's advice in *De officiis* 1.85–86.

73. Jacopo da Varagine, *Cronaca della città di Genova*, 31–44.

74. Discussed as the "baptism" of Janus in Petti Balbi, *Città e il suo mare*, 319–20, and Di Fabio, "Mito delle origini," 39.

75. Di Fabio and Besta, *Cattedrale di Genova*, 196–99. On the griffin as a civic symbol, see Bernabò di Negro, *L'araldica a Genova*; Cellerino, "Genova e il grifone"; and Petti Balbi, *Città e il suo mare*, 315–16. The standard work on Genoese money (which shows both gates [*ianuae*] and griffins) is Pesce and Felloni, *Monete genovesi*.

76. Along with Di Fabio and Besta, *Cattedrale di Genova*, 196–99, see Cellerino, "Genova e il grifone."

77. D'Oria, *Chiesa di San Matteo*, and Silva, Varaldo, and Origone, *Corpus inscriptionum medii aevi Liguriae*, vol. 3, inscription nos. 122 (1284; battle of Meloria, a Genoese victory over Pisa under Oberto Doria), 123 (1290; destruction of the Porto Pisano by Genoese under Corrado Doria), and 125 (1298; battle of Curzola, a Genoese victory over Venice under Lamba Doria). Further inscriptions (nos. 132, 134, and 139) date from 1323, 1353–54, and 1379.

78. For example, Grossi Bianchi and Poleggi, *Città portuale*, 106, and Epstein, *Genoa and the Genoese*, 176. The city's lack of open space was most likely an incidental result of the demographic pressure of a population crowded between mountains and sea, although it may also have affected the community's social dynamics.

79. "MCCCVII: Pastonus de Nigro et Nicoletus de Goano fecerunt renovari hoc opus de deceno legatorum." Silva, Varaldo, and Origone, *Corpus inscriptionum medii aevi Liguriae*, vol. 3, no. 25. I give catalogue numbers from the *Corpus* for fullness of reference, but the transcriptions and texts given throughout are my own, as its transcriptions are not always accurate. The circumstantial evidence of kin affiliations suggests that both di Negro and di Goano were Ghibellines.

80. For this practice in twelfth-century Rome, see Krautheimer, *Rome: Profile of a City*, 198. Inscriptions of 1157 and 1191–93 survive; Brezzi, *Roma e l'impero medievale*, reproduces the former as fig. 14, opposite p. 384.

81. "Ianus primus rex Ytalie, de progenie gigantium, qui fundavit Januam tempore Abrahe." Silva, Varaldo, and Origone, *Corpus inscriptionum medii aevi Liguriae*, vol. 3, no. 53.

82. Jacopo da Varagine, *Cronaca della città di Genova*, 341–42.

83. For Eusebius, see the discussion in chapter 1.

84. "MCCCXII: Filippus de Nigro et Nicolaus de Goano reparatores huius ecclesie fecerunt renovari hoc opus de deceno legatorum. Janus princeps Troianus astrologia peritus navigando ad habitandum locum querens sanum dominabilem et securum Janua iam fundata a Jano rege Ytalie pronepote Noe venit, et eam cernens mare et montibus tutissimam ampliavit nomen et posse." Silva, Varaldo, and Origone, *Corpus inscriptionum medii aevi Liguriae*, vol. 3, no. 25.

85. "Janua iam fundata a Jano rege Ytalie pronepote Noe." See previous note.

86. The inclusion of Janus, the Roman god, would presumably be harder to justify in a Christian cathedral.

87. Fusero, *Doria*; Imperiale di Sant'Angelo, *Jacopo d'Oria*; and *DBI*, 41:257–466. Especially relevant are the entries on Pietro (*DBI*, 41:449–52) and his sons Jacopo (41:391–96), Lamba (41:396–99), and Oberto (41:424–31). The Genoese nobility played a much larger role in local government than the nobility in many other cities did (for example, in Padua).

88. See previous note, as well as Epstein, *Genoa and the Genoese*, 156–78, and Grossi Bianchi and Poleggi, *Città portuale*, 169.

89. See note 77 above.

90. See Imperiale di Sant'Angelo's introduction to Jacopo Doria, *Annales Januenses*, xvii.

91. Ibid., xv–xviii. These have been edited in Puncuh and Rovere, *Libri iurium*.

92. *DBI*, 41:391–96; Epstein, *Genoa and the Genoese*, 163–66; and Imperiale di Sant'Angelo's introduction to Jacopo Doria, *Annales Januenses*, xxix–lxi.

93. Jacopo da Varagine, *Chronicon Januense*, 68, and *Cronaca della città di Genova*, 380–81.

94. "De mense ianuarii, facta est pax generalis et universalis in civitate Ianue inter illos qui dicebantur Mascarati, sive Gibelini, et illos qui dicebantur Rampini, sive Guelfi." Jacopo da Varagine, *Cronaca della città di Genova*, 502.

95. "Proh dolor!" Ibid., 503.

96. The riots lasted for approximately forty days from the end of December to early February: "Per vicos et plateas manu armata confligerent et diebus multis ad invicem hostiliter dimicarent. Ex quo secute sunt neces hominum, vulnerationes multorum, domorum incendia, rerum exspoliacio et rapina." (They fought armed battles in the streets and the piazzas, and struggled amongst themselves for many days like enemies. From this came the slayings of men, grave injuries to many people, homes set on fire, and the theft and looting of property.) Ibid., 503. For more on the riots, see Goria, "Lotte intestine in Genova," and Di Fabio and Besta, *Cattedrale di Genova*, 223–53.

97. Monleone discusses the "vast" manuscript tradition of the *Chronica* and describes at length the five early codices chosen as the basis of his edition in Jacopo da Varagine, *Chronicon Januense*, 1:343–96. One page from each codex is reproduced in vol. 2 as plates 1–5.

98. Monleone describes MS B (Genoa, Biblioteca Civica Berio, MS m.r.cf bis.4.2, *olim* D bis.7.6.20) in Jacopo da Varagine, *Chronicon Januense*, 1:366–73. Copies deriving from this codex are discussed at 1:429–44, and the text of the index is given at 2:414–22.

99. "Avari non erant Romanorum consules et ideo Res publica bene gubernabatur et augmentabatur, lib. VII, cap. IIII.

"Amicis aflictis debemus subvenire. exemplum in Romanis, qui rehedificaverunt Ianuam ab Africanis destructam, lib. II, cap. III.

"Fides etiam inimicis debet servari. Exemplum de Romanis, qui propter legalitatem et fidem, quam inimicis suis servabant et numquam pacta frangebant, fuerunt semper victores, et totum mundum sibi subiugaverunt, lib. VIII, cap. II.

"Humilitatem debet pretendere quilibet rector et quilibet victor, quapropter victoriam non debet in superbiam elevari, exemplum habes de Romanis, lib. VI, cap. III.

"Utilitati proprie preponenda est communis utilitas. exemplum de Marco Regulo Romano, lib. VIII, cap. III." Anonymous list, edited by Monleone in Jacopo da Varagine, *Chronicon Januense*, 2:414–22.

100. Medieval communities chiefly viewed civic virtue as a renunciation of self-interest in favor of maintaining collective *libertas*, especially as led under a republican government. Theorists such as Remigio de' Girolami and Ptolemy of Lucca considered examples from classical Rome at length. See, for example, Makdisi, Sourdel, and Sourdel-Thomine, *Notion de liberté*, especially the article by Benson, "*Libertas* in Italy"; Nederman, "Nature, Sin, and the Origins of Society"; Cammarosano, *Propaganda politica*; and Kempsall, *Common Good*.

Chapter 4

The epigraph is drawn from Lisini, "Lupa," 28. "Chi sale anche oggi in Campidoglio può osservare due lupi viventi che il Comune di Roma tiene come simbolo della eterna città. Questa costumanza fu assai nel medio evo. E come la vicina Firenze teneva un leone vivente presso la porta del Palagio pubblico, così i senesi fino a due secoli fa, vi tennero qualche lupa perchè stesse a simboleggiare la loro origine romana."

1. The legend is described in Douglas, *History of Siena*, 6–7.

2. Livy, *Ab urbe condita* 1.4–7.

3. These chronicles are edited in Lisini and Iacometti, *Cronache senesi*. The earliest incarnation of the Aschius and Senius legend occurs in a fifteenth-century chronicle that claims to have taken its information from certain much older chronicles written by one "Tisbo Colonnese." Banchi, *Origini favolose di Siena*, asserted that the legend was of fifteenth-century origin, but Rondoni, *Tradizioni popolari e leggende*, argued, based on its diction, that it dated at least from the fourteenth century, if not earlier. In their preface (esp. x–xiii), Lisini and Iacometti disagree with Rondoni on the diction and make a good case for placing the chronicle in the fifteenth century.

4. Stopani, *Via Francigena*, and Guidoni and Maccari, *Centri senesi sulla via Francigena*. Ascheri, *Spazio storico*, 115, contains a good map showing the path of the Via Francigena.

5. Bowsky, *Siena Under the Nine*, 4. On the Sienese contado and its governance, see Ascheri, *Spazio storico*, chapters 3 and 7, which both contain several useful maps.

6. See Ascheri, *Siena e Maremma*, especially the article by Borracelli, "Sviluppo economico di Grosseto," 115–78. Redon, *Uomini e comunità*, includes a number of interesting legal-political studies of the Sienese contado, and Bowsky, *Finance of the Commune of Siena*, 1–15 and 47–68, analyzes the Sienese state's financial arrangements.

7. Bowsky, *Siena Under the Nine*, 7–8. Bairoch, Batou, and Chèvre, *Population des villes*, 48, estimates the population of Siena at twelve thousand in 1200 and fifty thousand in 1300.

8. Bowsky, *Siena Under the Nine*, 159–74, provides an extensive analysis of Sienese foreign relations under the Nine, in particular their interactions with Florence.

9. Ibid., 5 and 11.

10. Bortolotti, *Siena*, contains a number of useful maps showing the city's urban development.

11. On Siena's problems with the port of Talamone, see Bowsky, *Siena Under the Nine*, 175–76; on the aqueduct, see Bargagli-Petrucci, *Fonti di Siena*, 1:33–46. Along with the aqueduct, a network of tunnels (called *bottini*) almost twenty-five kilometers long ran under the city and collected water; on these, see Balestracci et al., *Bottini medievali*.

12. On the factions of Guelf versus Ghibelline on a broader Italian scale, as well as the fortunes of Ghibellinism in the later thirteenth century, see the introduction to this study.

13. Bowsky, *Siena Under the Nine*, 23–85, deals at length with the holders of these offices and their duties. See also Waley, *Siena and the Sienese*, 42–64.

14. The oath of office administered to each group of Nine is reproduced in English translation in Bowsky, *Siena Under the Nine*, 55–56.

15. Ibid., 23.

16. Ibid., 56.

17. Norman, *Siena and the Virgin*, 1–43, addresses communal patronage and civic devotion. On the Sienese cathedral, see also Carli, *Duomo di Siena*, and van der Ploeg, *Art, Architecture, and Liturgy*. The recent collection by de Mattei, *Presenza del passato*, is also valuable.

18. Bowsky, *Siena Under the Nine*, 58.

19. Ibid., 276. See Ceppari Ridolfi, Ciampolini, and Turrini, *Immagine del Palio*, 64–67, for the early history of the Palio.

20. On the hospital, see Norman, *Siena and the Virgin*, 87–103. For the Sienese university, see Zdekauer, *Studio di Siena nel Rinascimento*, which publishes a number of related documents; Prunai expands on many of Zdekauer's points in "Studio Senese dalle origini" and "Studio Senese dalla 'migratio' Bolognese." Recent studies include Ascheri, *Università di Siena*, a broad history; P. Nardi, *Insegnamento superiore a Siena*, which focuses on the higher faculties; and Denley, *Commune and Studio*, which analyzes the university's relations with the commune. Frova, Nardi, and Renzi, "Maestri e scolari," is the Web site for a prosopographical study of students and masters at the universities in Siena and Perugia between 1250 and 1500; the Sienese half of the project contains a brief history of the university (with a sizeable bibliography) as well as searchable lists of masters and students.

21. Bowsky, *Siena Under the Nine*, 200. On roads generally, see Szabó, "Rete stradale," and Bowsky, *Siena Under the Nine*, 191–201. Szabó contains a foldout map showing the network of roads in the Sienese contado around 1300, which is reproduced in Ascheri, *Spazio storico*, 88–89.

22. Bowsky, *Siena Under the Nine*, 198–99.

23. See the diagrams in Carli, *Duomo di Siena*, 12, and Benton, "Siena and Florence Duomos," 133, plate 163; the latter is a much-improved version of Pietramellara, *Duomo di Siena*, plate 19.

24. Waley, *Italian City-Republics*, 158.

25. The single completed wall is still visible in the buildings around the cathedral piazza today. The best accounts of the fourteenth-century plans for cathedral improvement are in Carli, *Duomo di Siena*, 11–28; van der Ploeg, *Art, Architecture, and Liturgy*, 97–120; and Benton, "Siena and Florence Duomos."

26. Ascheri, *Siena nella storia*, 94–95, provides a good diagram of the "great building projects and definition of the urban fabric" that occupied the city at the turn of the fourteenth century, including fountains and churches as well as city walls and gates.

27. On the *Maestà* specifically, see Bellosi, *Duccio*. Satkowski and Maginnis, *Duccio di Buoninsegna*, have recently published the archival documents surrounding Duccio's life; the chronicle sources for the procession and celebration commemorating the placement of the finished work appear at 97–108. Agnolo di Tura's account is edited in Lisini and Iacometti, *Cronache senesi*, 313–14, and discussed at length in Norman, *Siena and the Virgin*, 20–43.

28. Larner, *Culture and Society*, has a good diagram showing the different stages in which the Palazzo was built; see plate 11, opposite p. 129. More generally, see Cairola and Carli, *Palazzo pubblico di Siena*, 7–68, and Brandi, *Palazzo Pubblico*, on the Palazzo's construction. On civic ideals as expressed in architecture, see also Cunningham, "For the Honor and Beauty," and Norman, "Glorious Deeds of the Commune."

29. Waley notes wryly how strategically useful it was for the Sienese to wait until 1297 to start building their town hall, so as to be sure of making it taller than those of their key competitors.

30. Guidoni, *Campo di Siena*, 75–77. Guidoni notes also (as one sees in contemporary documents like Agnolo di Tura's chronicle and the Sienese council minutes) that through the end of the thirteenth century, the Campo was usually referred to as the *campus fori*, echoing the classical *forum*. See also Franchina, *Piazza del Campo*.

31. The aqueduct was a monumental undertaking, which took six years longer to finish than the three years that the original engineer (Jacopo di Vanni Ugolini, a master stoneworker) had projected;

the celebration at its completion, then, must have been especially heartfelt. See the works cited in note 11 above.

32. The third story of the Palazzo on either side section is late seventeenth-century work, and the two small belfries on top of the main section date from the eighteenth century. The Palazzo as completed in 1310 consisted of the four-story main section, with nine merlons, or crenellations, along its top edge, and both two-story side sections, with merlons above them as well (since removed). The architectural molding that supported these lost merlons is, however, still visible, and the second-story merlons still exist on the left wing of the palace, which was added in 1325–41 to support the Torre del Mangia; see the works cited in note 28 above, especially the diagram in Larner, *Culture and Society*.

33. Cairola and Carli, *Palazzo pubblico di Siena*, 71–186, and Southard, *Frescoes in Siena's Palazzo Pubblico*.

34. See Leone de Castris, *Simone Martini*, esp. 12–24, and Norman, *Siena and the Virgin*, 48–65. Southard, "Simone Martini in the Palazzo Pubblico," is also useful.

35. On Lorenzetti's "Roman scenes," see note 78 below. The literature on Lorenzetti's frescoes in the Palazzo Pubblico is vast. The best analyses are Starn and Partridge, *Arts of Power*; C. Frugoni, *Distant City*; Skinner, "Lorenzetti's *Buon governo* Frescoes"; and Norman, "Love Justice." Starn's *Ambrogio Lorenzetti* is a good introduction with many illustrations.

36. For example, the "idealized" city has Siena's cathedral campanile and dome, as reproduced in Starn, *Ambrogio Lorenzetti*, 32, and Frugoni, Donato, and Monciatti, *Pietro and Ambrogio Lorenzetti*, 227–28. See the discussion in note 69 below, as well as C. Frugoni, *Distant City*, 181–88, and Starn and Partridge, *Arts of Power*, 46–50.

37. See de Wesselow, "Decoration of the West Wall," on this particular wall of the Sala, esp. 21–24 on the *Mappamondo* and 25–31 on Guidoriccio; see also Polzer, "Simone Martini's *Guidoriccio* Fresco," and Leone de Castris, *Simone Martini*, 265–73.

38. Tomei, *Biccherne di Siena*, has excellent plates of all of these; his introduction (esp. 35–53) is particularly helpful; see also the discussion in note 74 below.

39. The *Breves* of 1250 are edited in Banchi, "Breve degli officiali"; the Constitutions of 1262 are edited in Zdekauer, *Constituto del comune di Siena dell'anno 1262*, and the statutes of 1309–10 in Lisini, *Costituto del comune di Siena*. Those of 1337–39 remain unpublished; they are Siena, Archivio di Stato, Statuti 26. The council deliberations (*Deliberazioni del Consiglio generale*) are also unpublished. On both of these, see Ascheri, *Antica legislazione della Repubblica*.

40. On road legislation and maintenance, see Ciampoli and Szabò, *Viabilità e legislazione*, 3–67; on prostitution and further statutes related to urban planning, see Bowsky, *Siena Under the Nine*, 294–96, and Maginnis, *World of the Early Sienese Painter*, 172.

41. Maginnis, *World of the Early Sienese Painter*, 170–73, discusses this example and others as they relate to the broader concepts of beauty and order in trecento Siena.

42. The praetorship (the duties of which had very little in common with its Roman namesake) had been reinvented several times in the thirteenth century, as discussed in Zdekauer, "Per la storia del pretore Senese." The 1346 bill to revive the office is translated in Bowsky, *Siena Under the Nine*, 295.

43. See note 20 above.

44. Bowsky, *Siena Under the Nine*, 278.

45. English, *Enterprise and Liability in Sienese Banking*, provides a good analysis of the rise and fall of Sienese banking, centered on the major *compagnie* of the Bonsignori (which failed c. 1300–10) and the Tolomei (which failed c. 1310–20). See also Cardini and Cipolla, *Banchieri e mercanti di Siena*, especially the article by Cassandro, 109–60. Bowsky, *Siena Under the Nine*, 247–58, contains a detailed discussion of how the Sienese government dealt with bankruptcy.

46. Bowsky, "Impact of the Black Death," estimates that "the population loss in Siena was at least fifty per cent, and probably more" (18), based on a pre-plague population of "over 50,000" (11). He reaffirms these estimates in Bowsky, *Siena Under the Nine*, 7.

47. The fall of the Nine and the fortunes of the city after 1355 are discussed at the end of this chapter.

48. Bowsky, *Siena Under the Nine*, 293. See also Maginnis, *World of the Early Sienese Painter*, 196–97.

49. Such chapels are especially visible in Santa Maria Novella (Dominican) and Santa Croce (Franciscan), the mendicant churches that were in vogue in the fourteenth century.

50. See note 41 above.

51. Starn and Partridge, *Arts of Power*, 57–58.

52. On the classical legend of Remus, see Wiseman, *Remus: A Roman Myth*. Several other medieval foundation legends, many of them French, rested on the same pretext. One legend about the city of Reims, relying on the Reims/Remus similarity, claims that it was founded by Remus himself, only after which he went back to Rome and was killed by his brother. For this, Remus's son killed Romulus and reigned in Rome in his place. See Rondoni, *Tradizioni popolari e leggende*, 25–27; Graf, *Roma nella memoria e nelle immaginazioni*, 79; and Wiseman, *Remus: A Roman Myth*, 150.

53. The legend *Sena vetus* appears on twelfth- and thirteenth-century coins in Paolozzi Strozzi, "Iconografia monetale senese," 80–81 and figs. 6, 7, and 10. Sometime in the first half of the fourteenth century, the prevailing trend in coins expanded to *Sena vetus civitas virginis*, a variation of the acronym CSCV (Comune Senarum, Civitas Virginis) that appears in Lorenzetti's frescoes in the Palazzo Pubblico; see C. Frugoni, *Distant City*, 125, and note 70 below.

54. The Senones were a Celtic tribe originally from the Seine basin; Caesar refers to them in *Bellum Gallicum* 2.2 as a "civitas in primis firma et magnae inter Gallos auctoritatis" (a community established in prominence and of great authority among the Gauls). Their name survives in the modern French city of Sens. The mistaken etymology seems to have arisen from the confusion of Siena (in Latin, *Sena*) with Senigallia, another Italian city.

55. "Apud Trogum Pompeium in vicesimo reperitur, quod Senones Galli, commilitones Brenni cum in Italiam venissent, Tuscos a suis sedibus expulerunt, in ea condiderunt urbes egregias, Mediolanum, Cornum, Brixiam, Veronam, Bergamum, Tridentum atque Vincentiam. Nam quod urbem Senensium senibus suis, et valetudinariis, armentariisque, construxerint, non modo fides historiae, sed celebris traditio est, ex eo quidem validior, quod Senenses et lineamentis membrorum, venustate faciei, et coloris gratia, moribus quoque ipsis ad Gallos et Britones, a quibus originem contraxerunt, videntur accedere." John of Salisbury, *Policraticus* 6.17, ed. Migne, col. 613a. The only modern edition of the *Policraticus*, ed. Keats-Rohan, covers books 1–4; the next volume is in preparation. There is also an English edition of excerpts by Nederman.

Classical history recounts two Gauls named Brennus, one who led the Gallic sack of Rome in 390 B.C. and the other who invaded Greece in 278 B.C. As far as we know, Pompeius Trogus's text (John cites *Historiae Philippicae* 24) referred to the latter Brennus's adventures in Greece but did not mention his presence in Italy or the establishment of Gallic cities there. Seel, *Pompeius Trogus fragmenta*, 140–41, collates the remaining fragments of Pompeius Trogus (as preserved in collections like that of Valerius Maximus) with Justinus's third-century epitome.

56. "Senibus suis, et valetudinariis, armentariisque." John of Salisbury, *Policraticus* 6.17, ed. Migne, col. 613a.

57. "Et quicunque ceperit lupum aliquem vel lupam extra civitatem Senensem in comitatu et iurisdictione Senensi, dabo vel dari faciam pro qualibet lupa .x. sol., et pro lupo .v. sol., et pro quolibet lupicino .iii. sol." (Whoever captures a male or female wolf outside the city of Siena, in the territory and jurisdiction of Siena, shall receive for each female wolf 10 solidi, and for each male wolf 5 solidi, and for each pup 3 solidi.) Constitutions of 1262, 1.196, in Zdekauer, *Constituto del comune di Siena dell'anno 1262*, 80. The city's ideological connection with she-wolves might have made the reward for a female twice that of a male, but the practical consideration that male wolves do not bear young might also have made them less valuable. See also Carlen, *Wölfin von Siena*.

58. Zdekauer, *Vita privata dei Senesi*, 57.

59. Rondoni, *Tradizioni popolari e leggende*, 15 and 24–8. For Doria and Genoa, see chapter 3.

60. "Vedesi nelle muraglie un lacero avanzo d'una gran carta topografica dello Stato Sanese, posta quivi per ogni dimostrazione, che accedesse fare del sito de' luoghi soggetti, e dicesi, che in tal guisa fosse mal menata, e ridotta da certa Lupa domestica, che una volta in questa Sala si teneva." Gigli, *Diario sanese*, 2:223.

61. Cf. Hahn, *Tower Menagerie*, as well as Brucker, *Florence: The Golden Age*, 178, and P. F. Brown, *Venice and Antiquity*, 33–34. Villani narrates, "Nel detto anno, a dì XXV di luglio, il dì di santo Iacopo, nacquono in Firenze II leoncini del leone e leonessa del Comune, che stavano in istia incontro a San Pietro Scheraggio . . . e nacquono vivi e non morti, come dicono gli autori ne' libri della natura delle bestie, e noi ne rendiamo testimonianza, che con più altri cittadini gli vidi nascere, e incontanente andare e poppare la leonessa; e fu tenuta grande maraviglia che di qua da mare nascessono leoni che vivessono, e non si ricorda a' nostri tempi. Bene ne nacquono a Vinegia due, ma di presente morirono. Dissesi per molti ch'era segno di buona fortuna e prospera per lo Comune di Firenze." (In that year [1332], on the 25th day of July, the day of San Jacopo, were born in Florence two cubs to the Commune's pair of lions, who live *in istia* near San Pietro Scheraggio; and they were born alive and not dead, as authors claim in their books on nature and beasts, and I myself bear witness to this, since I saw them born, along with many other citizens; and immediately they began to walk and to nurse from their mother; and it was held a great marvel that lions born so far from the sea should live, which is a thing never seen in our times. Two were also born at Venice, but failed to live. Many people said that this was a sign of the great fortune and prosperity of the Commune of Florence.) Giovanni Villani, *Nuova cronica* 11.184, ed. Porta, 2:748.

62. See the introduction to this study.

63. Venturi, "Giovanni Pisano e le lupe-doccioni"; Paolozzi Strozzi, "Iconografia monetale senese," 116, fig. 60; and Brandi, *Palazzo Pubblico*, 57, which also contains a number of good illustrations.

64. On the iconographical development of the symbol of the wolf and twins, see the conclusion of this study.

65. Maginnis, *World of the Early Sienese Painter*, 131–32 and 171, notes other improvements to the city gates: a park was built inside the Porta Camollia in 1309 "for the delight and joy of citizens and foreigners," while images of the Virgin were added to other gates between 1309 and 1346. These would have contributed to the city's beauty and order, as well as having symbolic significance—like the she-wolf, the Virgin Mary was an official protector of the city.

66. Reproduced in Starn, *Ambrogio Lorenzetti*, 71, and Frugoni, Donato, and Monciatti, *Pietro and Ambrogio Lorenzetti*, 237–38.

67. The Torre del Mangia, now considered the city's major landmark, had not yet been completed when Lorenzetti painted his fresco.

68. Starn, *Ambrogio Lorenzetti*, 66, and Frugoni, Donato, and Monciatti, *Pietro and Ambrogio Lorenzetti*, 223.

69. This figure has been interpreted variously as the personification of the Sienese commune (C. Frugoni, *Distant City*, 119, esp. n. 3), the Common Good (Starn and Partridge, *Arts of Power*, 50), and the ideal magistrate of communal government (Skinner, "Ambrogio Lorenzetti," 42–43). The debate continues in C. Frugoni, *Distant City*, 193; Donato, "Ancora sulle 'Fonti' nel *Buon Governo*"; and Skinner, *Visions of Politics*, 2:39–117. These are subtle distinctions; as Starn and Partridge point out, the figure contains visual parallels to the usual representations of saints, kings, and civic magistrates, and contemporary theorists such as Remigio de' Girolami easily equate the Common Good with the Good Commune.

70. The letters currently read CSCCV, but the original inscription seems to have lacked the third C. See Skinner, "Ambrogio Lorenzetti," 42 n. 1.

71. See note 53 above. The Constitutions of 1262 are titled the *Constitutum Comunis Senarum* (Zdekauer, *Constituto del comune di Siena dell'anno 1262*, 25), and the city's official designation as *Civitas Virginis* occurred shortly after the battle of Montaperti in 1260. On the city's Marian connections, see Southard, *Frescoes in Siena's Palazzo Pubblico*, 48–49, and Norman, *Siena and the Virgin*, esp. 1–17.

72. Southard, *Frescoes in Siena's Palazzo Pubblico*, 274.

73. C. Frugoni, *Distant City*, denies this association: "Although undoubtedly a replica of the she-wolf of Rome, this image had long since become the autonomous emblem of Siena, and its use betrays no intention, contrary to the opinion of Rowley, *Ambrogio Lorenzetti*, 1:99, of vaunting a filiation with the eternal city. The twins are not Romulus and Remus but Aschio and Senio" (119 n. 4). I agree that the twins are Aschius and Senius but contend that the Roman connection stands, since the legend of Aschius and Senius automatically refers back to the original Roman set of twins.

74. Art historians disagree on whether Lorenzetti himself painted the cover or whether another painter copied his tableau from the Sala della Pace. Tomei, *Biccherne di Siena*, 150–51.

75. There are scattered rumors that the Sienese adopted the wolf and twins on the arms of the commune in 1297—for example, as mentioned in Larner, *Culture and Society*, 113, and Skinner, "Ambrogio Lorenzetti," 43—but I have found no direct evidence for this claim.

76. "Item Miccheli ser Memmi aurifici novem Lib., pro pretio unius sigilli argentei quod fecit pro Dominis Novem in quo est sculta quadam [*sic*] lupa et hoc per apodixam Dominorum Novem, . . . viiij lib." Lisini, "Impresa della lupa."

77. Among these citizens was Ciampolo di Meo degli Ugurgieri, a member of one of Siena's most prominent families, who created one of the earliest translations of the *Aeneid* into Italian in precisely this period; see the discussion in chapter 6.

78. Rowley, *Ambrogio Lorenzetti*, 1:94. Agnolo di Tura's text, which is translated in Rowley, reads, "Sanesi avendo fatto el palazzo co' la prigione nuova, e sopra la sala del consiglio fecero le camere de' signori e d'altri famegli nella sala del palazo del mezo, e fecelle dipegnare di fuore a storie romane di mano di maestro Anbruogio Lorenzetti di Siena." Agnolo di Tura, *Cronaca maggiore*, 518.

79. Donato, "Ciclo pittorico ad Asciano," and Ascheri, *Spazio storico*, fig. 6.

80. Rowley, *Ambrogio Lorenzetti*, 1:94–96, and Starn, *Ambrogio Lorenzetti*, 60–61 and 70–71.

81. Skinner, "Ambrogio Lorenzetti," 2–5. The more traditional view is that the frescoes emerged from the Aristotelian-Thomistic intellectual tradition; this is the view advanced by Rubinstein, "Political Ideas in Sienese Art," 182–89, and C. Frugoni, *Distant City*, 118–57. Starn and Partridge note cheerfully in *Arts of Power*, that "perhaps the clearest lesson to be drawn from these readings is that the frescoes lend themselves to a variety of learned interpretations—indeed, that they positively invite them" (39).

82. Starn and Partridge, *Arts of Power*, 35–45.

83. Wieruszowksi, "Art and the Commune," 28, and Southard, "Simone Martini's Lost Marcus Regulus." Hoch, "Antique Origins of an Emperor," notes that Simone Martini used Constantinian *solidi* as models for his depiction of the Emperor Julian in the Saint Martin chapel in the basilica of Saint Francis in Assisi: "[Julian] is the earliest image extant in Italian painting possessing an identifiable source based on antique numismatic portraiture" (43).

84. [Lisini], "Statua trovata in Siena." Regarding the "signature," art historians note that the statue was probably a Roman copy, since Lysippus never signed his work.

85. "Fu trovata nella città di Siena, della quale ne feciono grandissima festa et dagli intendenti fu tenuta maravigliosa opera, e nella basa era scripto el nome del maestro, el quale era excellentissimo maestro, el quale era Lisippo. . . . Questa non vidi se non disegnata di mano d'uno grandissimo pictore della città di Siena, il quale ebbe nome Ambruogio Lorenzetti; la quale teneva con grandissima diligentia uno frate antichissimo dell'ordine de' frati di Certosa; el frate fu orefice et ancora el padre, chiamato per nome frate Jacopo et fu disegnatore et forte si dilettava dell'arte della scultura et cominciommi a narrare come essa statua fu trovata, faccendo uno fondamento, ove sono le case de' Malavolti: come tutti gli intendenti et dotti dell'arte della scultura et orefici et pictori corsono a vedere questa statua di tanta maravigla et di tanta arte. . . . E con molto honore la collocorono in su la loro fonte, come cosa molto egregia. Tutti concorsono a porla con grandissima festa et honore et muroronla magnificamente sopra essa fonte." ([Another statue] was found in Siena; a great festival was held and the experts held it to be a marvelous work. It was signed on the base with the name of the excellent master, Lysippus. . . . I know this statue only from a drawing by Ambrogio Lorenzetti, a very great Sienese painter, which was preserved with the greatest care by a very old Carthusian named Fra Jacopo, a goldsmith like his father before him. Fra Jacopo was a draughtsman and took great pleasure in the art of sculpture, and he undertook to tell me how the statue had been found during the digging of a foundation where the houses of the Malavolti now stand, and how all the experts and all those learned in the art of sculpture, the goldsmiths, and the painters ran to see this admirable statue of such skill. . . . So they set it on their fountain as a work of great eminence. They flocked to put it up with great pomp and honor, and it was set magnificently above the fountain.) Lorenzo Ghiberti, *Commentarii* 3.3.2, ed. Bartoli, 108–9.

86. Gramaccini, *Mirabilia*, 206–17, and Rowley, *Ambrogio Lorenzetti*, 1:94–95.

87. Hanson, *Fonte Gaia*, 9. A parallel example of a classical statue erected on a public fountain (in this case still extant) occurred in Verona in 1368; Gramaccini, *Mirabilia*, 224–37.

88. Agnolo di Tura's description of this celebration is discussed in chapter 6.

89. "Avendo la terra moltissime aversità di guerra con Fiorentini et essendo nel consiglio ragunati el fiore de' loro cittadini, si levò uno cittadino et parlò sopra a questa statua in questo tenore: 'Signori cittadini, avendo considerato dapoi noi trouamo questa statua, sempre siamo arrivati male, considerato quanto la ydolatria è proibita alla nostra fede, doviamo credere tutte le aduersità noi abbiamo, Iddio ce le manda per li nostri errori. Et veggiallo per effecto che, da poi noi honoramo detta statua, sempre siamo iti di male in peggio. Certo mi rendo che per insino noi la terremo in sul nostro terreno, sempre arriveremo male. Sono uno di quelli consiglerei essa si ponesse et tutta si lacerasse et spezassesi et mandassesi a soppellire in sul terreno de' Fiorentini.' Tutti d'achordo, raffermarono el detto del loro cittadino et così missono in essecutione, et fu soppellita in su el nostro terreno." (They were suffering many reverses in their war with Florence and when the flower of the citizens met in council one of them rose and spoke of the statue, to this effect: "Respected citizens, considering that things have gone ill with us ever since we found this statue and considering that idolatry is forbidden by our faith, we must believe that God has visited us, for our errors, with these adversities. And in fact, ever since we honored this statue, things have gone from bad to worse. I am certain that while we keep it in our territory things will continue to go badly. I am one of those who advise taking it down and smashing it to pieces, sending the fragments to be buried in Florentine soil." They all agreed with this and so the plan was put into execution and it was buried in our lands [Ghiberti was Florentine].) Lorenzo Ghiberti, *Commentarii* 3.3.2, ed. Bartoli, 109.

90. The Sienese wolf and twins seem likely to have represented Aschius and Senius from their first appearance in the city, since even the earliest representations include twins with the wolf. The Capitoline wolf in Rome, the most likely model for such representations, had no twins at that date. For the history of the Capitoline wolf, see Presicce, *Lupa Capitolina*, 93–98, and Carruba, *Lupa Capitolina*. On the medieval practice of keeping antiquities (including the Capitoline wolf) at the Lateran Palace, see Krautheimer, *Rome: Profile of a City*, 191–97.

91. See the examples given in chapter 2.

92. Lorenzetti's composition of the inscriptions, if the attribution is correct, is notable, since most medieval artists were considered artisans rather than intellectuals; Starn and Partridge, *Arts of Power*, 33–34.

93. Ibid., 18–19.

94. Brucker, *Florence: The Golden Age*, 167–73.

95. Dino Compagni, *Cronica*, 78.

96. Giovanni Villani, *Nuova cronica* 2.9–19, ed. Porta, 1:75–82. Selfe and Wicksteed, *Villani's Chronicle*, translate only one of these on the city of Luni (34–35).

97. "La città di Siena è assai nuova città, ch'ella fu cominciata intorno agli anni di Cristo 670, quando Carlo Martello, padre del re Pipino di Francia, co'Franceschi andavano nel regno di Puglia in servigio di santa Chiesa a contrastare una gente che si chiamavano i Longobardi. . . . E trovandosi la detta oste de' Franceschi e altri oltramontani ov'è oggi Siena, si lasciaro in quello luogo tutti gli vecchi e quelli che non erano bene sani, e che non poteano portare arme, per non menarglisi dietro in Puglia; e quelli rimasi in riposo nel detto luogo, vi si comiciaro ad abitare . . . e l'uno abitacolo e l'altro era chiamato Sena, dirivando di quegli che v'erano rimasi per vecchiezza." Giovanni Villani, *Nuova cronica* 2.19, ed. Porta, 1:81–82.

98. Villani uses the word *Francia* to refer both to the pre-Carolingian territory of the Franks and to the medieval French kingdom in his own time. He also calls Charles Martel's soldiers *Franceschi*, the vernacular Italian word for "French." His word choice therefore clearly identifies the founders of Siena with the French of his own day.

99. This is particularly true since *non bene sani* has distinct overtones of "insane"; the term can mean mentally unwell as well as physically so.

100. Hanson, *Fonte Gaia*, esp. 25ff. Ferretti, *Fonte Gaia*, also discusses the fountain's recent replacement and restoration (the fifteenth-century panels and figures are now in the museum of Santa Maria della Scala).

101. Rubinstein, "Political Ideas in Sienese Art," 189–207. For *lupae*, see Popp, "Lupa Senese"; Presicce, *Lupa Capitolina*, 98–99, esp. figs. 6 (a statue by Giovanni and Lorenzo Turino, 1429) and 7 (a ceremonial plate by Giovanni Turino, 1427); Norman, *Siena and the Virgin*, 5, fig. 6 (the illuminated title page of the *Libro dei Censi*, c. 1405, which depicts the wolf and twins prominently in the center of the bottom border); and Paolozzi Strozzi, "Iconografia monetale senese," figs. 59 (cast iron gate, 1437), 61 (an intarsia panel by Domenico di Niccolò, mid-fifteenth century), and 66–71 (Sienese coins bearing the wolf and twins, sixteenth century).

102. Shown in Presicce, *Lupa Capitolina*, 98, fig. 6. The original is now kept in a case inside the Palazzo Pubblico, and a replica stands on the column outside the Palazzo.

103. See note 3 at the beginning of this chapter.

Chapter 5

The epigraph is drawn from the *Annali decemvirali* for 1293, edited in Mazzatinti, "Bonifacio da Verona," 559. "Magister Bonifacium de Verona magister in Estroloia et in versificando venit ad civitatem Perusii et velit solempne opus facere et librum antiquitatum et negotiorum Comunis Perusii et antiquitates reducere ad memoriam pro honore Comunis Perusii."

1. Blanshei, *Conflict and Change*, 7.

2. See the maps in Grohmann, *Città e territorio*, vol. 3, and Neri, "Perugia e il suo contado."

3. Blanshei, *Conflict and Change*, 15, and Nico Ottaviani, *Statuti, territorio e acque*.

4. Bairoch, Batou, and Chèvre, *Population des villes*, 46, and Blanshei, "Population, Wealth, and Patronage," 601.

5. Neri, "Perugia e il suo contado," and Grohmann, *Città e territorio*, vol. 2, esp. chapters 3 and 10.

6. On medieval Perugian economy and industry, see Blanshei, "Population, Wealth, and Patronage," and *Conflict and Change*, 16–21, as well as Grohmann, *Città e territorio*, vol. 1, chapters 5 and 7.

7. Grohmann, *Perugia*, esp. chapter 2.

8. On the various structures of Perugian internal politics, see Abbondanza, "Legislazione statutaria"; Marcacci Marinelli, *Liber Inquisitionum*; Grundman, *Popolo at Perugia*; and Giorgetti, *Ufficiali a Perugia*. Blanshei, *Conflict and Change*, 52–59, provides a good overall picture.

9. On the Papal States, see Partner, *Lands of St. Peter*, and Waley, *Papal State*. Waley in particular gives a good account of the negotiations between the papacy and each of its supposedly dependent communes, including Perugia (37ff.). The best-known case of effigy-burning took place in 1282.

10. See the works cited in note 8 above.

11. Fabretti, "Brevi annali," 56–59.

12. Blanshei, *Conflict and Change*, 38.

13. Ugolini, "Annali e Cronaca di Perugia in volgare," 145–54; Blanshei, *Conflict and Change*, 24–26; and Fabretti, "Brevi annali," 56–58.

14. Gurrieri, *Fontana Maggiore*, and Cavallucci, *Fontana Maggiore*, 11–40. "1276: In quisto millessimo, del mese del março, se començò el condutto de Monte Paciano per l'acqua, la quale venia ella fonte che stava en capo de la piaçça. . . . 1278: In quisto millessimo, dì xiij de ffebraio, venne l'acqua de Monte Pacciano ella ffonte de la piaçça de Peroscia." (1276: In this year, in the month of March, the aqueduct for water from Monte Pac[c]iano was begun, which came to the fountain at the head of the square. . . . 1278: In this year, on the thirteenth day of February, the water came from Monte Pacciano to the fountain in the Perugian square.) Ugolini, "Annali e Cronaca di Perugia in volgare," 154.

15. The Palazzo Nuovo is now known as the Palazzo dei Priori, after the priors who replaced the Consoli delle Arti early in the fourteenth century; Cavallucci, *Fontana Maggiore*, 146–52, and Riess, *Political Ideals in Medieval Art*, 5–24.

16. Abbondanza, "Legislazione statutaria" and *Notariato a Perugia*; also Bartoli Langeli, *Codice diplomatico*.

17. Vermiglioli, *Zecca e monete perugine*, and Pierotti, "Circolazione monetaria." See Fabretti, "Brevi annali," 57: "1255: Si comenzò a batter la moneta di Perugia" (the minting of Perugian money was begun).

18. Ermini, *Università di Perugia*, 1:8; see also Bellini, *Università a Perugia negli statuti cittadini*.

19. Blanshei, *Conflict and Change*, 24.

20. See note 9 above.

21. For example, F. Mancini, "Euliste della Fontana Maggiore," 329.

22. "Heulixstes" appears on the Fontana Maggiore; "Eulistes" and "Heulistes" in the *Eulistea*; and "Ulisste" in the *Conte di Corciano e di Perugia*, a vernacular prose romance written later in the fourteenth century.

23. The Samnite Wars are narrated by Livy in books 9 and 10 of the *Ab urbe condita*; Perugia's role in the civil wars appears in Appian of Alexandria, *Historia romana* 5.32–49.

24. "Perusini quoque originem ab Achaeis ducunt." Justinus, *Epitoma historiarum Philippicarum Pompei Trogi* 20.1.11.

25. "Hic Mantuam dicitur condidisse, quam a matris nomine appellavit: nam fuit filius Tiberis et Mantus, Tiresiae Thebani vatis filiae, quae post patris interitum ad Italiam venit. Alii Manto, filiam Herculis, vatem fuisse dicunt. Hunc Ocnum alii Aulestis filium, alii fratrem, qui Perusiam condidit, referunt: et ne cum fratre contenderet, in agro Gallico Felsinam, quae nunc Bononia dicitur, condidisse: permisisse etiam exercitui suo ut castella munirent, in quorum numero Mantua fuit." (Here [Ocnus] is said to have founded Mantua, which he called by the name of his mother, for he was the son of Tiber and Manto, the daughter of the Theban seer Tiresias, who came to Italy after the death of her father. Others say that Manto was the daughter of Hercules, and a seer herself. From this, some claim that Ocnus was the son [others, the brother] of Aulestes, who founded Perugia, and to avoid competing with his brother, he founded Felsina in the Gallic plain, which is now Bologna; and he allowed his army to fortify castles there, among which one was Mantua.) Servius, *In Vergilii carmina commentarii*, commentary on *Aeneid* 10.198–200.

26. "È probabile che la figura dell'eroe risulti da un adattamento della menzione serviana di Auleste . . . ai caratteri consolidati del personaggio di Ulisse." Galletti, "Materiali per una storia," 77.

27. The secondary literature on the Fontana Maggiore is considerable. See, for example, Fasola, *Fontana di Perugia*; Cavallucci, *Fontana Maggiore*; Dozzini, *Fontana Maggiore*; and Ottavi, *Fontana Maggiore*.

28. White, *Art and Architecture*, 70, and Gramaccini, *Mirabilia*, 186–205.

29. Cf. chapter 4 on Siena.

30. "Rappresenta uno dei più significativi esempi nel panorama della cultura gotica internazionale, ove si percepiscono in forme tangibili ideologie e istanze di una società che raggiunge uno dei massimi apici di sviluppo, coniugando felicemente le nuove esigenze politiche, economiche e sociali con gli insegnamenti tratti della memoria." Grohmann, "Fontana Maggiore," 50.

31. Moskowitz, *Italian Gothic Sculpture*, 41–44, and Cavallucci, *Fontana Maggiore*, 11–28. The relevant municipal documents regarding commissions and purchasing have been published in Fasola, *Fontana di Perugia*, 55–63.

32. White, "Nicola Pisano's Perugia Fountain," has been especially influential, but see also Hoffmann-Curtius, *Programm der Fontana Maggiore*. Sproviero, *Fontana Maggiore*, esp. 60–63, and Cenci, *Fontana Maggiore*, discuss the fountain's most recent restoration, in which the figures were replaced in White's proposed "original" arrangement.

33. "Heulixstes Perusine conditor urbis" on the north, "Augusta Perusia" on the south, "Roma capud mundi" on the west, and "Sanctus Johannes Baptista" on the east. King Solomon used to sit on the fourth axis point, now occupied by John the Baptist, but White argued that this arrangement could not be correct, based on the order of the various inscriptions. He explains that "to set Saint John the Baptist opposite Rome . . . is to refer not only to the replacement of the old law by the new, but to the continuation and transformation of the antique pagan Rome in the new Christian Rome," in preference to either of the other options: Solomon (on the fountain before 1998) or Saint Benedict (reconstruction by Cellini). White, "Nicola Pisano's Perugia Fountain," 81.

34. Fasola, *Fontana di Perugia*, 20 and 66, and Vermiglioli, *Zecca e monete perugine*.

35. Cavallucci, *Fontana Maggiore*, 42–45, and Santini, *Linguaggio figurativo*.

36. "Augusta Perusia fertilis in omnibus his." Fasola, *Fontana di Perugia*, 65, and Bartoli Langeli and Zurli, *L'iscrizione in versi*.

37. The Gospels present fish and grain as the basic necessities for survival; the miracle of the loaves and fishes appears in Matthew 15:32–38; Mark 6:35–44; Luke 9:12–17; and John 6:5–14.

38. "Mater Romuli" (mother of the Romuluses), that is, the mother of Romulus and Remus. The figures are illustrated in Cavallucci, *Fontana Maggiore*, 121–31.

39. Two manuscripts of the *Eulistea* are known; the more important is an early fourteenth-century paper manuscript (cited throughout this study) in the Istituto della filologia romanza in the Università di Perugia, which contains both poetic and prose versions of the work. Another fifteenth-century manuscript in the Biblioteca Nazionale Centrale di Firenze contains only the poetic version. Mazzatinti, "Bonifacio da Verona," 557, and Galletti, "Materiali per una storia," 85 n. 6, together give a good account of the text's transmission; see also Schmidt, "Epica latina." Most of the *Eulistea*, with the exception of the first two books, was poorly edited in 1850 by Bonaini, Fabretti, and Polidori; Anna Imelde Galletti of the Università di Perugia is said to be preparing a new edition of both versions of the work.

40. "Il poema giunge a conclusione e sigillo di un processo di costruzione dell'identità cittadina che ha già visto il consolidamento del culto del santo patrono, la fabbrica dei due grandi simboli araldici della città, il grifo e il leone, il compimento della Fontana Maggiore: altri linguaggi hanno già posto le basi di una sintassi del sentimento civico e politico." Galletti, "Materiali per una storia," 76. See also Galletti, "Scritture della memoria storica," 379–85.

41. "Incipiet namque ab Eulistis evenctu urbis fundatore augusto Perusie, victorias eiusque titulos insingnitos recitabit et fasces." Bonifacio da Verona, *Eulistea*, prose prologue, lines 20–22, MS p. 1.

42. "Et oves maneamus in Christo; et Romulidus populus cum suis rectoribus suum ingredi santuarium mereatur." Ibid., prose prologue, lines 9–10, MS p. 2.

43. Rex fuit ex Daneis trabeatus et yndole clara,
Non minus et lingua fulgens Ytacensis Ulixis,
Progenieque sua, priscis natalibus ortus:
Eulistes cui nomen erat, post dirupta longe
Pergama dardanicum, qui post et tempora multa
Postque annos mangnos Saturni postque potentis
Advenctum Enee, priusquam Roma fuisset,
Inciperent, eiusque lares, et menia starent
Venit in Ytaliam, fatis agitantibus illum.
Hic patrie primus, Perusine structor et urbis;
Fundatorque fuit et cur sic illa vocata.
Urbs fuerit, refert Dyo tot nuntia nostra.
Ibid., 1.77–88, MS p. 5.

44. Saturn was a mythical colleague of Janus during the earliest settlement of Italy; see chapter 3 of this study on Genoa.

45. Eulistes was "priscis natalibus ortus" (of ancient birth, line 79) and living "post dirupta . . . Pergama" (after the destruction of Troy, lines 80–81), but "priusquam Roma fuisset" (before Rome existed, line 83). Galletti, "Materiali per una storia," 77, notes that these details are two of the basic features of any foundation myth: the founder's own origin and the time period in which the foundation occurred.

46. "Tantoque triunpho / Eulistes iussit, sic urbs perusina vocari . . . // Eulistes hic urbem ergoque nomen ab ursa / Accipiet, statues sic voluunt et tua mangna." Bonifacio da Verona, *Eulistea* 1.169–76, MS p. 7. My translation of the last two lines is conjectural.

47. Virgil, *Aeneid* 8.82–83.

48. "Hec ut dicta patent Eulistes condere cepit / Urbem, ac murorum fabricas conducere giro / Et sic constructe sunt urbis menia tante." Bonifacio da Verona, *Eulistea* 1.190–92, MS p. 8.

49. "Ast ubi lege sua constructa ac ordine tali, / Urbs perusina fuit, memorant ut scripcta primorum / Ac exempla diu recitant, lactatus uterque / Nutritusque lupa frater processi ut inqui[t] / Fabula Romuleos propere tunc condere muros." Ibid., 2.1–5, MS p. 12.

50. "Inter romanos amor et perusina castra." Ibid., 2.47, MS p. 12.

51. "Hinc hodie rome perusine vigintum urbi / Fit soror atque parens et amica in fine dierum / Gloria romulidum sibi semper et eius aluna / Illa sibi sic forte data societ et arget / Fedus amititie, congnataque nomina mundo." Ibid., 2.90–94, MS p. 14.

52. " . . . Hic credite Romam; / Vos Romani estis, relevati tempore longo: / Hec urbis porte refer-unt, et pagina sculta: / Hec et Troya dum retinent exempla vetusta." Ibid., 3.224–27, MS p. 27; ed. Bonaini, Fabretti, and Polidori, 13.

53. *Romulidus* is a patronymic for Romulus, thus translating as "son of Romulus"; *Quirites* is an ancient term for the Roman people; and *lares* were the Romans' household gods. The other terms mean city, citizen, law, seer, province, faith, and fatherland, respectively.

54. "Nobilis Eulistes, Perusine conditor urbis, / Contra Troianos bella multa tulit. / Urbs Perusina vocor, Rome reparata vigore; / Fertilis et fortis sum, libera, pronta favore." Bonifacio da Verona, *Eulis-tea*, epilogue, MS p. 70; ed. Bonaini, Fabretti, and Polidori, 52. The diction clearly refers to the inscrip-tion accompanying the figure of Eulistes on the Fontana Maggiore; see note 33 above.

55. "Hec Heuliste tenent, bello qui mangnus et acer / Rex fuit, atque sue patrie fundator et urbis . . . // Et quamvis veniens Troyano sanguine purus, / Supponant alii, fuerit quod pinus Acthenis." Bonifacio da Verona, *Eulistea* 6.186–92, MS p. 49; ed. Bonaini, Fabretti, and Polidori, 35. Galletti, "Materiali per una storia," makes the interesting claim that *purus* (line 191) and *pinus* (line 192) should both be read *Pirrus*, implying a connection to the Perus who also occasionally appears in medieval sources as the founder of Perugia (in Latin, *Perusia*); the paleographical evidence of the manuscript, however, does not seem to support this idea.

56. Although the Perugian frescoes are not considered as artistically significant as (for example) the Lorenzetti frescoes in Siena, they encompass the same kind of encyclopedic themes. Compare Riess, *Political Ideals in Medieval Art*, 5–17, with *L'Uomo, la terra e gli astri* on Padua, and Starn and Partridge, *Arts of Power*, 46–58, on Siena.

57. Riess, *Political Ideals in Medieval Art*, xii.

58. Ibid., chapters 4 through 8.

59. The red and gold shield identifies ancient and medieval Romans in contemporary art and manuscripts, such as Giotto's *Stefaneschi Altarpiece* and copies of Giovanni Villani's Florentine chronicle (see, for example, Vatican City, Biblioteca Apostolica Vaticana, MS Chigi L.VIII.296, whose illustra-tions have been recently reproduced in C. Frugoni, *Villani illustrato*). The acronym had originally been revived, and the coat of arms created, by the Roman commune in the twelfth and thirteenth centuries; see Beneš, "Whose SPQR?"

60. The documents especially relevant to this study have been published respectively in Mazzatinti, "Bonifacio da Verona"; Fasola, *Fontana di Perugia*; and Blanshei, *Conflict and Change*.

61. Fasola, *Fontana di Perugia*, 55–57.

62. Such lists survive from both 1277 and 1285; Blanshei, *Conflict and Change*, 105–14.

63. Ibid., 102.

64. Ibid., 99–104.

65. The mendicant orders were considered knowledgeable in matters of engineering due to the emphasis they placed on education; Fasola, *Fontana di Perugia*, 55, for May 5, 1276.

66. Ibid., for Tuesday, February 16, 1277.

67. Ibid., 56, for Friday, February 26, 1277.

68. "Item dedit et solvit magistro Guidoni de Civitate Castelli pro xviiii diebus quibus stetit in civ-itate Perusii occasione providendi et examinandi aqueductum . . . vi libr. den." Ibid., 55, for February 16, 1277.

69. "Fontes complentur super annis mille ducentis / [s]eptuaginta [bis quat]t[uor] atque dabis." Ibid., 62–63.

70. Ibid., 56, for March 5 and 22, 1277, and 62, for August 7, 1287.

71. White, *Art and Architecture*, 91.

72. Moskowitz, *Italian Gothic Sculpture*, 21–44.

73. The same claim appears in chapter 4 of this study, regarding the Sienese wolf drain-spouts attributed to Giovanni Pisano; see also the bibliography cited in White, *Art and Architecture*, 659–60.

74. Fasola, *Fontana di Perugia*, 58, for September 10, 1277. The fountain was finished and Arnolfo paid in 1281.

75. Piastra, "Nota sull'*Annayde*" and "Nota sulla *Veronica*." De Braye died in 1282; see the discussion in chapter 6. Ubaldini (1214–1272), known among his contemporaries simply as "the Cardinal," was a notorious papal legate in charge of Romagna; he appears with Emperor Frederick II among the heretics in Dante's *Inferno*, canto 10.

76. "Die martis ultima Junii. Congregato consilio speciali et generali populi civitatis Perusii in sala domorum domini Vençoli more solito. . . . Item cum magister Bonifacium de Verona magister in Estroloia et in versificando venit ad civitatem Perusii et velit solempne opus facere et librum antiquitatum et negotiorum Comunis Perusii et antiquitates reducere ad memoriam pro honore Comunis Perusii, Si placet consilio quod dum stabit in civitate Perusii ad compilandum et conficiendum dictum opus, quod debeat habere expensas a Comuni et quod profecto dicto opere provideatur sibi quod videbitur Consulibus pro tempore existentibus et consilium populi consulatur." *Annali decemvirali* for 1293, in Mazzatinti, "Bonifacio da Verona," 559.

77. "[In reformatione consilii . . . stanciatum et reformatum fuit] quod de moneta Comunis Perusii fiant expense magistro Bonifacio et filio donec stabit et faciet librum de antiquitatibus Comunis Perusii et consules arcium predictas fieri faciant expensas ut eis videbitur convenire et perfecto opere predicto provideatur dicto Magistro Bonifacio pro remuneratione sui laboris sicut viderint convenire." Ibid.

78. See, in the previous note, "expense magistro Bonifacio et filio."

79. "Deliberarunt et ipsi sapientes iuris cum eisdem quod magister Bonifacius pro opere quod fecit suo dictamine de gestis Comunis Perusii habeat et habere debeat de avere Comunis Perusiiet a Comuni Perusine .xxv. flor. auri. . . . Et quod ipse magister Bonifacius teneatur et debeat ipsum opus prosaice distinguere et ordinare et componere Et pro dicto opere prosayce faciendo et ordinando per eum cum factum erit habere debeat de avere Comunis Perusii .xxv. flor. auri qui sibi exsolvantur de avere Comunis pro mercede laboris et opere supradicto si per eum fiet et ordinabitur ut dictum est et dare debeat Comuni dictos libros." *Annali decemvirali* for 1293, in Mazzatinti, "Bonifacio da Verona," 560–61.

80. The prose version is still in Latin, so it is not entirely clear how the commune intended to use each version. The poem's general impenetrability probably explains why it never reached a wide audience; as mentioned earlier, only two manuscript copies survive. Nonetheless, Zappacosta, "*Orationes de laudibus Perusiae*," 69–70, gives some indication of the legend's afterlife, especially in the guise of a short poem by the sixteenth-century Perugian humanist Francesco Maturanzio, written to accompany a series of fourteen frescoes of famous Perugians, of which Eulistes was one.

81. Mazzatinti, "Bonifacio da Verona," 560.

82. Ibid.

83. "Pro opere quod fecit in butinis et laborerio aqueductus hinc." Fasola, *Fontana di Perugia*, 58, for November 2, 1277.

84. As argued by Galletti, "Considerazioni," 323, "Non era solo manifestazione; era anche e sopratutto giustificazione e persuasione." ([The *Eulistea*] was not just a manifestation [of an ideal]; it was also and above all a justification and a persuasion.)

85. "Divengono simboli unitari della realtà comunale, 'monumenti pubblici' rappresentativi di ciò che si è stati, si è e si vuole essere, ove passato e presente, immaginario e concreto, mito e realtà si fondono continuamente." Grohmann, "Fontana Maggiore," 155.

86. White, *Art and Architecture*, 88–91; see also the discussion in chapter 4 of this study.

87. *Campanilismo* is closely related to that other axiom of Italian culture, *fare figura*—to make a good appearance, or present a good façade.

88. "Il Consiglio ascolta il parere di maestro Bonainsegna de Veneciis, qui fecit fieri fontem de Urbeveteri, il quale disse di poter fare l'aquedotto et etiam plus forte opus, plus securum quam non est illud opus fontis de Urbevetere." Fasola, Fontana di Perugia, 56, for February 26, 1277.

Chapter 6

The epigraph is drawn from Guidotto da Bologna, *Fiore di rettorica*, 150. "Fue maestro e trovatore della grande scienza di rettorica, cioè di ben parlare . . . la qual sormonta tutte l'altre scienze per la bisogna di tutto giorno parlare ne le valenti cose, sì come in fare leggi e piati civili e criminali, e ne le cose cittadine, sì come in fare battaglie e ordinare schiere e confortare cavalieri ne le vicende de l'imperii e regni e principati, in governare popoli e regni e cittadi e ville e strane e diverse genti, siccome conversano nel gran cerchio del mappamundo della terra. . . . E io, frate Guidotto da Bologna, cercando le sue magne vertudi, sì mmi mosso talento di volere alquanti membri del fiore di rettorica volgarezzare di latino in nostra loquenzia, siccome appartiene al mestiere de' ladici, volgarmente."

1. The profession was generally divided into notaries (*notari*) and judges (*giudici*), although these titles are imprecise and the two categories often overlapped. Modern historians frequently use the term "lawyer" or "jurist" when a member of the medieval legal profession's precise position is unclear. Armannino Giudice, to give one example, appears in a number of documents as *iudex* and *iudice*—that is, judge—but he held the office of notary in the city of Fabriano after moving there late in life; see Mazzatinti, "*Fiorita*," and *DBI*, 4:224–25.

In certain cities, such as Perugia and Siena, the two professions were incorporated in the same guild, and in others they were entirely separate. Paduan notaries had their own guild, while Paduan judges shared a *collegio* with the university's law professors; see Abbondanza, *Notariato a Perugia*, Catoni, *Statuti senesi dell'arte dei giudici e notai*; and Hyde, *Padua in the Age of Dante*, 122–23. Roughly speaking, both notaries and judges required formal legal training, but judges studied Roman law at university (usually Bologna). Because a university education was expensive, judges more often came from wealthier families than notaries.

2. Podestà of Vicenza was an official Paduan position, since Padua had conquered Vicenza and incorporated the city into the Paduan contado in 1266; hence, the Paduan commune appointed the city's podestà. See the discussion in chapter 2.

3. Recent studies on Guittone include Baldi, *Guittone d'Arezzo*; Picone, *Guittone d'Arezzo*; and Borra, *Guittone d'Arezzo*.

4. On Dante Alighieri (1265–1321), see Jacoff, *Cambridge Companion to Dante*, which includes a brief biography with bibliography by Giuseppe Mazzotta.

5. Randolph Starn refers to Lorenzetti as a "cultural bureaucrat"; Starn, *Ambrogio Lorenzetti*, 20.

6. Petrarch's "Letter to Posterity" (*Seniles* 18.1) explains his failure to finish his legal studies in this way: "I set out for Montpellier for the study of law, staying another four years there; then to Bologna where I spent three years and heard lectures on the whole body of civil law, and would have been a young man with a great fortune, as many thought, had I concentrated on the project. But I abandoned that subject altogether as soon as my parents abandoned me [because of their death]. Not that I did not like the dignity of the law, which is doubtless great and replete with Roman antiquity which delights me, but that practicing it is perverted by men's wickedness. It therefore irked me to master something I did not want to use dishonestly, and could scarcely use honestly." Petrarch, *Rerum senilium libri*, trans. Bernardo, Levin, and Bernardo, 2:674–75.

7. On Petrarch more broadly, see Mazzotta, *Worlds of Petrarch*, and Wilkins, *Life of Petrarch*. Stierle, *Francesco Petrarca*, contains a recent bibliography.

8. From Ceffi's unpublished translation; this citation from Florence, Biblioteca Riccardiana, MS 1899 (mid-fourteenth century). On Guido generally, see Chiàntera, *Guido delle Colonne*, although the various debates surrounding his life and works have been summarized more recently in Jensen, *Poets of the Scuola Siciliana*.

9. Black, *Education and Society*, esp. 190–205.

10. See Cino da Pistoia, *Rime* and *Lectura super Codice*, for his university lectures on the *Digest* (the main textbook of Roman law). Chiappelli, *Vita e opere giuridiche*, and Gagliardi, *Cino da Pistoia*, provide analytical perspectives. On the poets of the *dolce stil nuovo* (including Dante and Cino), see di Benedetto, *Rimatori del dolce stil novo*, and Marti, *Poeti del Dolce stil nuovo*.

11. On Rolandino Passaggeri and the various roles he played in Bolognese society, see Palmieri, *Rolandino Passaggeri*, and Giansante, *Retorica e politica nel Duecento*. For Rolandino's work as a notary, see his *Summa totius artis notariae* and *Atti e formule*, as well as Tamba, *Rolandino e l'ars notaria*.

12. On Ceffi, see *DBI*, 23:320–21, as well as Palma, "Redazione autografo delle *Dicerie*"; Buonocore, "*Heroides* di Filippo Ceffi"; and Giannardi, "*Dicerie* di Filippo Ceffi." The *Dicerie* have been edited by

228 NOTES TO PAGES 147–149

Biondi in *Dicerie di ser Filippo Ceffi*, but Ceffi's translation of Ovid's *Heroides* and its accompanying glosses remain unpublished. For Matteo dei Libri, see his *Arringhe*, along with Kristeller, "Matteo de' Libri."

13. Brunetto Latini, *Livres dou Trésor*, and Holloway, *Brunetto Latini* and *Twice-Told Tales*.

14. Pincus, "Andrea Dandolo and Visible History," and the bibliography cited in *DBI*, 32:433–40, especially Lazzarini, "*Dux ille Danduleus*," and Arnaldi, "Andrea Dandolo, Doge-cronista." On Venetian cultural relations with the mainland, see Folena, *Storia della cultura veneta*.

15. Marsilius (c. 1278–1342) completed legal studies at his local university in Padua before moving to Paris; *Defensor pacis*, 20–28, and Hyde, *Padua in the Age of Dante*, 165–68. On Bono Giamboni (c. 1240–after 1292), see *DBI*, 54:302–4.

16. Moskowitz, *Italian Gothic Sculpture*, 21–93, esp. 44–45 and 67–68.

17. *DBI*, 29:460–66.

18. Chapter 3 of this study deals extensively with the Doria family, but see also *DBI*, 41:257–466, especially on Pietro (41:449–52) and his sons Jacopo (41:391–96), Lamba (41:396–99), and Oberto (41:424–31).

19. The Ugurgieri played a major role in Sienese and church politics. Ruggiero degli Ugurgieri was bishop of Massa Marittima in 1231, and the family is also well known for the Castellare, the fortified castle they built on the edge of Siena in 1212. See Bowsky, *Siena Under the Nine*, 17, 66, and 278, and English, "Urban Castles in Medieval Siena." The Fiadoni were likewise members of the Lucchese merchant elite. One Omodeo, a near relative of Ptolemy, was elected into an elite *societas* of merchants in 1284; *DBI*, 47:317–20.

20. Granchi was twice regional head of the order in Pisa; *DBI*, 58:450–52.

21. Eighteenth- and nineteenth-century scholars thought that the Dominican author and translator Bartolomeo da San Concordio was also a member of the Granchi family; see, for example, Nannucci's introduction to Bartolomeo da San Concordio, *Ammaestramenti degli antichi*, 7. I have found no evidence for or against this theory.

22. See Davis, "Remigio de' Girolami's *De bono pacis*" and "Early Florentine Political Theorist," as well as de Matteis, "*De bono commune*" and *Teologia politica comunale*; Panella, "Priori di Santa Maria Novella"; and *DBI*, 56:531–41.

23. Hyde, *Padua in the Age of Dante*, 287; Boncompagno da Signa, *Assedio d'Ancona*, 46–48; and *DBI*, 28:563–68. Niccolò da Prato (Niccolò Albertini; *DBI*, 1:734–36) was a friend of Petrarch's father, Ser Petracco, and a patron of Convenevole da Prato, Nicholas Trevet, and Simone d'Arezzo; see further discussion below.

24. Chiappelli, *Vita e opere giuridiche*, 72–79.

25. Moskowitz, *Italian Gothic Sculpture*, 67, and Seidel, "Arnolfo e il suo rapporto."

26. *DBI*, 47:331–38, and "Per Galvano Fiamma"; see also Ferrai, "Cronache di Galvano Fiamma" and "Benzo d'Alessandria."

27. On Ferreti, *DBI*, 47:57–60. On the Alighieris (Dante and his sons Jacopo and Pietro), see *DBI*, 2:385–451 (Dante), 2:452–53 (Jacopo), and 2:453–54 (Pietro).

28. De Braye was created cardinal in the second creation by Urban IV (1262) and died in 1282; my thanks to Father Michael Sheehan of the Biblioteca Apostolica Vaticana for his help with this point. De Braye's tomb is reproduced in Napoli, *Arnolfo di Cambio*, 43. Arnolfo also designed the tombs of Cardinal Annibaldi (in Saint John Lateran, Rome) and Pope Adrian V (in Viterbo); see Moskowitz, *Italian Gothic Sculpture*, 44–67, for details of his career. On Bonifacio, see *DBI*, 12:191–92, and chapter 5 of this study.

29. Matteo da Correggio was podestà in Piacenza, 1250; Gubbio, 1252; Jesi, 1255; Florence, 1257; Padua, 1258–59; Bologna, 1261; Padua, 1263–64; Treviso (subject to Paduan control), 1265–66; Mantua, 1269–72 (with his brother Guido); Padua, 1269; Cremona, 1271–72; Mantua, 1274; Perugia, 1278; Padua, 1280; Bologna, 1282; Modena, 1283; Pistoia, 1286; and Parma, 1288. In addition to overseeing the construction of the Fontana Maggiore while podestà of Perugia (on which see chapter 5 of this study), he was commended by the chronicler Rolandino for having organized Padua's rout of the forces of Ezzelino while podestà there in 1258–59; *DBI*, 29:462–64.

30. *DBI*, 4:285–90, and Napoli, *Arnolfo di Cambio*.

31. Boncompagno da Signa, *Assedio d'Ancona*, and *DBI*, 11:720–25. On Convenevole, see Giuseppe Billanovich, "Ser Convenevole," and *DBI*, 28:563–68.

32. See works cited on Cino in note 10 above, especially Chiappelli, *Vita e opere giuridiche.*

33. *DBI*, 58:450–52.

34. *DBI*, 6:768–70.

35. The intellectual culture surrounding Santa Maria Novella in this period has been addressed chiefly by scholars dealing with specific individuals; no synthetic study exists. See Panella, "Priori di Santa Maria Novella"; Smalley, *English Friars and Antiquity*, esp. chapter 11; and Davis, "Education in Dante's Florence." On Remigio, see de Matteis, *"De bono commune,"* and on Nicholas Trevet, see *CTC*, 2:333; R. Dean, "Cultural Relations in the Middle Ages"; and Ziolkowski and Putnam, *Virgilian Tradition*, 750–73.

36. R. Dean, "Cultural Relations in the Middle Ages," 563; and Muttoni, "Simone d'Arezzo."

37. Ibid., and Giuseppe Billanovich, "Dal Livio di Raterio," 136ff.

38. *DBI*, 28:564.

39. Pasqui, "Biblioteca d'un notaro aretino."

40. Ibid., 253.

41. Now London, British Library, MS Harley 2493, and "m" in the editions; Giuseppe Billanovich, "Dal Livio di Raterio," 177.

42. R. Dean, "Cultural Relations in the Middle Ages," 563.

43. Jones, *Italian City-State*, 495–516.

44. The classics are Davis, "Education in Dante's Florence," and Wieruszowksi, "Rhetoric and the Classics," but see also the more recent Gehl, *Moral Art*, and Black, *Humanism and Education* and *Education and Society.*

45. As, for example, in Padua; Hyde, *Padua in the Age of Dante*, 35. Martines, *Power and Imagination*, 148, stresses how low these percentages are in absolute terms, but this emphasis strikes me as misleading. The Italian city-states never claimed to be democracies, and the level of citizen involvement in government they sustained over a period of centuries was strikingly unusual for the time.

46. On Perugia, see Blanshei, *Conflict and Change*; Grundman, *Popolo at Perugia*; and Giorgetti, *Ufficiali a Perugia*. On Siena, see Bowsky, *"Buon Governo* of Siena" and *Siena Under the Nine.*

47. See, for example, chapter 3's discussion of regime changes in Genoa, as detailed in Epstein, *Genoa and the Genoese.* Bornstein's introduction to Dino Compagni, *Chronicle of Florence*, xi–xxviii, is also helpful.

48. Cracco, *Società e stato*, chapters 3 and 4, and Lane, *Venice*, esp. 110–14.

49. Jacopo Doria, *Annales Januenses*, 4; see the discussion in chapter 3.

50. On Siena, see Rondoni, *Tradizioni popolari e leggende*, 15, and the discussion in chapter 4; on Perugia, see Galletti, "Scritture della memoria storica," 379, and the discussion in chapter 5.

51. "L'aqua de la fonte del Canpo di Siena vene la prima volta nel Canpo a dì . . . di giugno; . . . è incredibile a scrivere e narare le magnificenze che per ognuno era fatto. Sì per li Nove e così per li grandi e popolari e artifici d'ogni arti . . . nuovi giuochi e belli e svariati infiniti con grande spendio di cera e confetti e solenni vini e mangiari e cene senza alcuna parola di scandolo, che senpre con canti e balli e gioia e festa omini, done e fanciulli e religiosi e contadini tanto, che sarebe incredibile a scrivare." Agnolo di Tura, *Cronaca maggiore*, 537.

52. See also Hanawalt and Reyerson, *City and Spectacle*, especially Kempers, "Icons, Altarpieces, and Civic Ritual," 89–136. Carruthers and Ziolkowski, *Medieval Craft of Memory*, 3–4, discuss public oral presentations.

53. Dazzi, *Mussato preumanista*, 188–90. See the discussion in chapter 2.

54. Pope Gregory I's famous dictum that art was "the book of the illiterate" was well-known in late medieval Italy; Baxandall, *Painting and Experience*, 41, cites to this effect Giovanni Balbi's late thirteenth-century *Catholicon*, on which see chapter 3.

55. Maggini, *Primi volgarizzamenti*; Rinoldi and Ronchi, *Volgarizzamenti.*

56. With the possible exception of the materials on Troy and Julius Caesar—which could be considered historical as well as courtly—all of the translations discussed in Segre, *Volgarizzamenti*, are on moral and historical rather than chivalric subjects.

57. The mid-thirteenth-century *Faits* amalgamated Suetonius, Lucan, and Sallust into a pseudo-chivalric account of the late republican period, edited by Flutre and de Vogel in *Faits des Romains*. On the *Fatti dei Romani*, see Papini, "Fatti dei Romani," and Bénéteau, "Fatti dei Romani." See also Banchi's edition of the contemporary *Fatti di Cesare*.

58. *DBI*, 54:302–4. See Bono Giamboni, *Vegezio Flavio* and *Storie contra i pagani*; see also *CTC*, 6:177–80, on Vegetius, and the notes in Segre, *Volgarizzamenti*, 317–19, on Orosius. See Holloway, *Twice-Told Tales*, 8–10, on the friendship between Bono Giamboni and Brunetto Latini. Traditional scholarship, such as Chabaille (editor of Brunetto Latini, *Tesoro*), had attributed the Italian translation of Brunetto Latini's *Trésor* to Bono Giamboni, but recent scholars, including Holloway, have argued against this, maintaining that Latini wrote his own translation.

59. Andrea Lancia, *Compilazione della Eneide*. The *Aeneid* was valued in this period as much for its "historical" material as for its poetic style. See Parodi, "Rifacimenti e traduzioni italiani," which covers the extensive body of medieval pseudo-Virgilian literature; see also Gamba, *Diceria bibliografica*, and the discussion in Segre, *Volgarizzamenti*, 567–73.

60. Andrea Lancia, *Ordinamenti, provvisioni e riformagioni del Comune*, as well as Maggini, *Primi volgarizzamenti*. Casella, *Tra Boccaccio e Petrarca*, argues that the early fourteenth-century translations of Livy and Valerius Maximus, which had traditionally been attributed to Lancia, were actually made by a young Giovanni Boccaccio; see *CTC*, 3:297 and 5:297.

61. Segre, *Volgarizzamenti*, 283–313, contains a biographical note and book five of the text; the full text appears most recently in Battaglia, *Boezio e l'Arrighetto*.

62. See the works cited in note 12 above.

63. Ciampolo di Meo degli Ugurgieri, *Eneide di Virgilio*; see also note 19 above. According to Speroni's introduction to Guidotto da Bologna, *Fiore di rettorica*, there are four different contemporary redactions of the work; two of these are anonymous, and the other two attribute the work to Bono Giamboni and Guidotto da Bologna, respectively. Both men were well-known authors and translators. I have chosen to refer to the work as Guidotto's since I cite the introduction to "his" redaction in this chapter.

64. On Guido himself, see Canal, *Guido da Pisa* and "Venti anni di studi." Gamba and Puoti's 1834 introduction to Guido da Pisa, *Fatti di Enea*, xix, calls the work "la *Eneide* di Virgilio denudata di ogni fiore di poetica leggiadria" (Virgil's *Aeneid* denuded of every flower of poetic eloquence).

There are a number of nineteenth- and early twentieth-century editions of the *Fatti d'Enea*, but according to Fòffano's introduction in Guido da Pisa, *Fatti d'Enea*, vii, book one of Guido's history has only been published once, under the title *Fiore di mitologia* (Bologna, 1845). I have not been able to locate a copy of this edition.

65. On Giovanni Boccaccio (1313–1375) generally, see *DBI*, 10:838–56; on his translation activity, see Casella, *Tra Boccaccio e Petrarca*, and *CTC*, 5:297. See also note 60 above.

66. On Bonvesin da la Riva, see the introductory material in the recent edition of his *De magnalibus Mediolani* and *DBI*, 12:465–69. Bonvesin's other works include the *Expositiones Catonis* (a version of the *Disticha Catonis*) and *Volgari scelti* (vernacular poetry).

67. I have not been able to identify this particular Lamberto. If a contemporary of Bono, he cannot be the Lamberto degli Abati mentioned by Villani in connection with the dictatorship of the duke of Athens in 1343. The Abati family, however, were prominent members of Florentine society; they took part in the battle of Montaperti in 1260 and were included in the exile of the White Guelfs in 1302. See Brucker, *Florence: The Golden Age*, 167, and Dino Compagni, *Cronica* 2.25 and 3.8, ed. Cappi, 75 and 98.

68. Manetto Scali served at least once as captain of the Guelf party in Florence and figures prominently in Dino Compagni's chronicle. Compagni, himself a White Guelf, describes Scali as "strong in friends and followers" (Dino Compagni, *Cronica* 2.16, ed. Cappi, 63) and attributes the continued factional struggles in Florence at least partly to Scali's unwillingness to assert his influence. Scali was banished from Florence with Dante Alighieri and the rest of the White Guelfs in 1302. Due to these political setbacks and the king of France's notorious reluctance to repay his loans, the Scali family bank failed in 1326; Brucker, *Florence: The Golden Age*, 74–83, and Dino Compagni, *Cronica* 1.22, 2.5, and 2.22–25, ed. Cappi, 37, 48, and 70–74. On Compagni, see *DBI*, 27:629–47.

69. *DBI*, 40:594–95.

70. "Coppus Borgesis de Dominicis florentinus amantissimus reipublice, morum pater"; cited in Bruni, "Oral Memory and Written Tradition," 121. Bruni unravels the complex web of cultural associations among Boccaccio, Coppo, and Andrea Lancia, while Azzetta's introduction to Andrea Lancia, *Ordinamenti, provvisioni e riformagioni del Comune*, 18–20, inserts Giovanni Villani into the same cultural, literary, and political milieu.

71. "Al nobile e savio cavaliere Messer Geri degli Spini da Firenze" (to the noble and wise knight Messer Geri Spini of Florence). Bartolomeo da San Concordio, *Ammaestramenti degli antichi*, 13. The Spini family were Pope Boniface VIII's bankers, and Geri Spini (fl. 1285–1313) plays a major role in Dino Compagni's chronicle of the Florentine struggles of 1300–1313. He was one of the leaders of the Black Guelfs who first supported and then overthrew Corso Donati when the Black Guelf faction split apart.

72. *DBI*, 17:106–7, and Dino Compagni, *Cronica* 1.21–23 and 2.26, ed. Cappi, 34–39 and 76.

73. *DBI*, 17:106.

74. Compare, for example, Livy, *Ab urbe condita* 1.7, with Riccobaldo da Ferrara, *Compendium Romanae historiae* 1.52, ed. Hankey, 1:56, on the founding of Rome.

75. "Fateor quidem quod michi rationabiliter suasisti ut operem darem in attenuando molem operis et in stillum faciendo plebe[i]um, quippe multi volumina spernunt maiora propter impensam scribendi ac propter stilli maiestatem, que non congruit tenuit[er] litteratis." Riccobaldo da Ferrara, prologue to the *Compendium Romanae historiae*, ed. Hankey, 1:1.

76. An intriguing modern parallel is the proliferation in recent years of simplifications of influential texts: "Freud for Beginners" or "The Complete Idiot's Guide to Postmodern Literary Criticism." Their titles notwithstanding, such texts are usually reasonably good introductions to their topic; in this sense, Riccobaldo's *Compendium* could be considered a fourteenth-century "Ancient History for Dummies."

77. "Dolui rem tam dignam proborum cognitione virorum esse abditam ac perditam ut thesaurus suffossus. Proposui ad publicam utilitatem opus chronicum ordinare, non difficile intellegi et scriptura breviter moderatum." Riccobaldo da Ferrara, prologue to the *Compilatio chronologica*, ed. Hankey, 1–2.

78. "Sì mmi mosso talento di volere alquanti membri del fiore di rettorica volgarezzare di latino in nostra loquenzia, siccome appartiene al mestiere de' ladici, volgarmente." Guidotto da Bologna, *Fiore di rettorica*, 150.

79. "A onore e reverenza dell'alto Iddio Padre, da cui discende il sommo bene, e a frutto e utolità di tutti coloro che leggeranno, sì degli alletterati come de' laici." Ricordano Malispini, *Storia fiorentina*, 1.

80. See the definitions of *literatus/litteratus* in du Cange, *Glossarium*, and Niermeyer, *Mediae latinitatis lexicon minus*, as well as *letterato* in *Grande dizionario*; all translate as "cultured, literary, lettered" rather than "literate." Dictionaries of modern Italian such as the *Cambridge Italian Dictionary* still give an archaic meaning of *letterato* as "a Latinist" (1:439). See the discussion in Clanchy, *From Memory to Written Record*, 226–40, and Paul Gehl's discussion of the terms used to describe education in fourteenth-century Florence (*Moral Art*, 20–42, esp. 29–35).

81. "E l'uno e l'altro di questi libri è scritto per lettera molto sottilmente, sicchè gli uomini volgari non ne possono trarre utilità ne avere diletto. Onde io, sopra ciò pregato, sì mi brigherò di recarlo al volgare." Bartolomeo da San Concordio, *Catilinario e il Giugurtino*, 3–4.

82. "In questo proemio intende Sallustio di confortare e inanimare gli uomini ad operazione di virtù; Qui comincia il Proemio del Sallustio Giugurtino, nel quale intende dimostrare come per via di studio e di virtù d'animo s'acquista onore e gloria; et come principalmente è utile lo studio dele veraci storie." Ibid., 5 and 119.

83. Along with works by Ceffi and Lancia, the volume contains the *Intelligenza* and the *Istorietta Troiana*, on which see Gorra, *Testi inediti di storia troiana*, 61, and Parodi, "Rifacimenti e le traduzioni italiani," 359–60.

84. Early copies of the *Commedia* helped establish *mercantesca* as an acceptable literary bookhand, much as the poem itself did for the Italian language. On the role of *mercantesca* or chancery minuscule as a bookhand, see Petrucci, "Reading and Writing *Volgare*," 183–200.

85. See note 83 above.

86. "Redacta fuerunt igitur in scriptis facta maiorum, ut humana propago successivis uteretur exemplis, et cum audit quantam victoriosi gloriam reportabant, de virtute in virtutem ascendat; et dum intellegit quanto ludibrio criminosi et pusillanimes respergebantur, a similibus caveat, ne parem infamiam ex post facto incurrat." Boncompagno da Signa, *Assedio d'Ancona*, 114. This echoes Livy's instruction that "hoc illud est praecipue in cognitione rerum salubre ac frugiferum: omnis te exempli documenta in inlustri posita monumento intueri; inde tibi tuaeque rei publicae quod imitere capias, inde foedum inceptu, foedum exitu, quod uites." (From these [historical examples] you may choose for yourself and for your own state what to imitate; from these mark for avoidance what is shameful in the conception and shameful in the result.) Livy, preface to *Ab urbe condita*, 10.

87. The collections of excerpts by Valerius Maximus and Solinus also exposed medieval readers to authors whose full texts had been lost. Authors chiefly or only available in this way include Catullus, the *Laus Pisonis*, Publilius, Seneca's *Dialogues*, and Tibullus; see L. D. Reynolds, *Texts and Transmission*, xxxviii.

88. Folena, *Storia della cultura veneta*, 2:31–32, and Ullman, "Hieremias de Montagnone." The latter includes a list of all the manuscripts of Geremia's florilegium of which Ullman was aware (p. 109).

89. One of the most striking examples of this is Dante's appointment of Marcus Porcius Cato (the Younger), the famous late-republican Stoic and a non-Christian, as the guardian of Purgatory; Dante Alighieri, *Purgatorio* 1.31–93 and 2.118–23.

90. Black, *Humanism and Education*, 211–12.

91. Nederman, "Nature, Sin, and the Origins of Society," 9.

92. In the *Gesta Florentinorum*, Sanzanome refers to his fellow Florentines as having "sanguinem de libera nati" (blood of freeborn men, 29), while Bonvesin da la Riva, *De magnalibus Mediolani*, speaking of Milan, eulogizes the "huius civitatis naturalis libertas" (natural freedom of this city, 24).

93. "Omnino qui rei publicae praefuturi sunt duo Platonis praecepta teneant: unum ut utilitatem civium sic tueantur ut quaecumque agunt ad eam referant obliti commodorum suorum, alterum ut totum corpus rei publicae curent, ne, dum partem aliquam tuentur, reliquas deserant." Cicero, *De officiis* 1.85. See also Dyck, *Commentary on Cicero*, 220–23.

94. Skinner, "Rediscovery of Roman Values," 14–18.

95. "Non solum seditiones, sed etiam pestifera bella civilia." Cicero, *De officiis* 1.86.

96. "Nam concordia parvae res crescunt, discordia maxumae dilabuntur." Sallust, *Jugurtha* 10.6. As Beryl Smalley has demonstrated in "Sallust in the Middle Ages," Sallust's monographs were widely influential in the late medieval period, appearing in a number of historical compilations like the *Faits des Romains* as well as being copied on their own.

97. "Per loro superbia e per loro malizia e per gara d'ufici hanno così nobile città disfatta, e vituperate le leggi, e barattati gli onori in picciol tempo, i quali i loro antichi con molto fatica e con lunghissimo tempo hanno acquistato." Dino Compagni, *Cronica*, 5; English translation by Bornstein, *Chronicle of Florence*, 6.

98. "Et etiam a gentibus non exterminabitur, nisi in se ipsa divisa exterminetur." *Chronica de civitate Ravennae*, col. 575. Ranieri Granchi makes the same point to his fellow Pisans in specifically Roman terms; *De proeliis Tusciae*, 7, lines 1–4.

99. Molho, Raaflaub, and Emlen, *City States in Classical Antiquity and Medieval Italy*, esp. parts 2 and 3 on the practice of politics in classical antiquity and medieval Italy.

100. I do not mean to suggest that saints' lives were not widely read and enjoyed (Jacopo da Varagine's *Legenda aurea*, for example), but rather that there were nevertheless large parts of the medieval Italian urban experience to which the ideals of traditional saints' lives (such as withdrawal from the world, poverty, and self-mortification) did not speak.

101. Sanzanome, *Gesta Florentinorum*, 29.

102. "Cum animadverterem non solum gentes extraneas, verum quoque compatriotas meos in cuiusdam ignorantie dormientes deserto, nescientes Mediolani magnalia, oppinioni eorum succurrendum et consulendum fore exstimavi, ut vigilantes videant et videntes cognoscant qualis et quanti sit nostra civitas admiranda. . . .

"Ut omnes extranei Mediolanensium nobillitatem atque dignitatem scientes, eos ubique super omnes mortales revereantur et honorent, dilligant, et deffendant . . . ut mei concives in hoc speculo se intuentes et quante oriundi sint patrie contemplantes, a nobilitate nequaquam degenerent nec patriam suam dedecoroso regimine commaculent et diffament." Bonvesin da la Riva, *De magnalibus Mediolani*, 20 and 22.

103. Fasola, *Fontana di Perugia*, 56.

Conclusion

The epigraph is drawn from a 1725 edition of the early fourteenth-century *Chronica de civitate Ravennae*.

1. For two influential discussions of "truth" in historiography, see Morse, *Truth and Convention in the Middle Ages*, 85–124, and Veyne, *Did the Greeks Believe in Their Myths?*

2. D. Kelly, "Viking Saga Sets Sail."

3. Smalley, "Sallust in the Middle Ages," 167.

4. Martines, *Power and Imagination*, 22–29.

5. See the terms used in Fasoli, *Dalla 'civitas' al comune*, 155–89; Artifoni, "Podestà professionali," 690–98; and Dazzi, *Mussato preumanista*, 47. A. Frugoni, "*Renovatio Senatus* del 1143," discusses a similar case in twelfth-century Rome. Related to the use of such terms is the proliferation in manuscripts of vernacular lists explaining Roman offices and their functions—for example, "Tribuni fuoro officiali del popolo minuto" (tribunes were the officials of the "little people"), in Casella, *Tra Boccaccio e Petrarca*, 25. One such list, transcribed and discussed by Casella, appears with an Italian translation of Valerius Maximus in at least ten fourteenth-century manuscripts; a version of this list appears as part of book thirty of Armannino Giudice's unpublished *Fiorita*.

6. See, for example, Beneš, "Mapping a Roman Legend."

7. The dating of the Capitoline wolf—traditionally assumed to be an Etruscan work from the fifth century B.C.—has recently been challenged by Carruba, *Lupa Capitolina*, who claims that evidence from the bronze's production process attests to a medieval origin.

8. The only exception—and one probably not meant for public view—is the Rambona diptych, a small ivory (c. 900) now in the Vatican Museum. See Mazzoni, *She-Wolf*, 193–97.

Bibliography

Manuscript Sources

Cambridge, Corpus Christi College, MS 16
Florence
    Biblioteca Medicea-Laurenziana, MS Gaddi rel. 1, rel. 11, rel. 12, rel. 18, rel. 20, rel. 35, rel. 46, rel. 47, rel. 71, rel. 88, rel. 90, rel. 95; MS Martelli 2; MSS Plut. 61:33, 62:12, 62:26, 78:23, 89 inf.:50
    Biblioteca Nazionale Centrale, MSS II.II.60, II.II.73, II.II.124, II.II.154, II.III.135, II.IV.32, II.IV.44, II.IV.45, II.IV.46; MS Palatino 348; MS Panciatichi 13 [12]
    Biblioteca Riccardiana, MSS 816, 1538, 1554, 1821, 1899, 2268, 2418
Genoa
    Archivio di Stato, MS 84
    Archivio storico del comune di Genova, MS 352
    Biblioteca Universitaria, MS B.VII.21
    Biblioteca Civica Berio, MSS m.r.cf Arm.8, m.r.cf bis.4.1, m.r.cf bis.4.2
London, British Library, MSS Add. 11987, 15477; MS Egerton 2630; MSS Harley 2493, 3536A; Cotton MSS Nero D.I, Julius D.VII
Lucca, Archivio di Stato, MSS 53, 54
Milan, Biblioteca Ambrosiana, MSS B 24 inf., C 174 inf., D 11 inf., G 75 sup., G 111 inf., N 288 sup., Q 85 sup., T 32 sup.
New Haven, Yale University, Beinecke Library, MS Osborn fa. 33
Oxford, Bodleian Library, MSS Canon. Class. Lat. 212, Canon. Ital. 2, Canon. Ital. 146
Paris, Bibliothèque Nationale, MSS Ital. 6, 120, 590, 617, 16577; MSS Lat. 4931, 8027, 10136
Perugia, Università di Perugia, Istituto della filologia romanza, unnumbered MS (Bonifacio da Verona, *Eulistea* [*Liber antiquitatum comunis Perusii*])
Siena, Biblioteca Comunale degli Intronati, MSS I.VII.6, S.IV.11
Vatican City, Biblioteca Apostolica Vaticana, MSS Barb. Lat. 3923, 3992; MSS Chigi L.VIII.296, L.VIII.297, L.VIII.298, L.VIII.299; MSS Ottob. Lat. 92, 3336; MSS Pal. Lat. 939, 1644; MS Urb. Lat. 422; MSS Vat. Lat. 1769, 4834, 4941, 4949, 5261, 5271, 5287, 9448
Venice
    Biblioteca Nazionale Marciana, MSS Lat. X, 96 (3530), 169 (3847), 237 (3659), 263 (3661); MSS Zanetti Lat. CCCCI (1703), DXLIV, 169 (2030)
    Museo Civico Correr, Rip. Commissioni 326; Correr MS 887
Verona, Biblioteca Comunale, MS 209/1308

Cited Editions of Primary Sources

Agnolo di Tura. *Cronaca maggiore*. In *Cronache Senesi*, edited by Alessandro Lisini and Fabio Iacometti, 253–564. Rerum italicarum scriptores, n.s., 15.6. Bologna: Zanichelli, 1931–39.

Albertino Mussato. *Écérinide, épîtres métriques sur la poésie, songe*. Edited by Jean-Frédéric Chevalier. Paris: Les Belles Lettres, 2000.

———. *Ecerinis*. Translated by J. R. Berrigan. Munich: Fink, 1975.

———. *The Tragedy of Ecerinis*. Translated by R. W. Carruba. University Park: Pennsylvania State University Press, 1972.

Andrea Caffaro. *Annales Januenses*. Edited by Luigi T. Belgrano and Cesare Imperiale di Sant'Angelo in *Annali genovesi di Caffaro e de' suoi continuatori*, vol. 1. Fonti per la storia d'Italia 11. Rome: Istituto storico italiano per il medio evo, 1890.

Andrea Lancia. *Compilazione della Eneide di Virgilio fatta volgare in sul principio del secolo XIV da Ser Andrea Lancia, notaro fiorentino*. Edited by Pietro Fanfani. Florence: Stamperia sulle logge del grano, 1851.

———. *Ordinamenti, provvisioni e riformagioni del Comune di Firenze volgarizzati da Andrea Lancia, 1355–1357*. Edited by Luca Azzetta. Venice: Istituto Veneto di scienze, lettere, ed arti, 2001.

Das Anno-Lied. Edited by Martin Opitz. Heidelberg: Winter, 1961.

Appian of Alexandria. *Historia romana*. Edited by P. Viereck and A. G. Roos. Bibliotheca scriptorum Graecorum et Romanorum. Leipzig: Teubner, 1962.

Banchi, Luciano, ed. "Breve degli officiali del comune di Siena, 1250." *Archivio storico italiano*, 3rd ser., 3 (1866): 3–104.

Bartolomeo da San Concordio. *Ammaestramenti degli antichi*. Edited by Pier Giuseppe Colombi. Siena: Cantagalli, 1963.

———. *Ammaestramenti degli antichi, raccolti e volgarizzati per fra Bartolomeo da San Concordio*. Edited by V. Nannucci. Florence: Fraticelli, 1857.

———. *Il Catilinario e il Giugurtino, libri due di C. Crispo Sallustio, volgarizzati per frate Bartolomeo da S. Concordio*. Edited by Basilio Puoti. 2nd ed. Naples: Diogene, 1843.

———. *De origine civitatis Pisanae: Breviarium Pisanae historiae*. In *Rerum italicarum scriptores 6*, edited by Lodovico Muratori, cols. 163–65. Milan: Societas Palatina in Regia Curia, 1725.

Benzo d'Alessandria. *Chronicon*, chapters 136–67. Edited and translated by J. R. Berrigan in "Benzo d'Alessandria and the Cities of Northern Italy." *Studies in Medieval and Renaissance History* 4 (1967): 125–92.

Biagi, Guido, ed. *Lo Zibaldone Boccaccesco: Mediceo Laurenziano Plut. XXXI-8*. Facsimile ed. Florence: Olschki, 1915.

Boncompagno da Signa. *L'assedio d'Ancona (Liber de obsidione Ancone)*. Edited by Paolo Garbini. Rome: Viella, 1999.

———. *Boncompagno da Signa: The History of the Siege of Ancona*. Translated by Andrew F. Stone. Venice: Filippi Editore, 2002.

Bonifacio da Verona. *Eulistea (Liber antiquitatum comunis Perusii)*. *See* Manuscript Sources: Perugia.

———. *Eulistea*. Edited as "De rebus a Perusinis gestis" by Francesco Bonaini, Ariodante Fabretti, and Filippo-Luigi Polidori in "Cronache e storie inedite della città di Perugia da MCL al MDLXIII (1150–1563)." *Archivio storico italiano* 16 (1850): 1–52. [Selections.]

Bono Giamboni. *Delle storie contra i pagani di Paolo Orosio libri VII*. Edited by Francesco Tassi. Florence: Baracchi, 1849.

———. *Di Vegezio Flavio dell'arte guerra libri IV*. Florence: Marenigh, 1815.

Bonvesin da la Riva. *De magnalibus Mediolani (Meraviglie di Milano)*. Edited and translated by Paolo Chiesa. Milan: Scheiwiller, 1997.

———. *Expositiones Catonis: Saggio di ricostruzione critica*. Edited by Carlo Beretta. Pisa: Scuola normale superiore, 2000.

———. *Volgari scelti (Select Poems)*. Edited and translated by Patrick S. Diehl. New York: Peter Lang, 1987.

Brunetto Latini. *Li livres dou Trésor*. Edited by Paul Barrette and Spurgeon Baldwin. Tempe: Arizona Center for Medieval and Renaissance Studies, 2003.

———. *The Book of the Treasure (Trésor)*. Translated by Paul Barrette and Spurgeon Baldwin. New York: Garland, 1993.

———. *Il Tesoro*. Edited by François A. P. Chabaille as *Il Tesoro di Brunetto Latini volgarizzato da Bono Giamboni*. Bologna: Romagnoli, 1878. [Contemporary Italian translation of *Li livres dou Trésor*.]

Caesar (Gaius Julius Caesar). *Bellum Gallicum*. Edited by Wolfgang Hering. Leipzig: Teubner, 1987.

Carmen in victoriam Pisanorum. Edited by H. E. J. Cowdrey in "The Mahdia Campaign of 1087." *English Historical Review* 92 (1977): 1–29.

Catoni, Giuliano, ed. *Statuti senesi dell'arte dei giudici e notai del secolo XIV*. Rome: Centro di Ricerca Editore, 1972.

Chronica de civitate Ravennae. In *Rerum italicarum scriptores* 1.2, edited by Lodovico Muratori, cols. 574–79. Milan: Societas Palatina in Regia Curia, 1725.

Chronica de origine civitatis. In *Quellen und Forschungen zur ältesten Geschichte der Stadt Florenz*, vol. 1, edited by Otto Hartwig, 35–69. Marburg: N. G. Elwert, 1875.

Ciampolo di Meo degli Ugurgieri. *L'Eneide di Virgilio volgarizzata nel buon secolo della lingua*. Edited by Aurelio Gotti. Florence: Le Monnier, 1858.

Cicero (Marcus Tullius Cicero). *De officiis*. Edited by M. Winterbottom. Oxford: Clarendon Press, 1994.

Cino da Pistoia. *Lectura super Codice*. Edited by Giovanni Polara. 2 vols. Rome: Istituto giuridico Bartolo da Sassoferrato, Il Cigno Galileo Galilei, 1998.

———. *Rime*. Edited by Alberto Tallone. Paris: Mansart, 1948.

Il Conto di Corciano e di Perugia: Leggenda cavalleresca del secolo XIV. Edited by Franco Mancini. Florence: La nuova Italia, 1979.

Dante Alighieri. *Divina commedia*. Edited and translated by Charles S. Singleton as *The Divine Comedy: Inferno, Purgatorio, Paradiso*. 6 vols. Princeton: Princeton University Press, 1970.

De laude civitatis Laude. Edited by Alessandro Caretta. Lodi: Biancardi, 1962.

Dino Compagni. *Cronica*. Edited by Davide Cappi. Fonti per la storia dell'Italia medievale: Rerum italicarum scriptores 1. Rome: Istituto storico italiano per il medio evo, 2000.

———. *Dino Compagni's Chronicle of Florence*. Translated by Daniel E. Bornstein. Philadelphia: University of Pennsylvania Press, 1986.

Eusebius of Caesarea. *Chronicorum libri duo*. Edited by Alfred Schoene. 2nd ed. Berlin: Weidmann, 1967.

Fabretti, Ariodante, ed. "Brevi annali della città di Perugia dal anno 1194 sino al 1352." *Archivio storico italiano* 16 (1850): 53–68.

Li faits des Romains. Edited by Louis-Fernand Flutre and K. Sneyders de Vogel. 2 vols. Paris: Droz, 1938.

I fatti di Cesare. Edited by Luciano Banchi. Bologna: Romagnoli, 1863.

Ferreto de' Ferreti. *De Scaligerorum origine*. Vol. 3 of *Opere di Ferreto de' Ferreti*, edited by Carlo Cipolla. Fonti per la storia d'Italia 43 bis. Rome: Tipografia del Senato, 1920.

Filippo Ceffi. *Le Dicerie di ser Filippo Ceffi notaio fiorentino*. Edited by Luigi Biondi. Turin: Chirio e Mina, 1825.

Flodoard of Reims. *Historia Remensis ecclesiae*. Edited by Martina Stratmann. Monumenta Germaniae Historica: Scriptores 36. Hannover: Hahn, 1998.

Florentie urbis et reipublice descriptio. In *Die Loggia dei Lanzi*, edited by C. Frey, 199–223. Berlin: Wilhelm Hertz, 1885.

Francesco di Andrea. *Croniche di Viterbo*. In *Fontes rerum germanicarum*, edited by F. Boehmer, 4:686–722. Aalen: Scientia Verlag, 1969.

Frazer, R. M., trans. *The Trojan War: The Chronicles of Dictys of Crete and Dares the Phrygian*. Bloomington: Indiana University Press, 1966.

Galvano Fiamma. *Chronica Mediolani, seu Manipulus florum*. In *Rerum italicarum scriptores* 11, edited by Lodovico Muratori, cols. 537–740. Milan: Societas Palatina in Regia Curia, 1727.

Geoffrey of Monmouth. *The History of the Kings of Britain*. Translated by Lewis G. M. Thorpe. Baltimore: Penguin, 1966.

Gigli, Girolamo. *Diario sanese*. Siena: Quinza, 1723. Reprint, Bologna: Forni, 1974.

Giovanni Balbi. *Catholicon*. Mainz, 1460. Reprint, Westmead, UK: Gregg International, 1971.

Giovanni da Nono. *Liber de ludi fortunae*. Edited by Giovanni Fabris in "La cronaca di Giovanni da Nono." *Bollettino del Museo civico di Padova*, n.s., 8 (1932): 1–33; 9 (1933): 167–200; 10–11 (1934–39): 1–30.

Giovanni Villani. *Nuova cronica*. Edited by Giuseppe Porta. 3 vols. Parma: Fondazione Pietro Bembo/Guanda, 1990.

———. *Villani's Chronicle: Being Selections from the First Nine Books of the Croniche Fiorentine of Giovanni Villani*. Edited and translated by Rose E. Selfe and Philip Henry Wicksteed. 2nd ed. London: Constable, 1906.

Gloria, A., ed. *Monumenti della Università di Padova 1222–1318*. Venice: R. Istituto Veneto di scienze, lettere, ed arti, 1884.

———. *Statuti del Comune di Padova, dal secolo XII all'anno 1285*. Padua: Sacchetto, 1873.

Guglielmo da Pastrengo. *De viris illustribus et de originibus*. Edited by Guglielmo Bottari. Padua: Editrice Antenore, 1991.

Guido da Pisa. *I fatti d'Enea di Frate Guido da Pisa*. Edited by Francesco Fòffano. Florence: Sansoni, 1957.

———. *I fatti di Enea, estratti dalla Eneide di Virgilio e ridotti in volgare da Frate Guido da Pisa, carmelitano del secolo XIV*. Edited by Bartolommeo Gamba and Basilio Puoti. Naples: Del Fibreno, 1834.

Guido delle Colonne. *Historia destructionis Troiae*. Edited by Nathaniel Edward Griffin. Cambridge: Medieval Academy of America, 1936.

Guidotto da Bologna. *Fiore di rettorica*. Edited by Giambattista Speroni. Pavia: Università di Pavia, 1994.

Historia Tudertine civitatis. In *Le Cronache di Todi (secoli XIII–XVI)*, edited by G. Italiani, Claudio Leonardi, Franco Mancini, Enrico Menestò, Carlo Santini, and G. Scentoni, 66–93. Florence: La nuova Italia, 1979.

Isidore of Seville. *Etymologiae*. Edited by W. M. Lindsay as *Etymologiarum sive Originum*. 2 vols. Oxford: Clarendon Press, 1911.

———. *The Etymologies of Isidore of Seville*. Translated and edited by Stephen A. Barney, W. J. Lewis, J. A. Beach, and Oliver Berghof. Cambridge: Cambridge University Press, 2006.

Jacopo da Varagine. *Chronicon Januense*. Edited by Giovanni Monleone as *Jacopo da Varagine e la sua cronaca di Genova*. 3 vols. Fonti per la storia d'Italia 84–86. Rome: Tipografia del Senato, 1941.

———. *Cronaca della città di Genova dalle origini al 1297*. Translated by Stefania Bertini Guidetti. Genoa: ECIG, 1995.

———. *Legenda aurea*. Edited by Giovanni Paolo Maggioni. 2nd ed. 2 vols. Florence: SISMEL, 1998.

———. *The Golden Legend: Readings on the Saints*. Translated and edited by William Granger Ryan. 2 vols. Princeton: Princeton University Press, 1993.

Jacopo Doria. *Annales Januenses*. Edited by Cesare Imperiale di Sant'Angelo in *Annali genovesi di Caffaro e de' suoi continuatori*, vol. 5. Fonti per la storia d'Italia 14 bis. Rome: Istituto storico italiano per il medio evo, 1929.

John of Salisbury. *Polycraticus*. In *Patrologia Latina*, edited by J.-P. Migne, vol. 199, cols. 379–822. Paris: Garnieri, 1844–55.

———. *Policraticus*. Edited by K. S. B. Keats-Rohan. Corpus Christianorum Continuatio Medievalis 118. Turnhout: Brepols, 1993. [Books 1–4 only.]

———. *Policraticus*. Translated by Cary J. Nederman. Cambridge: Cambridge University Press, 1990. [Selections.]

Justinus (Marcus Junianus Justinus). *Epitoma historiarum Philippicarum Pompei Trogi*. Edited by Franz Rühl and Otto Seel. 2nd ed. Stuttgart: Teubner, 1972.

Libro fiesolano. In *Quellen und Forschungen zur ältesten Geschichte der Stadt Florenz*, vol. 1, edited by Otto Hartwig, 35–69. Marburg: N. G. Elwert, 1875.

Lisini, Alessandro, ed. *Il costituto del comune di Siena volgarizzato nel MCCCIX–MCCCX*. 2 vols. Siena: Lazzeri, 1903.

Lisini, Alessandro, and Fabio Iacometti, eds. *Cronache senesi*. Rerum italicarum scriptores, n.s., 15.6. Bologna: Zanichelli, 1931–39.

Livy (Titus Livius). *Ab urbe condita*. Edited by R. M. Ogilvie, C. F. Walters, R. S. Conway, A. H. MacDonald, S. K. Johnson, and P. G. Walsh. 6 vols. Oxford: Clarendon Press, 1965–.

Lorenzo Ghiberti. *I commentarii*. Edited by Lorenzo Bartoli. Florence: Giunti, 1998.

Macrobius (Ambrosius Aurelius Theodosius Macrobius). *Saturnalia*. Edited by James Willis. Leipzig: Teubner, 1963.

———. *Saturnalia*. Translated by Percival V. Davies. New York: Columbia University Press, 1969.

Marcacci Marinelli, Olga, ed. *Liber inquisitionum del Capitano del popolo di Perugia*. Perugia: Università degli studi di Perugia, 1975.

Marco. *Prima edificacio civitatis Venetorum*. Edited by Antonio Carile in "Aspetti della cronachistica veneziana nei secoli XIII e XIV." In *La storiografia veneziana fino al secolo XVI*, edited by Agostino Pertusi, 75–126. Florence: Olschki, 1970.

Marsilius of Padua (Marsiglio de Mainardini). *Defensor pacis*. Translated by Alan Gewirth. Edited by Cary Nederman. New York: Columbia University Press, 2001.

Matteo Ciaccheri. *Cronachetta di S. Gemignano composta da Fr. Matteo Giaccheri fiorentino l'anno mccclv*. Edited by Ettore Sarteschi. Bologna: Commissione per i testi di lingua, 1968.

Matteo dei Libri. *Le Arringhe*. Edited by Eleonore Vincenti. Naples: Ricciardi, 1974.

Meister, Ferdinand Otto. *Über Dares von Phrygien: De excidio Troiae historia*. Breslau: Druck von Grass Barth, 1871.

Niccolò Smereglo. *Annales civitatis Vincentiae*. Edited by G. Soranzo. Rerum italicarum scriptores, n.s., 8.5. Città di Castello: Zanichelli, 1921.

Origo civitatum Italie seu Veneziarum (Chronicon Altinate et Chronicon Gradense). Edited by Roberto Cessi. Fonti per la storia d'Italia 73. Rome: Tipografia del Senato, 1933.

Pace da Ferrara. *La festa delle Marie descritta in un poemetto elegiaco latino da Pace del Friuli*. Edited by Emmanuele A. Cicogna. Venice: Cecchini, 1843.

Padrin, Luigi, ed. *La dedizione di Treviso e la morte di Cangrande I: Carme del secolo XIV (per le nozze Tolomei-Frigerio)*. Padua: Tipografia del Seminario, 1896.

———, ed. *Lupati Lupatis, Bovetini de Bovetinis, Albertini Mussatis necnon et Jamboni Andreae de Favafuschis Carmina quaedam (per nozze Giusti-Giustiniani)*. Padua: Tipografia del Seminario, 1887.

Paulus Diaconus. *Historia Romana*. Edited by A. Crivellucci. Fonti per la storia d'Italia 51. Rome: Tipografia del Senato, 1914.

Petrarch (Francesco Petrarca). *De viris illustribus*. Edited by G. Martellotti. Vol. 1. Florence: Sansoni, 1964.

———. *Vita Julii Caesaris*. Edited by Luigi Razzolini in *Le vite degli uomini illustri di Francesco Petrarca, volgarizzate da Donato degli Albanzati da Pratovecchio*. 2 vols. Bologna: Romagnoli, 1874.

———. *Invectives*. Edited and translated by David Marsh. I Tatti Renaissance Library 11. Cambridge: Harvard University Press, 2003.

———. *Rerum familiarium libri (Letters on Familiar Matters)*. Edited and translated by Aldo S. Bernardo. 3 vols. Vol. 1, Albany: State University of New York Press, 1975. Vols. 2 and 3, Baltimore: Johns Hopkins University Press, 1982 and 1985.

———. *Rerum senilium libri (Letters of Old Age)*. Edited and translated by Aldo S. Bernardo, Saul Levin, and Reta A. Bernardo. 2 vols. Baltimore: Johns Hopkins University Press, 1992.

Pietro Alighieri. *Comentum super poema Comedie Dantis: A Critical Edition of the Third and Final Draft of Pietro Alighieri's Commentary on Dante's "The Divine Comedy."* Edited and translated by Massimiliano Chiamenti. Tempe: Arizona Center for Medieval and Renaissance Studies, 2002.

Powell, J. M., ed. *The "Liber Augustalis," or the Constitutions of Melfi Promulgated by the Emperor Frederick II for the Kingdom of Sicily in 1231*. Syracuse: Syracuse University Press, 1971.

Ptolemy of Lucca. *On the Government of Rulers: De regimine principum*. Edited and translated by James M. Blythe. Philadelphia: University of Pennsylvania Press, 1997.

Puncuh, Dino, and Antonella Rovere, eds. *I libri iurium della Repubblica di Genova*. Rome: Istituto poligrafico e zecca dello stato, Libreria dello stato, 1992.

Ranieri Granchi. *De proeliis Tusciae*. Edited by Celestino Meliconi. Rerum italicarum scriptores, n.s., 11.2. Bologna: Zanichelli, 1915.

Ranieri Sardo. *Cronaca di Pisa*. Edited by Ottavio Banti. Fonti per la storia d'Italia 99. Rome: Istituto storico italiano per il medio evo, 1963.

Remigio de' Girolami. *De bono communi* and *De bono pacis*. Edited by Emilio Panella in "Dal bene comune al bene del Comune: I trattati politici del Remigio de' Girolami nella Firenze del bianchi-neri." *Memorie domenicane* 16 (1985): 123–83.

Riccobaldo da Ferrara. *Chronica parva Ferrariensis*. Edited by Gabriele Zannella. Ferrara: Deputazione provinciale ferrarese di storia patria, 1983.

―――. *Compendium Romanae historiae*. Edited by A. Teresa Hankey. 2 vols. Fonti per la storia d'Italia 108. Rome: Istituto storico italiano per il medio evo, 1984.

―――. *Compilatio chronologica*. Edited by A. Teresa Hankey. Fonti per la storia dell'Italia medievale, Rerum italicarum scriptores 4. Rome: Istituto storico italiano per il medio evo, 2000.

Ricordano Malispini. *Storia fiorentina: Col seguito di Giacotto Malispini dalla edificazione di Firenze sino all'anno 1286*. Edited by Vincenzio Follini. Rome: Multigrafica, 1976.

Rolandino of Padua. *Liber chronicarum*. Edited by A. Bonardi as *Cronica in factis et circa facta Marchie Trivixane*. Rerum italicarum scriptores, n.s., 8.1. Città di Castello: Zanichelli, 1905.

―――. *The Chronicles of the Trevisan March*. Translated and edited by Joseph R. Berrigan. Lawrence, Kans.: Coronado Press, 1980.

Rolandino Passaggeri. *Atti e formule di Rolandino*. Bologna: Forni, 2000.

―――. *Summa totius artis notariae*. Bologna: Forni, 1977.

Sallust (Gaius Sallustius Crispus). *Jugurtha*. In *Opera*, edited by L. D. Reynolds, 54–149. Oxford: Clarendon Press, 1991.

Sanzanome. *Gesta Florentinorum*. In *Quellen und Forschungen zur ältesten Geschichte der Stadt Florenz*, vol. 1, edited by Otto Hartwig, 1–34. Marburg: N. G. Elwert, 1875.

Seel, Otto, ed. *Pompeius Trogus fragmenta*. Leipzig: Teubner, 1956.

Seneca (Lucius Annaeus Seneca, the Younger). *Ad Helviam de consolatione*. In *Dialogues*, vol. 3, *Consolations*, edited by René Waltz, 54–89. Paris: Les Belles Lettres, 1971.

Servius Grammaticus. *In Vergilii carmina commentarii*. Edited by Georg Thilo and Hermann Hagen. 3 vols. Leipzig: Teubner, 1881–1902. Reprint, Hildesheim: G. Olms, 1961.

Silva, Augusta, Carlo Varaldo, and Sandra Origone, eds. *Corpus inscriptionum medii aevi Liguriae*. Vol. 3, *Genova, Centro storico*, edited by Augusta Silva. Genoa: Istituto di medievistica, Università di Genova, 1987.

Solinus (Gaius Iulius Solinus). *Collectanea rerum memorabilium*. Edited by Theodor Mommsen. 1895. Reprint, Berlin: Weidmann, 1958.

Ugolini, Francesco, ed. "Annali e Cronaca di Perugia in volgare dal 1191 al 1336." *Annali della facoltà di lettere e filosofia della Università degli studi di Perugia* 1 (1964): 143–337.

Virgil (Publius Vergilius Maro). *Aeneid*. In *Opera*, edited by R. A. B. Mynors, 103–422. Oxford: Clarendon Press, 1972.

Wace (Master Wace). *Wace's Roman de Brut: A History of the British*. Edited and translated by Judith Weiss. Exeter: University of Exeter Press, 1999.

William Fitzstephen. *Norman London*. Edited and translated by F. M. Stenton. New York: Italica Press, 1990.

Wright, John, trans. *The Life of Cola di Rienzo*. Toronto: Pontifical Institute of Mediaeval Studies, 1975.

Zappacosta, G., ed. "*Orationes de laudibus Perusiae* di Francesco Maturanzio e Cristoforo Sassi." In *Studi e ricerche sull'umanesimo italiano*, 65–113. Bergamo: Minerva Italica, 1972.

Zdekauer, Lodovico, ed. *Il constituto del comune di Siena dell'anno 1262*. Milan: Hoepli, 1897.

Zorzi, M. A., ed. "L'ordinamento comunale padovano nella seconda metà del secolo XIII." *Miscellanea di storia veneta, R. Deputazione Veneta di storia patria*, 4th ser., 5 (1931): 1–245.

Secondary Works Cited

Abbondanza, Roberto, ed. *Il notariato a Perugia: Mostra documentaria e iconografica per il XVI Congresso nazionale del notariato (Perugia, maggio–luglio 1967)*. Rome: Consiglio nazionale del notariato, 1973.

———. "Primi appunti sulla legislazione statutaria di Perugia dei secoli XIII e XIV." *Archivio storico italiano* 120 (1962): 461–68.

Abulafia, David. *Frederick II: A Medieval Emperor*. London: Allen Lane, 1988.

———. "Kantorowicz and Frederick II." *History* 62 (1977): 193–210.

Airaldi, Gabriella. "Caffaro, storia di Genova, storia economica." In *Studi in onore di G. Barbieri*, 53–74. Pisa: IPEM, 1984.

———. *Genova e la Liguria nel Medio Evo*. Turin: UTET, 1986.

———. *Jacopo da Varagine: Tra santi e mercanti*. Milan: Camunia, 1988.

Albini, Giuliana, ed. *Le scritture del comune: Amministrazione e memoria nelle città dei secoli XII e XIII*. Turin: Scriptorium, 1998.

Alessio, G. C., and C. Villa. "Il nuovo fascino degli autori antichi tra i secoli XII e XIV." In *Lo spazio letterario di Roma antica*, edited by G. Cavallo, P. Fedeli, and A. Giardina, 473–511. Rome: Salerno Editrice, 1995.

Algazi, Gadi, Valentin Groebner, and Bernhard Jussen. *Negotiating the Gift: Pre-Modern Figurations of Exchange*. Göttingen: Vandenhoeck & Ruprecht, 2003.

Althoff, Gerd, Johannes Fried, and Patrick J. Geary, eds. *Medieval Concepts of the Past: Ritual, Memory, Historiography*. Cambridge: Cambridge University Press, 2002.

Andrews, Frances. "Albertano of Brescia, Rolandino of Padua, and the Rhetoric of Legitimation." In *Building Legitimacy: Political Discourses and Forms of Legitimacy in Medieval Societies*, edited by Isabel Alfonso Antón, Hugh Kennedy, and Julio Escalona, 319–40. Leiden: Brill, 2004.

Antonelli, Roberto, Costanzo di Girolamo, and Rosario Coluccia. *I poeti della scuola siciliana*. Milan: Mondadori, 2008.

Arnaldi, Girolamo. "Andrea Dandolo, Doge-cronista." In *La storiografia veneziana fino al secolo XVI*, edited by Agostino Pertusi, 127–268. Florence: Olschki, 1970.

———. "Il notaio-cronista e le cronache cittadine in Italia." In *La storia del diritto nel quadro delle scienze storiche*, 293–309. Florence: Olschki, 1966.

———. "Il primo secolo dello studio di Padova." In *Storia della cultura veneta*, vol. 2, *Il trecento*, edited by Gianfranco Folena, 1–18. Vicenza: Neri Pozza, 1976.

———. *Studi sui cronisti della Marca Trevigiana nell'età di Ezzelino da Romano*. Rome: Istituto storico italiano per il medio evo, 1963.

———. *Testi per lo studio di Rolandino di Padova*. Padua: Pàtron, 1964.

Artifoni, E. "I podestà professionali e la fondazione retorica della politica comunale." *Quaderni storici* 63 (1996): 687–719.

Ascheri, Mario. *Antica legislazione della Repubblica di Siena*. Siena: Il Leccio, 1993.

———. *Le città-stato*. Bologna: Il Mulino, 2006.

———, ed. *Siena e Maremma nel medioevo*. Siena: Betti, 2001.

———. *Siena nella storia*. Milan: Silvana, 2000.

———. *Lo spazio storico di Siena*. Milan: Silvana, 2001.

———. *L'Università di Siena: 750 anni di storia*. Milan: Silvana, 1992.

Azzetta, Luca. "Per la biografia di Andrea Lancia." *Italia medioevale e umanistica* 39 (1996): 121–70.

Bairoch, Paul, Jean Batou, and Pierre Chèvre. *La population des villes européennes, 800–1850: Banque de données et analyse sommaire des résultats.* Geneva: Droz, 1988.

Balard, Michel. *La mer Noire et la Romanie génoise: XIIIe–XVe siècles.* London: Variorum, 1989.

Baldi, Agnello. *Guittone d'Arezzo fra impegno a poesia.* Salerno: Società editrice salernitana, 1975.

Balestracci, Duccio, Daniela Lamberini, Mauro Civai, Paolo Galluzzi, and Bruno Bruchi. *I bottini medievali di Siena.* Siena: Alsaba, 1993.

Banchi, Luciano. *Le origini favolose di Siena secondo una presunta cronica romana di Tisbo Colonnese.* Siena: Tipografia all'Insegna di S. Bernardino, 1882.

Banti, Ottavio. "Studi sulla genesi dei testi cronistici pisani del secolo XIV." *Bollettino dell'Istituto storico italiano per il medio evo* 75 (1963): 259–319.

Bargagli-Petrucci, Fabio. *Le fonti di Siena e i loro acquedotti.* 2 vols. Siena: Olschki, 1906. Reprint, Siena: Periccioli, 1992.

Baron, Hans. *The Crisis of the Early Italian Renaissance: Civic Humanism and Republican Liberty in an Age of Classicism and Tyranny.* Princeton: Princeton University Press, 1955.

———. *In Search of Florentine Civic Humanism: Essays on the Transition from Medieval to Modern Thought.* 2 vols. Princeton: Princeton University Press, 1988.

Bartoli Langeli, Attilio. *Codice diplomatico del comune di Perugia: Periodo consolare e podestarile (1139–1254).* 3 vols. Perugia: Deputazione di storia patria per l'Umbria, 1983.

Bartoli Langeli, Attilio, and Loriano Zurli. *L'iscrizione in versi della Fontana Maggiore di Perugia (1278).* Rome: Herder, 1996.

Bascapè, G. C. "I sigilli dei comuni italiani nel medio evo e nell'età moderna." In *Studi di paleografia, diplomatica, storia e araldica in onore di Cesare Manaresi,* 59–123. Milan: Giuffrè, 1953.

Battaglia, Salvatore. *Il Boezio e l'Arrighetto nelle versioni del trecento.* Turin: UTET, 1929.

Baxandall, Michael. *Painting and Experience in Fifteenth-Century Italy.* 2nd ed. Oxford: Oxford University Press, 1988.

Beaune, Colette. *The Birth of an Ideology: Myths and Symbols of Nation in Late-Medieval France.* Translated by Fredric L. Cheyette. Berkeley and Los Angeles: University of California Press, 1991.

Becker, Marvin B. *Florence in Transition.* 2 vols. Baltimore: Johns Hopkins University Press, 1967.

Bellini, Erika. *L'università a Perugia negli statuti cittadini, secoli XII–XVI.* Perugia: Deputazione di storia patria per l'Umbria, 2007.

Bellosi, Luciano. *Duccio: La Maestà.* Milan: Electa, 1998.

Beneš, Carrie E. "Ancient and Most Noble: Catalogues of City Foundation in Fourteenth-Century Italy." In *Medieval Manuscripts, Their Makers and Users: A Special Issue of Viator in Honor of Richard and Mary Rouse.* Turnhout: Brepols, 2011.

———. "Cola di Rienzo and the *Lex Regia.*" *Viator* 30 (1999): 231–52.

———. "Many Januses in Search of Unity: Defining Civic Identity in Genoa, 1257–1312." *Studies in Medieval and Renaissance History,* 3rd ser., 6 (2009): 53–92.

———. "Mapping a Roman Legend: The House of Cola di Rienzo from Piranesi to Baedeker." *Italian Culture* 26 (2008): 53–83.

———. "Whose SPQR? Sovereignty and Semiotics in Medieval Rome." *Speculum* 84 (2009): 874–904.

Bénéteau, David P. "Per un'edizione critica dei 'Fatti dei Romani.'" *Italianistica: Rivista di letteratura italiana* 26, no. 3 (1997): 401–11.

Benson, R. L. "*Libertas* in Italy (1152–1226)." In *La notion de liberté au Moyen Age: Islam, Byzance, Occident*, edited by G. Makdisi, D. Sourdel, and J. Sourdel-Thomine, 191–213. Paris: Les Belles Lettres, 1985.

———. "Political *Renovatio*: Two Models from Roman Antiquity." In *Renaissance and Renewal in the Twelfth Century*, edited by R. L. Benson and Giles Constable, 339–86. Cambridge: Harvard University Press, 1982.

Benton, Tim. "The Design of Siena and Florence Duomos." In *Siena, Florence, and Padua: Art, Society, and Religion, 1280–1400*, edited by Diana Norman, 129–43. New Haven: Yale University Press, in association with the Open University, 1995.

Bernabò di Negro, G. F. *L'araldica a Genova: Origini e significati di une realtà storica e sociale*. Genoa: Liguria, 1983.

Berrigan, J. R. "Benzo d'Alessandria and the Cities of Northern Italy." *Studies in Medieval and Renaissance History* 4 (1967): 125–92.

———. "Riccobaldo and Giovanni Mansionario as Historians." *Manuscripta* 30 (1986): 215–23.

———. "A Tale of Two Cities: Verona and Padua in the Late Middle Ages." In *Art and Politics in Late Medieval and Early Renaissance Italy, 1250–1500*, edited by Charles M. Rosenberg, 67–80. South Bend, Ind.: University of Notre Dame Press, 1990.

Bertazzo, L., ed. *Vite e vita di Antonio di Padova: Atti del convegno internazionale sulla agiografia antoniana, Padova, 29 maggio–1 giugno 1995*. Padua: Centro studi antoniani, 1997.

Bertini, Stefania. "Il mito di Genova in Iacopo da Varagine tra storia e satira." *Studi umanistici piceni* 14 (1994): 63–69.

Bertini Guidetti, Stefania. "Contrastare la crisi della chiesa cattedrale: Iacopo da Varagine e la construzione di un'ideologia propagandistica." In *Le vie del Mediterraneo: Idee, uomini, oggetti, secoli XI–XVI, Genova, 19–20 aprile 1994*, edited by Gabriella Airaldi, 155–81. Genoa: ECIG, 1997.

———. "Iacopo da Varagine e le *Ystorie antique*: Quando il mito diventa *exemplum* della storia." In *Posthomerica I: Tradizioni omeriche dall'Antichità al Rinascimento*, edited by Franco Montanari and Stefano Pittaluga, 1–19. Genoa: Dipartimento di archeologia filologia classica e loro tradizioni, Università di Genova, 1997.

———, ed. *Il paradiso e la terra: Iacopo da Varazze e il suo tempo: Atti del convegno internazionale, Varazze, 24–26 settembre 1998*. Florence: SISMEL, 2001.

———. *Potere e propaganda a Genova nel Duecento*. Genoa: ECIG, 1998.

Berto, Luigi Andrea. *Il vocabolario politico e sociale della "Istoria Veneticorum" di Giovanni Diacono*. Padua: Il poligrafo, 2001.

Beschorner, Andreas. *Untersuchungen zu Dares Phrygius*. Tübingen: G. Narr, 1992.

Billanovich, Giuseppe. "Dal Livio di Raterio (Laur. 63, 19) al Livio del Petrarca (BM Harl. 2493)." *Italia medioevale e umanistica* 2 (1959): 103–78.

———. *I primi umanisti e le tradizioni dei classici latini*. Fribourg, Switzerland: Edizioni Universitarie, 1953.

———. "Ser Convenevole maestro notaio e chierico." In *Petrarca, Verona, e l'Europa: Atti del Congresso internazionale di studi (Verona, 19–23 settembre 1991)*, edited by Giuseppe Billanovich and Giuseppe Frasso, 367–90. Padua: Editrice Antenore, 1997.

———. "Tra Dante e Petrarca." *Italia medioevale e umanistica* 8 (1965): 1–44.

Billanovich, Guido. "Il Cicerone di Rolando da Piazzola." *Italia medioevale e umanistica* 28 (1985): 37–47.

———. "Il preumanesimo padovano." In *Storia della cultura veneta*, vol. 2, *Il trecento*, edited by Gianfranco Folena, 19–110. Vicenza: Neri Pozza, 1976.

———. "I primi umanisti padovani e gli epitafi di Seneca e Livio." *Italia medioevale e umanistica* 43 (2002): 115–46.

———. "*Veterum vestigia vatum* nei carmi dei preumanisti padovani." *Italia medioevale e umanistica* 1 (1958): 155–243.

Billanovich, Maria Pia. "Una miniera di epigrafi e di antichità: Il chiostro maggiore di S. Giustina di Padova." *Italia medioevale e umanistica* 12 (1969): 197–293.

Black, Robert. *Education and Society in Florentine Tuscany: Teachers, Pupils, and Schools, c. 1250–1500.* Leiden: Brill, 2007.

———. *Humanism and Education in Medieval and Renaissance Italy: Tradition and Innovation in Latin Schools from the Twelfth to the Fifteenth Century.* Cambridge: Cambridge University Press, 2001.

Blanshei, Sarah Rubin. *Perugia, 1260–1340: Conflict and Change in a Medieval Italian Urban Society.* Philadelphia: American Philosophical Society, 1976.

———. "Population, Wealth, and Patronage in Medieval and Renaissance Perugia." *Journal of Interdisciplinary History* 9, no. 4 (1979): 597–619.

Blythe, James M. "'Civic Humanism' and Medieval Political Thought." In *Renaissance Civic Humanism: Reappraisals and Reflections,* edited by James Hankins, 30–74. Cambridge: Cambridge University Press, 2000.

Bodon, Giulio. "L'immagine di Tito Livio a Padova nella tradizione artistica rinascimentale." *Bollettino del Museo civico di Padova* 78 (1989): 69–92.

Boje Martenson, Lars. "The Diffusion of Roman Histories in the Middle Ages." *Filologia Mediolatina* 6/7 (1999–2000): 101–200.

Bolisani, E. "Un importante saggio padovano di poesia preumanistica latina." *Atti e memorie dell'Accademia patavina di scienze, lettere ed arti* 66 (1953–54): 61–77.

Boone, Marc, and Peter Stabel, eds. *Shaping Urban Identity in Late Medieval Europe* [L'apparition d'une identité urbaine dans l'Europe du bas moyen âge]. Leuven: Garant, 2000.

Bordone, Renato. *La società urbana nell'Italia comunale: Secoli XI–XIV.* Turin: Loescher, 1984.

Borlandi, F. "La formazione culturale del mercante genovese nel medioevo." *Atti della società ligure di storia patria,* n.s., 3 (1963): 221–30.

Borra, Antonello. *Guittone d'Arezzo e le maschere del poeta: La lirica cortese tra ironia e palinodia.* Ravenna: Longo, 2000.

Borracelli, Mario. "Lo sviluppo economico di Grosseto e della Maremma nei secoli XII e XIII nell'ambito dell'area economica senese." In *Siena e Maremma nel medioevo,* edited by Mario Ascheri, 115–78. Siena: Betti, 2001.

Bortolami, S. "Da Rolandino al Mussato: Tensioni ideali e senso della storia nella storiografia padovana di tradizione 'repubblicana.'" In *Il senso della storia nella cultura medievale italiana (1100–1350): Atti del XIV Convegno di studi del Centro italiano di studi di storia e arte, Pistoia, 14–17 maggio 1993,* 53–86. Pistoia: Centro italiano di studi di storia e d'arte, 1995.

Bortolotti, Lando. *Siena.* Rome: Laterza, 1983.

Boscolo, Alberto. *Sardegna, Pisa e Genova nel Medioevo.* Genoa: Istituto di paleografia e storia medievale, Università di Genova, 1978.

Bowsky, William M. "The *Buon Governo* of Siena (1287–1355): A Medieval Italian Oligarchy." *Speculum* 37 (1962): 368–81.

———. *The Finance of the Commune of Siena, 1287–1355.* Oxford: Clarendon Press, 1970.

———. *Henry VII in Italy: The Conflict of Empire and City-State, 1310–1313.* Lincoln, Nebr.: Greenwood Press, 1960.

———. "The Impact of the Black Death upon Sienese Government and Society." *Speculum* 39 (1964): 1–34.

————. *A Medieval Italian Commune: Siena Under the Nine, 1287–1355.* Berkeley and Los Angeles: University of California Press, 1981.

Boynton, Susan. *Shaping a Monastic Identity: Liturgy and History at the Imperial Abbey of Farfa, 1000–1125.* Ithaca: Cornell University Press, 2006.

Bozzo, Gianni, and Giampaolo Bartolozzi. *Cattedrale e chiostro di San Lorenzo a Genova: Conoscenza e restauro.* Genoa: Sagep, 2000.

Braccesi, Lorenzo. *La leggenda di Antenore: Dalla Troade al Veneto.* 2nd ed. Venice: Marsiglio Editori, 1997.

Brandi, Cesare, ed. *Il Palazzo Pubblico di Siena: Vicende costruttive e decorazione.* Milan: Silvana, 1983.

Brezzi, Paolo. *I comuni medioevali nella storia d'Italia.* Turin: ERI, 1970.

————. *Roma e l'impero medievale (774–1252).* Bologna: Licinia Cappelli, 1947.

Britnell, R. H. *Pragmatic Literacy, East and West, 1200–1330.* Woodbridge, Suffolk, UK; Rochester, N.Y.: Boydell Press, 1997.

Brown, Patricia Fortini. *Venice and Antiquity: The Venetian Sense of the Past.* New Haven: Yale University Press, 1996.

Brown, T. S. "History as Myth: Medieval Perceptions of Venice's Roman and Byzantine Past." In *The Making of Byzantine History: Studies Dedicated to Donald M. Nicol,* edited by M. Beaton and C. Roueché, 145–57. London: Variorum, 1993.

Brucker, Gene A. *Florence: The Golden Age, 1138–1737.* Berkeley and Los Angeles: University of California Press, 1984.

————. *Renaissance Florence.* Berkeley and Los Angeles: University of California Press, 1983.

Bruni, Francesco. "Between Oral Memory and Written Tradition in Florence at the Beginning of the XIVth Century: Coppo di Borghese Domenichi, Andrea Lancia, and Giovanni Boccaccio." In *L'Histoire et les nouveaux publics dans l'Europe médiévale (XIIIe–XVe siècles): Actes du colloque international organisé par la Fondation européenne de la science à la Casa de Velasquez, Madrid, 23–24 avril 1993,* edited by Jean-Philippe Genet, 113–25. Paris: Sorbonne, 1997.

————. "Documenti senesi per fra Guidotto da Bologna." *Medioevo romanzo* 3 (1976): 229–35.

Buonocore, Marco. "Quattro nuovi codici vaticani con il volgarizzamento delle *Heroides* di Filippo Ceffi." *Studi umanistici* 4/5 (1993–94): 259–67.

Burckhardt, Jacob. *The Civilization of the Renaissance in Italy.* Translated by S.G.C. Middlemore. London: Penguin, 1990.

Burgess, R. W., and Witold Witakowski. *Studies in Eusebian and Post-Eusebian Chronography.* Stuttgart: F. Steiner, 1999.

Burke, Peter. *The Fabrication of Louis XIV.* New Haven: Yale University Press, 1992.

————. "History as Social Memory." In *Varieties of Cultural History,* 43–59. Ithaca, N.Y.: Cornell University Press, 1997.

————. *The Italian Renaissance: Culture and Society in Italy.* 2nd ed. Princeton: Princeton University Press, 1987.

Cabona, Danilo. *Palazzo San Giorgio.* Genoa: Sagep, 1991.

Caesar, Michael. *Dante: The Critical Heritage.* New York: Routledge, 1995.

Cairola, Aldo, and Enzo Carli. *Il Palazzo pubblico di Siena.* Roma: Editalia, 1963.

Cambridge Italian Dictionary. Edited by Barbara Reynolds. 2 vols. Cambridge: Cambridge University Press, 1981.

Cammarosano, Paolo, ed. *Le forme della propaganda politica nel Due e nel Trecento: Relazioni tenute al convegno internazionale organizzato dal Comitato di studi storici di Trieste, dall'Ecole francaise de Rome e dal Dipartimento di storia dell'Universita degli studi di Trieste (Trieste, 2–5 marzo 1993).* Rome: École française de Rome, 1994.

———. *Italia medievale: Struttura e geografia delle fonti scritte.* Rome: La nuova Italia scientifica, 1991.

Campana, Augusto. *Il "cippo riminese" di Giulio Cesare.* Rimini: Arnaud, 1933.

Canal, Antonio A. *Il mondo morale di Guido da Pisa interprete di Dante.* Bologna: Pàtron, 1981.

———. "Venti anni di studi e dibattiti su Guido di Pisa." *Studi medievali* 38 (1997): 931–44.

Cannon, Joanna, and Beth Williamson, eds. *Art, Politics, and Civic Religion in Central Italy, 1261–1352.* Aldershot, UK: Ashgate, 2000.

Caputo, Giacomo. "La tradizione etrusca del grifo e l'emblema di Perugia." *Studi Etruschi* 29 (1961): 417–22.

Cardini, Franco, and Carlo M. Cipolla. *Banchieri e mercanti di Siena.* Rome: De Luca, 1987.

Carile, Antonio. "Aspetti della cronachistica veneziana nei secoli XIII e XIV." In *La storiografia veneziana fino al secolo XVI,* edited by Agostino Pertusi, 75–126. Florence: Olschki, 1970.

———. "Il problema delle origini di Venezia." In *Le origini delle chiesa di Venezia,* edited by Franco Tonon, 77–100. Venice: Edizioni studium cattolico veneziano, 1987.

Carile, Antonio, and Giorgio Fedalto. *Le origini di Venezia.* Bologna: Pàtron, 1978.

Carlen, Louis. "Die Wölfin von Siena: ein Stadt- und Staatssymbol." In *Nit anders denn liebs und guets: Petershauser Kolloquium aus Anlaß des 80. Geburtstags von Karl S. Bader,* edited by Clausdieter Schott and Claudio Soliva, 35–38. Sigmaringen: Thorbecke, 1986.

Carli, Enzo. *Il Duomo di Siena.* Genoa: Sagep, 1979.

———. *Giovanni Pisano.* Pisa: Pacini, 1977.

Caro, Georg. *Genua und die Mächte am Mittelmeer: 1257–1311: Ein Beitrag zur Geschichte des 13. Jahrhunderts.* 2 vols. Aalen: Scientia-Verlag, 1967.

Carpegna Falconieri, Tommaso di. *Cola di Rienzo.* Rome: Salerno, 2002.

Carruba, Anna Maria. *La Lupa Capitolina: Un bronzo medievale.* Rome: De Luca, 2006.

Carruthers, Mary. *The Book of Memory: A Study of Memory in Medieval Culture.* Cambridge: Cambridge University Press, 1990.

Carruthers, Mary, and Jan M. Ziolkowski, eds. *The Medieval Craft of Memory: An Anthology of Texts and Pictures.* Philadelphia: University of Pennsylvania Press, 2002.

Casella, Maria Teresa. *Tra Boccaccio e Petrarca: I volgarizzamenti di Tito Livio e di Valerio Massimo.* Padua: Editrice Antenore, 1982.

Cassidy, Brendan. *Politics, Civic Ideals, and Sculpture in Italy, c. 1240–1400.* London: Harvey Miller, 2007.

Cavallucci, Francesco. *La Fontana Maggiore di Perugia: Voci e suggestioni di una comunità medievale.* Perugia: Quattroemme, 1993.

Cellerino, F. "Genova e il grifone." *Studi Genuensi,* n.s., 6 (1988): 109–13.

Cenci, Valeria. *La Fontana Maggiore di Perugia: Restauri e metodi conservativi.* Perugia: Fondazione Cassa di Risparmio di Perugia, 2006.

Ceppari Ridolfi, Maria A., Marco Ciampolini, and Patrizia Turrini. *L'immagine del Palio: Storia, cultura e rappresentazione del rito di Siena.* Siena: Banca Monte dei Paschi di Siena, 2001.

Chiàntera, Raffaele. *Guido delle Colonne.* Naples: Federico & Ardia, 1956.

Chiappelli, Luigi. *Vita e opere giuridiche di Cino da Pistoia.* Bologna: Forni, 1978.

Ciampoli, Donatella, and Thomas Szabò. *Viabilità e legislazione di uno stato cittadino del Duecento: Lo statuto dei viarii di Siena.* Siena: Accademia senese degli intronati, 1992.

Cimegotto, C. "La figura di Antenore nella vita, nella leggenda, e nell'arte." *Atti e memorie dell'Academia patavina di scienze, lettere, ed arti* 53 (1936–37): 20–43.

Cipolla, Carlo. Introduction to *Opere di Ferreto de' Ferreti*. 3 vols. Fonti per la storia d'Italia 43 bis. Rome: Tipografia del Senato, 1920.

Clanchy, M. T. *From Memory to Written Record: England, 1066–1307*. 2nd ed. Oxford: Blackwell, 1993.

Clarke, Paula. "The Villani Chronicles." In *Chronicling History: Chroniclers and Historians in Medieval and Renaissance Italy*, edited by Sharon Dale, Alison Williams Lewin, and Duane Osheim. University Park: Pennsylvania State University Press, 2007.

Coleman, Janet. *Ancient and Medieval Memories: Studies in the Reconstruction of the Past*. Cambridge: Cambridge University Press, 1992.

Coletti, Luigi. *Treviso: Catalogo delle cose d'arte e di antichità d'Italia*. Bergamo: Libreria dello stato, 1935.

Collins, Amanda. *Greater than Emperor: Cola di Rienzo (ca. 1313–54) and the World of Fourteenth-Century Rome*. Ann Arbor: University of Michigan Press, 2002.

Collodo, Silvana. *Una società in trasformazione: Padova tra XI e XV secolo*. Padua: Editrice Antenore, 1990.

Comparetti, Domenico. *Vergil in the Middle Ages*. Translated by E. F. M. Benecke, with a new introduction by Jan Ziolkowski. Princeton: Princeton University Press, 1997.

Consoli, Joseph P., ed. *Giovanni Boccaccio: An Annotated Bibliography*. New York: Garland, 1992.

La coscienza cittadina nei comuni italiani del Duecento: Atti dell' XI convegno del Centro di studi sulla spiritualità medievale. Todi: Accademia Tudertina, 1972.

Costamagna, G. *Il notaio a Genova tra prestigio e potere*. Rome: Consiglio nazionale del notariato, 1970.

Cowdrey, H. E. J. "The Mahdia Campaign of 1087." *English Historical Review* 92 (1977): 1–29.

Cracco, Giorgio, ed. *Nuovi studi ezzeliniani*. 2 vols. Rome: Istituto storico italiano per il medio evo, 1992.

———. *Società e stato nel medioevo veneziano (secoli XII–XIV)*. Florence: Olschki, 1967.

Cunningham, Colin. "For the Honor and Beauty of the City: The Design of Town Halls." In *Siena, Florence, and Padua: Art, Society, and Religion, 1280–1400*, edited by Diana Norman, 29–54. New Haven: Yale University Press, in association with the Open University, 1995.

Dale, Sharon, Alison Williams Lewin, and Duane Osheim, eds. *Chronicling History: Chroniclers and Historians in Medieval and Renaissance Italy*. University Park: Pennsylvania State University Press, 2007.

Davis, Charles Till. *Dante's Italy and Other Essays*. Philadelphia: University of Pennsylvania Press, 1984.

———. "An Early Florentine Political Theorist: Fra Remigio de' Girolami." *Proceedings of the American Philosophical Society* 104 (1960): 662–76.

———. "Education in Dante's Florence." *Speculum* 40 (1965): 415–35.

———. "Ptolemy of Lucca and the Roman Republic." *Proceedings of the American Philosophical Society* 118, no. 1 (1974): 31–50.

———. "Recent Work on the Malispini Question." In *Dante's Italy and Other Essays*, 290–99. Philadelphia: University of Pennsylvania Press, 1984.

———. "Remigio de' Girolami O. P. (d. 1319), Lector of S. Maria Novella in Florence." In *Le Scuole degli Ordini Mendicanti (secoli XIII–XIV): Atti del convegno 11–14 ottobre 1976*, 283–304. Todi: L'Accademia tudertina, 1978.

———. "Remigio de' Girolami's *De bono pacis*." *Studi danteschi* 36 (1959): 105–36.

————. "Roman Patriotism and Republican Propaganda: Ptolemy of Lucca and Pope Nicholas III." *Speculum* 50 (1975): 411–33.

Day, Gerald W. *Genoa's Response to Byzantium, 1155–1204: Commercial Expansion and Factionalism in a Medieval City.* Urbana: University of Illinois Press, 1988.

Dazzi, Manlio Torquato. *Il Mussato preumanista (1261–1329): L'ambiente e l'opera.* Vicenza: Neri Pozza, 1964.

Dean, Ruth J. "Cultural Relations in the Middle Ages: Nicholas Trevet and Nicholas of Prato." *Studies in Philology* 45 (1948): 541–64.

————. "The Dedication of Nicholas Trevet's Commentary on Boethius." *Studies in Philology* 63 (1966): 593–603.

Dean, Trevor. *Land and Power in Late Medieval Ferrara: The Rule of the Este, 1350–1450.* Cambridge: Cambridge University Press, 1988.

de Hamel, Christopher. *The Parker Library. Treasures from the Collection at Corpus Christi College, Cambridge, England.* Cambridge: Cambridge University Press, 2000.

Del Bello, Davide. *Forgotten Paths: Etymology and the Allegorical Mindset.* Washington, D.C.: Catholic University of America Press, 2007.

Deliyannis, Deborah M., ed. *Historiography in the Middle Ages.* Leiden: Brill, 2003.

de Mattei, Roberto, ed. *Presenza del passato: 'Political ideas' e modelli culturali nella storia e nell'arte senese.* Siena: Cantagalli, 2008.

de Matteis, M. C. "Il *De bono commune* di Remigio de' Girolami." *Annali dell' Università di Lecce* 3 (1965–67): 13–86.

————. *La "teologia politica comunale" di Remigio de' Girolami.* Bologna: Pàtron, 1977.

de Negri, Teofilo Ossian. *Storia di Genova.* Florence: Martello, 1986.

de Nino, Antonio. "Ovidio nella tradizione popolare di Sulmona." In *Tradizioni popolari abruzzesi,* edited by Bruno Mosca, 9–54. L'Aquila: Japadre, 1970.

Denley, Peter. *Commune and Studio in Late Medieval and Renaissance Siena.* Bologna: CLUEB, 2006.

de Nolhac, Pierre. *Petrarch and the Ancient World.* Translated by D. B. Updike. Boston: Merrymount Press, 1907.

Derbes, Anne, and Mark Sandona, eds. *Cambridge Companion to Giotto.* Cambridge: Cambridge University Press, 2004.

De Robertis, Francesco Maria. *Federico II di Svevia nel mito e nella realtà.* Bari: Editrice Tipografica, 1998.

de Wesselow, Thomas. "The Decoration of the West Wall of the Sala del Mappamondo in Siena's Palazzo Pubblico." In *Art, Politics, and Civic Religion in Central Italy, 1261–1352,* edited by Joanna Cannon and Beth Williamson, 19–70. Aldershot, UK: Ashgate, 2000.

di Benedetto, Luigi. *Rimatori del dolce stil novo.* Turin: UTET, 1944.

Di Fabio, Clario. "Il 'mito delle origini' e il nome di Genova nel medioevo." *Bollettino Ligustico* 31 (1979): 37–44.

Di Fabio, Clario, and Raffaella Besta. *La cattedrale di Genova nel medioevo: Secoli VI–XIV.* Genoa: Banca CARIGE, 1998.

Donato, Maria Monica. "Ancora sulle 'Fonti' nel *Buon Governo* di Ambrogio Lorenzetti: Dubbi, precisazioni, anticipazioni." In *Politica e cultura nelle repubbliche italiane dal medioevo all'età moderna,* edited by Simonetta Adorni Braccesi and Mario Ascheri, 43–79. Rome: Istituto storico per l'età moderna e contemporanea, 2001.

————. "Un ciclo pittorico ad Asciano (Siena): Palazzo pubblico e l'iconografia 'politica' alla fine del medioevo." *Annali della Scuola Normale Superiore di Pisa,* 3rd ser., 18 (1988): 1105–1272.

D'Oria, Jacopo. *La chiesa di San Matteo in Genova.* Genoa: Sordo-Muti, 1860.

Dotson, John. "The Genoese Civic Annals: Caffaro and His Continuators." In *Chronicling History: Chroniclers and Historians in Medieval and Renaissance Italy*, edited by Sharon Dale, Alison Williams Lewin, and Duane Osheim, 55–85. University Park: Pennsylvania State University Press, 2007.

Dotti, Ugo. *Vita di Petrarca.* Rome: Laterza, 1987.

Douglas, Langton. *A History of Siena.* London: John Murray, 1902.

Dozzini, Bruno. *La Fontana Maggiore di Perugia.* Assisi: Minerva, 1994.

du Cange, Charles du Fresne. *Glossarium mediae et infimae latinitatis.* Edited by Pierre Carpenter, Christoph Adelung, Leopold Favre, and G. A. Louis Henschel. Graz: Akademische Druck-u. Verlagsanstalt, 1954.

Dufour Bozzo, C. *La porta urbana nel medioevo: Porta Soprana di Sant'Andrea di Genova, immagine di una città.* Rome: "L'Erma" di Bretschneider, 1988.

Dyck, Andrew R. *A Commentary on Cicero, De Officiis.* Ann Arbor: University of Michigan Press, 1996.

Eco, Umberto, and Costantino Marmo, eds. *On the Medieval Theory of Signs.* Amsterdam: John Benjamins, 1989.

Edwards, Catharine. *Writing Rome: Textual Approaches to the City.* Cambridge: Cambridge University Press, 1996.

English, Edward D. *Enterprise and Liability in Sienese Banking, 1230–1350.* Cambridge: Medieval Academy of America, 1988.

———. "Urban Castles in Medieval Siena: The Sources and Images of Power." In *The Medieval Castle: Romance and Reality*, edited by Kathryn Reyerson and Faye Power, 175–98. Dubuque, Iowa: Kendall/Hunt, 1984.

Epstein, Steven. *Genoa and the Genoese, 958–1528.* Chapel Hill: University of North Carolina Press, 1996.

Ermini, Giuseppe. *Storia dell'Università di Perugia.* 2nd ed. 2 vols. Florence: Olschki, 1971.

Fabris, Giovanni. *Cronache e cronisti padovani.* Padua: Cittadella, 1977.

———. "Le demolizioni di S. Lorenzo e la tomba di Antenore." *Padova: Rivista del Comune* 10 (1937): 1–14.

———. "La tomba di Antenore." *Padova: Rivista del Comune* 6, no. 7 (1932): 13–26.

Fantelli, Pier Luigi, and Franca Pellegrini, eds. *Il Palazzo della Ragione in Padova.* Padua: Editoriale Programma, 2000.

Farmer, Sharon A. *Communities of Saint Martin: Legend and Ritual in Medieval Tours.* Ithaca: Cornell University Press, 1991.

Fasola, Giusta Nicco. *La Fontana di Perugia.* Rome: Libreria dello Stato, 1951.

Fasoli, Gina. *Dalla 'civitas' al comune nell'Italia settentrionale: Lezioni tenute alla Facoltà di magistero della Università di Bologna nell'anno accademico 1960–61.* Bologna: Pàtron, 1961.

Federico, Sylvia. *New Troy: Fantasies of Empire in the Late Middle Ages.* Minneapolis: University of Minnesota Press, 2003.

Federico II e l'antico: Esempi dal territorio. Foggia: Comune di Foggia, 1997.

Fentress, James, and Chris Wickham. *Social Memory.* Oxford: Blackwell, 1992.

Feo, Michelle. "The 'Pagan Beyond' of Albertino Mussato." In *Latin Poetry and the Classical Tradition: Essays in Medieval and Renaissance Literature*, edited by Peter Godman and Oswyn Murray, 115–47. Oxford: Clarendon Press, 1990.

Ferrai, L. A. "Benzo d'Alessandria e i cronisti milanesi del secolo XIV." *Bollettino dell'Istituto storico italiano per il medio evo* 7 (1889): 97–137.

———. "Le cronache di Galvano Fiamma e le fonti della *Galvagnana*." *Bollettino dell'Istituto storico italiano per il medio evo* 10 (1891): 93–128.

Ferrando Cabona, Isabella, and Alberto Lagomaggiore. *Palazzo San Giorgio: Pietre, uomini, potere (1260–1613)*. Milan: Silvana, 1998.

Ferretti, Massimo. *Fonte Gaia di Jacopo della Quercia*. Siena: Protagon Editori Toscani for Santa Maria della Scala, 2001.

Fischer, Marta, and Walter Pedrotti. *Le città italiane nel medioevo*. Colognola ai Colli: Demetra, 1997.

Fisher, Craig B. "The Pisan Clergy and an Awakening of Historical Interest in a Medieval Commune." *Studies in Medieval and Renaissance History* 3 (1966): 144–219.

Folena, Gianfranco, ed. *Storia della cultura veneta*. Vol. 2, *Il trecento*. Vicenza: Neri Pozza, 1976.

Foster, Kenelm. *Petrarch: Poet and Humanist*. Edinburgh: Edinburgh University Press, 1984.

Franchina, Letizia, ed. *Piazza del Campo: Evoluzione di una immagine, documenti, vicende ricostruzioni*. Siena: Archivio di stato, 1983.

Frova, Carla, Paolo Nardi, and Paolo Renzi. "Maestri e scolari a Siena e Perugia, 1250–1500: Una prosopografia dinamica del corpo accademico e studentesco." http://www.unisi.it/docenti/.

Frugoni, Arsenio. "Sulla *Renovatio Senatus* del 1143 e l'*Ordo equestris*." *Bollettino dell'Istituto storico italiano per il medio evo* 62 (1950): 159–74.

Frugoni, Chiara. *A Distant City: Images of Urban Experience in the Medieval World*. Translated by W. McCuaig. Princeton: Princeton University Press, 1991.

———, ed. *Il Villani illustrato: Firenze e l'Italia medievale nelle 253 immagini del ms. Chigiano L VIII 296 della Biblioteca Vaticana*. Florence and Vatican City: Le lettere and Biblioteca apostolica Vaticana, 2005.

Frugoni, Chiara, Maria Monica Donato, and Alessio Monciatti. *Pietro and Ambrogio Lorenzetti*. Milan: Le Lettere, 2002.

Fusero, Clemente. *I Doria*. Milan: Dall'Oglio, 1973.

Gagliardi, Antonio. *Cino da Pistoia: Le poetiche dell'anima*. Alessandria: Edizioni dell'Orso, 2001.

Galletti, Anna Imelde. "Considerazioni per una interpretazione dell'*Eulistea*." *Archivio storico italiano* 128 (1970): 305–34.

———. "Materiali per una storia del mito di fondazione di Perugia." In *Renaissance Studies in honour of Craig Hugh Smyth*, edited by Andrew Marrogh, 75–87. Florence: Giunti Barbèra, 1985.

———. "Mitografie della memoria urbana." In *Storiografia e poesia nella cultura medievale*, 299–324. Rome: Istituto storio italiano per il medio evo, 1999.

———. "Motivations, modalités et gestions politiques de la mémoire urbaine." In *L'historiographie médiévale en Europe, Paris, 29 mars–3 avril 1989*, 189–97. Paris: CNRS, 1991.

———. "Sant'Ercolano, il grifo, e le lasche: Note sull'immaginario collettivo nella città comunale." In *Forme e tecniche del potere nella città (sec. XIV–XVII)*, 203–16. Perugia: Università di Perugia, 1979–80.

———. "Le scritture della memoria storica: Esperienze perugine." In *Cultura e società nell' Italia medievale: Studi per Paolo Brezzi*, 367–92. Rome: Istituto storico italiano per il medio evo, 1988.

Gamba, Bartolommeo. *Diceria bibliografica intorno ai volgarizzamenti italiani delle opere di Virgilio*. Verona: Ramanzini, 1831.

Gasparotto, C. "Alla origine del mito della tomba di Antenore." In *Medioevo e Rinascimento veneto, con altri studi in onore di Lino Lazzarini*, 3–12. Padua: Editrice Antenore, 1979.

Geanakoplos, Deno John. *Emperor Michael Palaeologus and the West, 1258–1282: A Study in Byzantine-Latin Relations.* Hamden, Conn.: Archon, 1973.

Geary, Patrick J. *The Myth of Nations: The Medieval Origins of Europe.* Princeton: Princeton University Press, 2002.

Gehl, Paul F. *A Moral Art: Grammar, Society, and Culture in Trecento Florence.* Ithaca: Cornell University Press, 1993.

Giannardi, Giuliana. "Le *Dicerie* di Filippo Ceffi." *Studi di filologia italiana* 6 (1942): 5–63.

Giansante, Massimo. *Retorica e politica nel Duecento: I notai bolognesi e l'ideologia comunale.* Rome: Istituto storico italiano per il medio evo, 1998.

Giorgetti, Vittorio. *Podestà, capitani del popolo e loro ufficiali a Perugia: 1195–1500.* Spoleto: Centro italiano di studi sull'alto Medioevo, 1993.

Girardi, Giacinto. *Rolando da Piazzola.* Padua: Fratelli Drucker, 1909.

Golinelli, Paolo. *Città e culto dei santi nel medioevo italiano.* Bologna: CLUEB, 1991.

Goria, A. "Le lotte intestine in Genova tra il 1305 e il 1309." In *Miscellanea di storia ligure in onore di Giorgio Falco,* 251–80. Milan: Feltrinelli, 1962.

Gorra, Egidio. *Testi inediti di storia troiana.* Turin: Triverio, 1887.

Graf, Arturo. *Roma nella memoria e nelle immaginazioni del medio evo, con un'appendice sulla leggenda di Gog e Magog.* Turin: Giovanni Chiantore, 1923.

Gramaccini, Norberto. *Mirabilia: Das Nachleben antiker Statuen vor der Renaissance.* Mainz: Philipp von Zabern, 1996.

Grande dizionario della lingua italiana. Edited by Salvatore Battaglia. Turin: UTET, 1973.

Greenhalgh, Michael. *The Survival of Roman Antiquities in the Middle Ages.* London: Duckworth, 1989.

Grendler, Paul F. *Schooling in Renaissance Italy: Literacy and Learning, 1300–1600.* Baltimore: Johns Hopkins University Press, 1989.

Griffin, Nathaniel Edward. *Dares and Dictys: An Introduction to the Study of Medieval Versions of the Story of Troy.* Baltimore: J. H. Furst, 1907.

———. "Unhomeric Elements in the Medieval Story of Troy." *Journal of English and Germanic Philology* 7 (1907–8): 32–52.

Grohmann, Alberto. *Città e territorio tra Medioevo ed età moderna: Perugia, secoli XIII–XVI.* 3 vols. Perugia: Volumnia Editrice, 1981.

———. "La Fontana Maggiore: Sintesi dei fermenti economici e sociali della città a metà del Duecento." In *Il linguaggio figurativo della Fontana Maggiore di Perugia,* edited by Carlo Santini, 49–60. Perugia: Calzetti-Mariucci, 1996.

———. *Perugia.* Bari: Editoria Laterza, 1981.

Grossi Bianchi, Luciano, and Ennio Poleggi. *Una città portuale del Medioevo: Genova nei secoli X–XVI.* Genoa: Sagep, 1979.

Grundman, John P. *The Popolo at Perugia, 1139–1309.* Fonti per la storia dell'Umbria 20. Perugia: Deputazione di storia patria per l'Umbria, 1992.

Guidoni, Enrico. *Il Campo di Siena.* Rome: Multigrafica, 1971.

Guidoni, Enrico, and Paolo Maccari. *Siena e i centri senesi sulla via Francigena.* Florence: Giunta regionale, 2000.

Gurrieri, Ottorino. *La Fontana Maggiore e le altre fontane in Perugia: Una guida illustrata.* Perugia: Grafica, 1973.

Hahn, Daniel. *The Tower Menagerie: The Amazing 600-Year History of the Royal Collection of Wild and Ferocious Beasts Kept at the Tower of London.* New York: Penguin, 2004.

Hale, J. R. *Renaissance Venice.* London: Faber and Faber, 1973.

Hammer, William. "The Concept of the New or Second Rome in the Middle Ages." *Speculum* 19 (1944): 50–62.

Hanawalt, Barbara, and Kathryn Reyerson, eds. *City and Spectacle in Medieval Europe*. Minneapolis: University of Minnesota Press, 1994.

Hankey, A. Teresa. "Riccobaldo of Ferrara, Boccaccio, and Domenico di Bandino." *Journal of the Warburg and Courtauld Institutes* 21 (1958): 208–26.

———. *Riccobaldo of Ferrara: His Life, Works, and Influence*. Fonti per la storia d'Italia, Subsidia 2. Rome: Istituto storico italiano per il medio evo, 1996.

Hankins, James, ed. *Renaissance Civic Humanism: Reappraisals and Reflections*. Cambridge: Cambridge University Press, 2000.

Hanson, Ann Coffin. *Jacopo della Quercia's Fonte Gaia*. Oxford: Clarendon Press, 1965.

Hattendorf, John B., and Richard W. Unger, eds. *War at Sea in the Middle Ages and the Renaissance*. Rochester, N.Y.: Boydell Press, 2003.

Hen, Yitzhak, and Matthew Innes, eds. *The Uses of the Past in the Early Middle Ages*. Cambridge: Cambridge University Press, 2000.

Herrick, Samantha Kahn. *Imagining the Sacred Past: Hagiography and Power in Early Normandy*. Cambridge: Harvard University Press, 2007.

Hersey, George L. *The Aragonese Arch at Naples, 1443–1475*. New Haven: Yale University Press, 1973.

Hoch, A. S. "The Antique Origins of an Emperor by Simone Martini." *Paragone-Arte* 443 (1987): 42–47.

Hoffmann-Curtius, Kathrin. *Das Programm der Fontana Maggiore in Perugia*. Düsseldorf: Rheinland-Verlag, 1968.

Holloway, Julia Bolton. *Brunetto Latini: An Analytic Bibliography*. London: Grant and Cutler, 1986.

———. *Twice-Told Tales: Brunetto Latini and Dante Alighieri*. New York: Peter Lang, 1993.

Hortis, Attilio. *Cenni di Giovanni Boccacci intorno a Tito Livio*. Trieste: Austro-Ungarico, 1877.

Hughes, Diane. "Kinsmen and Neighbors in Medieval Genoa." In *The Medieval City: Essays in Honor of Robert S. Lopez*, edited by H. Miskimin, D. Herlihy, and A. L. Udevich, 95–111. New Haven: Yale University Press, 1977.

Hyde, John Kenneth. "Medieval Descriptions of Cities." *Bulletin of the John Rylands Library* 48 (1965–66): 308–40.

———. *Padua in the Age of Dante*. Manchester: Manchester University Press, 1966.

———. *Society and Politics in Medieval Italy: The Evolution of the Civil Life, 1000–1350*. London: Macmillan, 1973.

Imperiale di Sant'Angelo, Cesare. *Jacopo d'Oria e i suoi Annali: Storia di un'aristocrazia italiana nel duecento*. Venice: Emiliana editrice, 1930.

Iotti, Roberta, ed. *Gli Estensi*. 2 vols. Modena: Il Bulino, 1997–99.

Jacks, Philip. *The Antiquarian and the Myth of Antiquity: The Origins of Rome in Renaissance Thought*. Cambridge: Cambridge University Press, 1993.

Jacoff, Rachel. *The Cambridge Companion to Dante*. 2nd ed. Cambridge: Cambridge University Press, 2007.

Jaeger, Mary. *Livy's Written Rome*. Ann Arbor: University of Michigan Press, 1997.

Jenkyns, Richard. *The Legacy of Rome: A New Appraisal*. Oxford: Oxford University Press, 1992.

Jensen, Frede. *The Poets of the Scuola Siciliana*. New York: Garland, 1986.

Jones, P. J. *The Italian City-State: From Commune to Signoria*. Oxford: Clarendon Press, 1997.

Kallendorf, Craig. "Virgil, Dante, and Empire in Italian Thought, 1300–1500." *Vergilius* 34 (1988): 44–69.

Kantorowicz, Ernst H. *Frederick the Second, 1194–1250*. Translated by E. O. Lorimer. London: Constable, 1931.

Kedar, Beniamin Z. "Una nuova fonte per l'incursione musulmana del 934–935 e le sue implicazioni per la storia genovese." In *Oriente e occidente tra medioevo ed età moderna: Studi in onore di Geo Pistarino*, edited by Laura Balletto, 605–16. Genoa: Brigati, 1997.

Kelly, David. "Viking Saga Sets Sail in Utah Town." *Los Angeles Times*, August 31, 2003, 19.

Kelly, Samantha. *The New Solomon: Robert of Naples (1309–1343) and Fourteenth-Century Kingship.* Leiden: Brill, 2003.

Kempers, Bram. "Icons, Altarpieces, and Civic Ritual in Siena Cathedral, 1100–1530." In *City and Spectacle in Medieval Europe*, edited by Barbara Hanawalt and Kathryn Reyerson, 89–136. Minneapolis: University of Minnesota Press, 1994.

Kempshall, M. S. *The Common Good in Late Medieval Political Thought.* Oxford: Clarendon Press, 1999.

Kohl, Benjamin G. *Padua Under the Carrara, 1318–1405.* Baltimore: Johns Hopkins University Press, 1998.

Kohl, Benjamin G., and Alison Andrews Smith, eds. *Major Problems in the History of the Italian Renaissance.* Lexington, Mass.: D. C. Heath, 1995.

Krautheimer, Richard. *Rome: Profile of a City, 312–1308.* 2nd ed. Princeton: Princeton University Press, 2000.

Kretschmer, Marek Thue. *Rewriting Roman History in the Middle Ages: The "Historia Romana" and the Manuscript Bamberg, Hist. 3.* Leiden: Brill, 2007.

Kristeller, Paul Oskar. "Matteo de' Libri, Bolognese Notary of the Thirteenth Century, and His *Artes dictaminis.*" In *Miscellanea Giovanni Galbiati*, 283–320. Milan: Hoepli, 1951.

———. "Umanesimo e scolastica a Padova fino al Petrarca." *Medioevo* 11 (1985): 1–18.

Lane, Frederic Chapin. *Venice: A Maritime Republic.* Baltimore: Johns Hopkins University Press, 1973.

Larner, John. *Culture and Society in Italy, 1290–1420.* New York: Charles Scribner's Sons, 1971.

———. *Italy in the Age of Dante and Petrarch, 1216–1380.* New York: Longman, 1980.

Lazzarini, Lino. "*Dux ille Danduleus*: Andrea Dandolo e la cultura veneziana a metà del Trecento." In *Petrarca, Venezia, e il Veneto*, edited by Giorgio Padoan, 123–56. Florence: Olschki, 1976.

———. "La tomba di Antenore e il primo segno dell'Umanesimo." *Padova: Rivista del Comune* 10 (1937): 13–14.

Le Goff, Jacques. *History and Memory.* Translated by Steven Rendall and Elizabeth Claman. New York: Columbia University Press, 1992.

Leonardi, Claudio, and Birger Munk Olsen, eds. *The Classical Tradition in the Middle Ages and the Renaissance: Proceedings of the First European Science Foundation Workshop on "The Reception of Classical Texts," Florence, Certosa del Galluzzo, 26–27 June 1992.* Spoleto: Centro italiano di studi sull'alto Medioevo, 1995.

Leone de Castris, Pierluigi. *Simone Martini.* Milan: Motta, 2003.

Levine, Robert, ed. *France Before Charlemagne: A Translation from the Grandes Chroniques.* Lewiston, N.Y.: E. Mellen Press, 1990.

Liagre-de Sturler, Léone. *Les relations commerciales entre Gênes, la Belgique et l'Outremont, d'après les archives notariales génoises, 1320–1400.* 2 vols. Brussels and Rome: Institut historique belge de Rome, 1969.

Lifshitz, Felice. *The Norman Conquest of Pious Neustria: Historiographic Discourse and Saintly Relics, 684–1090.* Toronto: Pontifical Institute of Mediaeval Studies, 1995.

Lilley, Keith D. *Urban Life in the Middle Ages, 1000–1450.* Houndmills, UK: Palgrave, 2002.

[Lisini, Alessandro]. "L'impresa della lupa." *Miscellanea storica senese* 3 (1895): 195.

———. "Lupa." *Miscellanea storica senese* 1 (1893): 28.

[———]. "Una statua trovata in Siena nel secolo XIV." *Miscellanea storica senese* 5 (1898): 175–76.

Locati, Silvia. *La rinascita del genere tragico nel Medioevo: L'Ecerinis di Albertino Mussato*. Florence: F. Cesati, 2006.

Lorenzoni, Giovanni, and Giulio Bresciani Alvarez. *L'edificio del Santo di Padova*. Vicenza: Neri Pozza, 1981.

Lowenthal, David. *The Past Is a Foreign Country*. Cambridge: Cambridge University Press, 1985.

Lucianetti, Sergio. "Lo sviluppo della città medievale." In *La città di Padova: Saggio di analisi urbana*, 71–125. Rome: Officina, 1970.

Macconi, Massimiliano. *Il grifo e l'aquila: Genova e il regno di Sicilia nell'età di Federico II*. Genoa: Name, 2002.

Maggini, Francesco. *I primi volgarizzamenti dai classici latini*. Florence: Le Monnier, 1952.

Maginnis, Hayden B. J. *The World of the Early Sienese Painter*. University Park: Pennsylvania State University Press, 2001.

Maire Vigueur, Jean-Claude. *Cavaliers et citoyens: Guerre, conflits et société dans l'Italie communale, XIIe–XIIIe siècles*. Paris: Ecole des hautes études en sciences sociales, 2003.

Makdisi, G., D. Sourdel, and J. Sourdel-Thomine, eds. *La notion de liberté au Moyen Age: Islam, Byzance, Occident*. Paris: Les Belles Lettres, 1985.

Mancini, A. "Macrobio Parmense." *Archivio storico per le Province Parmensi*, n.s., 28 (1928): 1–9.

Mancini, Franco. "L'Euliste della Fontana Maggiore nel 'Conto di Corciano e di Perugia.'" In *Il linguaggio figurativo della Fontana Maggiore di Perugia*, edited by Carlo Santini, 329–38. Perugia: Calzetti-Mariucci, 1996.

Manfroni, Camillo. *Le relazioni fra Genova, l'impero bizantino, e i turchi*. Genoa: Società ligure di storia patria, 1898.

Mann, Nicholas. "The Origins of Humanism." In *The Cambridge Companion to Renaissance Humanism*, edited by Jill Kraye, 1–19. Cambridge: Cambridge University Press, 1996.

Marangon, Paolo. *Ad cognitionem scientiae festinare: Gli studi nell'Università e nei conventi di Padova nei secoli XIII e XIV*. Trieste: LINT, 1997.

Marti, Mario. *Poeti del Dolce stil nuovo*. Florence: Le Monnier, 1969.

Martines, Lauro. *Power and Imagination: City-States in Renaissance Italy*. New York: Knopf, 1979.

Mazzatinti, G. "Di Bonifacio da Verona, autore dell'*Eulistea*." *Bollettino della Società umbra di storia patria* 2 (1896): 557–61.

———. "La *Fiorita* di Armannino Giudice." *Giornale di filologia romanza* 3 (1881): 1–55.

Mazzino, Edoardo, Teofilo Ossian De Negri, and Leonard von Matt. *Il centro storico di Genova*. Genoa: Stringa Editore, 1969.

Mazzoni, Cristina. *She-Wolf: The Story of a Roman Icon*. Cambridge: Cambridge University Press, 2010.

Mazzotta, Giuseppe. *The Worlds of Petrarch*. Durham: Duke University Press, 1993.

Meister, Ferdinand Otto. *Über Dares von Phrygien: De excidio Troiae historia*. Breslau: Druck von Grass Barth, 1871.

Meredith, Jill. "The Arch at Capua: The Strategic Use of *Spolia* and References to the Antique." In *Intellectual Life at the Court of Frederick II Hohenstaufen*, edited by William Tronzo, 109–26. Washington, D.C.: National Gallery of Art, 1994.

———. "The Revival of the Augustan Age in the Court Art of Emperor Frederick II." In *Artistic Strategy and the Rhetoric of Power: Political Uses of Art from Antiquity to the Present*, edited by David Castriota, 39–56. Carbondale: Southern Illinois University Press, 1986.

Modesto, Diana. "Il Primo Popolo: A Monument on the Bargello." Florin Web site, created by Julia Bolton Holloway. http://www.florin.ms/beth2.html#modesto.

Molho, Anthony, Kurt Raaflaub, and Julia Emlen. *City States in Classical Antiquity and Medieval Italy: Athens and Rome, Florence and Venice*. Ann Arbor: University of Michigan Press, 1991.

Mommsen, T. E. "Petrarch and the Decoration of the Sala Virorum Illustrium in Padua." *Art Bulletin* 34 (1952): 95–116.

Mor, Carlo Guido. *Il Palazzo della ragione di Padova*. Venice: Neri Pozza, 1964.

Moreno-Riaño, Gerson. *The World of Marsilius of Padua*. Disputatio 5. Turnhout: Brepols, 2006.

Morse, Ruth. *Truth and Convention in the Middle Ages: Rhetoric, Representation, and Reality*. Cambridge: Cambridge University Press, 1991.

Moskowitz, Anita Fiderer. *Italian Gothic Sculpture, c. 1250–c. 1400*. Cambridge: Cambridge University Press, 2001.

———. *Nicola and Giovanni Pisano: The Pulpits: Pious Devotion, Pious Diversion*. London: Harvey Miller, 2005.

———. *Nicola Pisano's Arca di San Domenico and Its Legacy*. University Park: Pennsylvania State University Press, 1994.

Müller, Rebecca. *Sic hostes Ianua frangit: Spolien und Trophäen im mittelalterlichen Genua*. Weimar: VDG, 2002.

Mundy, John Hine. "In Praise of Italy: The Italian City-Republics." *Speculum* 64 (1989): 815–34.

Musto, Ronald G. *Apocalypse in Rome: Cola di Rienzo and the Politics of the New Age*. Berkeley and Los Angeles: University of California Press, 2003.

Muttoni, L. "Simone d'Arezzo canonico a Verona." *Italia medioevale e umanistica* 22 (1979): 171–207.

Napoli, Federico. *Arnolfo di Cambio: Profilo e confronto di un maestro*. Florence: Pietro Chegai, 2002.

Nardi, Bruno. *Mantuanitas Vergiliana*. Rome: Edizioni dell'Ateneo, 1963.

Nardi, Paolo. *L'insegnamento superiore a Siena nei secoli XI–XIV: Tentativi e realizzazioni dalle origini alla fondazione dello Studio generale*. Milan: Giuffrè, 1996.

Nederman, Cary J. "Nature, Sin, and the Origins of Society: The Ciceronian Tradition in Medieval Political Thought." *Journal of the History of Ideas* 49 (1988): 3–26.

Nederman, Cary J., and Mary Elizabeth Sullivan. "Reading Aristotle Through Rome: Republicanism and History in Ptolemy of Lucca's *De regimine principum*." *European Journal of Political Theory* 7 (2008): 223–40.

Needham, Paul. "Johann Gutenberg and the Catholicon Press." *Papers of the Bibliographical Society of America* 76 (1982): 395–456.

Neri, Maria. "Perugia e il suo contado nei secoli XIII e XIV: Interventi urbanistici e legislazione statutaria." *Storia della città* 3 (1977): 28–37.

Nicholas, David. *The Growth of the Medieval City: From Late Antiquity to the Early Fourteenth Century*. A History of Urban Society in Europe. London: Longman, 1997.

Nico Ottaviani, Maria Grazia. *Statuti, territorio e acque nel Medioevo: Perugia e Marsciano, Tevere e Nestóre*. Spoleto: Fondazione Centro italiano di studi sull'alto Medioevo, 2008.

Niermeyer, Jan Frederik. *Mediae latinitatis lexicon minus.* Edited by J. W. J. Burgers and C. van de Kieft. 2nd ed. 2 vols. Leiden: Brill, 2002.

Norman, Diana. "'The Glorious Deeds of the Commune': Civic Patronage of Art.'" In Norman, *Siena, Florence, and Padua,* 1:133–53.

———. "'Love Justice, You Who Judge the Earth': The Paintings in the Sala dei Nove in the Palazzo Pubblico." In Norman, *Siena, Florence, and Padua,* 2:145–67.

———. *Siena and the Virgin: Art and Politics in a Late Medieval City State.* New Haven: Yale University Press, 1999.

———, ed. *Siena, Florence, and Padua: Art, Society, and Religion, 1280–1400.* 2 vols. New Haven: Yale University Press, in association with the Open University, 1995.

Oldfield, Paul. *City and Community in Norman Italy.* Cambridge: Cambridge University Press, 2009.

Origone, Sandra. *Bisanzio e Genova.* Genoa: ECIG, 1992.

Ortalli, Gherardo, and Dino Puncuh. *Genova, Venezia, il Levante nei secoli XII–XIV: Atti del Convegno internazionale di studi, Genova/Venezia, 10–14 marzo 2000.* Genoa and Venice: Società ligure di storia patria e l'Istituto veneto di scienze, lettere, ed arti, 2001.

Osmond, Patricia J. "Catiline in Florence and Fiesole: The Medieval and Renaissance Afterlife of a Roman Conspirator." *International Journal of the Classical Tradition* 7 (2000): 3–38.

Ottavi, Lucia. *La Fontana Maggiore di Perugia: La storia, la iconografia.* Perugia: Era Nuova, 1999.

Palma, Marco. "La redazione autografo delle *Dicerie* di Filippo Ceffi." *Italia medioevale e umanistica* 16 (1973): 323–25.

Palmieri, Arturo. *Rolandino Passaggeri.* Bologna: Zanichelli, 1933.

Panella, Emilio. "Nuova cronologia Remigiana." *Archivum Fratrum Praedicatorum* 60 (1990): 145–311.

———. "Priori di Santa Maria Novella di Firenze, 1221–1325." In *Memorie domenicane* 17 (1986): 253–84.

Paolozzi Strozzi, Beatrice. "Qualche riflessioni sull'iconografia monetale senese." In *Le monete della repubblica senese,* edited by Beatrice Paolozzi Strozzi, Giuseppe Toderi, and Fiorenza Vannel Toderi, 73–169. Milan: Silvana, 1992.

Papini, Gianni A. "I *Fatti dei Romani*: Per la storia della tradizione manoscritta." *Studi di filologia italiana* 31 (1973): 97–155.

Parodi, E. G. "I rifacimenti e le traduzioni italiane dell'*Eneide* di Virgilio prima del rinascimento." *Studi di filologia romanza* 2, no. 4 (1887): 97–368.

Partner, Peter. *The Lands of St. Peter: The Papal State in the Middle Ages and the Early Renaissance.* Berkeley and Los Angeles: University of California Press, 1972.

Pasqui, Ugo. "La biblioteca d'un notaro aretino del secolo XIV." *Archivio storico italiano,* 5th ser., 4 (1889): 250–55.

Pauler, Roland. *Die deutschen Könige und Italien im 14. Jahrhundert: Von Heinrich VII. bis Karl IV.* Darmstadt: Wissenschaftliche Buchgesellschaft, 1997.

Pavoni, Romeo. *Liguria medievale: Da provincia romana a stato regionale.* Genoa: ECIG, 1992.

———. "I simboli di Genova alle origini del Comune." In *Saggi e documenti III,* 29–64. Genoa: Civico istituto Colombiano, 1963.

Pertusi, Agostino. *La storiografia veneziana fino al secolo XVI: Aspetti e problemi.* Florence: Olschki, 1970.

Pesce, G., and G. Felloni. *Monete genovesi: Storia, arte ed economia nelle monete di Genova dal 1139 al 1814.* Genoa: Stringa, 1975.

Petitmengin, Pierre, and Birger Munk Olsen. "Bibliographie de la réception de la littérature classique du IXe au XVe siècle." In *The Classical Tradition in the Middle Ages and the Renaissance: Proceedings of the First European Science Foundation Workshop on "The Reception of Classical Texts," Florence, Certosa del Galluzzo, 26–27 June 1992*, edited by Claudio Leonardi and Birger Munk Olsen, 123–42. Spoleto: Centro italiano di studi sull'alto Medioevo, 1995.

Petrucci, Armando. *Medioevo da leggere: Guida allo studio delle testimonianze scritte del Medioevo italiano.* Turin: Einaudi, 1992.

———. "Reading and Writing *Volgare* in Medieval Italy." In *Writers and Readers in Medieval Italy*, 169–235. New Haven: Yale University Press, 1995.

Petti Balbi, Giovanna. *Caffaro e la cronachistica genovese.* Genoa: Tilgher, 1982.

———. *Una città e il suo mare: Genova nel medioevo.* Bologna: CLUEB, 1991.

———. *L'insegnamento nella Liguria medievale: Scuole, maestri, libri.* Genoa: Tilgher, 1979.

———. "Il mito nella memoria genovese (sec. XII–XV)." *Atti della società ligure di storia patria*, n.s., 29 (1989): 211–32.

———. "Il presente e il senso della storia in Caffaro e nei suoi continuatori." In *Il senso della storia nella cultura medievale italiana (1100–1350): Atti del XIV Convegno di studi del Centro italiano di studi di storia e arte, Pistoia, 14–17 maggio 1993*, 31–52. Pistoia: Centro italiano di studi di storia e d'arte, 1995.

———. "Società e cultura a Genova tra due e trecento." In *Genova, Pisa, e il Mediterraneo tra due e trecento: Per il VII centenario della battaglia della Meloria*, 121–49. Genoa: Società ligure di storia patria, 1984.

Piastra, Clelia Maria. "Nota sull'*Annayde* di Bonifacio Veronese." *Aevum* 28 (1954): 505–21.

———. "Nota sulla *Veronica* di Bonifacio Veronese." *Aevum* 33 (1959): 356–81.

Picone, Michelangelo. *Guittone d'Arezzo nel settimo centenario della morte: Atti del Convegno internazionale di Arezzo, 22–24 aprile 1994.* Florence: Cesati, 1995.

Picone, Michelangelo, and Claude Cazalé-Bérard. *Gli zibaldoni di Boccaccio: Memoria, scrittura, riscrittura: Atti del seminario internazionale di Firenze/Certaldo, 26–28 aprile 1996.* Florence: Cesati, 1998.

Pierotti, Romano. "La circolazione monetaria nel territorio perugino nei secoli XII–XIV." *Bollettino della Deputazione di storia patria per l'Umbria* 78 (1981): 81–151.

Pietramellara, Carla. *Il duomo di Siena.* Florence: Edam, 1980.

Pincus, Debra. "Andrea Dandolo (1343–1354) and Visible History: The San Marco Projects." In *Art and Politics in Late Medieval and Early Renaissance Italy, 1200–1500*, edited by John van Engen, 191–206. South Bend, Ind.: University of Notre Dame Press, 1990.

———. "Venice and the Two Romes: Byzantium and Rome as a Double Heritage in Venetian Cultural Politics." *Artibus et historiae* 26, no. 13 (1992): 101–14.

Pistarino, Geo. *Libri e cultura nella cattedrale di Genova tra Medioevo e Rinascimento.* Genoa: Società ligure di storia patria, 1961.

Pluskowski, Aleksander. *Wolves and Wilderness in the Middle Ages.* Woodbridge, UK: Boydell, 2006.

Polizzi, Carlo Fisber. *Ezzelino da Romano: Signoria territoriale e comune cittadino.* Romano d'Ezzelino: Sezione cultura e ricerca storica del Comune, 1989.

Polonio, Valeria. *Istituzioni ecclesiastiche della Liguria medievale.* Rome: Herder, 2002.

Polzer, Joseph. "Simone Martini's *Guidoriccio* Fresco: The Polemic Concerning Its Origin Reviewed, and the Fresco Considered as Serving the Military Triumph of a Tuscan Commune." *RACAR (Canadian Art Review)* 14 (1987): 16–69.

Popp, Dietmar. "Lupa Senese: Zur Inszenierung einer mythischen Vergangenheit in Siena (1260–1560)." *Marburger Jahrbuch für Kunstwissenschaft* 24 (1997): 41–58.

Porta, Giuseppe. "Censimento dei mss delle cronache di Giovanni, Matteo, e Filippo Villani: I." *Studi di filologia italiana* 34 (1976): 61–123.

———. "Le varianti redazionali come strumento di verifica dell'autenticità dei testi: Villani e Malispini." In *La filologia romanza e i codici: Atti di convegno della società italiana di filologia romanza, Università di Messina, 19–22 dicembre 1991*, edited by Saverio Guido and Fortunata Latella, 2:481–529. Messina: Sicania, 1993.

Presicce, Claudio Parisi. *La Lupa Capitolina*. Milan: Electa, 2000.

Prosdocimi, A. "L'arca di Rolando di Piazzola sul sagrato del Santo." *Bollettino del Museo civico di Padova* 29/30 (1939–41): 19–31.

Prunai, Giulio. "Lo studio Senese dalla 'migratio' Bolognese alla fondazione della 'Domus Sapientiae,' 1321–1408." *Bullettino senese di storia patria* 57 (1950): 3–54.

———. "Lo studio Senese dalle origini alla 'migratio' Bolognese, sec. XII–1321." *Bullettino senese di storia patria* 56 (1949): 53–79.

Raffard de Brienne, Daniel. *Saint Antoine de Padoue*. Monaco: Rocher, 1998.

Rapisarda, Mario. *La signoria di Ezzelino da Romano*. Udine: Del Bianco, 1965.

Rashdall, Hastings. *The Universities of Europe in the Middle Ages*. Edited by F. M. Powicke and Alfred Brotherston Emden. 3rd ed. 3 vols. Oxford: Clarendon Press, 1987.

Redon, Odile. *Uomini e comunità del contado Senese nel duecento*. Siena: Accademia senese degli Intronati, 1982.

Remensnyder, Amy G. *Remembering Kings Past: Monastic Foundation Legends in Medieval Southern France*. Ithaca: Cornell University Press, 1995.

Reynolds, L. D., ed. *Texts and Transmission: A Survey of the Latin Classics*. Oxford: Clarendon Press, 1983.

Reynolds, Susan. *An Introduction to the History of English Medieval Towns*. Oxford: Clarendon Press, 1977.

Riess, Jonathan B. *Political Ideals in Medieval Art: The Frescoes in the Palazzo dei Priori, Perugia (1297)*. Ann Arbor: University of Michigan Research Press, 1981.

Rigon, Antonio. *Dal libro alla folla: Antonio di Padova e il francescanesimo medievale*. Rome: Viella, 2002.

Rinoldi, Paolo, and Gabriella Ronchi. *Studi su volgarizzamenti italiani due-trecenteschi*. Rome: Viella, 2005.

Roma antica nel medioevo: Mito, rappresentazioni, sopravvivenze nella Respublica Christiana dei secoli IX–XIII: Atti della quattordicesima Settimana internazionale di studio, Mendola, 24–28 agosto 1998. Milan: V & P Università, 2001.

Ronchi, O. "Padova che si rinnova: L'antica porta delle Torricelle, Vicende della strada dal Gallo al Prato." *Il Veneto* 24 (1911): 174ff.

———. "Vecchia Padova." *Bollettino del Museo civico di Padova* 56 (1967): 157–63.

Rondoni, Giuseppe. *Tradizioni popolari e leggende di un comune medioevale e del suo contado: Siena e l'antico contado senese*. 1886. Reprint, Bologna: Forni, 1968.

Rowley, George. *Ambrogio Lorenzetti*. 2 vols. Princeton: Princeton University Press, 1958.

Rubinstein, Nicolai. "Political Ideas in Sienese Art: The Frescoes by Ambrogio Lorenzetti and Taddeo Bartolo in the Palazzo Pubblico." *Journal of the Warburg and Courtauld Institutes* 21 (1958): 179–207.

Ruck, Germaid. "Brutus als Modell des guten Richters: Bild und Rhetorik in einem Florentiner Zunftgebäude." In *Malerei und Stadtkultur in der Dantezeit: Die Argumentation der Bilder*, edited by Hans Belting and Dieter Blume, 115–31. Munich: Hirmer, 1989.

Russell, Josiah Cox. *Medieval Regions and Their Cities*. Newton Abbot, UK: David and Charles, 1972.

Sabbadini, Remigio. *Le scoperte dei codici latini e greci ne' secoli XIV e XV*. Rev. ed. 2 vols. Florence: Sansoni, 1967.

Santini, Carlo, ed. *Il linguaggio figurativo della Fontana Maggiore di Perugia*. Perugia: Calzetti-Mariucci, 1996.

S. Antonio, 1231–1981: Il suo tempo, il suo culto e la sua città. Padua: Signum, 1981.

Sassi, R. "Documenti intorno ad Armannino Giudice." *Atti e memorie della Deputazione di storia patria per le Marche*, 4th ser., 1, no. 2 (1924): v–viii.

Satkowski, Jane, and Hayden B. J. Maginnis. *Duccio di Buoninsegna: The Documents and Early Sources*. Athens: Georgia Museum of Art, 2000.

Schmidt, Paul Gerhart. "L'epica latina nel secolo XIII: Notizie sul Bonifazio da Verona e la sua Eulistea." In *Aspetti della letteratura latina nel secolo XIII: Atti del primo Convegno internazionale di studi dell' Associazione per il medioevo e l'umanesimo latini (AMUL), Perugia 3–5 ottobre 1983*, edited by Claudio Leonardi and Giovanni Orlandi, 221–27. Perugia and Florence: Regione dell'Umbria and La nuova Italia, 1986.

Scovazzi, Italo. *Origini, miti, e leggende liguri e piemontesi*. Savona: Tipografia savonese, 1932.

Segre, C., ed. *Volgarizzamenti del Due e Trecento*. Turin: UTET, 1969.

Seidel, Max. "Arnolfo e il suo rapporto con Nicola Pisano." In *Arnolfo di Cambio e la sua epoca: Atti del Convegno Internazionale di Studi, Firenze–Colle di Val d'Elsa, 7–10 marzo 2006*, edited by Vittorio Franchetti Pardo, 57–64. Rome: Viella, 2006.

Il senso della storia nella cultura medievale italiana (1100–1350): Atti del XIV Convegno di studi del Centro italiano di studi di storia e arte, Pistoia, 14–17 maggio 1993. Pistoia: Centro italiano di studi di storia e d'arte, 1995.

Shepard, Laurie. *Courting Power: Persuasion and Politics in the Early Thirteenth Century*. New York: Garland, 1999.

Shopkow, Leah. *History and Community: Norman Historical Writing in the Eleventh and Twelfth Centuries*. Washington, D.C.: Catholic University of America Press, 1997.

Signorini, Rodolfo. "Two Notes from Mantua." *Journal of the Warburg and Courtauld Institutes* 41 (1978): 317–21.

Simioni, Attilio. *Storia di Padova: Dalle origini alla fine del secolo XVIII*. Padua: Randi, 1968.

Siraisi, Nancy G. *Arts and Sciences at Padua: The Studium of Padua Before 1350*. Toronto: Pontifical Institute of Mediaeval Studies, 1973.

Skinner, Quentin. "Ambrogio Lorenzetti's *Buon governo* Frescoes: Two Old Questions, Two New Answers." *Journal of the Warburg and Courtauld Institutes* 62 (1999): 1–28.

———. "Ambrogio Lorenzetti: The Artist as Political Philosopher." *Proceedings of the British Academy* 72 (1986): 1–56.

———. *The Foundations of Modern Political Thought*. 2 vols. Cambridge: Cambridge University Press, 1978.

———. "The Rediscovery of Roman Values." In Skinner, *Visions of Politics*, 2:10–38.

———. *Visions of Politics*. 3 vols. Cambridge: Cambridge University Press, 2002.

Smalley, Beryl. *English Friars and Antiquity in the Early Fourteenth Century*. Oxford: Oxford University Press, 1960.

———. "Sallust in the Middle Ages." In *Classical Influences on European Culture, AD 500–AD 1500*, edited by R. R. Bolgar, 165–75. Cambridge: Cambridge University Press, 1971.

Sòriga, Renato. "La tradizione Romana in Pavia e la statua del 'Regisole.'" In *Atti e memorie del primo congresso storico Lombardo (Como 21–22 maggio—Varese 23 maggio 1936)*, 33–44. Milan: Giuffrè, 1937.

Southard, Edna Carter. *The Frescoes in Siena's Palazzo Pubblico, 1289–1539: Studies in Imagery and Relations to Other Communal Palaces in Tuscany.* New York: Garland, 1979.

———. "Reflections on the Documented Work by Simone Martini in the Palazzo Pubblico." In *Simone Martini: Atti del convegno: Siena, 27–29 marzo 1985,* edited by Luciano Bellosi, 103–8. Florence: Centro Di, 1988.

———. "Simone Martini's Lost Marcus Regulus: A Document Rediscovered and a Subject Clarified." *Zeitschrift für Kunstgeschichte* 42 (1979): 217–21.

Spiegel, Gabrielle M. *The Past as Text: The Theory and Practice of Medieval Historiography.* Baltimore: Johns Hopkins University Press, 1997.

———. *Romancing the Past: The Rise of Vernacular Prose Historiography in Thirteenth-Century France.* Berkeley and Los Angeles: University of California Press, 1993.

Sproviero, Filippo. *La Fontana Maggiore di Perugia: Immagini di un restauro.* Perugia: Guerra, 1999.

Stadter, Philip A. "Planudes, Plutarch, and Pace of Ferrara." *Italia medioevale e umanistica* 16 (1973): 139–62.

Starn, Randolph. *Ambrogio Lorenzetti: The Palazzo Pubblico, Siena.* New York: George Braziller, 1994.

Starn, Randolph, and Loren W. Partridge. *Arts of Power: Three Halls of State in Italy, 1300–1600.* Berkeley and Los Angeles: University of California Press, 1992.

Steinberg, Justin. *Accounting for Dante: Urban Readers and Writers in Late Medieval Italy.* South Bend, Ind.: University of Notre Dame Press, 2007.

Stierle, Karlheinz. *Francesco Petrarca: Ein Intellektueller im Europa des 14. Jahrhunderts.* Munich: Hanser, 2003.

Stopani, Renato. *La via Francigena: Storia di una strada medievale.* Florence: Le lettere, 1998.

Szabó, Thomas. "La rete stradale del contado di Siena: Legislazione statutaria e amministrazione comunale nel Duecento." *Mélanges de l'École française de Rome: Moyen Age–temps modernes* 85 (1975): 141–86.

Tamba, Giorgio, ed. *Rolandino e l'ars notaria da Bologna all'Europa: Atti del Convegno internazionale di studi storici sulla figura e l'opera di Rolandino: Bologna, 9–10 ottobre 2000.* Milan: Giuffrè, 2002.

Thomas, Heinz. *Ludwig der Bayer, 1282–1347: Kaiser und Ketzer.* Regensburg: Styria, 1993.

Thompson, Augustine. *Cities of God: The Religion of the Italian Communes, 1125–1325.* University Park: Pennsylvania State University Press, 2005.

Tomea, Paolo. "Per Galvano Fiamma." *Italia medioevale e umanistica* 39 (1996): 77–120.

Tomei, Alessandro. *Le Biccherne di Siena: Arte e finanza all'alba dell'economia moderna.* Rome: Retablo-Bolis, 2002.

Tucci, Hannelore Zug. "Il carroccio nella vita comunale italiana." *Quellen und Forschungen aus italienischen Archiven und Bibliotheken* 65 (1985): 1–104.

Ullman, B. L. "Hieremias de Montagnone and His Citations from Catullus." In *Studies in the Italian Renaissance,* 81–115. Rome: Edizioni di storia e letteratura, 1955.

———. "The Post-Mortem Adventures of Livy." *University of North Carolina Extension Bulletin* 34, no. 4 (1945): 39–53.

L'Uomo, la terra e gli astri: Gli affreschi del Palazzo della ragione a Padova. 2nd ed. Padua: Istituto Poligrafico e Zecca dello Stato, 1989.

van der Ploeg, Kees. *Art, Architecture, and Liturgy: Siena Cathedral in the Middle Ages.* Groningen: Forsten, 1993.

van Houts, Elisabeth M. C. *Medieval Memories: Men, Women, and the Past, 700–1300.* New York: Longman, 2001.

Varanini, Gian Maria, ed. *Gli Scaligeri, 1277–1387*. Verona: Mondadori, 1988.

Venturi, A. "Giovanni Pisano e le lupe-doccioni del Palazzo Pubblico di Siena." *L'Arte* 26 (1923): 187–89.

Vermiglioli, G. B. *Della zecca e delle monete perugine*. Perugia: Francesco Baduel, 1816.

Verona e il suo territorio. Vol. 3, *Verona Scaligera*. Verona: Istituto per gli studi storici veronesi, 1960.

Veyne, Paul. *Did the Greeks Believe in Their Myths? An Essay on the Constitutive Imagination*. Chicago: University of Chicago Press, 1988.

———. *Le pain et le cirque: Sociologie historique d'un pluralisme politique*. Paris: Seuil, 1976.

Visser Travagli, Anna Maria, ed. *Ferrara nel medioevo: Topografia storica e archeologica urbana*. Casalecchio di Reno: Grafis, 1995.

Vitale, Vito. *Il comune del podestà a Genova*. Milan: R. Ricciardi, 1951.

Waley, Daniel P. *The Italian City-Republics*. 3rd ed. New York: Longman, 1988.

———. *The Papal State in the Thirteenth Century*. New York: St. Martin's Press, 1961.

———. *Siena and the Sienese in the Thirteenth Century*. Cambridge: Cambridge University Press, 1991.

Webb, Diana. *Patrons and Defenders: The Saints in the Italian City-States*. London: I. B. Tauris, 1996.

Weinstein, Donald. "The Myth of Florence." In *Florentine Studies*, edited by Nicolai Rubinstein, 15–44. London: Faber and Faber, 1969.

Weiss, Roberto. "Lovato Lovati (1241–1309)." *Italian Studies* 6 (1951): 3–28.

———. *The Renaissance Discovery of Classical Antiquity*. New York: Humanities Press, 1973.

———. *The Spread of Italian Humanism*. London: Hutchinson, 1964.

White, John. *Art and Architecture in Italy, 1250–1400*. 3rd ed. New Haven: Yale University Press, 1993.

———. "The Reconstruction of Nicola Pisano's Perugia Fountain." *Journal of the Warburg and Courtauld Institutes* 33 (1970): 70–83.

Wieruszowksi, Helene. "Art and the Commune in the Time of Dante." *Speculum* 19 (1944): 19–33.

———. "Rhetoric and the Classics in Italian Education of the Thirteenth Century." *Studia Gratiana* 11 (1967): 169–207.

Wilkins, Ernest Hatch. *Life of Petrarch*. Chicago: University of Chicago Press, 1961.

———. *Studies in the Life and Works of Petrarch*. Cambridge: Medieval Academy of America, 1955.

Wiseman, T. P. *Remus: A Roman Myth*. Cambridge: Cambridge University Press, 1995.

Witt, Ronald G. "Boncompagno and the Defense of Rhetoric." *Journal of Medieval and Renaissance Studies* 16 (1986): 1–31.

———. *In the Footsteps of the Ancients: The Origins of Humanism from Lovato to Bruni*. Leiden: Brill, 2000.

———. "Medieval Italian Culture and the Origins of Humanism as a Stylistic Ideal." In *Renaissance Humanism: Foundations, Forms, and Legacy*, edited by Albert Rabil, 29–70. Philadelphia: University of Pennsylvania Press, 1988.

———. "The Rebirth of the Concept of Republican Liberty in Italy." In *Renaissance Studies in Honor of Hans Baron*, edited by Anthony Molho and John A. Tedeschi, 173–99. Dekalb: Northern Illinois University Press, 1971.

———. "What Did Giovannino Read and Write? Literacy in Early Renaissance Florence." *I Tatti Studies: Essays in the Renaissance* 6 (1995): 83–114.

Yates, Frances A. *The Art of Memory*. London: Routledge, 1966.

Zaccaria, Vittorio. *Boccaccio narratore, storico, moralista, e mitografo.* Florence: Olschki, 2001.

Zampieri, G., ed. *Padova per Antenore: Atti della giornata di studio tenutasi il 14 dicembre 1989 presso il Museo Civico Archeologico agli Eremitani e altri interventi.* Padua: Editrice Programma, 1990.

Zanella, Gabriele. *Riccobaldo e dintorni: Studi di storiografia medievale ferrarese.* Ferrara: Bovolenta, 1980.

———. "Riccobaldo e Livio." *Studi petrarcheschi,* n.s., 6 (1989): 59–66.

Zanker, Paul. *The Power of Images in the Age of Augustus.* Ann Arbor: University of Michigan Press, 1988.

Zdekauer, Lodovico. "Per la storia del pretore Senese, 1231–1241." *Bullettino senese di storia patria* 7 (1900): 468–72.

———. *Lo studio di Siena nel Rinascimento.* Bologna: Hoepli, 1894. Reprint, Bologna: Forni, 1977.

———. *La vita privata dei Senesi nel Dugento.* Siena: Lazzeri, 1896. Reprint, Bologna: Forni, 1967.

Ziolkowski, Jan M., and Michael C. J. Putnam. *The Virgilian Tradition: The First Fifteen Hundred Years.* New Haven: Yale University Press, 2008.

Index

Page numbers in *italics* refer to illustrations.